Social History of Africa

MOBILIZING THE MASSES

Recent Titles in
Social History of Africa Series
Allen Isaacman and Jean Allman, Series Editors

"City of Steel and Fire": A Social History of Atbara, Sudan's Railway Town, 1906–1984
Ahmad Alawad Sikainga

"We Were All Slaves": African Miners, Culture, and Resistance at the Enugu
Government Colliery
Carolyn A. Brown

Running after Pills: Politics, Gender, and Contraception in Colonial Zimbabwe
Amy Kaler

"The Pygmies Were Our Compass": Bantu and Batwa in the History of West Central
Africa, Early Times to c. 1900 C.E.
Karin A. Klieman

Men and Masculinities in Modern Africa
Lisa A. Lindsay and Stephan F. Miescher, editors

Working with Gender, Wage Labor and Social Change in Southwestern Nigeria
Lisa A. Lindsay

Planting Rice and Harvesting Slaves: Transformations along the Guinea-Bissau Coast,
1400–1900
Walter Hawthorne

Landed Obligation: The Practice of Power in Buganda
Holly Elisabeth Hanson

Creative Writing: Translation, Bookkeeping, and the Work of Imagination in
Colonial Kenya
Derek R. Peterson

Slavery and Beyond: The Making of Men and Chikunda Ethnic Identities in the
Unstable World of South-Central Africa, 1750–1920
Allen F. Isaacman and Barbara S. Isaacman

Paradoxes of Power: The Kano "Mamluks" and Male Royal Slavery in the Sokoto
Caliphate, 1804–1903
Sean Stilwell

Re-creating Eden: Land Use, Environment, and Society in Southern Angola and Northern
Namibia
Emmanuel Kreike

MOBILIZING THE MASSES

GENDER, ETHNICITY, AND CLASS IN THE NATIONALIST MOVEMENT IN GUINEA, 1939–1958

Elizabeth Schmidt

Social History of Africa
Allen Isaacman and Jean Allman, Series Editors

HEINEMANN
Portsmouth, NH

Heinemann
A division of Reed Elsevier Inc.
361 Hanover Street
Portsmouth, NH 03801-3912
www.heinemann.com

Offices and agents throughout the world

ISBN: 0–325–07031–8 (cloth)
ISBN: 0–325–07030–X (paper)
ISSN: 1099–8098

Library of Congress Cataloging-in-Publication Data

Schmidt, Elizabeth.
Mobilizing the masses : gender, ethnicity, and class in the nationalist movement in Guinea, 1939–1958 / Elizabeth Schmidt.
    p. cm.—(Social history of Africa, ISSN 1099–8098)
    Includes bibliographical references.
    ISBN 0–325–07031–8 — ISBN 0–325–07030–X (pbk. : acid-free paper)
    1. Guinea—Politics and government—To 1958. 2. Nationalism—Guinea—History—20th century. 3. Sex role—Political aspects—Guinea—History—20th century. 4. Ethnicity—Political aspects—Guinea—History—20th century. 5. Social classes—Guinea— History—20th century. 6. Guinea—Social conditions—20th century. I. Title. II. Series.
DT543.75.S36   2005
966.52'03—dc22   2004028489

British Library Cataloguing in Publication Data is available.

Printed in the United States of America on acid-free paper.

08   07   06   05   04 SB 1 2 3 4 5 6 7 8 9

For my son,
Jann Albert Grovogui,
A story of his people

"Using colonial archives, especially police reports, and oral interviews, Elizabeth Schmidt has written a brilliant study of the nationalist movement in Guinea that focuses not on a handful of leaders, but on the mass of followers. By looking at the way different groups of people articulated their grievances against the colonial state, she provides a richly textured study of the end of colonialism in Guinea. The success of Sékou Touré and his collaborators was thus not in creating opposition, but in riding the waves of popular feeling and pulling together disparate strands of discontent into a powerful national movement."

Martin Klein
Emeritus Professor
University of Toronto

"[Schmidt] shows how the politics of independence [were] fired by the interests, grievances, and energies of women, male trade unionists and ex-soldiers after the Second World War. Their indigenous nationalism was not always united, but it carried great force, often to the alarm of the western-educated elites. By renewing the history of West African nationalism Schmidt has also given greater historical depth to the conflicts between 'ordinary Africans' and those who claim to speak for them."

John Lonsdale
Emeritus Professor
University of Cambridge

"This book is a major revision of former traditional political histories, in favor of grassroots analyses. It is courageous from three perspectives: because it tackles a difficult subject that has not been addressed in English in forty years (since Ruth Schachter Morgenthau, 1964); because it recognizes (indirectly) the political genius of Sékou Touré in his early days; and, above all, thanks to a conjunction of original sources, it proposes a "politics from the bottom" analysis of the social forces of protest. Grassroots activists—veterans, trade unions and workers, mobilized rural dwellers and women—shaped the RDA as a popular national movement. Only later did ethnicity and violence generate the growing divisions of today."

Catherine Coquery-Vidrovitch
Emeritus Professor
University of Paris–7 Denis Diderot.

CONTENTS

Illustrations   ix
Abbreviations   xi
Acknowledgments   xiii

Introduction   1
1. History, Culture, and War: The Roots of Guinean Nationalism,
   1939–1947   15
2. *Liberté, Égalité, Fraternité:* Military Veterans and the Postwar
   Nationalist Movement, 1940–1955   37
3. The Universal Worker: Organized Labor and Nationalist Mobilization,
   1946–1953   55
4. Rural Revolt: Popular Resistance to the Colonial Chieftaincy,
   1946–1956   91
5. Women Take the Lead: Female Emancipation and the Nationalist
   Movement, 1949–1954   113
6. Ethnicity, Class, and Violence: Internal Dissent in the RDA,
   1955–1956   145
7. Independence Now: The Resurgence of the Left and the Move toward
   Independence, 1956–1958   171
Conclusion   193

Notes   197
Bibliography   269
Index   279

ILLUSTRATIONS

MAPS

0.1	French Guinea	xvi
0.2	Africa, c. 1947	xvii

PHOTOGRAPHS

1.1 Tirailleurs Sénégalais on parade on the Champs-Élysées, Paris, July 14, 1939 19

1.2 Tirailleurs Sénégalais in an African training camp, December 4, 1939 19

1.3 Tirailleurs Sénégalais defending Dakar, Senegal, ca. September 1940–November 1941 20

1.4 Tirailleurs Sénégalais assuming their post, Dakar, Senegal, ca. September 1940–November 1941 21

1.5 Tirailleurs Sénégalais constructing shelters at Ouakan, Dakar, Senegal, ca. September 1940–November 1941 22

3.1 Constructing the Conakry-Niger railway, Koumi Pass 57

3.2 Plantation workers cutting bananas for export, Kindia 63

3.3 Child laborers transporting bananas in Benty (Lower-Guinea), January 1948 ... 64

3.4 Dock workers loading bananas, Conakry port, 1957 79

5.1 Market women selling fruit, Conakry 121

5.2 Market women selling their wares, Conakry, 1954 122

5.3 Market women crossing the Milo River with their produce, before the construction of the bridge, Kankan, November 1949 128

5.4 Market women selling their wares near the Milo River bridge, Kankan, 1950 129

6.1 Male weavers, Labé, Futa Jallon 150

6.2 Malinke women spinning and dying cloth 152

7.1 General de Gaulle greeted by a crowd on his arrival in Conakry, August 1958 187

7.2 Sékou Touré, president of newly independent Guinea, October 6, 1958 ... 191

ABBREVIATIONS

AACVGAOF	Association des Anciens Combattants et Victimes de Guerre de l'Afrique Occidentale Française
AGAGBAOF	Association Générale des Amputés et Grands Blessés de l'Afrique Occidentale Française
AOF	Afrique Occidentale Française
BAG	Bloc Africain de Guinée
CFTC	Confédération Française des Travailleurs Chrétiens
CGT	Confédération Générale du Travail
DSG	Démocratie Socialiste de Guinée
FLN	Front de Libération Nationale
FNPG	Fédération Nationale des Prisonniers de Guerre
FO	CGT-Force Ouvrière
FOM	France Outre-Mer
FSCA	Fédération des Syndicats des Cheminots Africains de l'A.O.F.
GEC	Groupes d'Études Communistes
PCF	Parti Communiste Français
PDG	Parti Démocratique de Guinée
PPG	Parti Progressiste de Guinée
PRA	Parti du Regroupement Africain
PRSG	Parti Républicain Socialiste de Guinée
PTT	Postes, Télégraphes, Téléphones
RDA	Rassemblement Démocratique Africain
RJDA	Rassemblement de la Jeunesse Démocratique Africaine
SIP	Société Indigène de Prévoyance
USCG	Union des Syndicats Confédérés de Guinée

ARCHIVES ABBREVIATIONS

AG	Archives de Guinée
ANS	Archives Nationales du Sénégal
CAOM	Centre des Archives d'Outre-Mer, Archives Nationales (de France)
CARAN	Centre d'Accueil et de Recherche des Archives Nationales (de France)
CRDA	Centre de Recherche et de Documentation Africaine
IFAN	Institut Fondamental d'Afrique Noire

PHOTO CREDITS

AFP	*Agence France-Presse*

ACKNOWLEDGMENTS

Writing a book is never a solo endeavor. Without the assistance of many people and institutions, this project would not have seen the light of day. As a historian of anglophone Southern Africa, I relied on the wisdom and experience of countless others as I retooled for my francophone West African journey. Siba N'Zatioula Grovogui introduced me to Guinea and, with his intriguing stories of market women in the nationalist struggle, helped to inspire this project. Using his extensive connections, he located aging former activists in the nationalist movement, collaborated on interviews conducted in French, interpreted those in Susu and Malinke, and transcribed and translated the African language tapes. He devised ingenious methods for obtaining microfilm in France and tracked down private photograph collections in Guinea.

Sidiki Kobélé Kéïta shared his vast knowledge of nationalist history and rare copies of his published work. Kéïta, along with Fatou Aribot, Jeanne Martin Cissé, Abdoulaye "Ghana" Diallo, and Idiatou Camara, identified a number of key informants, while Hawa Fofana helped us find "anonymous" female militants and convinced them to speak with us. Ouessou "Körö" Nabé, a great friend and enthusiastic supporter of the project, introduced us to relatives with sterling nationalist credentials and provided much-needed transport to interview sessions. Most important were the many informants who gave us their time and confidence and directed us to their colleagues in the nationalist struggle. Their names, too numerous to list here, are included in the bibliography.

The oral interviews were supplemented with archival research in three countries. For their invaluable assistance, I thank the staffs of the Archives de Guinée (AG) in Conakry; the Archives Nationales du Sénégal (ANS) and the Institut Fondamental d'Afrique Noire (IFAN) in Dakar; and the Archives Nationales in France, including the Centre d'Accueil et de Recherche des Archives Nationales (CARAN) in Paris and the Centre des Archives d'Outre-Mer (CAOM) in Aix-en-Provence. At CAOM, Frédéric Gilly helped immensely in the quest for historical photographs. At the Centre de Recherche et de Documentation Africaine (CRDA) in Paris, Vassiafa Touré went far beyond the call of duty. Besides invaluable professional assistance, he and his family offered their friendship and graciously welcomed us into their home. Hervé Raulet, at La Documentation Française, and Fanny Steeg, at *Agence France-Presse,* offered crucial aid in the search for historical photographs.

In the United States, a number of scholars have both inspired me with their work and been enormously helpful professionally. Frederick Cooper provided critical advice about archives in Senegal and France—and brought the CRDA's existence to my attention. Along with Steven Feierman, Allen Isaacman, and Susan Geiger, he wrote numerous letters to funding agencies on my behalf. Susan Geiger, Jean Allman, and Joseph Miller critiqued portions of the manuscript, while Allen Isaacman, Jean Hay, Thaddeus Sunseri, and anonymous Heinemann readers gave critical advice about the whole. (Allen, in his inimitable generosity, read several drafts of the manuscript in its various transformations.) Colleagues in the Loyola College History Department contributed important insights through faculty colloquia, lectures, and works-in-progress seminars.

Others ensured that this book would not languish as a manuscript and guided it through the publication process. At Heinemann, Allen Isaacman and Jean Allman, editors of the Social History of Africa Series, and Brien McDonald and Alexander Andrusyszyn, the African Studies editors, persevered to make this book a reality. Apex Publishing and editor Elizabeth Schueler coaxed the manuscript through the copyediting process. Rona Tuccillo, at Getty Images, helped me obtain rare photographs, and Malcolm Swanston produced excellent maps in record time.

This project could not have been realized without critical financial support. Toward that end, Louise Bedicheck, public affairs officer at the U.S. Embassy in Conakry, encouraged me to apply for a Fulbright in 1989. Since there was no senior Fulbright program in Guinea at the time, she helped to facilitate its establishment. During 1990–1992, my research in the Republic of Guinea, Senegal, and France was supported by a Fulbright Senior Research and Lecturing Grant and funds from the Joint Committee on African Studies of the American Council of Learned Societies and the Social Science Research Council.

Loyola College in Maryland has also supported this project in numerous ways. The college granted me a leave of absence in 1990–1991 so that I could begin research for the book. In the fall of 1993, Loyola's Center for the Humanities awarded me a Junior Faculty Sabbatical that enabled me to organize my research materials and transcribe my interview tapes. Successive deans of the College of Arts and Sciences provided summer monies in 1993 and 1998. The Faculty Development/Research and Sabbatical Committee awarded me a yearlong senior sabbatical in 1998–1999, a sabbatical research fund, and summer grants in 1994, 1999, 2003, and 2004 that allowed me to draft and revise the manuscript and travel to France to collect historical photographs.

Many friends and family members have provided encouragement and moral support. In particular, I owe a debt of gratitude to Mark Peyrot, my greatest enthusiast, who bolstered my spirits during the toughest times and served as a sounding board as I tried to sharpen my argument. My parents, Albert J. and Kathryn J. Schmidt, never wavered in their confidence and supported me through the most difficult periods. Joan McHugh Zang helped me get it all together. I could not have done it without her. Finally, I dedicate this book to my son, Jann Albert Grovogui, who made this work a labor of love, because it is a history of *his* people.

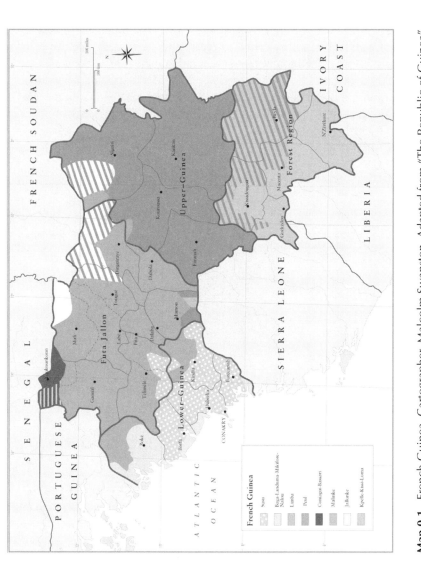

Map 0.1 French Guinea. Cartographer, Malcolm Swanston. Adapted from "The Republic of Guinea" (p. 433) in *Political Parties in French-Speaking West Africa* (1964) by Ruth Schachter Morgenthau. By permission of Oxford University Press.

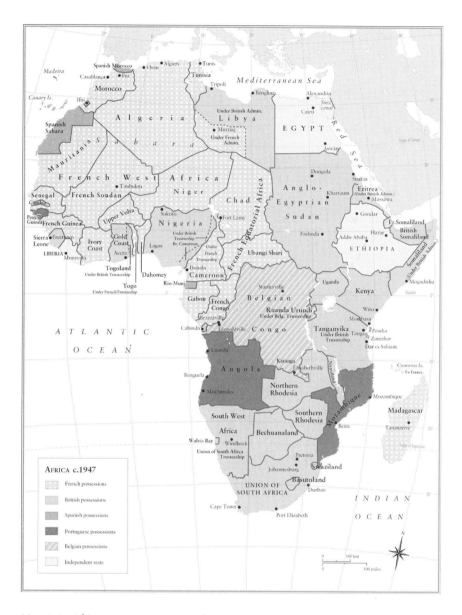

Map 0.2 Africa, c. 1947. Cartographer, Malcolm Swanston. Adapted from "The Political Map of Africa in 1935" (pp. 2–3). In *UNESCO, General History of Africa. Vol. 8, Africa since 1935* (1993), edited/translated by A. A. Mazrui. Copyright ©1993 UNESCO.

INTRODUCTION

On September 28, 1958, the population of Guinea voted overwhelmingly for complete and immediate independence from France, rejecting the proposed constitution for the Fifth French Republic that would have granted it junior partnership in the French Community. Of the 14 territories included in the great federations of French West and Equatorial Africa and the United Nations trusts of Togo and Cameroon, only Guinea voted "No." With 85 percent of the registered voters participating, 94 percent favored immediate independence, despite French threats to cut off all technical and economic assistance.[1] Spearheading the "No" vote was the Guinean branch of the Rassemblement Démocratique Africain (RDA).

Founded in 1946, the RDA was an interterritorial alliance of political parties with branches in each territory of the two federations and United Nations trusts. It promoted united action across colonial boundaries as a means of achieving its goals, which included greater political autonomy for the territories, as well as equality of political, economic, and social rights for colonial and metropolitan peoples.[2]

According to its detractors, the Guinean RDA was a party of prostitutes, school dropouts, and divorced women. It was derided as "a party of girls, social climbers—tasteless women who crudely mimic the upper classes."[3] It was dismissed as a party of illiterates, the unemployed, and the hungry, without an elite to call its own.[4] It was aggressively opposed by the French colonial administration, the so-called traditional chiefs who served as its spokesmen in the countryside, and the esteemed notable families of Guinea. Yet, it was this much-disparaged party that led Guinea to independence in 1958, advancing a wave of decolonization that ultimately swept across the African continent.

The RDA was one of many political parties active in Guinea during the postwar period. However, none approached the RDA in terms of numerical strength or ability to mobilize the masses. As its central proposition, this book argues that the RDA's overwhelming success was due to its ability to form a broad-based ethnic, class, and gender alliance, trumping rivals that were constrained by their narrow ethnic, regional, and elite male focus. While the movement's leadership was composed of Western-educated elites whose views of democracy and national self-determination were largely derived from European models, its strength lay in its solid support among the nonliterate masses. It was their grievances that drove the nationalist agenda and their energies that were harnessed in the struggle for national independence.

Linked to this thesis are four secondary propositions. First, the key to the RDA's success was its focus on groups that had already mobilized themselves. To build a broad anticolonial alliance, the party leadership targeted social groups already engaged in struggle against the state: military veterans and urban workers fighting for equality with their metropolitan counterparts, peasants burdened by the war effort and the demands of government-appointed chiefs, women unable to provide for their families' needs during the postwar economic crisis, and Western-educated elites agitating for a greater voice in political affairs. Embracing the particular causes of these social groups, the RDA enticed them into the broader nationalist movement.

Second, the party leadership forged this unlikely alliance through consistent focus on areas of common interest determined by these social groups: racial discrimination in wages, benefits, and social services; abuses by government-appointed chiefs; promotion of health, sanitation, and educational services; and expanded political representation and autonomy. While other political parties concentrated on so-called traditional male elites—chiefs, notables, and their allies—the RDA consciously focused on the majority of the population, polling their grievances and harnessing their discontent.

Third, unlike its rivals, the RDA was shaped primarily from the bottom up, rather than the top down. That grassroots actors left the strongest imprint on the party's goals is evident in three ways. First, the party attained its strength by addressing preexisting popular grievances and promoting solutions for them. Thus, it was local-level actors who determined many of the basic claims on the nationalist agenda. Second, these actors resisted some aspects of the program that was presented to them and contested fundamental components of their leaders' vision. Grassroots militants and the party leadership struggled continuously over issues of gender, ethnicity, class, and political violence. While the appearance of a broad-based nationalist alliance was maintained, serious rifts constantly threatened the movement. Third, as the RDA's interterritorial and territorial leadership grew more conservative, seeking power within the limits imposed by France, grassroots activists in Guinea continued to push the party to the Left. Ultimately, it was grassroots sentiment that carried the day, as rank-and-file militants swept aside party officials who were not prepared to follow their lead.

Fourth, if the grassroots membership defined the party's major objectives, it also determined its methods. Although print media contributed to the spread of nationalist ideas in nineteenth-century Europe, books and newspapers were less significant in Guinea, where mass education had yet to be established.[5] Mobilizing the largely nonliterate masses required new methods of communication, notably songs, symbols, and uniforms. While some local forms, images, and cultural practices were co-opted by elites and presented to the populace, the people themselves brought others to the movement. Thus, the masses were not simply an "audience" for elite-inspired nationalism, nor the "transmitters" of a message formulated for them.[6] Party leaders did not compose songs and slogans to communicate with the nonliterate population; rather, people without formal education composed their own. They used songs and slogans to communicate among themselves, to transmit their own messages to the party leaders, and to interpret the leaders' messages in terms meaningful to themselves.

SIGNIFICANCE OF THE PROJECT: AFRICA AND BEYOND

The significance of this project extends far beyond Guinea. It raises important theoretical and methodological issues that, when taken together, fundamentally alter the way in which we understand anticolonial nationalism in the non-Western world.[7] Building upon the work of earlier scholars, it pushes historical investigations of nationalism in new directions, illuminating the ways in which grassroots activists shaped the movements' visions, objectives, and strategies.

The historiography of anticolonial nationalism has evolved considerably during the past half century. In the post–World War II period, anticolonial movements in Africa and Asia waged scores of successful struggles for national independence—sparking new interest in what previously had been considered a uniquely European phenomenon. African historiography expanded in new directions as scholars explored nation-building endeavors across the continent. Written before social history gained ground in the discipline, most of the early studies paid scant attention to the involvement of peasants, workers, and women in anticolonial struggles. These works were, by and large, institutional histories, exploring the structure and internal struggles of the nationalist parties, the ins and outs of negotiations and constitutional proposals, and the compromises and concessions that ultimately led to self-rule and political independence. Their subjects were primarily the Western-educated male elites who led the nationalist movements and eventually assumed power.[8]

In the early 1970s, as social history achieved prominence in the discipline, African peasants and workers became important subjects of historical inquiry. With a new understanding of historical agency, scholars of African nationalism began to shift their focus to "the role of ordinary . . . Africans." Notable among them was John Lonsdale, who argued that "scholarly preoccupation with *élites* will only partially illumine the mainsprings of nationalism."[9] He claimed that "the pressures of the peasantry at the periphery were at least as important in breaking down the colonial governments' morale as the demands of the élite at the centre."[10] In the post–World War II era, increased government intrusion into the lives of ordinary Africans "resulted in a national revolution coalescing from below, co-ordinated rather than instigated by the educated *élite*." According to Lonsdale, it was the grassroots that "provided much of [the movement's] dynamism and direction."[11]

In the decades that followed, other scholars built upon these insights. While "ordinary Africans" protesting specific colonial policies were mobilized by elites into an explicitly nationalist movement, such scholars observed, they were not passive recipients of the nationalist message. In her pathbreaking work on colonial Tanzania, Susan Geiger argued that the nonliterate majority did not "learn nationalism" from the Western-educated male elites who dominated party politics. Instead, people without formal education brought to the party

an ethos of nationalism already present as trans-ethnic, trans-tribal social and cultural identity. This ethos was expressed collectively in their dance and other organizations, and reflected in their families of origin as well as in marriages that frequently crossed ethnic divisions.[12]

Despite the new focus on "ordinary Africans," until the mid-1970s, women's voices remained decidedly muted. "Ordinary Africans" were generally presumed to be male. Then, following the birth of "women's history" in the West, a number of assumptions concerning twentieth-century African social and economic history were drastically revised. Analyses sensitive to the centrality of women gradually superseded the presumption that men alone were the agents of African "modernization"—the backbone of emergent peasantries, capitalist farming sectors, and nascent entrepreneurial and working classes.[13]

These revisions were accompanied by a similar reevaluation of the "absence" of women from nationalist struggles, as well as a redefinition of the terms of the debate. While many earlier studies emphasized women's contributions to male-dominated nationalist movements,[14] more recent scholarship has emphasized their independent and formative roles.[15] In Geiger's words, African women were "a major force in *constructing, embodying,* and *performing* . . . nationalism."[16] They were not simply auxiliaries to the male-envisioned and constructed cause. The incorporation of women's vantage points into analyses of nationalist movements has dramatically altered our understanding of the premises of these struggles, their organization, dynamics, and objectives.

The importance of mass mobilization to the Guinean nationalist movement has received some attention. Ruth Schachter Morgenthau, Jean Suret-Canale, and Claude Rivière concentrate on colonial reforms and electoral politics, but touch upon the movement's popular aspects. In particular, they examine the party's trade union base and the impact of worker organization on broader political mobilization. While Morgenthau makes note of ethnic, regional, and class cleavages and the party's attempts to overcome them, she does not explore these issues in detail. None of these works focus exclusively on the Guinean nationalist movement. As a component of broader investigations, the analysis of the Guinean independence struggle is necessarily superficial.[17]

Guinean historian Sidiki Kobélé Kéïta has written the most comprehensive, if largely uncritical, account of the Guinean nationalist movement.[18] His laudatory study devotes considerable attention to elite electoral politics, with some discussion of the struggle's popular roots. The interaction of the postwar labor and nationalist movements is highlighted, and veterans', peasants', and women's roles are superficially treated, but the specific tactics of mass mobilization are not scrutinized. Although Kéïta mentions the crucial nature of women's involvement, neither the dynamics of their participation nor the controversy surrounding it is explored in depth. Finally, Kéïta's treatment of the "masses" is broad and undifferentiated. The complex ethnic tensions that at times seemed ready to derail the movement are completely ignored.

Although some other works remark upon the central role of Guinean women, few offer an analysis of women's motivations, methods, and visions of a transformed society. Few discuss their role in shaping the nationalist movement and defining the terms of the debate.[19] A notable exception to this generalization is Idiatou Camara's unpublished undergraduate thesis, which demonstrates the ways in which urban women helped to construct Guinea's nationalist movement and were critical to its success. Unfortunately, this unique work, preserved in Guinea's national archives, is available only in that country.[20]

Since Kéïta and Camara investigated Guinea's nationalist movement some two decades ago, no scholar has reassessed and utilized archival documents on this subject. Apart from Morgenthau, who interviewed male party elites, and Camara, who interviewed only female participants, few have conducted oral interviews. This book reconsiders archival sources in light of its new focus on grassroots activism. It fills lacunae and corrects distortions in the written record with oral interviews. Informants include both women and men from the lower echelons of party leadership and the rank and file.

Building upon and refining the work of earlier scholars, this book approaches the Guinean nationalist movement from the perspective of social history. However, in contrast to Kéïta, it does not treat "ordinary Africans" as a homogeneous mass. Rather, "common people" are considered in terms of the ethnic, class, and gender factors that divided as well as united them. Special attention is paid to the role of women, whose unique involvement in the Guinean nationalist movement was so crucial to its definition and its success. It investigates the ways in which preexisting "cultural systems," such as women's organizations, ethnic associations, and transethnic regional associations, fundamentally shaped the postwar nationalist movement.[21] Finally, African voices and perspectives, gleaned from numerous oral interviews as well as written sources, are given a prominent position in the analysis.

An examination of the Guinean case leads to three theoretical conclusions with far-reaching historical implications. First, anticolonial nationalism, in many instances, belongs to a progressive political tradition that one might call inclusive nationalism.[22] Embracing a heterogeneous population that is ethnically and religiously diverse, inclusive nationalism is frequently a starting point for a more broadly based internationalist perspective. Second, while anticolonial nationalist movements were led by educated elites, elites did not instigate the anticolonial protests. Rather, they built their base among popular groups already engaged in struggle against the colonial state. They identified issues around which the masses were already mobilizing and incorporated them into the nationalist agenda. These agendas were successful largely because they were deeply rooted in mass concerns rather than imposed from above or outside.

Third, conceptualizing the nation was a two-way street. Masses as well as elites had an impact on the ideas, objectives, strategies, and methods of the nationalist movement. While elites brought European ideas and models of nationalism to the table, the nonliterate majority brought others that were embedded in indigenous histories, practices, and beliefs.

Finally, an assessment of the Guinean case leads to a methodological observation with broad ramifications. Elite mobilization of the masses is now recognized as key to the success of any nationalist endeavor. Yet, the mechanisms and processes by which such mobilization occurred have rarely been identified. This book takes up the challenge and demonstrates *how* grassroots mobilization actually came about. It explores the ideology and methods that were used to appeal to the general population, as well as the actual dynamics of mass mobilization. What we have learned from Guinea can help us to understand the processes of nationalist mobilization elsewhere in the colonized world.

ORGANIZATION OF THE BOOK

Incorporating gender, ethnicity, and class into a broader historical analysis, this book investigates the Guinean nationalist movement from several perspectives. It explores the roles played by reform-minded colonial officials and Western-educated African elites whose ideas were rooted in the Enlightenment, the French Revolution, and nineteenth-century European nationalist movements. It examines the interaction of these elites with four popular groups already engaged in anticolonial agitation: military veterans, trade unionists, peasants, and women. To facilitate analysis, these groups are treated as discrete entities. However, none of these groups was homogeneous, and their memberships often overlapped. Military veterans, for instance, were exclusively male and primarily of rural peasant origin. Trade unionists, who were generally urban and male, ran the gamut from Western-educated civil servants to nonliterate laborers. Peasants were both male and female. Women were both rural and urban. Most women involved in the nationalist movement were not of elite status.

Although this book is primarily a popular history, it makes reference to elite politics, whose story already has been told.[23] Its purpose is not to retell that story but to use elite politics as a reference point for the grassroots history, integrating the two historical strands in order to create a more accurate and informative whole. Elections to elite bodies frequently served as focal points for mass mobilization. It was the RDA's extraordinarily effective grassroots organization that resulted in unprecedented electoral successes at the municipal, territorial, federal, and metropolitan levels. These victories, in turn, permitted the abolition of the colonial chieftaincy and paved the way to independence.

Chapter 1 sets the stage for the emergence of the postwar nationalist movement. It examines the roots of Guinean nationalism in the precolonial and colonial eras, concentrating on three major issues. First, it argues that the Guinean movement led by the RDA belonged to the progressive political tradition of the European revolutionary era (1789–1848).[24] It was not only vehemently anticolonial but also very consciously nationalist. A broad-based ethnic and class alliance that incorporated multiple religious and linguistic groups, the RDA envisioned an inclusive political community based on a shared history rooted in both the precolonial and colonial past.

Second, it investigates the ways in which mobilization for the war effort (1939–1945) augmented the burden of colonialism through forced labor, crop requisitions, and military conscription. It argues that increased civilian hardship in the rural areas laid the groundwork for postwar protest in the countryside. Similarly, the experience of military combat, contact with French civilians, and the disparate treatment of African and metropolitan soldiers set the stage for veterans' subsequent challenges to the colonial state.

Third, it examines the impact of imperial reforms on postwar political action. Dependent upon the colonies for its execution of the war, France promised to enact a series of reforms in its aftermath. Although it hoped to reshape imperialism in order to save it, France lost control of the process as African actors put forth their own demands and mobilized popular support to realize them. Military veterans, trade unionists, peasants, and women were critical to these endeavors.

Military veterans were among the first historical actors to challenge the French state. Chapter 2 explores the role of these veterans, politicized by their wartime experiences, in popular mobilization against colonial institutions. Myron Echenberg's pioneering work on French West Africa and Nancy Lawler's on the Ivory Coast have helped to shape the contours of this investigation.[25] Proud of their service to France and its ideals of "Liberty, Equality, and Fraternity," returning veterans were embittered by their unequal treatment and challenged the state to make good on the promises of reformed imperialism. Rallying under the slogan "Equal sacrifices, equal rights," they employed the new French rhetoric of equality to claim pay and benefits previously denied to African soldiers.[26] In the rural areas, military veterans increasingly spearheaded opposition to the chiefs, who had enforced the demands of the war effort. Endowed with a new confidence and sense of themselves as important men, they provided alternative leadership to their rural communities. Recognizing an opportunity to expand its operations into the countryside, the RDA embraced the veterans' cause. Building upon preexisting discontent, the party championed veterans' rights, promoted them in opposition to existing authority structures, and rallied veterans to the nationalist program. Although veterans were early leaders in the anticolonial struggle, once their immediate objectives were achieved, they retreated into the background and threw in their lot with the colonial paymaster.

African trade unionists were the second major group to challenge French authority. Like postwar veterans' associations, the French West African trade union movement latched onto French claims of universalism and enlightened imperialism, demanding that African workers be incorporated into the same labor system as their metropolitan counterparts. As citizens rather than subjects of the revamped empire, African workers demanded equal pay and benefits.[27]

Chapter 3 focuses on postwar trade union actions and labor's role in launching the nationalist movement. Worker protest in Guinea began as rural resistance to forced labor and widespread desertion from public and private work sites. This momentum was captured by organized labor in the urban areas, most notably the RDA-associated Confédération Générale du Travail (CGT). Guinean trade unionists were a heterogeneous group, ranging from relatively privileged civil servants—postal, telegraph, and telephone (PTT) workers; teachers; clerks; and medical personnel—to nonliterate laborers, dock workers, and domestic servants. Thus, the Guinean labor movement crossed class boundaries, including both intellectual elites and members of the working class.

In his pivotal book on labor and decolonization, Frederick Cooper explores French attempts to justify their continued colonial claims in the post–Atlantic Charter era by introducing a number of political and labor reforms.[28] Cooper's framework is key to understanding significant labor actions in Guinea: the French West African railway strike in 1947–1948, Guinea's general strike in 1950, and the French West African general strike in 1953. These strikes, in turn, catalyzed the nationalist movement. Although few women were wageworkers during this period, they were keenly aware of the impact of men's wage and benefit packages on their families' well-being. They were critical to the sustenance of urban communities during the strikes. The 1953 general strike, in particular, served as women's entrée into explicitly anticolonial activity. Once again, the RDA followed in the wake of the trade union actions, linking workers' grievances to a broader anticolonial cause and mobilizing male workers and their female allies into the nationalist movement.

African peasants were the third popular group to rally against the colonial state. Chapter 4 investigates rural mobilization against the chieftaincy, one of the most notorious colonial institutions. The 1939–1945 war effort had a major impact on postwar nationalist activity in the rural areas. The wartime burden of heavy taxes, forced labor and crop production, and military conscription generated immense popular hostility toward the colonial power. Because government-appointed chiefs were the minions who collected taxes, requisitioned crops, and forcibly recruited labor and military conscripts, popular anger was first manifest in agitation against the colonial chieftaincy. While peasant resistance—including both men and women and a disproportionate number of military veterans—predated RDA activity in the countryside, the party was quick to recognize the opportunity for rural mobilization. Responding to peasants' grievances and articulating demands on their behalf, the RDA capitalized on homegrown antigovernment sentiment. In this way, the party was able to expand beyond its urban base and establish itself in the interior, harnessing peasant discontent to its postwar political cause.[29] The chiefs responded in kind, victimizing RDA members and ensuring the party's electoral defeat. Campaigns against the chieftaincy became central to the RDA's rural strategy.

Women were the fourth and final grassroots constituency to mobilize for the nationalist cause. Chapter 5 explains why women, particularly those without formal education (market women, cloth dyers, seamstresses, and peasants) were attracted to the RDA. Assuming roles never before even contemplated, they violated gender norms—speaking out in public, traveling without escorts in the countryside, leaving their husbands and children, sometimes even resorting to divorce—to mobilize for a political party. While other parties ignored women or opposed their political involvement, the RDA listened to women's demands and targeted issues of particular concern to them—especially those that affected their families' well-being. Acknowledging the power inherent in women's social relations and the relevance of their cultural associations, the RDA supported women's use of these resources in mobilizing their families and communities, even when they violated long-standing gender norms. Women reveled in their new roles and the respect they gained through political work. The RDA, in turn, gained an immense activist force snubbed by other political parties.

Women, more than any other popular group, transformed the mobilizational methods of the nationalist movement. This chapter explores the ways in which women adapted their preexisting organizations, practices, and beliefs to serve the nationalist cause, and the ways in which the party was shaped by women.

Having considered the major groups of local actors and their specific roles in nationalist mobilization, chapter 6 examines some of the movement's weaknesses, which also emanated from its base. The RDA's strategy of attracting marginalized social groups and classes contributed to its strength. However, this strategy backfired when new recruits challenged the leadership on issues of ethnicity and violence. While territorial leaders promoted ethnic inclusiveness as a crucial component of the RDA's nation-building project, local activists frequently held a more particularist perspective. Fissures emerged as RDA leaders sought to rein in grassroots militants, demanding that they refrain from political and ethnic violence. Such disputes deeply divided the party.

Chapter 7 concludes the story. It examines growing divisions within the party and the ways in which grassroots militants, both nonliterate and elite, pushed the leadership to a more radical stance. Differences between party leaders and local activists were exacerbated by the RDA's rise to power under a new system of limited self-government. Determined to "rule responsibly," party leaders demanded strict adherence to the law. Class tensions emerged when the RDA, having built its base among the lower classes, began to seek more "qualified" candidates for government office. As their leaders became part of the system, rank-and-file members continued to act the part of the opposition—deepening rifts between the upper and lower segments of the party.

In 1958, the party rank and file gained the upper hand as previously sidelined Leftists moved to the fore. Critiquing the compromises of self-government and the opportunism of the leaders who benefited from it, trade unionists, teachers, students, and other youth increasingly pushed the party to the Left. Bowing to these forces, the Guinean RDA rejected France's 1958 constitution and opted for immediate independence. When the populace voted a resounding "No" to the constitutional project, Guinea became the sole French territory to claim independence. Once again, the party had followed the people.

A NOTE ON THE SOURCES

While all historical sources include strengths and limitations, those pertaining to Guinean nationalist history are particularly problematic.[30] First, there are serious lacunae in the documentation. The French burned huge quantities of government documents when they left precipitously in 1958.[31] Moisture, insects, rodents, and mold have damaged many more beyond repair. Much of what remains at the Archives de Guinée (AG) is in terrible disarray. From 1989 to 1991, I found heaps of unsorted, moldy documents decomposing in the Archives' back rooms. The Annual Political Reports of the circle commandants existed only for the years 1947–1949. Those of the governor had been lost completely. Other documents, particularly RDA party files, were destroyed, lost, or stolen after the military coup in 1984. Some of the latter have migrated into private collections, for personal use or as a precaution against destruction by the government.

The problem of missing documents has been remedied to some extent by other archival collections. The most important of these is the collection of the Federation of French West Africa, housed in the Archives Nationales du Sénégal (ANS) in Dakar. Far more comprehensive than the collection in Guinea, the federal archives include copies of many of the documents that were lost or destroyed in Guinea—most notably, the political reports and correspondence of the governor. While the most detailed political analysis from the local level, written by circle commandants for the governor, has been lost, the territorial reports, written by the governor and transmitted to the high commissioner in Senegal, have survived. The territorial reports, which include excerpts from the lost commandants' reports, provide the broad outlines of political activities in Guinea.

Unlike the circle commandants' reports, which remained in Guinea, police informants' daily bulletins were carbon copied to Dakar. Written by Africans who spied on political and trade union meetings on behalf of the colonial government, these reports provide invaluable information about political and labor activities, as well as individuals central to both movements.

The second problem pertains to the sources themselves. Government documents contain inherent biases against nationalist and trade union actors. Local police and administrative reports on grassroots political and labor activities betray their hostility to the RDA and associated trade unions. African informers, dependent upon their employers' goodwill, rendered interpretations that conformed to their patrons' expectations; they generally reported what their bosses wished to hear. While such sources should not be discarded, they must be treated with caution.

Other written records contain biases of a different nature. The Centre de Recherche et de Documentation Africaine (CRDA) in Paris, and to a lesser extent, the federal archives in Dakar, include collections of RDA and trade union letters, speeches, and reports. The CRDA and the Institut Fondamental d'Afrique Noire (IFAN) in Dakar house extensive collections of party and trade union newspapers. While these documents are a source of unfiltered African voices, they promote the perspectives of Western-educated leaders at the interterritorial, territorial, and local levels. While the views of African teachers, clerks, and medical personnel serve as a corrective to the colonial record, they do little to illuminate the sentiments and views of the nonliterate majority. Yet, it is precisely those grassroots activists—military veterans, peasants, women in the informal sector, and the labor rank and file—who constitute the focus of this study.

Without the corrective of African voices, both popular and elite, this book would present a distorted view. It is only through oral interviews that the muted voices of nonliterate peasants, workers, soldiers, and women can be heard. Dozens of interviews with male and female participants in the nationalist and labor movements provided insight into the values, beliefs, and perspectives of ordinary Africans.[32]

Oral research entails yet another set of problems. How does one find the "historically voiceless" whose names do not appear in the written record? This problem proved particularly difficult in the case of women. My research assistant and I began with the Western-educated male elites who served in leadership positions, requesting the names of nonliterate women who had participated in the nationalist movement. The male leaders agreed that women had, indeed, been central to the movement's success. They remembered with great enthusiasm the women's uncontested leader, Mafory Bangoura, who had died a decade and a half earlier. However, none could remember a single other woman's name. Without a trace of irony, some men told us that those forgotten actors, deemed central to the movement, could not tell us anything of consequence about history; they were simply illiterate old women.

After three months of searching, the women's anonymity began to fade. Hawa Fofana, the dean of social sciences at the University of Conakry, had worked with grassroots women's organizations in the 1970s. Some of their members must have been politically active in the 1950s, she correctly surmised. After much coaxing, a few of these women agreed to speak with us. Once we had gained their confidence, they provided the names and whereabouts of several former colleagues who, in turn, led us to other sources. Our long search had begun to bear fruit.

Putting names on anonymous participants and seeking out informants were but the first of many difficulties that arose during the interview process. Conducting oral interviews in a country run by a brutal, ethnically based military regime proved to be another. When I arrived in Guinea, I naïvely assumed that my research project was not politically sensitive. After all, I would be raising questions concerning events that had transpired nearly 40 years before, when women and men collectively resisted the colonial state. True, the nationalist movement had been spearheaded by Sékou Touré and the Guinean branch of the RDA, both of which had been demonized by the military regime. However, it seemed to me that no matter how reactionary the military government, even it could not openly champion colonialism over national independence. Even the generals had to publicly concede that the nationalist struggle had been a fundamentally positive force.

As I began my investigation, I realized that I had gravely underestimated the cardinal rule of oral history research: the present is inextricably linked to the past. Present conditions, values, and interests affect the way in which people remember—or fail to remember—past experiences.[33] Having overlooked this fundamental principle, there were a number of considerations I had not foreseen. First, in a situation of tremendous political and economic stress, with the menace of civil unrest never far beneath the surface, the notion that someone had resisted state authority in the past—even the colonial state— was extremely threatening. That person was viewed as capable of resisting state authority in the future, articulating popular grievances and demands, and mobilizing urban workers and rural peasants against an unpopular government—in this case, the ruling military regime.

Second, association with Sékou Touré—whether the trade union and nationalist leader of preindependent Guinea or the autocratic ruler of the late 1970s—was an extremely dangerous proposition. Again, our experiences with women were instructive. Elderly women, proud of their fundamental contribution to the nationalist movement, were frequently silenced by their adult children who condemned their willingness to expose themselves to outsiders—particularly foreigners.

Third, mobilization across ethnic and class lines, one of the most striking, if imperfect, achievements of the nationalist era, had been replaced by narrow ethnic chauvinism—at the instigation of the military government. Constant harangues on state-run radio and television warned the coastal population that there was a Malinke (or Peul) plot to take over the government. The government rightfully belonged to the Susu, the speakers argued, since the coast was their historic home, and other ethnic groups were allowed to live there at their sufferance.

The power of the ethnic card was driven home when we interviewed Susu market women and cloth dyers, who had been central to the movement on the coast. These women felt compelled to choose between their past support of a Malinke leader, Sékou Touré, and their current loyalty to General Lansana Conté and his predominantly Susu ruling clique. Frequently their children, well placed in the Conté government, admonished their mothers to keep silent about the past. Out of respect—and fear—for their children's well-being, they frequently did so.

Fourth, in the early 1990s, Guinea was in the midst of a reactionary backlash against women and the political, economic, and social gains they had made during the first two and one-half decades of independence. The military regime criticized the way in which Sékou Touré and the RDA allegedly had destroyed the family, broken homes, and violated African culture and Muslim traditions by emancipating women. To acknowledge that they had resisted male authority was risky business for women, especially those who had joined the ranks of the elderly *hadjas,* who had made their pilgrimages to Mecca and were finally enjoying the prestige of age and religious respectability.

In undertaking to research the nature of grassroots mobilization in the Guinean nationalist movement, I had anticipated a range of problems: the notorious absence of women and other nonelites from archival documents; colonial biases in official sources; and gaps in written documentation resulting from archival destruction by departing French officials in 1958, military rulers after 1984, and through general neglect. I had anticipated weak or faulty memories and the need to reconcile conflicting accounts. What I had not anticipated was the wholesale erasure of Guinean history.

Most striking to me was the fact that Sékou Touré's name and that of the Guinean branch of the RDA were rarely spoken in public. People referred vaguely to the period "before" (the military coup) or to "the previous state president." Independence day was celebrated annually without a single reference to the RDA or its leadership. Old RDA songs were sung on the state-run radio but with new lyrics that lauded the military regime. Frescoed portraits of Sékou Touré had been effaced in towns and cities across the country, leaving only the recognizable contours of his silhouette. His famous quotes still adorned the walls of government buildings, but his initials had been blotted out—the vague outlines still showing through the whitewash. It was as if nearly four decades of Guinean history had never occurred.

Such circumstances were bound to affect people's willingness to speak about their past involvement in the nationalist struggle. And present conditions were bound to influence the way in which people presented that which they were willing to discuss at all. Changed perceptions about the legitimacy of resisting state, class, and patriarchal authority, and the changed life situations of the informants and their children inevitably altered descriptions of past actions. Having jettisoned the RDA's transethnic nation-building project, the military regime blatantly manipulated ethnicity for political ends. This also affected popular renditions of the past. Members of the Susu ethnic group, often at the behest of their well-positioned children, were sometimes reluctant to associate themselves with a Malinke leader of the past. They feared that this connection would somehow link them to one of President/General Lansana Conté's most feared political opponents, Alpha Condé, who also happened to be Malinke.

The strong impact of the present on the past does not mean that the past is completely irretrievable. It simply means that the job of delving into nationalist history, deciphering the complex codes, and trying to determine the nature and extent of present influence on the past was a far more difficult task than I had anticipated.

1

HISTORY, CULTURE, AND WAR: THE ROOTS OF GUINEAN NATIONALISM, 1939–1947

The nationalist movement that emerged in Guinea after World War II was deeply rooted in the past. This chapter considers three aspects of Guinean history that set the stage for the movement's birth. The first pertains to the book's central proposition, that it was the RDA's ability to build a broad-based alliance, overcoming regional, ethnic, gender, and class differences, that allowed it to triumph over rival political parties. The chapter begins by exploring some of the commonalities successfully promoted by the party. Of those ties that bound them together, the people's shared history was the most important.

Second, while the Guinean nationalist movement emerged in the aftermath of World War II, its seeds were sown during the war. State mobilization for the war effort had a major impact on both men and women, hitting the peasantry especially hard. The wartime burden of forced labor, military conscription, and crop requisitions, compounded by shortages and inflation, generated immense popular hostility toward the colonial power. Women, who found it increasingly difficult to provide for their families, resented the onerous labor and crop exactions. Forced laborers, embittered by poor pay and working conditions, deserted their work sites in droves. Whole villages absconded across territorial boundaries to avoid military and labor recruiters. Military veterans, who returned home with a new sense of confidence and entitlement, sought new ways to assert their masculinity and took the lead in articulating rural grievances. Imposed by government-appointed chiefs, the wartime exactions laid the groundwork for rural rejection of chiefly authority and, by extension, colonial rule more generally. This section provides the historical framework for the postwar revolt led by military veterans (chapter 2), trade unionists (chapter 3), peasants (chapter 4), and women (chapter 5).

Third, France gave impetus to its imperial demise by implementing reforms designed to save the empire. In order to stimulate more dedicated commitment to the war effort, France promised a series of reforms at the war's end. While French leaders assumed they would control the process, African actors seized the opportunity to establish institutions that would ultimately imperil the colonial state. This chapter introduces the rhetoric and reforms that would be embraced and transformed by military veterans, trade unionists, and Western-educated elites in the postwar period.

CONSTRUCTING A BROAD-BASED NATIONALIST ALLIANCE

The political movement that led Guinea to independence in 1958 was part of a progressive political tradition that swept Europe between 1789 and 1848.[1] To the Guinean RDA, the nation was not narrowly premised on ethnic and linguistic homogeneity. It was not exclusionary or chauvinistic. What made a person "Guinean" was broadly conceived. In Benedict Anderson's seminal work, *Imagined Communities: Reflections on the Origin and Spread of Nationalism,* he describes the nation as "an imagined political community" that is sovereign and contained within defined territorial boundaries. The community is "imagined" because most of its members are strangers to one another, yet consider themselves to be bound together in emotional solidarity as well as in a sovereign political entity.[2] Contesting the nineteenth-century German romantic notion of the nation as a primordial, ethnically and culturally bound entity, Miroslav Hroch argues that the nation is not an "eternal category, but . . . the product of a long and complicated process of historical development." It cannot be reduced to an ethnic or language group.[3]

According to these more nuanced definitions of the nation, Guinea in the postwar period was unquestionably a nation in the making. The nationalist movement, spearheaded by the RDA, was a broad-based ethnic and class alliance that incorporated Muslims, Christians, and practitioners of indigenous religions. Although characterized by its opponents as a party of Malinke and Susu, the RDA prided itself on its multiethnic membership, appealing especially to the lower classes. It included speakers of Maninka, Susu, Pulaar, Kissi, Kpelle, and Loma—as well as those who spoke languages indigenous to other French African territories. More than any other Guinean party, the RDA consciously and successfully shaped a national rather than an ethnic identity.[4]

If nations do not require ethnic or linguistic homogeneity, they do require a shared history. Thus, the RDA embarked upon an ambitious program of nation building that hearkened to the precolonial and colonial past. Party leaders stressed that much of the population shared a precolonial history. A large proportion shared a religion. All had mutually understood experiences and grievances resulting from French colonialism. Together, these formed a common basis that allowed a nation to be forged from a multilingual, ethnically heterogeneous population.

Parts of Guinea had been incorporated into multiethnic economic, religious, and political systems long before European conquest. For centuries, Malinke trading networks and their associated Muslim communities had connected diverse parts of what would become modern Guinea. Jallonke (Susu, Limba, Landuma, Baga, Bassari) and Fulbe (Peul and Tukulor) residents of the Futa Jallon traded extensively with coastal peoples.[5] In the eighteenth century, the Fulbe jihads brought the Futa Jallon under unified political and religious control.[6] In the nineteenth century, the politico-religious empires of the Tukulor leader El-Hadj Umar b. Said Tall and the Malinke leader Samori Touré brought together vast expanses of territory that included much of modern Guinea and its neighbors.[7] Many Guineans had, in E. J. Hobsbawm's words, "the consciousness of . . . having belonged to a lasting political entity."[8] This legacy of political, economic, cultural, and religious interaction linked Guineans to one another and to peoples in neighboring territories.[9]

Religion was an important unifying factor in Guinea. Although ethnically diverse, the territory was predominantly Muslim—conservatively estimated at 70 percent.[10] Christian missionaries, primarily Roman Catholics, had generally avoided proselytizing in Upper-Guinea and the Futa Jallon, convinced that they would make little headway among devout Muslims in these regions. However, they managed to attract some converts among the Baga (subsequently incorporated into the Susu) in the coastal areas, as well as in the forest region, which Islam had largely failed to penetrate. Other Christians in Guinea included civil servants from other parts of the French empire who had settled, or were the descendants of settlers, in Guinea. Apart from Muslims and Christians, a minority, particularly in the coastal and forest regions, continued to practice indigenous religions.[11]

If religion and precolonial political history were ties that bound, Guineans also held in common a history of French colonialism. Like other imperial powers, France failed to recognize the potency of shared suffering under colonialism and its power as a unifying force. To the French, Guinea represented a simple "administrative unit," with no natural claim to nation-statehood.[12] From the perspective of ethnicity, linguistics, and geography, its borders were arbitrary. Historically, the logic of its boundaries corresponded with nothing more than the extent of imperial conquest and "effective occupation," legitimized by the treaty of the Berlin Conference of 1884–1885.[13] However, Hobsbawm writes, "The unity imposed by conquest and administration might . . . produce a people that saw itself as a 'nation.'"[14]

Such was the case for Guinea, whose people experienced French colonialism as Guineans—not as Malinke, Susu, or Peul. As Guinean natives, they were subjected to taxation, forced labor, military conscription, and the arbitrary "justice" of the *indigénat*. As indigenous peoples, they participated in the same political and economic systems, within geographic boundaries created by the colonial power. Despite their variety in language and ethnicity, they shared symbols, memories, and events in history that permitted them to communicate more effectively with other Guineans than with outsiders. Increasingly, during the 1950s, this shared experience was reflected in their collective consciousness, the consciousness of themselves as Guineans.[15]

If the shared history of Guinean peoples extended into the precolonial past and was strengthened by the common experience of colonialism, the identity of Guinea as a nation was not yet fully developed during the colonial period. Colonial powers were notorious for maintaining control through policies of divide and rule. France was no exception. Existent social cleavages, often along ethnic and class lines, were reinforced—and new ones created—by colonial policies. Layers of African intermediaries—government-appointed chiefs, colonial soldiers, and police—became the focal points of popular anger, diverting attention from the Europeans at the reins of power. Guinea's nationalist leaders needed to shift the focus and demonstrate common cause.[16]

WORLD WAR II: THE SEEDS OF NATIONALISM

The anticolonial movement in Guinea began to germinate during World War II. The war effort under both Vichy and the Free French imposed severe hardships on the rural population. Mandatory military conscription, civilian labor, and crop requisitions resulted in increased hostility toward the colonial administration and its African allies. Much of this animosity was directed at the canton and village chiefs who enforced colonial policies in the countryside.

While the population at home grew increasingly hostile, African soldiers in the French armed forces imbibed wartime messages championing the Allied cause. Convinced that they were fighting for freedom, they were proud of their service on the front lines and their survival of German prison camps. Many had tasted a semblance of equality with Frenchmen, both in the trenches and in civilian life. Returning to an unchanged colonial situation, disenchanted veterans would play a major role in the anticolonial movement of the postwar period, their nationalist fervor rooted in their wartime experiences.

Military Conscription

Every year from January to March, a mobile draft board moved through each of Guinea's 19 circles (administrative districts). Since the passage of the Conscription Law of 1919, three years of military service had been compul-

Photo 1.1 Tirailleurs Sénégalais on parade on the Champs-Élysées, Paris, July 14, 1939. (AFP/Getty Images)

Photo 1.2 Tirailleurs Sénégalais in an African training camp, December 4, 1939. (AFP/Getty Images)

sory for all male subjects of the French Empire. Paris had mandated an annual levy of 10,000 to 12,000 men for the Tirailleurs Sénégalais, the colonial army recruited from the eight territories constituting French West Africa. From his seat in Dakar, the governor-general of the federation had determined that Guinea, with a population of 2 million people, would provide 1,577 of those men: 23 to 166 men per year from each circle.[17]

Heightened call-up during World War II meant that 25,000 to 30,000 soldiers per year were recruited from French West Africa, with the Guinean contingent growing accordingly.[18] In total, some 18,000 to 20,000 Guinean men were recruited into the armed forces during the war years, while another 38,153 were assigned to the "second portion of the contingent," where they worked as laborers on public works projects.[19] As part of the national defense effort, they built and maintained the railroads, airfields, ports, and roads.[20] Canton chiefs were required to supply the requisite number of military recruits, under threat of punishment for noncompliance.[21]

The effects of military conscription were felt not only by the recruits, but also by those left behind. Because the ill and unfit were rejected, military conscription removed large numbers of able-bodied, economically productive adult males from the countryside. This had dire effects on rural production.[22] Even the governor admitted that "each year, the recruitment of soldiers resulted in the appropriation of the most robust and dynamic elements of the

Photo 1.3   Tirailleurs Sénégalais defending Dakar, Senegal, ca. September 1940–November 1941. (ABC Photo/*La Documentation Française*)

population."[23] Thousands of these soldiers died. Of those who returned to Guinea, many were permanently disabled.[24] Soldiers who survived their ordeal frequently returned with infectious pulmonary ailments, especially tuberculosis and pneumonia; others brought back venereal disease.[25]

Soldiers recruited in French West Africa were shipped to combat zones in Europe, North Africa, and the Middle East.[26] While the French High Command vehemently denied that African troops were put at greater risk in order to preserve the lives of Frenchmen, the vast majority of Tirailleurs Sénégalais served in the infantry, were frequently on the front lines, and were called upon to cover the retreat of French soldiers. Many believed they had fought more courageously than their French counterparts.[27] The magnitude of their wartime sacrifices inspired many of the veterans' postwar demands for official recognition and just compensation.

Photo 1.4   Tirailleurs Sénégalais assuming their post, Dakar, Senegal, ca. September 1940–November 1941. (ABC Photo/*La Documentation Française*)

Proud of their performance on the battlefield, African soldiers also learned important lessons. The war provided many with their first experience of integration. When Tirailleur and French companies were combined to form Régiments d'Infanterie Coloniale Mixtes Sénégalais, African and French soldiers fought side by side. Accustomed to a highly stratified and segregated colonial society, African soldiers experienced in combat a semblance of equality that was unthinkable at home.[28] Their experience with French civilians had further leveling effects. Unlike settlers and officials in the colonies, French people in the *métropole* were generally hospitable and welcoming. They provided African soldiers with food, clothing, and entertainment and invited them into their homes. African soldiers drank and talked with Frenchmen in local cafes, and some found French girlfriends and wives.[29]

Photo 1.5   Tirailleurs Sénégalais constructing shelters at Ouakan, Dakar, Senegal, ca. September 1940–November 1941. (ABC Photo/*La Documentation Française*)

Returning veterans thus viewed the French empire from a new perspective. The discriminatory treatment meted out to them upon their reentry drove home the point that while they had fought to liberate France, they themselves were not free.[30] Moreover, having witnessed a weakened and defeated France, they learned that the imperial power was indeed vulnerable.[31] These lessons had a strong impact on their subsequent political development; angry veterans would be a major force in the postwar nationalist movement.

Crop Requisitions: Forced Cultivation and Collection

Military conscripts and their families were not the only Guineans affected by the European war. From the war's outbreak in 1939, rural civilians were subjected to a harsh labor regime in the interest of the war effort. They labored on behalf of the Paris government until its fall in June 1940, for the Vichy government through November 1942, and for the Free French until the war's end in 1945.[32]

Foremost among the labor requirements was the forced cultivation or collection of crops deemed critical to the war effort. Under both Vichy and the Free French, peasants were required to meet specific quotas and to sell at prices fixed by the government.[33] The colonial administration set quotas for the collection of honey, wax, and wild rubber—rubber being especially important for military purposes. It requisitioned large quantities of oil-producing plants such as peanuts, palm, shea, castor, and sesame to be used for fuel, industrial purposes, cooking, and soap production. Required to provision the urban populations of Guinea and France, as well as the French armed forces, peasants were taxed in rice, millet, fonio, and maize. They also furnished beef, potatoes, fruits, vegetables, pepper, coffee, cotton, sisal, indigo, and tobacco.[34]

Guinea's transfer to the Free French in late 1942 brought no relief. René Pleven, the Free French commissioner for the colonies, urged the peasant population to make "a maximum economic contribution to the effort of liberation and general relief after the war." Like his Vichy predecessor, the Free French governor-general of French West Africa called for the "intensification of production of vegetable oils, rubber and all products useful for the war."[35] Under Free French authority, quotas for food crops and rubber doubled. Recruitment quotas, for both military and forced labor, also increased by 100 percent.[36] The Guinean population was subjected to the most brutal forms of forced labor—to liberate France.

In 1943, the Free French governor noted that crop requisitions had increased dramatically since Vichy's departure. Rubber production in Guinea had augmented from 944 tons in 1942 to 1,323 tons in 1943. The production of valuable oils also had grown considerably. While the Guinean population produced 7,131 tons of oil-bearing palm kernels in 1942, it generated 17,000 tons in 1943. Similarly, rice production had increased substantially, rising from 2,000 tons in 1942 to 13,474 tons in 1943. Nearly all of the rice crop was earmarked for export.[37]

If peasants were unable to meet their quotas, or if the desired products were unavailable locally, they were forced to buy goods on the black market—at prices far greater than those they received from the colonial administration.[38] Circles that produced no rubber were forced to purchase it from those that did. In 1941, Kissidougou circle rendered nine tons of rubber to the colonial authorities, but most of it had been purchased elsewhere. The people of the Dialakoro canton furnished 566 kilos of rubber, but 476 kilos had been purchased from the neighboring circles of Kankan and Kouroussa, at a rate of 40 to 50 francs per kilo. Likewise, the people of Tinki canton bought 345 kilos out of a total of 360 kilos rendered, paying 80 francs per kilo.[39]

Writing of the Free French period in 1943, Jacques Richard-Molard described the impossible nature of colonial demands:

> One circle is required to produce so many tons of liana rubber, even though there is no liana in their territory. The native is therefore forced to travel on foot, sometimes very far, to buy rubber elsewhere, regardless of cost, in order to escape the hand of "justice." He must sell this to the commandant at the official price, which is many times lower than the purchase price.
>
> [In Guinea] another circle is taxed in honey. None is produced there. The commandant is punished for telegraphing his government: "AGREE TO HONEY. STOP. SEND BEES."[40]

If quotas were not met, the chiefs were held accountable. On May 20, 1945, the Kissidougou circle commandant warned his subordinate canton chiefs:

> I give you until 31 May at the latest to deliver your quota of millet for the current trading season to the Société commercial de l'Ouest africain.
>
> On 15 May . . . kilos still remained to be delivered. Unless you fulfil this order within the term stipulated, you will be brought physically to Kissidougou and subjected to the necessary sanctions until the quota of your canton is fulfilled.

Sanctions included dismissal, imprisonment, and the outright suppression of the canton. Chiefs, therefore, subjected the local populations to extreme pressures.[41]

Under threat of severe sanctions, men, women, and children were forced to abandon all other work in order to cultivate, collect, and process the products demanded by the state. Rubber collection, a particularly labor-intensive operation, diverted massive quantities of labor from food production, jeopardizing the people's nutritional base.[42] Women and children were forced to engage in the laborious task of crushing palm and shea nuts in order to extract the oil-bearing kernels.[43] In 1941, the Vichy governor noted that African farmers had cultivated substitute crops for local consumption, allowing the exportation of large quantities of rice.[44] Manioc, a common rice substitute, required far less labor than the grain crop. However, it was significantly less nutritious.[45] Inevitably, food rationing was introduced. As more crops were requisitioned to feed the troops and the *métropole,* peasant families went hungry. In some areas, famine occurred.[46]

Forced Labor

Mandatory crop production was not the only form of forced labor imposed on the peasant population during the war. Wartime restrictions on imports had resulted in severe shortages of cloth, blankets, gasoline, tools, hardware, and other consumer goods. With nothing to buy, Africans were not volunteering for wage labor, resulting in a serious labor crisis.[47] In 1941, the governor of Guinea proclaimed that if Africans did not offer their services voluntarily, the government would requisition civilian labor.[48] With few volunteers, the administration increasingly resorted to force. Canton and village chiefs were expected to provide the required number of so-called volunteers.[49]

Forced labor on behalf of the war effort encompassed both the public and private sectors. Peasants were compelled to cut and haul wood to fuel the Conakry-Niger railway line and to work as laborers on European-owned plantations and in the fields of the circle commandants. Women as well as men were put to work on coffee and banana plantations and in road construction.[50] Throughout the war years, tens of thousands of the most physically fit men were uprooted from their homes and made to work for others, rather than for their families. Forced laborers were often removed from their homes for long periods of time, jeopardizing their own economic base. Men forcibly recruited in Upper-Guinea and the forest region were sent to work on banana plantations in the coastal areas, hundreds of miles from home. Similarly, tens of thousands of men from the Futa Jallon and the circles of Boké (Lower-Guinea) and Siguiri (Upper-Guinea) were sent to work in the Senegalese peanut fields.[51] In 1942, the Kouroussa circle commandant noted that the demands of forced labor were taking a heavy toll. With an official population of 67,450 people,

> the circle at present supplies: 490 labourers for the Conakry-Niger railway line (tree-felling at Nono and Tamba); 80 labourers for the Baro plantation (Kankan circle); 80 labourers for the Delsol plantation; 15 labourers for the African Banana plantations; 40 labourers for the Linkeny banana planta-tions; 200 labourers for public works at Kankan; 100 labourers for charcoal

burning at Conakry; 100 labourers for road-repair work—making a total of 1,105.[52]

Forced labor also took other forms. With coal- and gasoline-powered vehicles inoperative due to the unavailability of imported fuel, the old system of head portage was reintroduced on a large scale.[53] In 1943, the Free French governor noted that the means of motorized transport were "so reduced, so precarious, that they will not suffice for assuring the evacuation of the products, and thousands of porters must be substituted for idle gasoline-powered vehicles."[54] Head portage was a particularly brutal form of forced labor. According to Richard-Molard,

> To transport one ton of rice to the nearest railway station, 300 km. away, 600 men were requisitioned, who each carried 15 kilos on their heads for twelve days, their return journey on foot taking another ten days; so for a total of more than three weeks they ate only what they found along the road.[55]

Taxed in food from their own reserves, overworked and underpaid, the Guinean population was also faced with demands for so-called voluntary subscriptions to support the war effort. These contributions were officially characterized as "gifts given for the Defense of the Empire."[56] In 1943, the governor of Guinea lauded the population's "magnificent effort of generosity . . . in contributing close to 100 million francs" to the defense of France.[57] Chiefs exerted enormous pressures on their subjects to contribute in cash and kind. There was little pretense that the subscriptions were, in fact, voluntary. In official reports, they were grouped with taxes, forced labor, and the obligatory provision of foodstuffs.[58]

Resistance: Desertion and Flight

Active opposition to state demands began during the war. Large numbers of workers resisted onerous working conditions—and the very principle of forced labor—by deserting their workplaces and returning home. In 1943, the inspector of labor reported that a number of European-owned plantations in Lower-Guinea were experiencing massive desertions due to low wages and inadequate rations.[59] Public work sites were also affected. Working in isolated areas with relatively little supervision, men cutting wood for the Conakry-Niger railway were especially prone to take flight.[60]

If forced laborers resisted wartime exactions by deserting the workplace, rural populations engaged in similar forms of resistance on an even grander scale. Throughout the war years, official reports document the widespread exodus of rural populations across territorial boundaries to avoid taxes, forced labor and rubber collection, and military recruitment. In 1943 alone, the Mali subdivision (Futa Jallon) lost more than 8,000 inhabitants, including some 6,000 eligible taxpayers, who had taken up residence in Senegal.[61] The governor observed that,

> most flee the furnishing of rubber and other products they are required to gather, or the increase in work resulting from the extension of agricultural production. But some also leave to avoid the extortions of their village or canton chief, and their absence lasts until a new chief is appointed.[62]

In Lower-Guinea inhabitants of Boké circle fled into Portuguese territory to avoid furnishing large quantities of rice and rubber. Despite what the governor termed "a very poor harvest," rice quotas were not diminished, and local food supplies suffered. Similarly, in the forest region, the N'Zérékoré circle commandant anticipated an exodus toward Liberia, provoked by the military recruitment campaign.[63]

By the end of the war, it was estimated that one-tenth of the population of the Faranah subdivision (Upper-Guinea) had fled their homes. In N'Zérékoré circle (forest region), 7,000 to 8,000 people had migrated to Liberia; all of the frontier cantons were depopulated. In Forécariah circle (Lower-Guinea), 5,000 to 6,000 people fled their homes between 1941 and 1946. Other border circles were similarly affected: Gaoual in the Futa Jallon, Boké and Kindia in Lower-Guinea, and Guéckédou and Macenta in the forest region.[64]

Although they masked their concern in praise for those African cultivators who had remained loyal, colonial officials were aware that the war effort placed intolerable burdens on the rural population. In 1943, the governor of Guinea acknowledged that "the production of the great products necessary for the war economy have been developed to the extreme limit of possibilities."[65] Similarly, the governor-general of French West Africa noted that while African cultivators throughout the federation had furnished a great deal toward the war effort, in Guinea and Togo, especially, the maximum had been attained.[66] The population could bear no further burdens.

The existence of an overworked yet impoverished peasantry had obvious political ramifications. Colonial officials were well aware that local disenchantment could escalate into more generalized political discontent, particularly as French subjects compared their lot to that in British colonies. At the war's end, the fear of nationalist ferment in the countryside increasingly overshadowed other government concerns. In 1945, the governor-general of French West Africa warned,

> The African peasant finds that the prices he receives for his products are too low and the prices of imported products, cloth in particular, are too high. He is aware, in seeing the poorly provisioned trading stations, that he is badly

recompensed for his effort. He compares his situation to that of his neighbor in the Gold Coast, Nigeria, Sierra Leone. It is indispensable that this
astonishment does not become discontent.[67]

All of these hardships resulted in increased tensions between rural civilians
and French authorities. These tensions would come to a head in the postwar
period.

ENLIGHTENED IMPERIALISM AND THE POSTWAR POLITICAL ORDER

Just as anticolonial sentiment began to proliferate during World War II, so
too did imperial strategies to combat it. African leaders argued that their people deserved increased political rights and economic compensation for their
wartime sacrifices. The United States, emerging as a world power, pressed for
the breakup of colonial empires—in the name of free trade and, to a lesser
extent, self-determination of peoples. Under pressure on the home front and
in the international arena, France hoped to deter more radical solutions by
promising a reformed imperialism at the war's end. It declared that the rights
of French citizenship were universal and would be extended to the colonized.
Employing the language of assimilation, it justified continued colonial domination. The result was "enlightened" imperialism, an innovation that breathed
new life into the old empire but also gave African activists room to maneu-
ver.[68] Whether through naïveté or arrogance, France expected to control the
assimilation process. Newly minted citizens of the overseas territories would
be integrated according to a pace and to the degree desired by France. The
imperial power did not expect its words to be turned against it, or to be used
for gains it never had envisioned.[69]

The postwar framework in which France was obliged to operate had been
initiated by the United States and Britain during the war. In the summer of
1941, Britain had been desperate for American assistance in the Allied war
effort. It needed American money, supplies, weaponry, and troops. Thus, the
old European imperial power was forced to make concessions to the emerging economic giant. Under the banner of free trade, the United States sought
access to European colonies in Africa and Asia for the purchase of raw materials, the exploitation of markets, and the establishment of military bases. In
August 1941, four months before the United States entered World War II,
American president Franklin Roosevelt and British prime minister Winston
Churchill met on a ship off the coast of Newfoundland. Their purpose was to
outline the principles they hoped would serve as the bedrock of the postwar
international order.[70]

The result of this meeting was the Atlantic Charter, a broad set of principles
that championed a variety of liberal rights and liberties and addressed Ameri-

can economic concerns. The Atlantic Charter underscored the right of all nations to free trade and "access, on equal terms, . . . to the raw materials of the world which are needed for their economic prosperity." It further declared "the right of all peoples to choose the form of government under which they will live" and the "wish to see sovereign rights and self-government restored to those who have been forcibly deprived of them."[71] These principles were endorsed by 26 nations in January 1942.[72]

In calling for the restoration of "sovereign rights and self-government," Europeans, faced with the Nazi/Fascist threat, had only themselves in mind. Americans, seeking an open door to world trade, assumed that colonial states in Africa and Asia would ultimately give way to independent ones. However, under pressure from the British government, later bolstered by concerns about growing Soviet influence, the United States conceded the notion of increased self-government within reformed European empires, as long as the reforms included free trade. Thus, "enlightened" imperialism was born.[73]

In 1941 and 1942, France was under the authority of Nazi Germany and the Vichy collaborationist state, neither of which had any interest in an "enlightened" empire. Thus, it was left to Charles de Gaulle and the Free French to devise a French version of the Atlantic Charter. It was hoped that promised future reforms would both spur on and justify the intensified demands of the war effort in the colonies, undermine incipient communist and nationalist movements, satisfy American requirements for modernized colonial rule, and stave off American encroachments on the French domain. Reforms would thus guarantee France's continued hold on its empire and its tenuous claim to "Great Power" status in the postwar order. In order to rally support in the colonies, the Free French cause was increasingly described as one of democracy and republicanism opposing fascism and racism.[74]

In terms of the war effort, the years 1944 and 1945 were the most difficult for French colonial subjects. Demands for labor, crops, and conscripts had intensified under the Gaullist regime. However, with the last vestiges of Vichy cleansed from the French West African administration, the stage was set for fundamental reforms in colonial policy. It was in this context that de Gaulle, as leader of the Free French and president of its provisional government, convened the Brazzaville Conference in the French Congo on January 30, 1944.[75] Attending the weeklong conference were 44 French colonial officials, as well as economic and religious leaders. Although the purpose of the conference was to sketch the outlines of French postwar colonial policy, not a single African representative was invited.[76]

The final recommendations of the Brazzaville Conference made clear that Africans' increased "management of their own affairs" was not synonymous with self-government; nor was any future outside the French empire conceivable.[77] However, there would be greater colonial representation in the important political bodies in Paris and in the Constituent Assembly charged with drafting a new French constitution.[78]

Colonial subjects were also slated to play a broader political role on the home front—albeit largely consultative. The conference recommended the establishment of regional and district councils composed of African notables. Incorporating indigenous chiefs, as well as other important personages, these councils would have only advisory functions. At the territorial level, assemblies composed of both European and African representatives would be elected—by universal suffrage wherever feasible. The territorial assemblies would be consultative in terms of legislative and regulatory matters, but deliberative in terms of budgetary ones.[79]

The Brazzaville Conference also recommended a number of social reforms. More substantial trade union rights should be extended to the colonies. The hated systems of forced labor and arbitrary justice (the *indigénat*), both of which applied exclusively to Africans, should gradually be abolished.[80]

The reforms outlined at Brazzaville were implemented slowly and were not fully realized until the adoption of universal suffrage in 1956 and the establishment of local self-government in 1957.[81] The first steps toward reform were taken in August 1944, when legally recognized trade unions were permitted in the colonies, and minimum standards for African workers were established.[82] In August 1945, a dual college electoral system was instituted in French West and Equatorial Africa. However, suffrage was far from universal. Voting rights were extended to "qualified"—that is, assimilated—subjects, or *évolués*. Those deemed properly assimilated by French authorities included "veterans, those who had French decorations or distinctions, those who had school certificates higher than and including the primary school certificate, chiefs of ethnic groups, members of unions or professional groups and civil servants." French citizens voted in the first electoral college, while qualified subjects voted in the second.[83]

Constituent Assemblies and Constitutions, 1945–1946

Carrying through on the promises of Brazzaville, the French government permitted some colonial representation in the Constituent Assembly of 1945, the body charged with drafting the constitution for the Fourth Republic. The Constituent Assembly was composed of 586 representatives, including 10 from French West Africa.[84] Of the latter, two were from Guinea, one elected through each college. With a population of nearly 2.5 million African subjects and 5,000 French citizens, Guinea's registered electorate numbered fewer than 20,000.[85]

The Constituent Assembly met in Paris from November 1945 to May 1946. By April, the assembly had drafted a constitution that clearly reflected the position of the French Left.[86] The people, rather than the nation, were deemed the source of sovereignty, and a unicameral, popularly elected National Assembly dominated a weak presidency.[87] Subjects of the old empire, now called the French Union, would be transformed into citizens of France, who would enjoy all the rights and freedoms that citizenship entailed. Suffrage would be universal. The Union would be "freely consented to" by its members through ratification of the constitution. Thus, in contrast to pronouncements at Brazzaville, the door to eventual independence appeared open, should any members subsequently decide to withdraw their consent.[88] That test never came to pass. The French citizenry rejected the constitution in a May 5, 1946, referendum in which colonial subjects were not allowed to vote.[89]

Despite the failure of the April 1946 Constitution, some movement toward reform was made. The Brazzaville Conference had proposed the gradual abolition of forced labor and the *indigénat*.[90] African representatives to the Constituent Assembly pressed for laws enacting these reforms. On February 20, 1946, the *indigénat* was suppressed. The Houphouët-Boigny Law of April 11, 1946, outlawed most forms of forced or obligatory labor. On May 7, 1946, the Lamine Guèye Law erased the legal distinction between French citizens and subjects by abolishing the category of subject. Henceforth, all Africans would be citizens, not subjects, of France.[91] However, certain distinctions remained. Individuals of European ancestry were automatically *citoyens de statut français*, which meant that they were subject to French civil law. Most Africans, in contrast, were *citoyens de statut local* and subject to African customary law.[92]

Alarmed by the reformist atmosphere in Paris and the liberal provisions that narrowly escaped enactment in the April constitution, settler and commercial interests lobbied hard during the campaign for the second Constituent Assembly.[93] As a result, the second assembly, elected on June 2, 1946, produced a far more conservative constitutional draft. Provisions that had favored the colonies were weakened or eliminated.[94] For instance, although "all subjects of overseas territories" were now deemed citizens, they were declared citizens of the French Union, not of the French Republic.[95] The Lamine Guèye Law, which distinguished between citizens based on their personal status, was incorporated into the proposed constitution, entrenching differential treatment in a number of domains.[96] In elections determined by a dual electoral college, citizens of French civil status voted in the first electoral college, while the large majority of African voters voted in the second.[97]

The second draft constitution contained other disparities. Suffrage remained highly restrictive for African citizens. The representation of overseas territories in the French National Assembly was disproportionately small relative to their populations. While metropolitan France was allotted one deputy for every 75,000 people, overseas territories were permitted one deputy for every 700,000 to 850,000 people. There was no longer reference to a Union "freely consented to." The door to eventual withdrawal of consent and, hence, to independence had slammed shut. Moreover, the new constitution made it clear that the overseas territories were deemed an integral part of the "indivisible" French Republic, rather than simply "associated" with it. Thus, any agitation for independence would be tantamount to secession—or treason.[98]

Nonetheless, some positive provisions remained in the new draft. For elections to the National Assembly, French West Africa would no longer utilize a dual college system. Guinea would henceforth have two deputies, both elected on a common voter roll. While French territorial governors would continue to operate with enormous executive powers, they would be advised by general councils, subsequently renamed "territorial assemblies." Due to settler pressure, however, the latter were elected according to the dual college system in which citizens of French civil status were disproportionately represented.[99]

Despite the obvious deficiencies, the second constitutional draft was the best that could be obtained under the circumstances. Thus, all the African delegates to the second Constituent Assembly voted for the revised constitution—although their feelings of anger and betrayal ran deep. The compromise draft was approved by a referendum composed solely of first college citizens on October 13 and officially adopted as the constitution of the Fourth Republic on October 28, 1946. Second college citizens had not been allowed to vote.[100]

The Congress of Bamako and the RDA

On September 15, 1946, as the final provisions of the constitution were being debated, all 22 African representatives to the Constituent Assembly signed a manifesto calling for equality of rights between peoples of the colonies and those of the *métropole*.[101] In order to protect the rights and liberties acquired since 1945 and to promote their extension, the document called for a congress of African parties and delegates, selected by the people of each territory, to be held in Bamako, capital of the French Soudan. The ultimate goal of the Bamako Congress was to form an interterritorial movement to press for African political rights and liberties, as well as economic and social reforms.[102]

The Guinean delegation to the Bamako Congress was politically and ethnically diverse. It included representatives from numerous bodies established since the 1944 Brazzaville Conference. Among these were delegates from the Parti Progressiste de Guinée (PPG), established in March 1946 as an outgrowth of the Parti Communiste Français (PCF)-sponsored Groupes d'Études Communistes (GEC). As the only party grouping both Africans and Europeans, the PPG delegation included a handful of French men and several young African men. While most African party members were civil servants, few had more than primary school education—the highest level available in Guinea—and, consequently, held only low-ranking government positions.[103] The Guinean delegation also included a dozen representatives of ethnic and regional associations, along with members of trade unions, particularly those affiliated with the CGT, which, in turn, was closely associated with the PCF.[104]

Guinea's delegation was led by Madéïra Kéïta, secretary-general of the PPG and a technical aide at the Institut Français d'Afrique Noire. A colonial civil servant originally from the French Soudan, Kéïta was posted in Guinea. The delegation also included Sékou Touré, a young Malinke postal clerk and secretary-general of the militant PTT workers' union, who, in March 1946, had founded the Union des Syndicats Confédérés de Guinée (USCG), which grouped together all CGT-affiliated unions in Guinea.[105]

The most significant event at the Bamako Congress was the formation of the RDA on October 20. An interterritorial alliance of parties that would soon boast branches in each of the territories of French West and Equatorial Africa, as well as in the United Nations trust territories of Togo and Cameroon, the RDA proposed united action across territorial boundaries as a means of achieving its goals.[106]

The RDA was not a radical organization; it embraced the notion of French universalism and sought African emancipation through assimilation rather than secession.[107] Its stated purpose was to win greater political autonomy for the colonies, as well as equality of political, economic, and social rights for colonial and metropolitan peoples. The party advocated increased local autonomy, not independence, which it considered premature. However, it rejected the notion that African territories constituted an integral part of an "indivisible" French Republic and noted that to be legitimate, the French Union must be "freely consented to" by all its members.[108] The RDA would dominate the political scene in French West Africa throughout the decade that followed.[109]

Ethnic Associations and the Guinean RDA

When the RDA entered the political scene, there were few political parties in Guinea. Those that existed were relatively weak and newly established. The political arena was dominated by regional and ethnic associations promoting the interests of their particular constituencies: Peul, Malinke, Susu, and people from the forest region. Although they sometimes formed temporary alliances with other groups, none of the associations was able to fully transcend regional or ethnic particularisms, thereby developing a national perspective. Led by notables of the "traditional" or "modern" (Western-educated) elites, none had a coherent political program or organization capable of mobilizing a mass base.[110]

Thus, it was in a social and political arena dominated by ethnic and regional associations that the RDA began to operate in Guinea—with an explicitly nonethnic national message. On October 12, 1946, the day after the conclusion of the Bamako Congress, a preliminary meeting was held in Conakry. In attendance were Madéïra Kéïta, secretary-general of the PPG, Sékou Touré, representing the Union du Mandé as well as the CGT, and members of the Union Forestière, Union des Métis, GEC, Comité d'Études Franco-Africain de Résistance, and the Mouvement Républicain Démocrate.[111] It was this group, with the Parti Progressiste at its center, that within a few months would form the core of the Guinean branch of the RDA.[112]

On May 14, 1947, Guinean delegates to the Bamako Congress, members of various ethnic associations, and other representative bodies met to draw up a constitution and charter for the Guinean RDA.[113] Although it assumed the name Parti Démocratique de Guinée (PDG) from its second party congress in October 1950, the Guinean branch continued to be known in Guinea as the RDA.[114] The constitution and charter were adopted on June 14, and the first board of directors was elected two days later. Madéïra Kéïta won the post of secretary-general.[115] The four undersecretaries included representatives from each of the major ethnic associations: Union du Mandé (Malinke); Union de la Basse-Guinée (primarily Susu); Amicale Gilbert Vieillard (Peul); and Union Forestière (forest peoples).[116]

The police reported that on June 16, the Union du Mandé, Union Forestière, and Amicale Gilbert Vieillard "practically fused with the RDA," which seemed intent upon uniting all ethnic groups.[117] This was, in fact, the party's goal. It aimed to unite all inhabitants of the territory, without distinction as to race, ethnicity, region, or religion, in the struggle for political and economic emancipation.[118] In the local party newspaper, Doudou Guèye explained:

> The R.D.A. is the alliance of our young intellectuals—the products of French schools—of our cultivators from the bush, of fishermen, peasants, customary chiefs, their slaves of yesterday, their griots, wives, sorcerers. . . . It is an alliance of *all* socio-economic strata in the exploited world. It is an alliance of those who want to break the chains of subjugation with the forces of democracy in the *métropole*—to assure the grandeur and future of the French community.[119]

Conferences were held to organize RDA subsections in Conakry and Kindia (Lower-Guinea); Mamou, Labé, Pita, and Dabola (Futa Jallon); and Kankan, Bissikrima, and Kouroussa (Upper-Guinea). Most of the ethnic associations encouraged their members to join.[120] By the end of 1947, the governor reported that apart from two or three circles in Lower-Guinea, the RDA had established subsections in all the circles and important urban centers of the territory.[121]

CONCLUSION

Guinea's postwar nationalist movement was rooted in the experience of war. On the home front, peasants were burdened by crop requisitions, forced labor, and military conscription, extracted from them by government-appointed chiefs. Abroad, Guinean soldiers, largely of rural origin, made tremendous sacrifices for the liberation of France. They returned home with a new sense of confidence and entitlement. This perception of worthiness and grievance permeated the countryside, laying the groundwork for subsequent nationalist activities.

In the face of mounting challenges to its imperial project, France attempted to reform its empire in order to save it. However, the imperial power lost control of the process. Western-educated elites seized the opportunities offered by "enlightened" imperialism, demanding the rights promised to them at Brazzaville, rallying for a more liberal constitution, and organizing political parties to advance their agendas. The most successful of these parties, the RDA, promoted an avowedly nationalist, rather than a simply anticolonial, agenda. With a message of unity that hearkened to a shared precolonial past and common grievances under colonialism, it rapidly trumped the ethnic associations that were limited by their narrow vision and base. Among the party's earliest adherents, military veterans were among the first to articulate anticolonial grievances and to organize to secure their rights. These returning servicemen spearheaded the RDA's penetration into the countryside. Their role in nationalist mobilization is the subject of the next chapter.

2

LIBERTÉ, ÉGALITÉ, FRATERNITÉ: MILITARY VETERANS AND THE POSTWAR NATIONALIST MOVEMENT, 1940–1955

The RDA's success was largely due to its organization of groups that had already mobilized themselves. Military veterans, primarily of rural origin, were among the first groups to join the party. Although they had long been the bulwark of the colonial administration, African soldiers, politicized by their wartime experiences, were at the forefront of postwar agitation against colonial institutions. After fighting side by side with Frenchmen, African veterans suffered discriminatory treatment upon their return home. Hearkening to the new French rhetoric of universalism, they demanded pay and benefits equal to those of their metropolitan counterparts. In the interior, they emerged as alternative leaders, challenging the chiefs who had enforced the government's war effort. Recognizing an opportunity to expand its base, the RDA embraced the veterans' cause in the political arena and followed their lead in the countryside.

Thus began a battle between the RDA and the French state for the veterans' allegiance. In an attempt to court this powerful constituency, the government gradually met the veterans' demands. As a result, by the end of the first postwar decade, military veterans had largely reconciled with the colonial regime. Better off than the vast majority of their rural brethren, they increasingly shied away from anticolonial protest. While they played a significant role in the early years of the nationalist struggle, military veterans had withdrawn from the political scene by its final stages.

This chapter focuses on veterans' grievances, the ways in which they organized themselves, and their leadership in rural resistance to the colonial chieftaincy. It concludes with an assessment of the RDA's successful courtship, the government's subsequent challenge, and the veterans' ultimate retreat from the political scene.

THE EXPERIENCE OF WAR

The Battle of France had officially ended with the signing of the Franco-German armistice on June 22, 1940. Three-fifths of France was occupied by German troops, while the collaborationist Vichy regime controlled the rest. Tens of thousands of Tirailleurs Sénégalais, including some 9,000 Guineans, were detained in prison camps in Occupied France or in Germany.[1] Conditions in the camps were treacherous—more so for African than for European prisoners. Thousands of Africans were summarily executed or died of hunger, malnutrition, cold, or disease. For survivors, dysentery and frostbite were constant problems.[2] Most Africans held in Germany were eventually transferred to work camps in northeastern France, where they were forced to contribute to the German war effort by cutting wood and working in the mining and arms manufacturing sectors.[3] While African prisoners were paid for their work, according to the stipulations of the Geneva Convention, their paltry pay was less than that of European prisoners.[4] Some POWs were imprisoned for as long as five years—until they were liberated by Allied armies in 1944 and 1945.[5]

Other African soldiers were called upon to carry on the fight. After France's defeat, General Charles de Gaulle rallied the Free French, assembled a truncated army, and vowed to continue the struggle.[6] From the fall of France in June 1940 until its liberation in the summer of 1944, French West and Equatorial Africans constituted the most important elements of the Free French forces. French West Africans were among those who fought in North Africa between 1940 and 1943. They were among the Allied forces that invaded Italy in the summer of 1943 and southern France in August 1944. The 20,000 African soldiers who participated in the Allied landings in southern France constituted 20 percent of the First French Army. Having liberated Toulon, Marseille, and Lyon, the First French Army was poised for an offensive on the Rhine when African soldiers were suddenly recalled from the front.[7]

By replacing African with French troops, de Gaulle hoped to bolster the morale of deeply humiliated Frenchmen. Having suffered defeat by the Germans, the French could not bear further insults. The prospect of African subjects gloating over their role in the liberation of France was completely unacceptable. Moreover, as self-described liberators, African veterans might make extraordinary and unprecedented political demands.[8]

De Gaulle's denigration of African soldiers' role in the war effort is perhaps most striking in his three-volume war memoirs. While the books include passing reference to the presence of sub-Saharan African troops in the war theaters, the critical nature of their role in the defense and liberation of France, the extent of their sacrifices, and the impact of the war effort on the African home front are not even mentioned.[9] De Gaulle's determination to minimize the significance of the Tirailleurs Sénégalais set the stage for the events that followed.

By the end of 1944, all of France had been liberated from German occupation. While French troops celebrated their victory with their countrymen, tens of thousands of African soldiers, including recently freed POWs, were herded into camps in central and southern France. For months they awaited transport home. Food, shelter, and clothing were woefully inadequate, the situation worsened by the confiscation of uniforms. While French soldiers were given back pay and discharged, Africans, denied their wages, continued to be subjected to tough military discipline. According to Echenberg, some ex-POWs were forced to engage in unpaid labor, exchanging German "stalags for French military camps; hard labor in the German war industry for construction work under French military supervision." While the Germans had paid African workers minimal wages, French authorities continued to deny them back pay owed for the period of their imprisonment.[10]

Reports of unrest aboard Africa-bound troop ships worried French authorities. Fearing a large concentration of angry soldiers in Dakar, René Pleven, the commissioner for the colonies, ordered the French West African governor-general to repatriate the returning troops as quickly as possible. In November 1944, Pleven warned, "The [former] prisoners of war may be a factor in stirring up discontent among the people."[11]

In fact, miserable conditions and discriminatory treatment did lead to a number of incidents, foreshadowing the demands of postwar veterans' movements. Most incidents involved *tirailleurs* who had been "whitened" out of the First French Army or ex-POWs recently freed from German camps. Grievances generally focused on inadequate food, clothing, and shelter, along with failure to receive back pay and demobilization premiums. While most incidents occurred in France, others occurred on African soil. The most notorious of these took place at the Thiaroye barracks on the outskirts of Dakar on December 1, 1944—shortly after Pleven issued his warning.[12]

At Thiaroye, angry ex-POWs roughed up their officers, and colonial troops and police were called in to put down the disturbances. Thirty-five protesters were shot dead and an equal number seriously wounded. Hundreds more were injured. Thirty-four ex-POWs were arrested, tried, and convicted of charges only slightly less serious than mutiny—despite pleas for leniency due to their outstanding military service. Sentences ranged from 1 to 10 years in prison, with fines of 10,000 francs—a hefty sum for an African *tirailleur.* Among those receiving an average of 5 to 10 years were six men from Guinea. Karimou Sylla, who was fingered as a particularly militant mutineer, probably came from Guinea or the French Soudan.[13]

A STAKE IN THE SYSTEM

Although wary of the veterans' increasingly vocal demands, the colonial state historically had considered African soldiers to be among its most loyal retainers. Unwilling to lose its long-standing allies, it made feeble attempts at co-optation, playing to veterans' views of themselves as an emerging new elite. It played off differences among them, promoting some at the expense of others. It privileged career soldiers over conscripts, and ex-POWs, the severely wounded, and a narrowly defined group of ex-combatants over others who had suffered in the service of France. It hoped that token privileges would mitigate against the influence of more radical elements, and that a stake in the system would outweigh the promise of something more substantial.

Although the term "veteran" applied to all soldiers who had served in the French armed forces during the war, there were important distinctions among them. These distinctions determined their access to cash income, primarily in the form of pensions, and it was access to pensions that divided veterans from one another and from their rural compatriots. A small minority of veterans had served as career soldiers *(anciens militaires),* who enlisted for 15 to 25 years and were entitled to pensions, which commenced upon discharge. If they had married according to civil—as opposed to customary—law, their pensions could be paid to their widows. However, very few women benefited since civil marriages were exceedingly rare, even among these relatively elite Africans.[14]

The vast majority of African soldiers were conscripts who served three-year terms before returning to their rural homes. Among conscripts, only those who had been at the front for 90 consecutive days *(anciens combattants)* were entitled to pensions upon reaching age 60. Their widows were not eligible to receive them. POWs who had been held for at least six months, soldiers who had been severely disabled by their wounds, and amputees were eligible for further benefits.[15]

Whatever their relative status within the group, returning veterans of all kinds rapidly emerged as a self-styled elite in the rural areas. With their worldly experience, access to cash income and consumer goods, and command of the French language, veterans developed new criteria of masculine status.[16] Although many were the descendants of slaves and other low-status groups, they aspired to leadership positions and "big man" stature, previously inaccessible to them.[17] If their long absence, low status, and prior poverty had prevented them from accumulating the land, livestock, wives, children, and junior male followers required for "big man" status, they could compensate with their new cash income. Bereft of young men who owed allegiance to them, many hired help to cultivate their land. Others used their newfound wealth to build up patronage networks.[18] Spearheading rural resistance to the local chiefs, many veterans sought appointment in their place.[19] Both embracing and redefining the norms of "dominant masculinity," returning veterans sought positions of respect, prestige, and leadership in their local communities.[20]

Eager to bolster its ties to this important constituency, the colonial administration granted veterans a number of rights and privileges that distinguished them from other Africans, even as it denied them pay and benefits equal to those of French soldiers. Military veterans were among the few Africans accorded the vote in the postwar political order. Given the highly restrictive nature of the franchise, they formed a significant proportion of the African electorate.[21] They were given special consideration in filling village and canton chieftaincies. The colonial archives are filled with petitions by veterans to replace existing chiefs, particularly those who were illiterate or had poor French language skills.[22] The government also offered veterans limited agricultural assistance and preference for a number of reserved jobs in both the public and private sectors.[23]

Some veterans were seduced by these enticements. In contrast to those who agitated for equality with their metropolitan counterparts, this group simply aspired to higher status within the colonial system.[24] Seeking to distinguish themselves from the more parochial peasant masses, these men viewed themselves as a new type of *évolué* who had adopted Western attire, ate bread and rice, and consumed alcohol and tobacco. As "modernizers," they sought Western education for their children and administrative positions for themselves.[25] As such, they were more susceptible to government, rather than nationalist, appeals.

THE POLITICIZATION OF AFRICAN VETERANS

Despite these promising developments, even the most loyal veterans suffered disappointment. Very few African veterans had the education and skills required for the reserved jobs. Thus, only about 10 percent of the returnees were able to take advantage of the job preference policy. Moreover, European veterans were offered far more governmental assistance in the reintegration effort. These disparities greatly angered African ex-servicemen.[26] Already, in the course of the 1946 elections, colonial authorities detected a change of attitude in the veteran population, particularly among the higher ranks. In Guinea, the security services reported,

For the non-elite indigenous people, forming the mass of *tirailleurs,* the elections boil down to an ethnic struggle, as they are for the civilians. . . . As for the indigenous cadres of noncommissioned officers, among certain elements, a sharp change in their frame of mind (in the bad sense) and in their attitude vis-à-vis European cadres have been observed.[27]

The uprising at Thiaroye and its repression also had a dramatic impact in French West Africa. Thiaroye became a rallying cry for indignant military veterans, who were outraged at the slaughter and imprisonment of soldiers who had suffered to defend and then liberate France.[28] African soldiers had imbibed French claims of universalism. As they saw it, they had made sacrifices equal to, if not greater than, their French counterparts. Upon their return home, they simply had demanded the rights and benefits that were due to them.[29] To their dismay, they found that French claims were not all they appeared to be. When disparate, prejudicial treatment continued, irate veterans moved to the forefront of the political struggle. Noncommissioned officers often assumed leadership positions, while ex-POWs, who had suffered particularly unjust treatment, and severely disabled veterans, who could not be reintegrated into civilian economic life, were among the most militant.[30]

Returning veterans, primarily conscripted rather than career soldiers, constituted an influential group within the French West African federation. Five years after the war's end, there were some 16,222 veterans of the campaigns of 1939–1945 in Guinea alone.[31] Some migrated to the urban areas, where they had greater access to reserved jobs, consumer goods, and a "modern" lifestyle. Many of these became important players in the urban-based regional and ethnic associations that formed the nucleus of postwar political parties. The vast majority, however, returned to their rural villages.[32]

Most soldiers, whether career or conscript, came from extremely modest backgrounds. In the Futa Jallon, especially, many were the descendants of slaves and other low-status groups. The association of military life with low social status deterred the more privileged from volunteering, and well-connected elites used their wealth and social ties to escape the draft.[33] Thus, it was primarily rural men with little or no access to Western education who formed the bulk of the colonial armed forces. Although some had engaged in migrant labor, religious pilgrimages, or trade, many had not previously traveled far from their homes.

The war had broadened their horizons and reshaped their perspectives. The soldiers had journeyed to distant places—France, Germany, Italy, and Indochina. Some had served in integrated regiments, including both French and African soldiers. Many had been welcomed into French homes. They had witnessed French humiliation and defeat and no longer thought of the colonial empire as invincible.[34] Returning soldiers were struck by the disparity between the relatively egalitarian circumstances they had experienced in

France—from French families and fellow soldiers—and their miserable treatment by the French at home.[35] The experience of the former POWs at the Thiaroye barracks pointedly reminded all veterans of the nature of the system to which they were returning. Having fought for freedom and democracy in Europe, they were even more determined to achieve them at home.

The government's initial response to veterans' claims was to scrutinize their activities with suspicion. French intelligence services kept close tabs on returned soldiers, especially former POWs. Their newly established associations were carefully monitored for signs of subversion. Police spies attended their meetings. Their attitudes, actions, and effects on the local population were duly noted in regular and frequent reports by circle commandants and police officials. Postal censors intercepted veterans' mail—searching for "disquieting" correspondence between African men and French women, as well as subversive political attitudes.[36] While social distance between the colonizer and the colonized had been bridged slightly during the war, the government vowed to turn back the clock.

POSTWAR VETERANS' ASSOCIATIONS AND THE POLITICS OF PENSIONS

Very few French officials understood the impact of wartime experiences on the psyche of African veterans—or their profound change in attitude toward the imperial power.[37] Few recognized the extent to which the African soldiers, from dozens of ethnic groups in numerous colonies, "had acquired a heightened consciousness of themselves as Africans" united across village, ethnic, and regional lines by their shared experiences and common purpose.[38] Newly established veterans' associations contributed to this growing sense of solidarity.

As World War II drew to a close, metropolitan veterans' associations founded branches in French West Africa, bringing together conscripted and career soldiers, Africans and Europeans. They provided federation-wide communication networks that facilitated mobilization around specific grievances. The most important of these organizations, the Association des Anciens Combattants et Victimes de Guerre de l'Afrique Occidentale Française (AACVGAOF), was established in Dakar in October 1945. Members included European and African veterans, former POWs, and amputees. With its headquarters in Dakar, this large umbrella organization maintained branches in all the territorial capitals of the federation.[39] Within two years of its formation, the AACVGAOF had established subsections in nearly all the circles of Guinea.[40]

A second, more radical organization, the Association Générale des Amputés et Grands Blessés de l'Afrique Occidentale Française (AGAGBAOF), was founded the same year. Its metropolitan counterpart was closely linked to the

PCF. A third body, which was more conservative, obeisant to imperial France, and far less popular than the others, was the French West African branch of the Fédération Nationale des Prisonniers de Guerre (FNPG), also linked to a metropolitan parent organization.[41]

While these three associations were officially recognized by the colonial state, others were not. Many of the latter were locally instigated and African led. Without affiliation to metropolitan parent bodies, they were more independent in pursuing specifically African interests.[42] Concerned about the subversive potential of autonomous organizations, the governor of Guinea urged the circle commandants to push for the creation of AACVGAOF subsections—under government supervision.[43]

The AACVGAOF newspaper, *La Voix des Combattants et Victimes des Guerres de l'A.O.F.,* established on April 1, 1948, disseminated veterans' demands and grievances. Keeping its audience abreast of veterans' activities in the various territories of the federation, it also printed the texts of relevant parliamentary debates, laws, and decrees.[44]

The grievances of African veterans were many. Deep, structural racial discrimination had long existed in the French armed forces. Compared to their metropolitan counterparts, African soldiers received inferior rations, wages, benefits, and pensions. During the war, in order to boost the fighting spirit, the French government had promised to remedy these disparities. After the war, those promises were ignored.[45]

To bolster their cause, African veterans quickly latched onto the universalistic, egalitarian claims of postwar reformed imperialism. Campaigning under the banner "Equal sacrifices, equal rights," African veterans charged that they were entitled to the same benefits as Europeans. They sought redress through their newly established associations, which became leading crusaders for equality between African and European veterans.[46]

The primary cause of veteran discontent was their military pensions. While African veterans were financially better off than most rural Africans, compared to their metropolitan counterparts they suffered serious discrimination. Under pressure from veterans' associations and newly elected African parliamentarians, the French government made some attempt to ameliorate the situation. A decree of January 16, 1947, raised African military pensions to half the value of metropolitan pensions; cost-of-living increments were to increase by the same percentages as those in the *métropole*.[47]

Like trade unionists agitating during the same period, African veterans were not satisfied. Taking to heart the fact of French citizenship and the rhetoric of universalism, they rejected the status of second-class citizen.[48] They demanded complete equality between African and metropolitan veterans in pensions and other benefits. As long as this issue remained unresolved, there was potential for serious popular unrest. In 1949, the governor of Senegal expressed the concerns of many in the French West African administration:

The African military veterans continue their efforts to benefit from the same rights as the metropolitan military veterans. This question, which is taking long to be resolved, especially in that which concerns the payment of different pensions to Africans according to their origin, is creating a malaise in this milieu that is worthy of interest.[49]

In the new era of "enlightened" imperialism, the failure of the French state to fulfill its promises to African veterans was embarrassing—and potentially explosive. Inadequate and unequal pensions were one grievance; the failure to secure them at all was another. In July 1947, the French West African high commissioner (formerly, governor-general) noted that Guinean veterans in Macenta circle were stirring up trouble due to the long delay "in the payment of demobilization gratuities and the determination of their pensions."[50] In 1948, more than 12,000 French West African career soldiers had been waiting a decade to receive the pensions due to them. A typical case occurred in Guinea, where 20 letters were sent over three years before one career soldier's pension was granted in principle, and another two years before he received payment.[51]

With signs of unrest surfacing, the governor of Guinea sent an urgent letter to the high commissioner, requesting his intervention:

Numerous African soldiers, discharged one or even two years ago, have been deprived until now of the booklet for advances on their pensions. . . . the delays brought about in this domain are giving rise to grave manifestations of discontent on the part of the discharged soldiers. For reasons of political order, it is desirable that the pension advances be agreed to with the least possible delay.[52]

The government had reason to be concerned. On March 3, 1947, about 250 military veterans, all of whom had seen action during World War II, met in the Conakry home of Soriba Dama. Since 1940, Dama, a career soldier, had been president of the local Association des Anciens Militaires Africains de Guinée. Frustrated that the local Association des Anciens Combattants de la Guinée Française, which included both Africans and Europeans, was not adequately representing its interests, the group planned to form a new association under African direction. The new organization, presently named the Association des Anciens Combattants et Anciens Militaires Africains de la Guinée, would embrace all African war veterans—career soldiers and conscripted men—without distinction as to rank, class, or branch of service.[53]

Ex-Lieutenant Youldé opened the March 3 meeting. According to a police informant, Youldé decried

the oblivion in which the military veterans of Guinea find themselves (lack of employment, negligence of the responsible authorities concerning payment of disability and retirement pensions, the granting of decorations and awards, etc . . .) and he recalled the sufferings that they had to endure on the battle fields.

The purpose of the new organization would be to assist, morally and materially, veterans who had been severely wounded, as well as war widows and orphans. It would assure payment of pensions and monitor the granting of decorations and awards.[54] Besides the central organization in Conakry, the members hoped to create local subsections in the interior of the country, which would attempt to resolve the particular problems of veterans in the circles and subdivisions.[55]

The colonial government regarded the March 3 meeting with some alarm. The payment of military pensions had been temporarily suspended due to a lack of provisionary notebooks. In a March 10 letter to the quartermaster general of French West Africa, the governor warned, "I permit myself to draw your attention to the manifestations of discontent that these delays have wrought on the Territory."[56]

LAMINE KABA, THE KANKAN REVOLT, AND RESISTANCE TO THE CHIEFTAINCY

While veterans in some parts of the territory resigned themselves to the long, slow process of the colonial bureaucracy, many were unwilling to wait. In January 1947, under the leadership of Muslim scholar and political activist Lamine Kaba, African veterans in Kankan revolted. The unrest lasted for the better part of a week, reaching its pinnacle in a half-hour siege of the circle's administrative offices, during which virtually all communication between the circle commandant and the exterior was severed. The government charged that 1,500 militants, many of them armed, surrounded the building. Other sources indicate that veterans and their supporters controlled the city for several hours and declared a short-lived republic.[57]

Among the reasons for the revolt, most were only indirectly related to veterans' grievances. Although the governor charged that Kaba agitated among "discontented military veterans" and exploited their resentments, far more important was Kaba's ability to harness general rural hostility toward the colonial chieftaincy.[58] In 1945 and 1946, Kaba had run unsuccessfully for elected office.[59] Focusing on popular discontent with the canton chiefs, notably their role in crop requisition and tax collection, he had rallied a significant amount of rural support.[60] Chagrined by his defeat in four successive elections and the domination of the elected bodies by chiefs and notables, Kaba and his supporters charged fraud.[61] Kaba's attacks on the chieftaincy resonated among military veterans, who rapidly moved to the forefront of the protests.

Kaba may have appealed to the veterans for other reasons as well. In his study of military veterans in San, a market town in the French Soudan, Gregory Mann found that in the mid-1950s, many became devout followers of a dissident Muslim holy man named Ousmane Sidibe.[62] During their long absence in military service, the veterans had been bypassed by other men who had acquired the necessary accoutrements of senior male status, which, besides land, livestock, wives, children, and junior male followers, included specialized religious knowledge.[63] Sidibe's unorthodox teachings, which challenged the local Muslim elite, offered the veterans an alternative route to religious knowledge and practice—and thereby, to senior male status.[64] Although not a religious rebel like Ousmane Sidibe, Lamine Kaba was also a Muslim scholar and teacher.[65] A respected cleric who protested the abusive powers of established "big men," Kaba appealed to rural veterans who both embraced the accepted norms of senior male status and sought to carve out new ones, presenting themselves as alternative leaders in the process.

When the government ordered Kaba's arrest in January 1947, 2,000 to 3,000 demonstrators marched through the streets of Kankan in a well-organized protest. Noting that the revolt was "guided and disciplined," the governor warned that it was led by an organization that could be called to order at any moment. Assembled in groups of 50, "encircled by former noncommissioned officers and *tirailleurs,* [the demonstrators] marched in columns by three." Among their most troubling cries were those of "Long live Black Africa!" and "Long live Lamine Caba!"[66] With the experience of the war effort in the not-too-distant past, Kaba's partisans, en route to the city, had destroyed the homes of several canton chiefs.[67]

Most of Kaba's supporters had come from the rural areas surrounding the city. According to the governor, those involved in the revolt were primarily "former *tirailleurs* and the inhabitants of certain villages of the circle of Kankan." Other members of his shock troops came from the adjacent circle of Beyla.[68] Apart from these participants in the revolt, Kaba's partisans had made significant inroads into the Upper-Guinea circles of Kankan, Kouroussa, and Siguiri, and the forest circles of Beyla, Kissidougou, and Macenta.[69]

In Beyla circle, hostility to the colonial chieftaincy motivated much of the postwar agitation. In the canton of Beyla-Faranah, the commandant wrote, adherents of Kaba's Parti Républicain Socialiste de Guinée (PRSG) were engaged in "intrigues against the chief." Similarly, in the canton of Guirila, "many former soldiers and partisans of Lamine Caba contest the authority of the Chief." In one Guirila village, the people succeeded in having appointed as chief a straw man representing a leading Laminist partisan who had been denied the position. The canton of Karagoua, maladministered by a habitually drunken chief, was also fertile ground for "Laminist propaganda."[70]

Returning veterans not only refused to recognize the authority of village and canton chiefs, they also frequently spearheaded popular campaigns against them.[71] The linkage of military veterans and popular resistance to the chieftaincy became an increasingly common theme in official reports. In the forest region, the N'Zérékoré circle commandant lamented the presence of "military veterans who appear to consider themselves independent of the indigenous chieftaincies, in the name of a citizenship recently [obtained]."[72] The Macenta circle commandant warned that veterans were stirring up resistance to involuntary "customary" labor:

> The state of mind of the military veterans . . . is frankly disastrous. They have been told too often that they are the "staff of Indigenous Society" and they have wrongly understood that they are its "chiefs." They do not work, even when it is a matter of public interest [such as fighting fires or rebuilding washed-out bridges]. Moreover, under political pretexts, too-well heeded, they are leading an opposition to the chiefs even more virulent than it has been for several years.[73]

In the Upper-Guinea circle of Kouroussa, widespread resistance to local chiefs persisted from 1945 through 1948. Former noncommissioned officers, spurred by ambition and angered by the limits imposed upon them, frequently led the popular revolts. In the canton of Sankaran, the governor remarked on "demonstrations against the chieftaincy by a 'clan' of military veterans, notably, a number of retired sergeant-majors." The veterans refused to recognize as chief anyone who was not from among their own ranks. A number of former sergeant-majors were imprisoned for their activities.[74]

Veterans' anti-chief activities also affected the Futa Jallon. In Dabola circle, legal action was taken against two former sergeant-majors who refused to recognize their village chief's authority.[75] In the Tougué subdivision of Labé circle, 2,000 military veterans were reportedly anxious to "shake off 'the tyranny of the chiefs.' "[76] The Labé circle commandant worried that the veterans' "indiscipline and intrigue against their canton and village chiefs" would infect the rural population more generally.[77]

In an attempt to limit the damage, the government recognized the legitimacy of some of the complaints. Corrupt chiefs would be removed, and veterans could help by identifying them. During a visit to Kankan in March 1947, the French West African high commissioner appealed to the veterans' sense of pride and loyalty:

> You are brave people who fought courageously for the liberty of France and the French Territories. You have obtained it. Your duty is to organize your country on the road to progress. Vis-a-vis your people, you must be the interpreters, the representatives of France. It is you who must give advice to

your brothers, encouraging them to work. The chiefs must be respected, because where there are no chiefs, there is no progress. But there are also chiefs who do not conform to the rules; do not hesitate to point them out. They will be revoked.[78]

Unfortunately, the police noted, the high commissioner's words were badly misinterpreted: "In the milieu of military veterans, it is said that the [high commissioner] gave full powers to the military veterans to have revoked Chiefs who are not to their liking."[79]

Anti-chief activity escalated following the high commissioner's visit. In April, the police reported, "In all the cantons of the Circle of Kankan, there are 'Laministes'. . . . In these cantons, the population does not listen to the Chiefs."[80] The police noted with alarm that the "Laministes" were "military veterans, cultivators, and hunters, regularly in possession of guns . . . who, on every occasion declare, 'We are with Lamine Caba until death.'"[81] Writing to his counterpart in the security services, the Kankan police commissioner noted,

All the indigenous people have sabers, machetes in their homes. This is an old custom. Certain soldiers possess firearms; a few military veterans [have] revolvers or military weapons that they concealed in their baggage on their return from France. These arms will serve should the occasion arise.[82]

The potential for violence was considerable, given the prominence of military veterans, who had both grievances and arms.

To counter the growing radical influence, the government engaged in manipulation and fraud. It first destroyed Kaba's political party, then targeted the veterans' association that was sympathetic to it. In the aftermath of the Kankan revolt, Lamine Kaba had been arrested and sentenced to two years' imprisonment and five years' exile from Guinea.[83] His party, however, had continued to thrive. After Kaba's imprisonment, the PRSG was dominated by a group of military veterans, notably ex–Sergeant-Major Sako Condé. Condé was also vice president of the newly formed Comité des Anciens Combattants de la Section de Kankan, which was composed largely of Kaba partisans.[84] In April 1948, the government dissolved Kaba's political party.[85] Then, on Bastille Day, 1948, a new executive committee of the veterans' association was elected. The assistant circle commandant reported unabashedly that, "With skill, the Administration managed to have elected military veterans without much influence, perhaps, but in any case, non-Laministes."[86]

By May 1950, government-recognized veterans' organizations in Kankan were no longer under radical leadership. The police reported that the Kankan subsection of the Association Unique des Anciens Combattants et Victimes de la Guerre de la Guinée, which included both African and European veterans, had recently assumed a more moderate and loyal stance.[87] While the organization's previous executive committee had included "partisans still faithful to Lamine Kaba," the current one refrained from engaging in any political activity whatsoever.[88]

As established veterans' organizations succumbed to state control, the more radical elements increasingly turned to the RDA. Police spies had already learned that Kankan RDA leader Moricandian Savané had enlisted Diémory Dioubaté, a griot and former partisan of Lamine Kaba, to recruit military veterans in the rural areas.[89] Kankan police reported on this trend with growing concern:

> a strong proportion of the military veterans of the circle of Kankan have been influenced by the R.D.A. and if they must some day orient themselves toward a political party, it will be toward the R.D.A. which has already successfully recruited all the former partisans of Lamine Kaba.[90]

Having decimated Lamine Kaba's organizations, the state was now faced with a much more serious problem: the RDA was rapidly filling the power vacuum.

MILITARY VETERANS AND THE RDA

Deep-seated veterans' grievances provided fertile ground for political organizing, and the RDA was determined to occupy it. Wartime sacrifices—and the consequent debt owed by France—figured heavily in the party's postwar demands. In April 1947, Mamady Kourouma, general councillor and vice president of Guinea's new, all-African Association des Anciens Combattants et Anciens Militaires Africains de la Guinée, spoke to an RDA gathering in Kindia. "In 1914 and in 1939," he cried, "Africa sent its best children, who fought heroically. France, victorious and grateful, gave us our rights of liberty."[91] However, those rights, enshrined in the 1946 constitution, had yet to be realized. In June 1947, Kourouma was elected to the Guinean RDA's first board of directors.[92] In July, the police reported that large numbers of veterans were joining the Kindia RDA subsection and paying their dues on the spot.[93]

Building upon preexisting discontent and the base established by Lamine Kaba, the RDA called for equality of rights, wages, pensions, and other benefits for all servicemen, no matter what their race, civil status, or national origin. In the overseas territories and in metropolitan France, the RDA rapidly assumed the role of spokesman for the veterans' cause.[94]

The RDA's efforts met with considerable success. When RDA militant Léon Maka toured Kankan in October 1949, he was besieged by 300 military veterans who requested RDA membership cards.[95] In the Futa Jallon, the

RDA recruited among military personnel at the Labé airfield and used veterans' organizations, with their large pool of low-status members, as a launching pad for its recruitment drives.[96] With growing concern, French army intelligence noted that throughout the French West African federation, veterans were "profoundly influenced" by the RDA and were joining the party in large numbers. Veterans served on the executive bodies of nearly all local RDA committees. In terms of both leadership and rank-and-file membership, the AACVGAOF and the RDA overlapped considerably.[97]

Veterans' grievances were frequently discussed in the columns of *Réveil*, the organ of the interterritorial RDA. Its May 13, 1948, issue included the text of a resolution presented in the Assembly of the French Union by RDA councillors, French Communists, and their allies.[98] Recounting the long and bitter history of veterans' efforts, the resolution described the persistent refusals of the French National Assembly to equalize their benefits. It urged the government "to put an end to the shocking inequalities existing between the pensions paid to military veterans of metropolitan origin and those paid to [veterans] from the Overseas Territories."[99]

In the French National Assembly, the chief advocate for the veterans' cause was Hamani Diori, the RDA deputy from Niger. In April 1949, Diori introduced an amendment, jointly sponsored by the RDA and the PCF, that would have instituted pension equality for all military veterans. The amendment was soundly defeated. Two months later, the RDA proposed a unified statute for all soldiers and veterans serving France. Had it passed, the unified statute would have instituted equality for all military veterans in wages, pensions, loans, and all other monetary matters. However, this bill was also defeated.[100]

While RDA parliamentarians lobbied in Paris, unrest continued at the grassroots. In March 1950, police in Kankan noted that former *tirailleurs* were still making "energetic demands concerning their pension arrears."[101] The N'Zérékoré circle commandant worried about the continued loyalty of a large group of military veterans in his area who "complain, and for good reason, [about] the incredible delays in the regularization of their pensions."[102]

In September 1951, the military police in N'Zérékoré reported that military pensions remained an important theme in RDA election campaigns. In preparation for the March 1952 Territorial Assembly (formerly, General Council) elections, the RDA had rallied a large number of military veterans under the banner "Equality of military pension rates for Europeans and Africans." The veterans now supporting the RDA had once been the epitome of loyalty to France and its institutions, the military police lamented: "If one considers that these same servicemen, in years gone by, formed the reinforcements of the canton and village chieftaincies, it is to fear that in the days to come, the latter will meet with certain difficulties in the exercise of their functions."[103]

In fact, the veterans' actions threatened the very basis of colonial authority in the rural areas. Just as the RDA championed veterans' rights in the upper echelons of the political arena, rural-based veterans led RDA campaigns at the grassroots level. Most notably, they helped to organize peasant resistance to unpaid compulsory labor—and to the village and canton chiefs who enforced it. As esteemed men in their villages who did not cower before the chiefs and circle commandants, veterans were in a premier position to mobilize for the RDA.[104] Léon Maka recalled that "former *tirailleurs* were usually at the core of RDA actions. They protested before the chiefs, before the circle commandants." If the veterans could not oust the chiefs through official means, they simply usurped chiefly functions. According to Maka, the veterans

> took the initiative to detach from the chieftaincies. They formed committees to collect taxes and send the taxes directly to the circle commandants, bypassing the chiefs who enriched themselves from these taxes.
>
> Instead of giving the taxes to the village chiefs and the canton chiefs, they sent them directly to the circle commandants—in order to undermine the chiefs and to keep some of the money in the area [for local development]. As a result, the influence of the chiefs diminished. It no longer had any importance.[105]
>
> The military veterans began this process. The RDA thought it was a good idea and decided to have village committees that would make the village chiefs redundant.
>
> Why the military veterans? Because they were the people who had traveled, served in France. They had seen how whites acted at home and in the colonies. They saw that there was a difference. They always had a white commander, even if they were competent to do the job for themselves. They understood the system of colonization, and they were angry.[106]

THE GOVERNMENT FIGHTS BACK

If the government had been concerned about Lamine Kaba and his regional influence, it was even more wary of the RDA, with its territory-wide and interterritorial impact. Having engaged in manipulation and fraud to defeat Kaba, it used co-optation and appeasement to undermine the RDA. Time and time again, the administration attempted to distinguish—and distance—veterans from the peasant masses, appealing to them as an elite, chosen to guide the people in the proper ways of the colonial system. In his annual report for 1948, the Kankan circle commandant detailed his administration's continued efforts in this regard:

> In the course of its missions in the bush, the Administration addressed itself to the military veterans, appealing to their experience, their sense of discipline and order, by showing them the role of good counselors that they must

fulfill and by putting them on guard against jealousy, envy of the commander or opposing the action of established chiefs.[107]

However, the government was also aware that such appeals would fall on deaf ears if the veterans' grievances were not resolved. "It is essential to neutralize the milieu of former *tirailleurs,*" the governor warned.[108]

Initially, the government's approach was piecemeal. In September 1947, the French West African high commissioner requested a list of former POWs in Guinea—in order to send them "significant sums" due to them as a result of their status as "prisoner of colonial war." He was determined to satisfy the veterans, particularly the militant ex-POWs, before they were seduced by the promises of subversive political parties.[109]

In 1948, faced with a brewing political crisis, the French government initiated a campaign to register African military veterans throughout French West Africa. A commission led by Henri Liger was to conduct a village-by-village census of all African veterans of World Wars I and II and to ensure that they and their survivors received whatever back pay and pensions were due to them. By July 1950, the Liger campaign had registered 21,855 veterans and their survivors in Guinea, including 4,259 veterans from the period 1914–1938 and 16,222 from the period 1939–1945, as well as 1,374 families of deceased veterans. Another 10,016 cases were pending, and an estimated 1,594 veterans and their survivors had not yet been seen. By the end of 1952, more than seven years after the war's end and four years after the commencement of the Liger campaign, all the French West African cases from World War II had been processed.[110]

As a result of tremendous political pressure from veterans' associations and African political parties, particularly the RDA, African veterans achieved a semblance of equality with their European counterparts. Parity between African and metropolitan veterans was finally granted in the Equality Law of August 8, 1950. It was parity in principle only, however. In practice, discrimination continued. African veterans, unlike European veterans, did not benefit from loans, cash advances, and overseas indemnities. Moreover, the French government continued to pay African soldiers in local currency and to calculate their pensions in the less valuable metropolitan francs.[111] In a final push for the veterans' allegiance, a decree issued on October 19, 1955, ruled that all French citizens, irrespective of race or personal status, should have access to all ranks of the military hierarchy. Until that time, African and European servicemen had belonged to different companies, served at different ranks, and thus earned different salaries.[112]

If the colonial administration was slow to realize the importance of retaining the veterans' loyalty, it did learn eventually. In a fierce competition for the veterans' support, it battled the RDA, each side claiming to better represent the ex-servicemen's interests. With more resources at its disposal, and through the strategic implementation of laws and decrees, the administration was able to buy the veterans' backing. Its tactics were frequently heavy-handed. In Dinguiraye, for example, ex-Lieutenant Abdou Karim accepted an offer of a reserved job in the local government—in exchange for his resignation from the RDA.[113] With the completion of the Liger campaign (1948–1952) and the passage of the Equality Law (1950), the state rapidly gained ground on the RDA.[114]

By the mid-1950s, the majority of veterans' demands had been satisfied. However inequitably treated, military veterans generally were better off than most of their rural compatriots. Thus, the greatest number sought accommodation with the colonial government. The veterans' cause was no longer prominent on the RDA agenda, and the colonial state no longer worried that African veterans would lead an uprising against it.[115]

In fact, by the mid-1950s, African military veterans were once again considered to be a bulwark of the colonial system. In his annual report for 1955, the governor of Guinea noted that while rebellious toward the chiefs, military veterans generally had "an excellent attitude vis-a-vis French authority. . . . [They] almost always have natural reflexes of deference in regard to authority."[116] That same year, the governor described the veterans as possessing "indisputable loyalty" to France. Armistice Day "was celebrated with fervor and was the occasion of an excellent day of comradeship in arms between French and African veterans."[117]

CONCLUSION

Despite their later retreat from the nationalist movement, military veterans made significant contributions to its ultimate success. Active in the countryside before the RDA, veterans helped to define the issues and shape the party's agenda. As ambitious new elites imbued with a sense of authority and entitlement, they spearheaded popular resistance to the chiefs, the cornerstone of state power in the rural areas. Demanding equal benefits for equal sacrifices, they challenged France to make good on the promises of reformed imperialism. As early agents of the RDA, they helped the party to take root in the interior. Equally important, military veterans' claims to equality and their insistence on being treated like Frenchmen would find resonance in the emerging trade union movement—the next pillar of Guinean nationalism.

3

THE UNIVERSAL WORKER: ORGANIZED LABOR AND NATIONALIST MOBILIZATION, 1946–1953

If a key segment of the Guinean RDA emerged from the military veterans' milieu, another emanated from the postwar labor movement. African workers, like military veterans, had begun to mobilize themselves before the RDA entered the scene. Like the veterans, they had taken their cue from the promises of "enlightened" imperialism that, despite French intentions, had opened up new spaces for African actors. Brazzaville and the Houphouët-Boigny Law had pledged an end to forced labor. Citizenship meant that African workers increasingly compared their wages, benefits, and working conditions to those of their metropolitan counterparts. Owning the language of assimilation, African trade unionists, like military veterans, seized upon French claims of universalism—and the divergent reality—to demand equal treatment. The most significant postwar labor actions revolved around issues of equal pay and benefits for equal work.[1]

Deep-seated workers' grievances, like those of African veterans, provided fertile ground for political organization. While wages had been frozen during the war, inflation had run rampant.[2] Living conditions had declined, even as hopes were raised by the rhetoric of reformed imperialism. The exigencies of the war effort resulted in significant discontent in the rural areas. When forced labor was suddenly abolished in 1946, rural workers deserted their work sites in droves. Building on this momentum, metropolitan-based trade unions, particularly the PCF-affiliated and RDA-associated CGT, organized increasingly vocal urban workers into local branches. Harnessing preexisting discontent, they channeled worker activity into new forms of organization. The result was a wave of labor mobilization and significant territory-wide and interterritorial strikes that incorporated political as well as economic demands. Championing the workers' cause as its own, the RDA successfully drew trade unionists into the party. Workers, like military veterans, were important catalysts for the emerging nationalist movement.

If the RDA's overwhelming success was due to its ability to form a broad-based ethnic, class, and gender alliance, it was in workers' struggles that this alliance first emerged. Elite civil servants and nonliterate laborers of multiple ethnicities banded together in trade union federations and jointly organized strikes. Although few African women earned wages during the postwar period, they played a critical role in labor actions. Ultimately responsible for their families' health and well-being, women stood behind their husbands' demands for equitable wage and benefit packages. They were particularly adamant about family allowances, which provided monetary supplements for each child. During the strikes, women sustained urban communities in myriad ways. It was in this self-ascribed role that women were first noticed by the RDA. Impressed by their decisive role in labor actions and aware that they were an untapped resource, the party consciously mobilized African women into the nationalist movement.

Unlike the military veterans, African workers did not retreat from the political scene. Even as their demands for more equitable wages and working conditions were satisfied, they became more militant in the political arena. As veterans' influence waned in the mid-1950s, that of organized labor soared. Although some unions eventually accommodated the colonial regime, the largest trade union federation, the Communist-affiliated CGT, did not. CGT workers, who constituted the bulk of organized labor in Guinea, plus autonomous teachers' and railway workers' unions, continually pushed the RDA to the Left. Radical trade unionists would be a critical factor in the party's push for independence in 1958.

THE END OF FORCED LABOR

Anticipating a reformed variant of imperialism in the postwar world, the Brazzaville Conference had recommended the discontinuation of forced labor and its gradual replacement by free wage labor, beginning in 1944. Due to the requirements of the war effort, however, that plan was quickly abandoned. The number of forced laborers in Guinea actually increased twofold between 1944 and 1945.[3] When the war ended, implementation of the Brazzaville recommendations was again postponed. This time, dire economic circumstances were blamed.[4] Thus, when the Houphouët-Boigny Law, abolishing forced labor in the French overseas territories, was enacted on April 11, 1946—and immediately implemented—both employers and colonial administrators were caught off guard.[5]

On May 7, 1946, another new law sent shock waves through the French empire. The Lamine Guèye Law granted French citizenship to all inhabitants of the overseas territories. With forced labor abolished and legal distinctions between inhabitants of metropolitan and overseas France upended, a new labor code was desperately needed. While forced labor was outlawed in April 1946, the controversial and much-debated labor code was not adopted until December 1952. During the six-and-one-half-year interim, there was no systematic set of rules and regulations governing African labor in French West Africa.[6]

That uncertain situation provided fertile ground for labor action, both spontaneous and organized. In Guinea, workers quickly demonstrated their hostility toward the forced labor regime. Circle commandants and administrative heads of service were informed of the Houphouët-Boigny Law on April 24, 1946. By April 26, rural workers were deserting their stations en masse. According to Inspector of Colonies Pruvost, "the news spread like wildfire into the depths of the bush." So great was worker determination to stop work and return home that local authorities anticipated "the massive departure of

Photo 3.1   Constructing the Conakry-Niger railway, Koumi Pass. (CAOM)

all non-voluntary workers from the plantations, mines, major work sites (public works and private enterprises), in other words the 'long-term recruits' transplanted far from their residences."[7]

Official records reveal an extraordinary picture of labor unrest throughout the territory. By the end of April 1946, 9,028 forced laborers in the public sector had abandoned their workplaces. Especially affected were public works (road construction and maintenance), agriculture, and woodcutting for the railways. By the end of June, another 6,139 public-sector workers had returned home. In the private sector, 2,021 workers had fled their jobs by the end of April, joined by another 2,853 by the end of June.[8] The inspector of labor concluded,

> The general abandonment of the public works sites can be explained by the fact that the workers employed at these sites were virtually all "forced" laborers. . . . Famine wages, irregularly paid, incessant displacements, persecution by the chiefs, brutality of the [circle] guards or supervisors, meager pittances, isolation from the [urban] centers—it was in fact the abhorred regime of obligatory services. . . . The announcement of free labor provoked a veritable explosion of joy. The laborers abandoned their work without even waiting for their pay. For them the time of liberty had finally struck. The same causes explain the massive abandonment of certain agricultural sites in Upper-Guinea [and the Futa Jallon].[9]

Rural anger, stemming from the hardships imposed by the war effort and the ongoing regime of forced labor, led to massive workplace desertions as soon as the opportunity allowed. This rural-based labor activity predated the trade union organizing that swept the urban areas in the late 1940s and early 1950s. While they focused on the urban rather than the rural areas, trade unions attempted to harness this popular discontent. They were especially successful in the public sector and in the towns that served as circle administrative centers, both recently depleted of involuntary laborers.

EARLY TRADE UNION ORGANIZING

While the French Popular Front government of the prewar period had recognized the right of Africans to organize trade unions in 1937, the Vichy regime had put an end to virtually all trade union activity in French West Africa. In 1943, shortly after the federation switched to the Free French, metropolitan unions, particularly the Communist-affiliated CGT, initiated contacts with African workers. A government decree in August 1944 reiterated the right of African workers to organize. In the wake of the Brazzaville Conference, newly constituted unions, led by Western-educated African elites, began to demand more equitable opportunities and pay.[10]

The first African trade union in Guinea was established by PTT workers on March 18, 1945. Part of a federation-wide body with branches across French West Africa, the CGT-affiliated Syndicat Professionel des Agents et Sous-Agents Indigènes du Service des Transmissions de la Guinée Française was led by Sékou Touré, who held the position of secretary-general.[11] Five relatively well-educated postal clerks served on the trade union's executive committee. The ethnic composition of the leadership, like the rank and file, was diverse, including Guineans of Malinke and Susu origin, nationals from other territories in the French West African federation, and one man of Guadeloupean ancestry. In terms of religion, both Muslims and Christians were represented.[12]

The union was self-consciously inclusive. Joseph Montlouis, who convened the organizing meeting at his Conakry home, had been approached by his department head, a French CGT member, who proposed that Montlouis initiate the African workers' union. Montlouis's grandfather was a native of Guadeloupe, a French territory in the Antilles. A customs officer, the grandfather had been posted in French West Africa. Montlouis's father had been born in Senegal, and Montlouis himself in Guinea. His department head believed that Montlouis would not favor one ethnic group over another, as a consequence of his ancestry. According to Montlouis, "He saw that I was not a member of any ethnic group here—or, that I was a member of all the ethnic groups here! I have relatives who are Peuls. I have relatives who are Malinkes. I have relatives from all the ethnic groups!"[13]

Although Montlouis had been asked to form the union, duly wrote the charter, and held the organizing meeting in his home, he did not relish the position of secretary-general. Refusing to accept the nomination, he urged his colleagues to elect instead Sékou Touré, a relatively unknown 23-year-old postal clerk with a lower-primary school certificate and technical school diploma. Sékou Touré, he recalled, was younger and more aggressive than he and, Montlouis was convinced, had the makings of a promising leader.[14]

Under the leadership of Sékou Touré, Guinean PTT workers joined a federation-wide strike on December 20, 1945, under the banner of "Equal pay for equal work." While the strike lasted for only a few days in most of French West Africa, in Guinea it lasted until January 4, 1946, paralyzing government services in the major urban centers of Conakry, Kindia, Mamou, and Kankan. While government operations were brought to a standstill and commercial enterprises suffered, strikers in various urban centers communicated among themselves via the telegraph services they now controlled.[15]

In Guinea, as elsewhere in colonial Africa, trade unions did not focus exclusively on wages and working conditions. From the outset, they entertained political questions and became increasingly politicized with time. Montlouis recalled that trade unions naturally took on political functions in 1945, because "at that time, political activities were forbidden," and Guinea had no political parties.[16]

A central theme of the PTT workers' strike was equality between African and metropolitan workers. In addition to federation-wide demands for an established minimum wage for various categories of workers, higher and more equitable wages and benefits throughout the job hierarchy, greater job security, integration of auxiliary workers into the regular civil service ranks, and general promotion of African workers, Guinean leaders included overtly political demands. These included the abolition of forced labor and suppression of the *indigénat*. Laws abrogating both of these systems were passed the following year.[17]

Participants in the strike included not only the relatively well-educated clerks and supervisors in the regular civil service ranks (the cadres), but also auxiliary workers, including mail carriers, mechanics, guards, laborers, and chauffeurs, who had little job security or recourse.[18] Like many subsequent strikes in Guinea, the PTT workers' strike crossed class lines.

In the strike's aftermath, some improvements were made in workers' conditions, but nothing approaching the parity they had demanded. More importantly, the stage was set for more expansive and radical trade union action. On March 23, 1946, less than three months after the conclusion of the PTT workers' strike, Sékou Touré organized the Union des Syndicats Confédérés de Guinée, which brought under one umbrella all the Guinean affiliates of the CGT. In contrast to its predecessors, which tended to group workers by rank—for example, civil servants of the *cadre commun secondaire* (the highest grade possible for those with African diplomas), civil service auxiliaries, and so forth—the CGT unions united all workers of a single industry or service without regard to rank. Focusing on common ground rather than competing interests, CGT unions were particularly suited to broad-based, well-coordinated collective action.[19]

THE FRENCH WEST AFRICAN RAILWAY WORKERS' STRIKE, 1947–1948

Railway workers, like their PTT colleagues, were among the first to organize. Their geographic concentration and the ease of communication along railway lines permitted railway workers and those at the associated ports and wharves to mobilize quickly.[20] Most of the French West African trade unions established during the postwar years were affiliated with the French CGT and thus indirectly connected to the RDA. However, the Fédération des Syndicats des Cheminots Africains de l'A.O.F. (FSCA), an alliance of African railway workers' unions from across French West Africa, chose to remain autonomous of all French trade union federations and political parties.[21] While the vast majority of African unions would break from their French parent bodies in the 1950s, the FSCA called for African leadership in support of African interests as early as 1946.[22] As a multiethnic, trans-territorial African association, the railway workers' union played a crucial role in the development of national and international identity and solidarity.

Like many other unions of the period, the FSCA's membership crossed class lines. Bringing together all African workers in the railway industry, the union included everyone from engineers and office workers to mechanics and manual laborers. Permanent employees (the cadres) and auxiliary workers were grouped in a single organization.[23] The vast majority of railway workers were manual laborers, however, whose common interests made them relatively easy to unite.[24] While most railway workers were nonliterate, manual laborers in the auxiliary workforce, the union leadership was drawn from the Western-educated elite. Ibrahima Sarr, the FSCA's secretary-general, was a secondary school graduate. Adama Diop, secretary-general of the Guinean branch, had an upper-primary school certificate. The union's board of directors also included a number of military veterans who had fought for France and were inspired by the veterans' slogan "Equal sacrifices, equal rights."[25]

Although it was not a CGT union, the FSCA and its method of organizing quickly attracted the RDA's attention. The railway workers' union, like the postwar veterans' associations, was a strong, multiethnic, interterritorial body with tremendous potential for political mobilization. If it understood the importance of forming broad-based ethnic and class alliances, the FSCA also grasped the importance of gender. It consciously drew on women's work and resources to sustain its 1947–1948 strike. When the union struck in 1947, the RDA was anxious to demonstrate common cause.

Like their counterparts in the postal and telecommunications industry, African railway workers agitated for wages, benefits, and working conditions on par with those of their European peers. One of their early demands was the integration of African and European workers into a single staff system, a nonracial hierarchy of positions that included the same wages and benefits for people of equal ranks. These benefits included family allowances and cost-of-living supplements. The railway workers also demanded that the distinction between cadre and auxiliary be abolished and that all auxiliary workers be integrated into the single staff system.[26]

In April 1947, the French West African administration, pushed by its own rhetoric of equality and a three-day federation-wide strike, agreed to the principle of a single staff system. A parity commission composed of railway administration and African and European worker representatives was charged with working out the details.[27] Anxious to cut costs, which a single staff system would send soaring, the railway administration rejected the commission's proposal. The union charged betrayal, and strike mobilization began.[28]

On September 8, 1947, the FSCA put forth a list of demands that expertly exploited the rhetoric of French universalism. Among the demands were the establishment of an equitable single staff system, including identical European and African cost-of-living and family allowances, and the abolition of other race-based disparities in worker treatment. The FSCA warned that if these demands were not satisfied, a federation-wide railway workers' strike would begin at midnight on October 10, 1947.[29] In Guinea, police reports warned of increased activity among African railway personnel and noted that a strike for parity with European workers was inevitable.[30]

Two weeks after the demands' publication, the governor of Guinea circulated a secret memo on internal security and military preparedness. He advised his circle commandants to pay close attention to the political sentiments of the local populations, monitoring their reactions to both internal and external events. He urged them to follow "the activities and propaganda" of political and trade union organizations, taking note of possible linkages between them. Unusual activities, including arms trafficking, should be reported to him—and to the military authorities in their circles.[31]

Given the large number of personnel and the geographic expanse of the rail network, the government had reason to be concerned. The impact of a work stoppage could be enormous. In early 1947 there were approximately 17,277 Africans working in the French West African railway network. The vast majority, 15,586, were permanent auxiliary workers, while the remaining 1,691 were managerial staff. Another 3,302 Africans worked at the ports and wharves. The number of European workers was comparatively small: 442 on the railways and 52 at the ports and wharves.[32]

When October 10 came, compliance with the strike was nearly 100 percent. Three weeks later, only 525 railway workers were on the job, including 487 European workers (whose numbers had been bolstered) and 38 Africans, 18 of whom were from Guinea.[33] Thus, with only slight exaggeration, Guinea's inspector of labor reported that in conformity with union instructions, African railway workers "in their totality stopped work on October 10." Moreover, all the African workers in the shipyards, public works, and at the Conakry port had walked off the job. Rail traffic had come to a standstill. By November 19, not a single worker had asked to be rehired.[34]

The colonial administration was clearly unprepared for the high level of discipline and cross-class organization demonstrated by the African railway workers' union. The inspector general of labor marveled that the strike order was followed not only by workers directly affected by the contract under discussion, that is, permanent staff and auxiliaries previously scheduled to be integrated into the staff system, but also by "the mass of ordinary auxiliaries, mostly manual laborers, and by the personnel of the wharves, whose situation was not at issue."[35]

For the duration of the strike, October 10, 1947, through March 18, 1948, economic activity in French West Africa was seriously disrupted. Ordinarily, it was the vast rail network that carried cash crops such as peanuts, bananas, cocoa, and coffee to the coast for export and migrant laborers from the interior to work on European plantations. During the strike, perishable crops rot-

Photo 3.2   Plantation workers cutting bananas for export, Kindia. (CAOM)

ted; inadequate roads were clogged with trucks; and import and export goods accumulated at the ports and wharves, awaiting the arrival of European strike-breakers.[36] The effectiveness of the strike was enhanced by the fact that it coincided with the harvest period, when cash crops were normally transported to the ports and when food crops were plentiful.[37] Its timing was such that it was at once most damaging to the colonial economy and least damaging to the workers and their families.

The Conakry-Niger line, which connected the territory of Guinea to that of Niger, linked the port of Conakry to the towns of Kindia, Mamou, Dabola, Kouroussa, and Kankan in the interior.[38] From Conakry to Kankan, the line was 661 kilometers and included 40 stations or stops and 69 metal bridges of more than 15 meters.[39] Ordinarily, tens of thousands of tons of pineapples, citrus fruits, oil-bearing palm products, coffee, and bananas especially were evacuated from the interior by rail. During the strike, however, the highly perishable banana and citrus crops, among Guinea's most valuable exports, had to be transported to Conakry by road. Although European planters loaned some trucks for this purpose, road transport was extremely expensive due to the high cost of gasoline.[40]

In early January 1948, African planter and merchant classes in the Ivory Coast, whose economic interests suffered as their products languished, successfully pressured Ivorian workers to return to their jobs. This breaking of ranks

Photo 3.3   Child laborers transporting bananas in Benty (Lower-Guinea), January 1948. Photographer, M. Mischkind. (CAOM)

was spearheaded by the RDA's interterritorial president, Félix Houphouët-Boigny, who was a wealthy planter himself.[41] Similarly, in Guinea, the Socialist deputy to the French National Assembly, Yacine Diallo, urged his fellow Peuls to return to work.[42] The first of many class cleavages in the labor and nationalist movements, this behind-the-scenes maneuvering by African elites contributed to the denouement of the strike.

From the outset, the administration charged that the union had violated arbitration procedures, rendering the strike illegal.[43] It warned that strikers who did not resume work immediately would be permanently replaced and evicted from company housing.[44] Union leaders were arrested, convicted, and sentenced to fines and imprisonment. To drive home its point, the government recruited scab labor: previously dismissed railway workers, French railway workers, untrained workers from other lines of employment, petty criminals, and soldiers.[45] Strikebreakers were brought to Guinea as early as November 20, 1947. Among them were active and retired railway workers from all parts of France.[46]

The scab labor was not particularly effective. Unskilled workers, including a detachment from the Marine Nationale, were completely unprepared to work with sophisticated railway equipment. Even skilled French railway workers, numbering in the hundreds, proved disappointing. Cooper writes that "the

French locomotive drivers were not familiar with the steam locomotives still in use in Africa," machines that were well known to striking African drivers.[47] Diop claims that in Guinea, "The French workers did not know the business and were not used to the heat. As a result, there was a big accident, a derailment at Dabola, Kilometer 417. There was much destruction of life and property."[48]

The deadly derailment of the Mikado train on January 6, 1948, resulted in government accusations of sabotage.[49] The administration charged that striking workers had oiled the tracks, intentionally causing the derailment that killed four and injured six. Yayé Diané and Jacques Traoré, members of the Guinean trade union's executive committee, were arrested, as were Faciné Touré and Mamby Diawara, secretaries of the Mamou and Kankan subdivisions, respectively. The leadership of the Guinean union was devastated. Rank-and-file members and supporters from Kindia, Mamou, and Kankan were also imprisoned.[50] The telegraphist Almamy Soumah and other PTT workers were arrested and charged with aiding and abetting the alleged sabotage by transmitting messages on behalf of the railway workers' union.[51]

Responding to charges leveled against the union leadership, Adama Diop blamed the crash on the inexperience of the scab labor force. He noted that Mamadou Kéïta, Mikado's engineer, had been described in *Paris-Dakar* as an ex-convict who was unfamiliar with the Conakry-Niger line, especially the difficult region between Dafila and Dabola where the derailment had occurred. Due to that area's heavy participation in the strike, the tracks had not been maintained since the strike began.[52]

Community Support for the Railway Strike

Popular mobilization before and during the strike was extensive. In railway communities throughout the federation, the strike had been well planned and widely discussed. The union leadership had visited railway towns in all the territories, publicizing the issues around which the strike would revolve.[53] Ibrahima Sarr, the FSCA's secretary-general, personally toured the railway towns in Guinea, Ivory Coast, Dahomey, and Senegal.[54] Attacking the inequalities inherent in the old colonial system and justifying African workers' claims for equal pay and benefits, Sarr made frequent references to Africans' role in the defense of France during the war and to the common work of African and European railway workers.[55] On September 21, 1947, he addressed workers in Conakry, where he was introduced by Adama Diop. A native of Senegal who was not familiar with the local languages, Sarr addressed the crowd in French, the vernacular of the interterritorial labor and nationalist movements. He explained the union's desire to obtain for African workers the same wages and benefits as their European counterparts. Jacques Traoré translated Sarr's remarks into Susu, for the benefit of the many unschooled workers not conversant in French. At the meeting's conclusion, the pro-strike vote was enthusiastic and unanimous.[56]

At each of his stops, Sarr attempted to allay workers' fears by promising that the union would provide them with food and money. At the same time, he routinely urged workers to carry out the strike peaceably, to stay at home, refrain from public demonstrations, and avoid sabotage. Even colonial police reports admit that Sarr's orders were "strictly observed by strikers."[57] Similarly, the board of directors of the union's Guinean branch appealed for "absolute calm" and respect for railway property.[58]

Throughout the federation, open meetings were held during the strike to discuss worker and community concerns.[59] Adama Diop recalled that meetings were held daily in the Guinean towns along the railway line. Because the government had prohibited meetings in public places, and the railway administration had prohibited them on railway property, the meetings were held in private homes.[60]

The police in Kankan noted that railway workers from as far away as Conakry and Dakar periodically came to Upper-Guinea to encourage continued support for the strike.[61] In Conakry, the police noted that handwritten placards had been posted "by unknown persons" on the night of November 26, 1947, bearing the following message: "African Railway workers: Respond to the loyal appeal of your union. The Railway Administration has fired you. To capitulate is to betray the future; it is to be servants of the colonialists!"[62] Some placards had been plastered over the election posters of the right-wing Gaullist Rassemblement du Peuple Français, which had won an overwhelming majority in the French municipal elections of October 1947, largely as a result of its opposition to colonial reforms.[63]

French colonial officials had anticipated a quick end to the strike, believing that poorly paid auxiliary workers could not have substantial resources in reserve. Initially, most officials failed to consider African practices of reciprocity and solidarity and the importance of family and community to daily survival. Only belatedly did some recognize the crucial social support networks so important to the success of the strike. In an unusually clairvoyant report, Pierre Pélisson, the inspector general of labor for French West Africa, remarked that in Africa, "the means of defense are much different—and singularly more effective—than is the case with metropolitan strikes because the roots of the wage-earners [in the urban areas] are less profound and their needs less pressing in Africa than in Europe."[64]

In the urban areas, African railway workers were linked by family and neighborhood to small-scale market traders as well as to more prosperous shopkeepers and merchants. They maintained close ties to rural family members engaged in agricultural production. The rural households they so often subsidized now assisted them through the provision of foodstuffs. In some cases, workers returned to their ancestral villages to farm. Those who remained in the railway towns sustained their families on fish and produce from the kitchen gardens tended by household members. Others progressively sold their meager possessions.[65]

Women were the crucial links between railway workers and the community. As market traders, kitchen gardeners, and rural agriculturalists, they played a critical role in sustaining the strike. Mobilizing through trade and kinship networks, market women provided food, largely grown by female farmers, to the striking workers and their families. They made monetary donations and collected funds for the strikers. In the absence of male wages, their own income-generating activities grew in importance. Finally, they played a crucial role in building morale and maintaining solidarity by singing songs in support of the strike—and others that publicly humiliated strike-breakers.[66]

Despite the hardships imposed on the community—notably in the diminution of rice and other foodstuffs from the interior and gasoline and other imports from the coast—community support for the strikers was strong.[67] PTT workers supported their colleagues on the rail lines by sending coded telegraphic communications about future strike actions.[68] The police reported that a number of Lebano-Syrian merchants and African civil servants had contributed sums of 300 to 500 francs in support of the striking workers.[69] Apart from monetary contributions, merchants provided credit to needy families and contributed large quantities of food to the strikers. Others lent trucks, which, along with private cars and taxis, served as a means of communication and mobilization, as well as a way to transport food.[70] Although a rumored general strike in support of the railway workers failed to materialize, such discussions foreshadowed subsequent more generalized action against the colonial state.[71]

The railway workers' strike was a consciously political one. It found support among other workers and community members who understood its broader implications. According to Guinean CGT leader Soriba Touré, "The struggle of the railway men is the struggle of all African people against the [forces of] reaction, and this is why the railway men must achieve victory."[72] This politicization of the workers' struggle would be echoed many times in the future. Moreover, it was the broad reach of the movement that made room for the RDA.

Among the parties represented in French political bodies, only the RDA and the PCF supported the strike, even though the railway union was not formally associated with either party. RDA politicians proposed countless resolutions in favor of a positive strike resolution, while party branches contributed financially. *Réveil,* the RDA's interterritorial organ, campaigned in support of the railway workers and made donations garnered from special newspaper sales.[73] The RDA-associated CGT unions also declared common cause. In Guinea, a CGT motion of support, signed by Sékou Touré and Soriba Touré, was reprinted in

Réveil. In France and French West Africa, CGT unions demonstrated solidarity through meetings and speeches, as well as financial contributions.[74] In this way, the RDA gained the support of workers who had already mobilized themselves.

Resolution of the Railway Workers' Strike

By the time the strike ended on March 19, 1948, French West African railway operations had been seriously disrupted for more than five months. The railway administration had lost hundreds of millions of francs. The colonial economy of French West Africa, and to a lesser extent, metropolitan France, had been similarly affected.[75] While anxious to end the strike, the government was aware that the final settlement would have far-reaching ramifications. It wished, at all costs, to avoid setting dangerous precedents. In Guinea, the inspector of labor noted that the CGT, which gave moral and material support to the railway workers, "represents the large majority of civil servants' unions." He warned that civil servants' future demands concerning cost-of-living allowances would be linked to the railway workers' success on this point.[76]

Workers were equally aware that the final settlement would affect far more than the railway workers. Declaring victory, Adama Diop claimed that the triumph of the railway workers "was a victory for all the trade unions of Africa."[77] Other unions would regard the federation-wide railway strike both as a precedent and a turning point in colonial labor struggles.

The outcome of the strike was a victory for African workers, if only a partial one. Threatened sanctions against striking workers were annulled, although workers were not paid for their days absent. The administration agreed to reintegrate Africans from the permanent staff, hiring them back in their original positions. Auxiliaries who had already returned to work would keep their jobs. Those auxiliaries who had remained on strike until the end were to be taken back in order of seniority until the agreed-upon staffing limits were reached. The principle of the single staff system was again accepted, although numerous privileges for European workers were retained. (For instance, the administration refused to provide comparable cost-of-living allowances for African and European workers; failure to treat African and European families equally would be one of the focuses of the 1953 general strike.) Finally, workers were given a 20 percent increase in wages and most allowances to compensate for spiraling inflation and the freezing of wages during World War II.[78]

Across French West Africa, thousands of auxiliaries were integrated into the single staff system. However, the majority retained their auxiliary status, and thousands more lost their jobs altogether. Agreed-upon staff reductions, plus the hiring of replacement workers during the strike, exacerbated the problem.[79] Of the 2,190 African workers on the Conakry-Niger line at the time of the strike, 92 were laid off in August 1948.[80]

THE GENERAL STRIKE OF JUNE 9–10, 1950

Stimulated by the successful federation-wide railway strike, the French West African trade union movement grew in leaps and bounds. As workers challenged France to keep the promises of "enlightened" imperialism, the CGT and other unions mobilized to achieve these ends. The early 1950s witnessed a proliferation of successful strikes, most of them led by the CGT. The implementation of egalitarian reforms was their central objective.

The rise of the trade union movement coincided with intense state repression against the RDA, largely due to its association with the PCF. Arrest and imprisonment on trumped-up charges and the suspension, dismissal, or transfer of civil servants were practices commonly used against RDA activists.[81] Fear of reprisals took a heavy toll on the RDA. The number of resignations mounted, and membership declined.[82] Virtually paralyzed by the government crackdown and resulting resignations, the party shifted its focus to the trade union movement, where it hoped to attract a mass constituency.

In French West Africa, and especially in Guinea, 1950 was a pivotal year in the labor movement. That year, the second Lamine Guèye Law was approved by the French National Assembly, mandating equal benefits for all civil servants and equal wages for all civil servants of the same grade. Affected benefits included family allowances, which provided a fixed supplement for each child and had been mandated for French workers since 1932. (Although African civil servants had won the right to family allowances after their 1946 strike, their benefits had not been equal across the ranks.)[83] As the cost of living skyrocketed during the postwar period, wages, and especially family allowances, became a heavily contested terrain of struggle. The 1950 general strike in Guinea would revolve around the minimum wage, while family allowances would be central to the general strike of 1953.[84]

In 1950, the dominant trade union federation in Guinea was the CGT-affiliated Union des Syndicats Confédérés de Guinée (henceforth, CGT), led by Sékou Touré. The 18 member unions included those representing Western-educated civil servants such as PTT workers, government clerks, and teachers, as well as African police and public works employees. CGT unions also represented elite and nonelite private-sector employees, including commercial and domestic workers, chauffeurs, and mechanics. In 1950, the Guinean CGT counted 20,000 members. The much-smaller Guinean branch of the French Confédération Française des Travailleurs Chrétiens (CFTC), financially supported by the Catholic missions, had four member unions in industry, commerce, and mining.[85] Despite their philosophical differences, the CGT and CFTC formed a strong alliance in 1950 and, together with the autonomous railway workers' union, mounted the June 9–10 general strike.[86] Due to the unions' diverse class base, the general strike, by definition, crossed class lines.

The strike was preceded by a motion, voted on May 31, 1950, by a joint committee of CGT, CFTC, and FSCA representatives, as well as thousands of public- and private-sector workers. Taking note of spiraling inflation and the government's failure to enact price-stabilizing measures, the unions demanded a decree ensuring unskilled laborers—the lowest category of urban wageworkers—a minimum wage of 134 francs per day and a 67.5 percent across-the-board increase for all other categories of workers in both the public and private sectors. These increases were to be enacted in Conakry and all the zones of the interior, where wages were significantly lower. If these demands were not acceded to by June 8, the motion warned, a 48-hour general strike by all public- and private-sector workers would be called for June 9–10, 1950.[87]

The dire nature of the workers' situation was described by a joint CGT-CFTC-FSCA document distributed at the end of May. According to the unions, unskilled Conakry laborers had received a minimum of 46 francs per day in 1946. By 1950, the minimum daily wage in the capital city had risen to 80 francs. However, as a result of the terrific increase in the cost of daily necessities, purchasing power had declined precipitously. While the minimum wage had risen by 74 percent between 1946 and 1950, the cost of living had increased by 500 percent.[88]

Hearkening to the rhetoric of assimilation, the unions noted the disparity in African and European workers' wages. In category after professional category, European workers received four to five times more than African workers with the same qualifications. Moreover, French workers received accommodations, whereas African workers did not. Calling for equal pay for equal work and an end to discrimination, the unions declared,

> We will defend our rights and our interests. We want to live, and enable our families to live, with dignity. . . . We fight to assure our livelihoods, and those of our wives and children. We fight so that the colonialists who are starving us can no longer trample on our rights. We fight for progress, happiness, and the evolution of our country.[89]

Reporting to his superior in Dakar, Governor Roland Pré described the strike as "partial" on June 9 and "almost total" on June 10.[90] The inspector general of labor for French West Africa noted that, "The totality of unskilled workers of the public and private sectors, commercial, industrial, and construction workers, workers on the ports and those in bakeries and butcher shops, as well as domestic workers, participated in this movement." Of an estimated 6,000 to 6,500 wageworkers in Conakry, 4,500 to 5,000—or 75 percent—went on strike. About half of these were unskilled laborers directly affected by the minimum wage. The remainder understood that a victory concerning the minimum wage, which would result in corresponding increases in other categories, was in their interest as well.[91]

The immediate outcome of the strike was an increase in the minimum wage and some benefits for unskilled workers, but not a daily minimum of 134 francs nor the across-the-board egalitarian measures demanded by the unions. Over the long term, however, the June 1950 general strike resulted in a clear victory for the unions. The increase in the minimum wage for unskilled workers, and the strike's ripple effect, resulted in territory-wide increased wages for skilled workers in construction, industry, commerce, banking, and insurance, as well as for bakers, chauffeurs, and domestic servants.[92] Moreover, within a year, the minimum wage had increased to 134 francs per day for almost all categories of unskilled workers.[93] This figure, 30 francs more than proposed by employers and 38 francs more than decreed by the government in June 1950, was precisely the amount demanded by the unions prior to the general strike.[94]

The RDA and the 1950 General Strike

The government's concern about the strike extended far beyond fears of damage to European commercial interests—or even to the economy in general. Its greatest worry in 1950 was communist subversion by means of the CGT and the RDA. In fact, the RDA was intensely interested in the labor movement. African trade unionists, like military veterans, were already engaged in struggle against the colonial state. The unions' militant, well-organized membership constituted a class alliance that was ready-made for political mobilization. Intense state repression had forced the RDA to shift tactics, moving from overt political to trade union activity. Taking advantage of the skills, organization, and momentum of the postwar unions, the RDA would build a mass political movement from the trade union ranks. Seizing the opportunity to champion the workers' cause, the RDA would ride to victory on the coattails of the labor movement.

Preoccupied with the RDA's communist ties, colonial officials minimized the strength and independence of the trade union movement. Behind every successful labor action, they saw the work of political activists and evidence of communism's long arm. The high commissioner, for instance, charged that the general strike was "organized and directed by active elements of R.D.A. Conakry, following the instructions of this movement to substitute trade union action for political action."[95] The inspector general of labor charged that tracts carrying the strike motion had been reproduced on an RDA duplicator. Those distributed prior to and during the strike included "terminology of the Rassemblement Démocratique Africain." Moreover, he concluded,

> The exploitation by meetings, tracts and whispered propaganda of the impatience of workers to see the reevaluation of their wages, the calculated whipping up of emotions . . . make it clear that the agitation was conducted

in a political as much as a trade union sense by the leaders of the Union des Syndicats C.G.T. of Guinea, active elements of the R.D.A. This activity is, moreover, in the line of conduct given to its militants by the R.D.A. to pass from political action to trade union action.

Implying communist influence, the inspector general charged that the Guinean CGT had designated "commissars" to enforce respect for the strike order. The anticolonial stance of the strikers was evident in their rallying of domestic workers and cooks to their cause, "with the goal of holding the European population and the restaurants at their mercy."[96] Finally, even after the strike ended, the CGT continued to demand a 134 franc minimum wage through "vehement articles" published in *Réveil.*[97]

In an attempt to thwart the growing influence of the CGT/RDA, the government sought moderate allies within the workers' milieu. Officials pinned their hopes on the Catholic mission-spawned CFTC, whose more conservative brand of trade unionism focused on wages and working conditions but shunned their linkage to broader political questions. According to the inspector general of labor,

> The C.F.T.C. has situated itself exclusively on the trade union plane in view of a reconsideration of the minimum wage. The same does not go for the C.G.T. which, through the R.D.A. representatives to the General Council, has transposed the problem onto the political plane.[98]

Unfortunately for the government, on May 14, 1950, the Guinean CFTC leader, David Soumah, was called to Paris by his superiors. He did not return until June 13—three days after the strike's conclusion. According to the inspector general of labor, the CGT took advantage of Soumah's absence and assumed direction of the initiative for an increased minimum wage. Within two weeks of Soumah's departure, the CGT had reoriented the movement and planned a program of direct action—the general strike of June 9–10. The inspector general concluded that the CGT leaders knew that the Guinean government could not satisfy their steep demands. By pressing the issue, they were "necessarily instigating the mass movement desired by political forces."[99]

The inspector general further noted that the May 31 intertrade union meeting had been initiated by the CGT, which dominated the event. Although the strike motion was presented in the name of all three union organizations (CGT, CFTC, FSCA), it was, the official implied, a CGT document. At the meeting, Sékou Touré had proposed "violently and in the habitual style of the R.D.A., recourse to strike." Between May 31 and June 9, the CGT held numerous private meetings, made contact with other unions, provoked demands, and organized the work stoppage. Meetings were convened at the homes of local RDA militants, including Sékou Touré, Amara Soumah,

Madéïra Kéïta, Baba Camara, and Ray Autra. "The direction of this movement by the C.G.T./R.D.A. is clearly apparent," the inspector concluded.[100]

In fact, workers were unabashed in their use of political avenues to promote their cause. On June 13, the government raised the daily minimum wage in Conakry to 96 francs. That same day, Amara Soumah, RDA councillor for Conakry, urged the General Council to request the governor's intervention to raise the daily minimum wage from 96 to 120 francs.[101] Complaining about CGT/RDA tactics, the inspector general charged that their actions and arguments in the General Council transformed a social issue into a political one.[102]

When the governor refused to act, Framoï Bérété, president of the General Council's Permanent Commission, wrote to the governor's superior in Dakar. In his June 26 letter to the high commissioner, Bérété recommended acceptance of the RDA proposal. The workers' demands were justified, he wrote. More importantly, if the proposal were not accepted,

> Would this not render the territory susceptible to the accomplishment of evil designs in regard to the masses . . . ? Will the workers disassociate their material interests from political tendencies, if the public powers do not give them the impression that they are themselves looking to distinguish between them?

On behalf of the Permanent Commission, Bérété urged the high commissioner to intervene to put the matter right.[103]

Bérété's request is remarkable only because he was not a member of the RDA. In fact, as a member of the vociferously anti-RDA Comité d'Entente Guinéenne, he was vehemently opposed to it. Another RDA rival, Barry Diawadou, was vice president of the Permanent Commission.[104] Yet even that conservative body was able to recognize the political explosiveness of rampant inflation and the large wage gap between public- and private-sector workers and between African and European workers with the same qualifications.[105] As matters stood, any political explosion in Guinea would be to the detriment of conservative African bodies—and to the benefit of the RDA.

The inspector general of labor also placed hope in mollifying tactics. As the ripple effect of the increased minimum wage was felt, and skilled workers were able to negotiate increases in their collective bargaining contracts, the official expressed relief: "These wage reevaluations should result in the definitive appeasement necessary to annihilate the efforts of the CGT/RDA to incite an agitating spirit, favorable to their political goals."[106] However, the government had not won the war. The battle over the minimum wage was part of a larger struggle for a comprehensive overseas labor code. The RDA would join the trade unions in that struggle as well.

THE FRENCH OVERSEAS LABOR CODE

Laws regulating African labor had been rendered obsolete by the first Lamine Guèye Law and the October 1946 constitution, which abolished the category of *indigène* and granted citizenship to former subjects.[107] Wishing to contain labor unrest by definitively settling controversies over the maximum number of hours in a workweek, overtime pay, and paid holidays, some colonial officials pressed for an overseas labor code—similar, but not identical, to the one that regulated labor in metropolitan France. As they severed their rural ties, African workers, like those in metropolitan France, needed some sort of social security system, these officials argued.[108] Employing the government's own language of assimilation, African trade unions pressed for a labor code that recognized no distinction between African and metropolitan workers. They demanded equal pay for equal work and benefits identical to those received by their French counterparts.[109]

Despite the apparent urgency, it was not until November 8, 1950, that the National Assembly as a whole began to consider a draft labor code.[110] On December 8, the Guinean CGT convened a large public meeting in Conakry's municipal stadium to discuss the proposed code. The meeting concluded by calling for a democratic labor code that would abolish all restrictions on trade union rights; recognize the right of workers to participate in crafting collective bargaining agreements; recognize unconditionally the right to strike and suppress all constraints on the free exercise of this right; mandate a 40-hour workweek for all workers; strictly apply the principle of equal pay for equal work; abolish all forced labor by closing the remaining loopholes; and require the absolute independence of labor inspectors with regard to the local administration. The meeting also moved that the draft labor code be discussed, enacted into law, and promulgated by January 1, 1951.[111]

Despite the appeals of African workers, it was not until April 1951 that the National Assembly approved an initial draft of the labor code. The draft was then submitted to the Council of the Republic, the second chamber of the French parliament. Forces of the Right gutted the text of liberal propositions, removing provisions guaranteeing free wage labor, the unrestricted right to form trade unions, the right to strike, and the possibility of instituting family allowances by (local government) decree. In April 1952, an unrecognizable version of the labor code was returned to the National Assembly for a second reading.[112]

In August 1952, frustrated by the backsliding and delays, Guinean workers seized the initiative. Meeting in Conakry, a joint committee of CGT, CFTC, and railway workers called for a federation-wide trade union conference to plan labor actions that would pressure the government to adopt a democratic labor code—similar to that approved by the National Assembly in April 1951.[113] The result was a meeting in Dakar on October 6–8 of some 70 trade union leaders, representing CGT, CFTC, FSCA, and other autonomous unions from each of the territories of French West Africa. Only the anticommunist trade union federation, CGT-Force Ouvrière (FO), composed exclusively of European workers, refused to participate.[114]

The conference delegates planned a three-step protest. First, in late October, there would be a day of demands, with demonstrations and speeches in all the major urban centers of French West Africa. Second, on November 3, there would be a one-day general strike throughout the federation. Third, if a democratic labor code were not passed by January 5, 1953, there would be a three-day general strike on January 12–14, 1953. The trade unionists also demanded the restoration of the text adopted by the National Assembly in April 1951—before the code was gutted by right-wing forces in the Council of the Republic.[115]

The federation-wide general strike of November 3, 1952, prompted by parliamentary delays in enacting and promulgating a democratic overseas labor code, was widely viewed as a remarkable success in every territory except Niger and Mauritania.[116] While noting massive work stoppages in Senegal, the Ivory Coast, Upper Volta, Dahomey, and the French Soudan, *West Africa* magazine observed that "the strike seems to have been the most complete in French Guinea."[117] The military police affirmed that Mamou had been brought to a standstill, with virtually all of the public- and private-sector workers adhering to the strike call.[118] In the capital, a police commandant noted with concern, "We witnessed in Conakry the birth of an African proletariat that will necessarily become a struggling proletariat with a class consciousness."[119]

Three days after the general strike, the National Assembly began what would become its final consideration of the overseas labor code. The impact of the general strike, plus the threat of a three-day strike in January 1953, prompted the government to reinstate most of the progressive provisions deleted by the Council of the Republic, including that which recognized the principle of family allowances for African workers. The codification of equal treatment for African and metropolitan workers, fundamental to trade union demands, was partially realized.[120] The National Assembly adopted the definitive text of the overseas labor code on November 22, 1952. It became law on December 15 and was effective in French West Africa from December 24, 1952.[121]

The overseas labor code applied to all wageworkers in the public and private sectors, including those in industry, commerce, and agriculture. Most of these workers were male. It excluded from its provisions "customary labor," a category that included sharecroppers; labor tenants; and the unpaid family labor of peasant women, junior men, and children, as well as rural subjects working for their chiefs.[122] It also excluded informal sector workers in the urban areas, including seamstresses, cloth dyers, and market women. In Guinea, the vast majority of the population fell into the "customary labor" or informal sector categories. Women in particular were defined outside the category of "worker."[123]

Workers covered by the labor code—those in the relatively small capitalist economic sector—were guaranteed a number of rights and protections. Using the metropolitan labor code as its model, the overseas code granted workers the right to one day off per week. Forty hours became the legal length of the workweek in all public and private establishments. Beyond that, employers were required to pay overtime. The principle of equal pay for equal work was underscored; wages were to be determined by workers' qualifications and job categories—not by race or civil status. While civil servants had obtained equal family allowances with the Lamine Guèye Law of 1950, private-sector workers were now eligible for family allowances, equal or otherwise, to be implemented by local government decree. Public- and private-sector workers were guaranteed paid holidays and clean, safe workplaces. Their right to organize trade unions was reaffirmed; procedures for conciliation and arbitration were spelled out, as were the circumstances for legal strikes and lockouts.[124]

The lengthy debates over the labor code had focused on a handful of key issues. One was the duration of the standard workweek. In the major cities of French West Africa, the normal workweek was 48 hours. In other parts of the federation, it was often longer. However, in metropolitan France, the workweek was 40 hours. Hence, the RDA, the PCF, and others argued that 40 hours should be the standard overseas. They demanded strict application of the 1946 Constitution, which accorded equal rights to inhabitants of the *métropole* and the French Union. As Cooper observes, the French parliament was ultimately forced to accept the consequences of its own assimilationist language.[125]

Unsettled was the question of pay. African representatives argued that wages for a 40-hour week should at least guarantee subsistence—that is, the amount necessary to provide for basic needs—with higher rates for overtime work.[126] If the length of the workweek were reduced, the hourly rate would have to increase accordingly—or workers would lose money in the process. The implementation of the 40-hour workweek and the amount that workers would be paid for it would be central issues in the 1953 general strike.

A second debate revolved around the issue of family allowances, one of the most contested benefits in the overseas labor code. Since 1932, metropolitan workers had received guaranteed family allowances in the form of a supplementary bonus for each child. Colonial officials argued, however, that African and European societies were totally different in nature. The practice of marrying multiple wives and the demands of the elastic African family would rapidly consume benefits intended only for monogamous nuclear families. Moreover, who would pay for such a fabulously expensive system? Yet, the receipt of family allowances was more important to African workers than any other single issue. It was significant philosophically—African and European families were of equal value—and materially—child supplements were critical to the survival of the large families of minimum wage earners.[127]

Implementation of the labor code was left to the colonial governments, which were generally ill disposed toward equalizing African and European benefits. It was the implementation of the overseas labor code—rather, the failure to implement it—that set the stage for the next phase of the struggle. Who would interpret the law, and how would it be applied?[128] African workers and their unions, colonial officials, and owners of commerce and industry attempted to dominate the ensuing contest.

THE GENERAL STRIKE OF 1953

In the crusade to force a favorable application of the labor code, Guinean trade unions were again in the vanguard, proposing a federation-wide trade union conference to determine strategy. Meeting in Bamako in early 1953, the conference delegates attempted to seize control of the interpretation process by introducing several demands. First, since the labor code had decreased the standard workweek by 20 percent (reducing it from 48 to 40 hours), the minimum hourly wage should be increased by an equal amount. Second, the territorial governments should immediately issue decrees instituting family allowances. Third, the same family allowances should apply to all workers, regardless of when they commenced wage work. If the colonial authorities failed to accede to these demands, the Bamako conference recommended a series of strikes.[129]

During the year that followed, the federation's principal urban centers were plagued by strikes. The most intensive labor actions occurred in Guinea, where trade unions were especially strong and the RDA had consolidated its position in the urban areas, largely due to its championship of the overseas labor code.[130] Trade union and party membership increasingly overlapped, and workers effectively transferred their discipline and organizational and leadership skills from the trade union to the political arena. The trade union–RDA alliance had been cemented in 1952, when Sékou Touré, secretary-general of the CGT's Union des Syndicats Confédérés de Guinée, was also elected secretary-general of the RDA's Guinean branch.[131]

As the year wore on and the French West African administration failed to implement the labor code, preparations were made for a federation-wide general strike. At a September 7 meeting, the Guinean CGT, CFTC, and railway workers' union, led by Sékou Touré, David Soumah, and Adama Diop, respectively, voted in favor of a motion for an unlimited general strike.[132] Although the unions' fundamental concern was the rapid implementation of the labor code, they also had other claims. While the 40-hour workweek had officially begun on August 16, 1953, the issue of wages still had not been resolved. The unions thus reiterated their demand that workers receive the same minimum pay for a 40-hour workweek as they previously had received for 48 hours. In other words, the minimum hourly wage should increase by 20 percent, with comparable increases for the other wage categories. Further, they demanded that the provision for family allowances, determined on the same basis for African and European workers, immediately be implemented.[133]

Negotiations began even before the onset of the strike. In response to the workers' demand for a 20 percent minimum hourly wage increase, employers countered with an offer of 14.3 percent. While the unions held firm on 20 percent for the minimum hourly wage, the CGT, at least, was willing to negotiate for the other wage categories. Sékou Touré suggested a minimum hourly wage increase of 20 percent, with a 14.3 percent raise for the other echelons. In a telegram to the high commissioner, the governor of Guinea argued against accepting the offer. While acceding to the CGT proposition might forestall the strike, he wrote, it would "recognize explicitly the thesis of the workers' union." This, the governor concluded, was politically unacceptable.[134]

On September 21, 1953, the federation-wide general strike began. It included skilled and semiskilled workers in the public and private sectors, represented by the CGT and CFTC, as well as quasi–public-sector workers in the FSCA. Like the railway strike of 1947–1948, the 1953 strike affected most of the territories of French West Africa, and its duration was not predetermined; workers were to boycott their jobs until union demands were satisfied.[135]

In Guinea, the capital city was the most severely affected. By eleven o'clock on the morning of September 21, there were no African workers on construction sites or in the mines. Only a few isolated railway workers were on the job. The ports functioned with the help of scab labor recruited on the spot. With the exception of the banks, commercial enterprises were shut down. The governor estimated that 80 percent of Conakry's private sector was on strike. In the interior, however, only Mamou reported extensive strike action.[136]

Having been elected to the Territorial Assembly on August 2, 1953, Sékou Touré had a new venue from which to champion the workers' cause.[137] However, his appeals fell on deaf ears. Notoriously conservative, the Territorial Assembly was composed primarily of chiefs, notables, and other elites.[138] Because RDA councillor Amara Soumah had defected from the party in April 1952, Sékou Touré was the sole RDA representative in the assembly.[139] On the evening of October 19, Sékou Touré reproached the body for its failure to support the striking workers and announced that the strike would be extended to the territory's interior.[140]

With no end in sight, the governor appealed to the territory's African elites. On October 24, he urged a group of eminent Conakry personages to use their

Photo 3.4 Dock workers loading bananas, Conakry port, 1957. (*La Documentation Française*)

influence against the strike. In a subsequent meeting convened in a Conakry mosque, the notables reproached Sékou Touré and David Soumah for their refusal to compromise. Yet, when El Hadj Konaté asked Sékou Touré to authorize a return to work, it was clear that even the religious elders recognized the superior influence of the 31-year-old trade union leader.[141] According to a police report, "The interview became spirited when the CGT chorus stationed outside the mosque began to hurl abuse at the notables, accusing them . . . of being paid by the administration to sabotage the strike." Despite their status, the notables were derided by the crowd. As partisans of the notorious RDA defector Amara Soumah, they had little standing among the striking workers.[142]

While the elders were not respected, their religion was. Recognizing the powerful hold of Islam on the local population, Sékou Touré took steps to win religious support for the strike. On October 30, he journeyed to Kankan to seek the patronage of the grand chérif Fanta Mady, hoping that this widely revered figure would back the strike with his religious authority.[143] Although he had vehemently opposed the RDA in 1949 for what he perceived to be its "anti-French" attitude, Fanta Mady's opposition had melted into "benevolent neutrality" by 1953. The CGT and RDA were anxious to receive his blessing.[144]

More important than the appeal to the grand chérif, however, was grassroots mobilization. As in previous strikes, the trade unions actively solicited community support. Military veterans, particularly those affected by racial discrimination, were invited to join the strikers. The local population was urged to boycott a reception for the French minister of veterans' affairs, resulting in an embarrassingly low turnout.[145] Although they anticipated no personal gain, their grievances having been resolved by the second Lamine Guèye Law, African civil servants waged a three-day solidarity strike on October 29–31.[146] Messages of support poured in from trade unions in neighboring territories, the unions' federal headquarters in Dakar, and from unions affiliated with the metropolitan CGT.[147]

Popular education and mobilization were critical to the strike's success. Sékou Touré and other trade unionists spoke daily in Conakry neighborhoods, providing news and circulating slogans, inspiring determination and invoking discipline. Urging the population to rise above petty feuds and ethnic infighting, Sékou Touré constantly referred to the common bonds between all workers and the irrelevance of ethnic origin.[148] The military police reported frequent meetings on the public roads, which generated crowds of several thousand people.[149]

Meanwhile, the strike had become an issue in the struggle for political ascendancy in Conakry. The Lower-Guinea regional association Union de la Basse-Guinée had recently split, with the original, more conservative body attracting older and rural supporters, and the new Foyer des Jeunes de la Basse-Guinée appealing to a younger, primarily urban group of dissidents.[150] The RDA and the Foyer des Jeunes supported the strike leader Sékou Touré against the RDA renegade Amara Soumah, who was president of the Union de la Basse-Guinée.[151] Discussions took on a political tone as workers' demands were increasingly couched in language that challenged the authority of French law and institutions. At an intertrade union rally of 2,000 on November 14, David Soumah, the relatively moderate CFTC leader, declared to the crowd, "They are refusing us this 20 percent [wage increase] for political reasons. . . . We want the honest application of a law voted by the sovereign Assembly. We must know if the institutions still hold value."[152]

Concerned that a concession on the wage issue would be perceived as political weakness, the high commissioner instructed territorial governors to decrease the prices of certain basic goods in lieu of increasing wages. The trade unions were equally determined in their defense of the 20 percent wage hike. Standing firm on a matter of principle, Adama Diop responded that the issue of the 40-hour week had nothing to do with the cost of living. Price controls would not satisfy the workers, whose primary demand remained the strict and egalitarian application of the labor code.[153] As the strike wore on, Guinean workers strengthened their determination not to accept anything less than 20 percent. They rejected numerous, incrementally better offers from owners of industry and commerce and the government. With an eye to the international arena, they consistently compared the proposals to better ones put forward in other French West African territories.[154]

In spite of worker indifference, the high commissioner launched a campaign of price controls on November 19. Even the government was dubious that it would satisfy workers' demands. On the second day of the campaign, one official wrote,

> The position of the representatives of the C.G.T. has not changed. . . . For them the problem of prices and the problem of the Labor Code are independent, and if the results of the price decrease are convincing, the fact remains that the reduction of the length of work from 48 to 40 hours implies an augmentation of 20 percent, demanded by all the workers.[155]

Meanwhile, the Grand Council of French West Africa recommended that the government decree a 40-hour week while maintaining the minimum hourly earnings of the 48-hour week. Any retreat from the 20 percent wage increase would be "a violation of the law." If the government did not take heed, the Grand Council concluded, the result could be "social troubles capable of dangerously compromising the order and the economy of the Federation."[156]

Worried about workers' perceptions of the administration and the political consequences of circumventing the law, the high commissioner telegraphed his concerns to his superior in Paris. Flagrant violation of the labor code carried a high political price; concession to the workers was equally troubling. If people concluded that the trade unions had won and the government had been forced into submission, the strike would be but the beginning:

> There will be very grave inconveniences if this final decision concerning the application of the Labor Code appears here as having been imposed on an executive suspected of wishing to violate the law. The attempts made to resolve the question at the local level . . . would be interpreted as a maneuver of the administration foiled by the trade unions. Far from being an appeasement, the success brought in this way by trade union action would quickly reinforce the spirit of making demands.

In order to avoid such developments and the obvious political ramifications, the administration must recapture the initiative.[157]

In urging that the government cut its losses, forestalling an even worse scenario, the high commissioner was not alone. The inspector general of labor for French West Africa enjoined the administration to quickly meet the union demand for a minimum hourly wage increase of 20 percent, permitting the existing subsistence level to be achieved within a 40-hour workweek. If the government demurred, he warned, the trade unions might begin to raise questions about the *quality* of food, clothing, and shelter used in calculating African subsistence levels. Once that occurred,

> there would no longer be any reason for claims to cease, along with agitation, until a minimum budget identical to that of the metropolitan workers were accepted, a budget already proposed by certain unions in the Ivory Coast and Guinea, under the pretext that this basic document for the determination of the minimum wage cannot be tainted by racial discrimination and thus must respond to the minimum needs of the European as well as the African.[158]

The inspector general's comments betrayed the belief commonly held by Europeans that Africans and Europeans had fundamentally different needs. This supposed difference in basic requirements was used to justify the wide disparity between European and African workers in allocations for food, clothing, and accommodations, not to mention the contested family allowances. It was this notion of difference that African workers challenged, using the French language of assimilation and universality to do so.[159]

The workers won their point. In an unacknowledged about-face, the high commissioner urged the overseas minister to increase the French West African minimum hourly wage by 20 percent in order to forestall more serious developments.[160] On November 28, the overseas minister accepted the recommendation. The strike was over.[161]

In Guinea, the general strike had lasted 67 to 71 days, with workers returning to their jobs from November 27 to December 1, 1953.[162] The strike's resolution weighed heavily in the workers' favor. Their central demand had been met; the 20 percent minimum wage increase was an unequivocal victory. Moreover, strikers were guaranteed reemployment in their previous positions.[163] Politically, the strike enhanced Guinea's standing in the West African labor scene and strengthened the trade union movement. Throughout the federation, Guinean trade union leaders were credited with the 20 percent minimum hourly wage increase. Inspired by the unions' success, workers joined in droves. The number of trade union members in Guinea skyrocketed from 4,600 at the beginning of 1953 to 20,000 in 1954 and 44,000 in 1955.[164] Popular memory of the strike's positive outcome remains vivid and sometimes overstated. According to RDA militant Fatou Kéïta,

After the strike, the things they had agreed to were implemented. Wages went up. Workers got family allowances. Rations of white rice were added to the monthly wages. . . . This was the first time they had had this kind of rice. Each worker got 15 kilos of rice per month.[165]

Because it had been a key demand, some informants associated the receipt of family allowances with the 1953 general strike. However, it was not until 1956 that France implemented a regime of family allowances in French West Africa that extended to African wageworkers outside the civil service.[166] The 1953 general strike had been a major victory for workers, but not a total one.

Just as the administration had feared, the workers' victory did not bring an end to demands but stimulated new ones. On December 15, the governor signed the decree increasing the minimum wage in Guinea by 20 percent. The ink was hardly dry when he was approached by a delegation of workers who requested that *all* wages be increased by 20 percent, in accordance with the first article of the overseas labor code, which stipulated that all wages be raised in proportion to an increased minimum wage. The frustrated governor referred the matter to a commission of employers and workers, charging that employers must shoulder some responsibility for the matter rather than looking to the government to resolve all their problems.[167]

The workers' response to victory—demanding even more—was precisely what the high commissioner had feared. In Guinea, he wrote to the overseas minister, the strike had concluded after "very laborious negotiations that will leave behind a bad social climate." Concessions would only stimulate further demands. Of even greater concern, the strike had reinforced the linkage between metropolitan and local trade unions. The African unions had received numerous French visitors and a constant stream of encouragement. These well-developed contacts boded ill for the future. The next strike, which could be unleashed simultaneously in all the territories of the federation, promised to be even more widespread. Finally, the high commissioner warned, there were few, if any, prospects that the new alliance between unions of diverse tendencies could be broken.[168]

Women's Role in the 1953 General Strike

The Guinean general strike had lasted more than 70 days, some two months longer than in the other French West African territories.[169] As with the railway strike of 1947–1948, community support was crucial to the strike's longevity and ultimate success. In 1953, Guinea's population was predominantly rural and agrarian. In the urban areas, informal sector activity surpassed wage work as the primary means of household support. With wage earners constituting only 3 percent of the population, there were significant community resources to draw upon.[170] Key to the mobilization of human and material resources were Guinean women.

Although many Guinean women eventually challenged circumscribed gender roles, their entrance into labor and nationalist politics was marked by its conservative nature. "Women got involved in the struggle because they were unable to fulfill their social roles," Kadiatou Meunier recalled. When economic conditions or colonial policies threatened their ability to raise their children and sustain their families and communities, women took action. "It was *not* to have equal access to resources, to have a political vocation," Meunier asserted. "They believed it was the role of women to support men in the society."[171] Drawing on the image of women preparing for a strenuous task— or to fight—Néné Diallo noted, "Women tightened their wrappers to help their husbands achieve their goals."[172] Relying on long-standing practices of female solidarity and collective action, they challenged the forces that prevented them from carrying out their duties.

In Conakry especially, the workers' grievances were widely publicized: colonial economic policies endangered the welfare of their families. The wives of wageworkers were aware that their husbands did not receive pay equal to that of their French counterparts. According to Fatou Kéïta, "There was oppression that they could see. It was not difficult to see the unequal relations between whites and blacks. They could see the difference in salaries—that they were being exploited." Moreover, in public meetings organized by labor leaders, women learned of the discriminatory nature of family allowances: French workers received them; Africans did not. The women realized "that when their husbands did not get family allowances, the children would suffer," Kéïta recalled. It was the suffering of their children in the long term that encouraged them to support the strike.[173]

Urban women agitated for family allowances attached to male wage packets, even though the formula implied that men alone were breadwinners and reinforced male dominance in the household. In Guinea, as in much of sub-Saharan Africa, women were deemed responsible for their children's sustenance. Food production was considered a preeminently female task. As the initiators of life, women were expected to nourish their children either by growing food or acquiring it in some other way. Most urban women were engaged in income-generating activities, particularly market trading, sewing, and cloth dying. With the proceeds, they contributed a substantial amount to household income.[174] Yet, as Lindsay found among women in southwestern Nigeria, Guinean women supported male trade unionists' demands for family allowances, predicated on the male breadwinner norm, because the result was a larger household income, part of which could be claimed for women's and children's benefit.[175]

Néné Diallo is a case in point. A cloth dyer whose husband resided in Senegal, Diallo clearly played a significant role in her children's support. Yet, she implied that male wage earners were their families' mainstay and described women as their husbands' subordinates. Although her own husband was not present during the general strike, Diallo described women's role in the strike as ancillary to that of their husbands, a term she used interchangeably with "worker." Thus, she said, "The worker toils for money . . . to support the family—to clothe the family, to feed the family. . . . When workers don't work, nobody eats." More equitable treatment of male wage earners, she concluded, would enable "them to support themselves and us."[176] Diallo's sentiments were echoed by other married working women, among them Tourou Sylla, a cloth dyer; Fatou Kéïta, a seamstress; and Mafory Bangoura, who was both a cloth dyer and seamstress.[177]

If inadequate wages and the lack of family allowances jeopardized the population's well-being, the strike itself caused more immediate suffering. As negotiations stalled and days mounted into weeks, food supplies dwindled. Conakry had come to a standstill. Boats were not being unloaded; work at the port had stopped completely. The railroad was not functioning. Even the markets were barely operating. Because men were not receiving their wages, their families were badly hit. "People's blood was being sucked," Fatou Kéïta recalled. The men's morale began to flag, and some contemplated returning to work so they could feed their families. Public meetings were held to decide whether or not to call off the strike. Fatou Kéïta, representing the women, spoke to the assembled crowds. She urged the unions to continue the strike until their conditions were met. If the men were not given family allowances, their children would have nothing to eat; their children's education would be at risk.[178]

Although their stance was less public, other women also encouraged their husbands to hold fast.[179] Recalling the strike in Mamou, Tourou Sylla noted that several of her male relatives were railway workers. It was their involvement in the strike that pulled her into the support movement. Sylla recounted how, when the men began to show weakness, women took the initiative. The fear of public humiliation—being married to a strikebreaker—was an important motivation:

> You know, it was the men who began to have doubts about what they were doing. The whites had said that the workers who stuck with the strike would be dismissed. Nobody would receive his wages. Some men began to get discouraged. When the women saw this air of despair, they realized they would be embarrassed before their peers. The women told their husbands not to worry about the daily food allowance. They said, "I will use the existing allowance to buy and resell oil, rice, spices or even to cook food to sell—all to help you maintain your determination. Do not give up until there is a dignified settlement."[180]

The first order of business was to replace the daily food allowance women customarily received from their husbands. Rural women helped to support their urban relatives by contributing rice—a staple food—as well as manioc, potatoes, maize, and fonio.[181] Taking advantage of kin and market networks, urban women brought products from the countryside and resold them in the urban areas, using the proceeds to support their families.[182] They sold oil, rice, spices, smoked fish, fruit, vegetables, cooked food, firewood, and other small items. Some women sold their jewelry, clothing, and cooking utensils so their husbands could continue the strike.[183] Urban market women took up collections and fed striking workers and their families without charge.[184] Fatou Kéïta recalled that small groups of women combed the neighborhoods collecting rice and money for the strikers' families. "It was easier for women than men to collect money from men," she recalled. "Men were ashamed if a woman asked for money and they did not have it."[185]

Instead of purchasing fish at the market, many women began to fish for themselves. Louis Marquis Camara remembered that women went in groups to fish on the rocks by the sea. They caught crabs and small fish in circular nets or scooped them up in calabashes. With their daily catch, they made soup for their families.[186] Fatou Kéïta recalled that Conakry women fished in teams along the coast, from the women's strike headquarters in downtown Tombo to the suburb of Camayenne:

> When it was low tide, the women went behind the rocks and caught small fish in round nets. The women's organization taught the women how to boil these small fish and prepare them with fresh pounded manioc. It was during this time that this dish was popularized.

Rice was a rarity during the strike, and manioc, a "famine food," was cheap. When mixed with fish, it was also nutritious. "This is how the women fed their families during the strike," Kéïta concluded.[187]

Kéïta also recalled that the dish was easy to make, which gave the women more time for organizing. While they fished, they discussed what they would do after their cooking obligations were finished. These were their strategy meetings, Kéïta said. "The women did all this in joy. Fishing, talking together—this kept them out of the house for a long time. They had fun. It was the men who were unhappy during the strike. This was the women's first sign of independence!"[188]

During their gatherings, women composed songs of support that urged men to keep on with the strike, boosted morale, and conveyed crucial information.[189] Aissatou N'Diaye remembered one such song:

> Courage was thrust upon Guinea once
> The cause of *Syli*
> Which women embrace
> The cause of the strike
> Women were for.[190]

Questioning the piety of El Hadji Alkaly Ibrahima Soumah, a government-appointed chief who was notoriously hostile to trade unions and the RDA, the women also sang:

> The chief of the neighborhood of Coronthie
> Is not an El Hadj
> Enemy of the workers
> He was bribed by the Administration
> To sabotage the strike.[191]

Finding food was not the only difficulty women faced. They had to devise innovative ways to clothe their families. Aissatou N'Diaye recalled that during the strike,

> There was lots of suffering in the land. . . . There was suffering, hunger, and people went naked. No one could afford to buy clothes. This was the result of the strike called by Sékou. The masses were having second thoughts about it. Men began giving their wives their full pants, made with lots of material. The women would take out the seams, tie the cloth into a scarf, and then take the cloth to a tailor to be sewn as a dress. That is what women resorted to, so as not to go about naked. The strike was very hard on people.[192]

"Women clothed their husbands and did everything so that the strike might succeed," Néné Diallo remembered.[193]

Besides supporting their husbands and families, women also engaged in acts of resistance. They ostracized strikebreakers, refusing to allow male scabs into their homes.[194] Obeying the appeals of strike leaders, they boycotted European-owned stores.[195] Market women refused to sell chicken, eggs, and milk to French colonialists.[196] They sent pointed messages to opponents of the strike. Amara Soumah, the RDA renegade, was a particular target, perhaps because he once had been so esteemed by the market women. It was during the 1953 strike that they renamed their wares to suit the political situation; cut-up chunks of bread, symbolizing ethnic and regional factionalism, were touted as *pain Amara Soumah,* while the whole loaf, representing national unity, was called *pain Sékou Touré.*[197]

The women who participated in the strike movement were, for the most part, without formal education.[198] In 1953, few African women had received Western schooling. Only a handful of these female elites—primarily civil servants working as schoolteachers and midwives—became politically involved. According to Kadiatou Meunier, "The intellectual women were highly privileged. From this position of privilege, it was very difficult for them to see the need to fight colonialism. They were sheltered from the hardships of colonialism and had the illusion that they had made it."[199]

Mafory Bangoura, the RDA women's leader whose political involvement began with the general strike, was a member of the town-based dissident group Foyer des Jeunes de la Basse-Guinée. She was a cloth dyer and seam-stress by profession.[200] Aissatou N'Diaye recalled her humble origins: "You must know that Mafory was only an intelligent woman; she was not literate. I was not literate either. But there was nothing we could do about that. Sékou had already taught us about politics."[201] Léon Maka elaborated:

> Mafory was a conscientious leader who always had the right word at the right moment. Her discussions with men were always very logical. Very often, her point of view triumphed. She was a worthy woman. She wasn't educated. She never spent a day in school. She didn't know how to read. She didn't know how to write. But she spoke, and she spoke frankly. She said what she thought.[202]

Aissatou N'Diaye explained how she and Mafory Bangoura became involved in the general strike. The people suffered from great hardship during the strike, she said. Then,

> One day—listen to me! One day we went to see the young man, Sékou. At that time he was living here [in the Conakry neighborhood of Sandervalia, by the sea]. It was Mafory's initiative. She said to me, "Asstou, let's go see this young man. You know this [situation] is becoming worrisome." She said, "Let's go see the young man."

Sékou Touré asked Bangoura and N'Diaye to mobilize women in support of the striking workers.[203] Together with Fatou Kéïta, they helped to form a women's wing of the strike committee. According to Fatou Kéïta, she and other women leaders made contacts through the women's auxiliaries of the ethnic associations. Cutting across ethnic lines, they brought women together to support the strike.[204]

As negotiations intensified, workers came under increasing pressure to end the strike. "They held a meeting at Cinéma Rialto—at the movie theater near here," N'Diaye continued. "Workers were getting discouraged because there was no way out of the deadlock."[205] At the Rialto meeting, the community weighed the pros and cons of a return to work. The strike committee's women's wing made its first public appearance, bringing together more than 500 supporters.[206] Fatou Kéïta was chosen to speak for the women. Standing before the crowd, she urged the workers not to call off the strike until their demands were met. If the men were not granted family allowances, she warned, the children would have nothing to eat. Their education would be jeopardized.[207] Mounting the rostrum, Mafory Bangoura also articulated the women's views. She urged the men not to give in; their wives would support them, even if the strike lasted for a year or more. However, she declared, if the men were afraid, the women had tightened their wrappers and were prepared to fight in their place.[208]

The success of the 1953 general strike was a turning point not only for the trade unions, but also for the RDA and for women in the nationalist struggle. Women's critical role in the strike was recognized, particularly by Sékou Touré, the rising star of both the labor and nationalist movements. According to Aissatou N'Diaye, "Soon after [the strike ended], things heated up once again. That is when the RDA gained strength. The RDA really took off. And women had [Sékou Touré's] trust, because women had been supportive of him. The struggle really began in 1953, '54, '55."[209] Aissatou N'Diaye recalled how women's efforts during the strike resulted in their mobilization into the RDA:

> Mafory came to tell me that [Sékou Touré] had asked to see us. Upon our arrival, he requested our help in mobilizing women. He said that when one asks for help from women, one has equally called upon their children. He said he needed help from the women, but that he had nothing material, not money nor gold, to offer in return. If the women would help him, they would do it for the love of Allah, His Envoy, and their cause. . . . It was then that he sent us the membership cards. . . . That day I was among those who collected the cards. We began mobilizing the women.[210]

Just as many male nationalist leaders began their careers as labor organizers, the general strike of 1953 was, for many Guinean women, their entrée into the broader anticolonial struggle. "After the strike, the ethnic associations disbanded," Fatou Kéïta recalled. "However, the women stayed together, as RDA women, rather than women of different ethnic groups." Following the strike, Fatou Kéïta was included in a delegation of trade union and party leaders that toured Guinea for three months, mobilizing for the RDA. She was the sole woman in the contingent. However, she was not tapped as the RDA women's leader. Rather, Mafory Bangoura was chosen because she was older, and therefore more respected, than Néné Diallo, Aissatou N'Diaye, N'Youla Doumbouya, or Kéïta herself.[211] "That's when the women got Mafory," Néné Diallo recalled, stressing that Bangoura was a respected leader, but only the first among equals:

> She stood up and tightened her wrapper. The women gathered to make her their leader, the top leader. . . . Mafory set up local committees accountable to her. But she did not set up the one where I lived. I would say that out loud on the radio for everyone to hear. I am Néné Diallo! *I* set up my neighborhood committee![212]

Without the rank and file, even the women's leader had no power.

CONCLUSION

Throughout French and British Africa, the immediate postwar period was one of tremendous political and labor ferment.[213] Invariably, workers' demands were explicitly linked to the role Africans had played during the war and to the wartime promises of reformed imperialism. During the federation-wide railway strike, workers' speeches frequently underscored Africans' strong defense of France during the war. African railway workers, who had worked side by side with their French colleagues, thus deserved equal pay and benefits. These demands bore a striking resemblance to those of military veterans, who were simultaneously rallying under the banner "Equal sacrifices, equal rights."[214] Other workers soon took up the cry.

The early 1950s were a low point for the RDA, which suffered from intensified state repression and a consequent wave of resignations. Far from enduring a similar fate, the trade union movement blossomed. Skillfully employing the French language of assimilation, as well as forceful strike action, African workers obtained many of the benefits heretofore reserved for their metropolitan counterparts. By the mid-1950s, a revitalized RDA would use the labor movement and its broad ethnic and class alliance as a launching pad for its revised political program. Guinean women, who had performed crucial functions that enabled their communities to withstand lengthy strikes, were enthusiastically drafted into the nationalist movement.

4

RURAL REVOLT: POPULAR RESISTANCE TO THE COLONIAL CHIEFTAINCY, 1946–1956

Just as the RDA emerged from the postwar veterans' and labor movements, it also gained strength from popular protests against the colonial chieftaincy that had begun during the war. Peasants, who had suffered the intensified burdens of the war effort, resisted with the limited means at their disposal. Women refused to labor in the chiefs' fields. Men recruited as forced laborers deserted their work sites in droves. Whole villages absconded across territorial boundaries to avoid military and labor recruiters. Rural men and women of diverse ethnic groups were thus central to yet another wave of anticolonial protest—resistance to the chiefly authorities who held sway in the countryside.

Rural-based mobilization against village and canton chiefs—often under the leadership of military veterans—predated RDA activities in the countryside. Once again, the RDA was able to capitalize and expand upon preexisting anticolonial sentiment. The party encouraged peasants in their refusal to pay taxes, engage in unpaid labor, and recognize chiefly authority more generally. Responding to peasants' grievances and articulating demands on their behalf, the RDA was able to expand beyond its urban base and establish itself in the interior. The chiefs retaliated by targeting RDA activists and rigging elections to ensure the party's defeat. Since the party's ability to hold the populous rural areas depended upon undermining chiefly power, the anti-chief campaigns became central to the RDA's grassroots strategy.

CHIEFS AS AGENTS OF COLONIAL RULE

From the onset of colonization, government-appointed chiefs played crucial intermediary roles between the colonial government and the rural population. As agents of the colonial state, their primary tasks were to collect taxes, recruit labor and military conscripts, and enforce the collection or cultivation of cash crops. They also transmitted the orders of European circle commandants and subdivision chiefs to the local population.[1]

Since 1897, all African men and women over 18 years of age were required to pay a personal tax to cover the costs of colonial administration. Initially, subjects were permitted to pay their taxes in kind, with rubber especially welcome as a cash substitute. Hoping to expand the wage labor force, the government soon required that taxes be paid in cash. A second portion of the tax was to be rendered in the form of unpaid labor. Peasants were compelled to donate their labor to build and maintain roads, trails, and culverts, and to care for the circle commandants' fields.[2]

To most rural and urban dwellers, it was the chiefs who starkly represented the evils of colonial rule.[3] While European circle commandants informed the canton chiefs how much money they were expected to accrue, canton chiefs supervised the tax collection in their jurisdictions, directing village and urban neighborhood chiefs to produce the requisite amounts. Thus, it was the chiefs, rather than the European administrators, who had the most direct impact on the rural population.[4]

While village and neighborhood chiefs were viewed by their subjects as instruments of colonial oppression, they, too, were victimized by their superiors in the administrative hierarchy. If local chiefs failed to fill their tax quotas, they were severely punished. In scenes that were both humiliating and painful, negligent village chiefs were whipped by the commandant's circle guards or the canton chief's strongmen. Some were imprisoned, others relieved of their positions.[5]

If local chiefs were thorough in collecting revenues, however, it was not only for fear of punishment. A number of benefits ensued from their tax-collecting role. Since a portion of the tax receipts was reserved for them, it was in their interest to accomplish their duties with diligence.[6] It was also in their interest to abuse their powers. The more revenue the chiefs collected, the greater the value of their share. Moreover, canton chiefs often embezzled portions of the revenues owed to village chiefs.[7] Thus, in order to get what they considered their due, village chiefs frequently inflated their tax lists, retaining the names of those who had emigrated or died. Minors, who were not yet obliged to pay taxes, were inscribed on the tax registers, as were the elderly who had passed the age of tax eligibility and women with four or more children, who were theoretically exempt from taxation. In order to meet the inflated tax quota, eligible residents were forced to pay a larger amount.[8] Tax abuses were among the major grievances that provoked rural resistance to the colonial chiefs in the postwar period.

While admitting that there were "unmistakable and abusive errors" in the census, leading to abuses in the tax system, the colonial administration took little corrective action. In June 1948, it seemed more concerned with increasing tax revenues than forestalling rural revolt. Thus, the inspector of administrative affairs counseled one circle commandant to

> avoid massive diminutions in the number of taxable subjects, which will result in a significant decline in anticipated revenues from the personal tax. All diminution that is too keen and insufficiently justified will bring me to reduce, in the same proportions, the credits allocated to your circle.[9]

Two months later, the governor of Guinea sent a similar warning to all circle commandants and subdivision chiefs:

> It seems necessary to remind you that the essential resources of the territorial budget derive from the personal tax, and it is indispensable, for the execution of public works programs, that we collect the maximum. . . . I insist on the necessity of "chasing down" taxable subjects who were not counted in the census; these exist in most of the villages, and it is your responsibility to make the canton chiefs understand that it is imperative that they assist you in ferreting them out. Each village chief must be made responsible for the inhabitants of his village. The taxable subjects who did not register themselves during the census or as soon as they settled in a village will be taxed under the rubric of migrant population. I will in no way allow a diminution in the number counted in the census and in taxable subjects while the population of Guinea is actually growing.[10]

It was with the explicit consent of the governor that tax abuses continued. In the same memo, the governor noted that in the villages of Yandi and Madina-Kouta (Mali subdivision, Labé circle), the census indicated that there were 1,719 inhabitants. Seventy-eight of these were registered as mothers of four children and thus exempt from taxation. The governor warned the subdivision commandant that women would be struck from the exempt list if their children's births were not recorded in the circle's register of vital statistics.[11] In remote rural areas, which included most of the Mali subdivision, the registration of vital statistics was difficult and thus highly unusual. As a result of the governor's stipulations, many nonliterate women without means of transportation would be unjustly forced to pay taxes because they were unable to register their children's births.

Over and above colonial taxes, the African population was expected to pay so called customary dues or fees to the village and canton chiefs. Writing in

1941, the governor of Guinea noted, "The canton and village chiefs continue to benefit widely from the unpaid assistance of their subjects for the execution of diverse works and labor services."[12] Rural dwellers, especially women, were expected to labor without pay for the chiefs, cultivating and harvesting their fields. Some women also were required to perform domestic services. Others were forcibly taken by chiefs as concubines or wives. Men were expected to build and repair the chiefs' huts and fences. Others were required to serve as messengers or chiefs' representatives to the circle commandants. This unremunerated work could occupy from a few days to one month per year. Subjects who were unable to work were made to contribute gifts in kind: eggs, chickens, sheep, cows, or large sums of money. Despite the appellation of "customary," only some of these duties had their origins in the precolonial period. Many were relatively new and were arbitrarily imposed by the chiefs for their personal benefit, with the consent of the colonial administration.[13]

Along with "customary" fees and their portion of the personal tax, chiefs also demanded large, so-called contributions on feast days, French national holidays, and during census taking. They levied death taxes and confiscated the inheritances of those who did not pay. Often, they left widows destitute.[14]

Maintaining official salaries at a minimum, the colonial administration relied on the rural population to provide the bulk of the chiefs' material needs. According to the governor,

> The [customary] services furnished to the chiefs are indispensable to them
> in accomplishing the numerous charges inherent in the exercise of their
> duties (their official remuneration is minute, out of proportion with the
> duties and expenses imposed by custom).[15]

As long as they collected the requisite amount of taxes and recruited the necessary complement of laborers, chiefs were generally permitted to extort money and labor from the population under their jurisdiction.[16] The limits historically imposed upon chiefs' powers by assemblies of free men (in the Futa Jallon), elders' councils, or powerful rival families disappeared under the colonial system.[17]

Under the circumstances, the posts of village, neighborhood, and canton chief were highly coveted, and contenders went to great lengths to obtain these positions. Canton chiefs were appointed by the governor, on the recommendation of the appropriate circle commandant. In order to enhance their popular legitimacy, canton chiefs were selected from traditional hierarchies wherever possible. However, if such chiefs proved to be inept or rebellious, they were replaced by more efficient or malleable men, without pretense of traditional rights to the position.[18] Village chiefs were, in theory, chosen by the circle commandants. In practice, canton chiefs were given relatively free rein to select their underlings, and they frequently sold the offices to the highest bidder.[19]

THE CRISIS OF CHIEFLY AUTHORITY

It was the increased hardship resulting from the war effort, more than any other single factor, that led to a crisis of authority in the rural areas. Although chiefs had long been resented for their role in colonial administration, World War II brought matters to a head. Men were forcibly conscripted for both military service and nonmilitary labor. Women were forced to sacrifice their own families' needs to grow food for the armed forces and for French citizens in the *métropole*. Severe shortages of goods, high inflation, and a dramatic decline in living standards contributed to the devastating effects of war.[20] According to RDA militant Léon Maka,

> The "war effort" consisted of demanding from the population grain—even money—through the intermediary of the canton chiefs. They were supposed to turn over things that the administration lacked. . . . There was always something—collection of money, collection of rice—to send to the *Tirailleurs.*[21]

Implemented by the chiefs on behalf of the administration, the war effort took a tremendous toll on the indigenous population.

During the war, peasants from all parts of Guinea had engaged in massive resistance to wartime exactions. They had refused to pay taxes, carry out their unpaid labor obligations, and provide the requisite crops on demand. They had sold their crops on the black market and smuggled them across territorial boundaries.[22] After the war, resistance continued. In 1946, the governor reported attacks against certain chiefs in Gaoual and Labé circles (Futa Jallon) as a result of the burdens they had imposed on the local populace during the war. Since the end of the war, the governor noted, "the mass of the population has lived only with the hope of seeing the immediate end of the constraints of all sorts that have weighed very heavily on it, particularly the furnishing—one could say the impositions—of rice and rubber, rightly unpopular."[23]

The heavy demands of the war effort resulted in mounting tensions between African villagers and colonial authorities, especially the canton chiefs. Since government demands for rubber, food crops, forced labor, and military recruits were enforced by the canton chiefs, the people held them responsible for their plight.[24] Other African representatives of the administra-

tion, including circle guards, soldiers, and police, also bore the brunt of popular hostility.[25] After all, it was African agents, not European officials, who
were in daily contact with the population, forcing rural inhabitants to comply
with government demands.

In the midst of postwar inflation and economic hardship, chiefs were particularly despised for their ostentatious consumption. The chiefs of the Futa
Jallon, many of whom hailed from a long line of aristocrats, were among the
most notorious in this regard. Their large American cars and numerous wives
drove home their social distance and increased the population's hostility
toward them.[26] Circle commandants in the Futa often commented on the
chiefs' wealth. In 1948, the Binani canton chief (Gaoual circle), who oversaw
12 villages with a population of approximately 14,100, was described as having "six wives and nine children." Another Gaoual canton chief, who also
served as a general councillor, possessed 5 wives, 80 head of cattle, and a
Peugeot truck.[27] Tierno Ibrahima Bah, a general councillor and the Timbi-
Touni canton chief (Pita circle), was a wealthy proprietor of two banana plantations. He also owned numerous trucks and a car.[28]

Implication in the war effort, conspicuous consumption in the face of
poverty, and abuse of power were only some of the factors that undermined
chiefly authority after the war. Another was the chiefs' lack of popular legitimacy. While many chiefs boasted aristocratic blood, a growing number had
little traditional claim to their positions. Ambitious new elites used their
knowledge of French and their proximity to Europeans to challenge "traditional" incumbents. Colonial agents, including government interpreters, circle police, military veterans, and even cooks and "house boys," were assigned
to the positions if no "traditional" candidates were available or acceptable to
the government.[29]

The government sought chiefs who would understand European ways,
speak their language, and respect their authority. The household employees of
colonial officials provided one pool of prospective chiefs. Western-educated
elites, including teachers and government clerks, provided another.[30] In theory, the latter should have included a large proportion of chiefs' sons. The
original intent of colonial education had been to educate the sons of chiefs in
order to create an echelon of African intermediaries who could implement
colonial policies. From the early days of the empire, school attendance and
study of the French language had been compulsory for these future chiefs.[31]
However, in the first years of occupation, chiefs often substituted slaves' sons
for their own, refusing to subject aristocratic lineages to the deleterious influences of "infidel" Christian schools. Thus, in the Futa Jallon, the sons of Jallonke slaves *(captifs),* rather than the Peul aristocracy, became the new elite,
comprising a large percentage of the first teachers and other civil servants.[32]

Other nontraditional candidates for the chieftaincy emerged from the ranks
of military veterans. Many veterans, particularly career soldiers, were also the

descendants of slaves. In the late nineteenth and early twentieth centuries, Tirailleurs Sénégalais were heavily recruited from densely populated regions with little room for agricultural expansion and from among the ranks of land-less slaves, former slaves, and their descendants. Because of the low status associated with the occupation, Echenberg writes, "few volunteers from the higher strata of African society" became career soldiers.[33] Low-status men also dominated the conscript army. RDA militant Ibrahima Fofana observed, "In the Futa Jallon, the society was highly stratified. When the colonial administration imposed obligatory military service, the notables sent slaves' sons instead of their own."[34]

The increasing prominence of low-status soldiers and civil servants brought turmoil to the Futa Jallon. The upheaval began during World War I, when the first "sons of chiefs" finished their studies and entered into the colo-nial administration. At the same time, three-quarters of Guinea's military recruits were of slave descent. When the war ended, decorated ex-combatants returned in glory. In a cash-poor society, they had access to pensions.[35] Thus, French-educated civil servants and military veterans, often from the lower strata of precolonial society, formed a new class of male elites with a deeper knowledge of European ways than the old ruling class. Seeking alternate avenues to "big man" status, they rapidly entered into fierce competition with the traditional aristocracy.[36]

The situation intensified after World War II as a growing number of low-status veterans sought chiefly positions. After the war, Ibrahima Fofana recalled,

> Men from slave families came back home as lieutenants and colonels. And when the opportunity arose, they presented themselves to the colonial administration as candidates for canton chieftaincies. The French, of course, were pleased, considering these men to have served France well. Often, the military veterans were appointed as chiefs.[37]

The Binani canton is a case in point. In 1948, the Gaoual circle commandant recommended that the presiding chief of Binani canton be replaced with a military veteran, ex–Sergeant-Major Cellou. While the incumbent neither spoke nor understood the imperial language, the ex–sergeant-major "speaks and writes French," the official noted. Moreover, as the president of the local veterans' association, he represented a constituency the government wished to woo.[38]

Although the government had created a strata of intermediaries that was indebted to it for its position, the low-status origin of many appointees threat-ened to alienate the government's traditional base. In October 1948, a mem-ber of Guinea's General Council, a body dominated by chiefs and notables, decried the government's practice of appointing domestic servants as chiefs.

These chiefs did not come from noble families, he protested. "The children of these former boys or cooks must not take the place of the children of the reigning family."[39] Ibrahima Fofana recalled that eventually the government was forced to make some concessions to the "traditional" elites:

> The notables went to the French administrators and told them, "If you want us with you, and do not want an uprising, then you will have to get rid of those slave chiefs. We will not be ruled by slaves. They have no right to rule us." And the French duly removed the chiefs they had appointed in this way and appointed the "legitimate" sons of the notables in their place.[40]

Wishing to forestall unrest at all costs, the government bowed to local exigencies.[41]

While "traditional" elites opposed some of the government's choices, most hostility toward the chiefs emanated from the lower echelons of society. In some cases, popular discontent focused on individual chiefs who were particularly abusive. In others, the institution, imposed by outsiders, was the target. In the forest region, for instance, centralized political chieftaincies had not existed prior to colonization. While village chieftaincies had existed, canton chieftaincies were established and officeholders installed only after conquest. These chiefs were granted formidable new powers, unchecked by elders' councils, which had been abolished by the colonial government.[42] Without basis in traditional authority structures, forest canton chieftaincies were relentlessly opposed by the local population.[43]

The crisis of authority was particularly notable in the forest circle of Macenta. The circle was composed of 23 cantons, each headed by a chief with only shallow roots of legitimacy. In the forest region, the circle commandant explained,

> The canton chiefs have nothing in common with those of the Futa. They have neither personal prestige, nor wealth, nor aristocratic traditions. . . . Their authority is weak. As auxiliaries, they are for us, for the most part, a source of vexations, because we must constantly support their authority, which is ceaselessly attacked. It is difficult to find among these 23 puppets, a few "enlightened despots."[44]

While lamenting the diffuse, democratic governing structures of the indigenous, animist Loma, the Macenta circle commandant praised those of the more hierarchical Malinke who, as long-distance Muslim traders, had settled in the forest region:

> If the Malinke cantons, under the influence of Islam, have generally conserved a semblance of respect for their chiefs, the Loma populations, his-

torically given to crumbling [small political domains] and anarchy, have for the most part returned to the conception of village-state in which the canton chief serves as a buffer between the inhabitants and the commandant.

He determined that it was his duty to give "these customary chiefs a piece of the authority and prestige that will permit them to fulfill their important social and political functions that are owed to them by right."[45]

Throughout Guinea, the crisis in chiefly authority escalated in the postwar period. In some areas, government appointees with little popular legitimacy or legal claim to the title filled the position of chief. In areas that historically had no canton chiefs, the positions themselves were contrived. In general, chiefs were granted unprecedented powers, without checks and balances, which they wielded tyrannically. Few refrained from abusing their subjects, even in times of economic hardship. Their demands for cash, goods, and services were relentless. Their unscrupulous practices in support of lifestyles marked by conspicuous consumption inspired deep resentment from the local populations.

POPULAR RESISTANCE TO THE CHIEFS

The authority crisis in the rural areas increasingly spawned outright resistance to the chieftaincy.[46] In 1945, the police reported widespread anti-chief sentiment and activity. Throughout the territory, the superintendent wrote, "One finds the same slogan everywhere: do not accede to administrative requisitions; oppose the obligatory furnishing of raw materials. . . . no longer recognize the chiefs and French authority."[47] In 1948, the Boké circle commandant noted that popular resistance to the chiefs was mounting. Grievances deriving from recent hardships were exacerbated by long-standing ethnic and class tensions:

> The policy called "the war effort," in demanding of many producers more than they were able to give, in leaving all powers to the chiefs to pressure their subjects at will to extract rubber from them, has reanimated old quarrels between the conquering and vanquished ethnic groups, amalgamated, for better or worse, by will or by force, in the texts organizing or reorganizing the chieftaincies.[48]

Once again, the forest region was the site of extensive anti-chief activity. Flight was a common mode of resistance. Populations on the international frontiers frequently fled from unpopular chiefs and their demands. Sometimes flight was temporary; often it was seasonal—during periods of taxation or the mandatory rendering of cash crops. Thus, the Macenta circle commandant reported, "During the period of obligatory furnishing [of raw materials], of rubber, in particular, which plagues a great deal of the population, a few hundred people crossed [the frontier] into Liberia."[49] The residents of Bouzié canton refused to supply their quota of rice for trade and seriously delayed their tax payments. Some notables declined to pay altogether and were sentenced to prison for having "refused to obey the exercise of legitimate authority."[50]

Some people resisted passively—withholding recognition of individuals appointed by the government. In 1947, the Macenta circle commandant remarked that, "On the occasion of the nomination of a new canton chief, we recently found ourselves faced with the systematic refusal to recognize as chief the designated person."[51] Similarly, in 1949, the N'Zérékoré circle commandant reported that the Vepo canton was "in complete anarchy." In 1944, the administration had appointed as chief an outsider from a neighboring canton. The new chief, Fahan Togba, was a government clerk, well educated in the colonial system. Like most of his subjects, he was a member of the Kpelle ethnic group. However, unlike the largely animist and Christian population, he was a Muslim. In 1947, the brothers and uncle of his predecessor had united behind the eldest male in their family, the elderly Gbato Duoulou, and demanded that he be named chief in place of "the stranger and man of the other religion." The majority of inhabitants supported Gbato's chieftaincy. Worried about unrest—as well as the possibility of flight—the circle commandant concluded, "This canton, already vulnerable as a result of its proximity to the Ivory Coast, is completely gangrenous."[52]

The perceived rot was not limited to the forest region. In Lower-Guinea, inhabitants of Samou canton (Forécariah circle) submitted petitions to the circle commandant, demanding the removal of Lamine Sylla, their canton chief.[53] In Upper-Guinea, five village chiefs in Kouroussa circle were dismissed for failing to halt popular uprisings against the canton chiefs.[54] In the Upper-Guinea circle of Kankan, the commandant complained of the widespread movement of "Laministes" in all the cantons under his jurisdiction:

> In these cantons, the population does not listen to the chiefs, considering them to be anti-Laministes. This movement against the chiefs is reinforced by the populations who heard the circle commandants tell the canton chiefs to remove themselves from the collection of taxes and to leave it solely in the hands of the village chiefs. Thus, most of the population concluded that the chieftaincy had become null.[55]

Their anti-chief message striking a resonant chord, Lamine Kaba's partisans had gained a large following in the Upper-Guinea circles of Kankan, Kouroussa, and Siguiri, and in the forest circles of Macenta, Beyla, and Kissidougou.[56] In Macenta circle, three Malinke-dominated cantons—Bouzié, Kononkoro-Malinké, and Mandougou—were engaged in tumultuous resistance to the colonial chiefs.[57] In Beyla circle, the most difficult cantons were those that included large villages and trading centers. With significant Malinke populations, these cantons were generally in direct contact with the political activities of Kankan and, hence, of Lamine Kaba.[58]

As hostilities toward the chiefs intensified, the governor complained that the population had misinterpreted the postwar political and social reforms:

> The ill-considered hopes that germinated in the minds of a population poorly prepared to assimilate these liberal reforms were cunningly exploited by a whole category of *arrivistes* without scruples (retired Malinke traders, . . . embittered civil servants, . . . former noncommissioned officers desirous of recapturing in civil attire the prestige conferred upon them by uniforms and stripes, marabouts pressed to cash in on their moral authority).

The portion of the population that followed these malcontents considered "the chiefs as the enemy," the governor concluded.[59] Thus, the administration conceded that the rural populace, long derided as "backward," was intensely aware of elite-inspired reforms in the political arena. Rural people were equally determined to exercise their newly granted rights—particularly their freedom to disengage from forced labor demands. Only belatedly did the government realize that elite-inspired reforms at the parliamentary level drew much of their impulse from intense popular sentiment at the grassroots.

The liberal reforms of 1946, especially the abolition of the *indigénat* and forced labor, exacerbated the authority crisis in the rural areas.[60] According to the governor, "The chiefs and the notables are the principal victims of the new institutions." The population, having been granted new political liberties, immediately used them to agitate against the colonial administration, which, during the war, had "shown itself to be somewhat exacting." As a result, "the authority of the customary chiefs is shaken."[61] Moreover, the governor observed, "The abusive interpretation of 'free labor' has gained ground; the wind of independence and of passive resistance to the orders of the chief, has blown too strongly for all things to instantly become normal again."[62]

One "abusive interpretation" of the Houphouët-Boigny Law included refusal to recognize its official limits. Certain types of involuntary labor, including "customary" dues owed to the chiefs, although without legal foundation, were specifically excluded from the provisions of the free labor law.[63] Although touted as traditional practices with deep historical roots, many of the so-called customary obligations had their origins in the colonial era.[64] When the administration refused to include this type of unremunerated labor in the forced labor ban, rural Africans took matters into their own hands. Claiming that they were now free, they rejected the legal limitations and simply refused to work for the chiefs. Military veterans often spearheaded this resistance.[65]

Shortly after the promulgation of the free labor law, the governor decried peasants' refusal to render canton chiefs their "customary" goods and services.[66] Given that the *indigénat,* requiring obedience to chiefly commands, and forced labor were abolished almost simultaneously, the governor was at a loss when it came to enforcing "customary" obligations: "Until now, the refusal to furnish these goods and services fell under the dispositions of the *indigénat* or the native penal code (opposition to the chiefs, ill will in the execution of certain services, etc.). There is not a single available sanction today."[67]

POPULAR RESISTANCE TO TAXES

Frequently linked to protest against the colonial chieftaincy was collective resistance to taxation. Of all the grievances of the rural population, excessive taxation was perhaps the most serious. Besides the personal tax, there were additional levies on income, patents, licenses, firearms, horses, nonmotorized vehicles, and even kola nuts. There were fees for a variety of permits— including those for hunting, trading, and cutting wood. There were charges for identification cards, work record books, and alien record books. Finally, rural dwellers were required to contribute to the Société Indigène de Prévoyance (SIP), a government-run insurance fund in which they had no voice.[68]

To meet their tax obligations, peasants often had to sell significant portions of their harvests or livestock, frequently at disadvantageous prices. Some offered their daughters in marriage to wealthy men in exchange for bridewealth. Others pawned their children in return for loans.[69] Popular hatred for colonial taxes and the destruction they caused were frequently represented in song:

> Tax collector's office
> It destroys our homes
> For the tax
> Tax collector's office
> It makes us work to death
> We will die for the tax.[70]

In the postwar period, rural resistance to the chiefs frequently focused on their role as tax collectors. In some instances, military veterans and other rural leaders usurped the chiefs' functions in order to undermine their authority. Such was the case when veterans formed committees to collect taxes, which they sent directly to the circle commandant—bypassing the village and canton chiefs.[71] In 1948, the Boké circle commandant noted that people in three villages were demanding the replacement of their chiefs, whom they charged with embezzling tax monies. To underscore their point, they were refusing to render taxes to those chiefs, although they would to other functionaries.[72] A similar situation existed in neighboring Boffa circle, where the population in Koba canton refused to submit its taxes to the village chiefs but appeared willing to pay by another route.[73]

Such actions demonstrated low regard for particular chiefs. Others focused on the taxes themselves. As an increasing number of peasants refused to pay taxes altogether, Lamine Kaba's partisans again took the lead. During the 1946 General Council election campaign, Kaba reportedly told his followers that with his party's membership card, they would no longer have to pay taxes or purchase train tickets.[74] Whether or not Kaba actually made such promises, by February 1947 it was evident that many people in Upper-Guinea were not planning to pay. No taxes had been rendered by the end of the month, and the police believed the tax protest to be a consequence of Kaba's electoral campaign.[75] In October 1947, Kaba's partisans were still traversing the bush, attempting to rejuvenate their jailed leader's party and urging people not to pay their taxes.[76]

In the face of the burgeoning tax protest, the government cracked down. A decree of January 8, 1947, imposed severe punishments for collective refusal to cooperate in census taking—a necessary preliminary to tax collection—and collective refusal to pay taxes.[77] The new penalty for tax resistance was three months to two years of imprisonment and a fine of 1,000 to 10,000 francs.[78] Despite these measures, the government had little success in quelling the resistance. Nearly nine years later, in his year-end report for 1955, the governor continued to lament the rural populace's refusal to pay taxes.[79]

RDA MOBILIZATION AGAINST THE CHIEFS

The crisis of chiefly authority was exacerbated by the RDA's penetration into the countryside. Determined to build a mass base in the rural areas, the RDA zeroed in on existent grievances and made the challenge to local authority structures a focal point of its message. According to RDA militant Léon Maka,

When one creates a political party, this party is created thanks to an ideology. There must be a force to mobilize people to rally around a certain point. What was the ideology? What provoked this ideology? It was the comportment of the colonial authorities vis-a-vis the people.[80]

The colonial authorities who had the most direct contact with the rural populace were, of course, the village and canton chiefs, whom the RDA disparaged as the circle commandants' domestic servants.[81]

The chiefs' political base consisted of the colonial administration and the notables who dominated the ethnic associations and government-backed political parties. Their narrow support network rarely extended beyond their own ethnic groups.[82] Most chiefs vehemently opposed the RDA, which fought against the deeply rooted hierarchies of gender, age, and class, as well as special birthrights and ethnic exclusivism. They were disturbed by the prominence of young men, women, and people of low social status in positions of political leadership, traditionally the domain of elite senior men.[83] According to RDA activist Aissatou N'Diaye,

> The canton chiefs, who had been appointed by the French, were afraid for their positions. They wanted the Europeans [to retain power]. In all the areas where Sékou went, none of the chiefs wanted to hear about the RDA. However, there was not much they could do, because there was pro-RDA sentiment among their own population. The population wanted the RDA.[84]

Initially, the RDA did not agitate for the chieftaincy's abolition. Rather, between 1947 and 1954, the party urged reform. It proposed that the chieftaincy be democratized through the popular election of chiefs, who would be assisted by elected councillors. According to the RDA proposal, chiefs would no longer be designated by European authorities but elected by universal suffrage. Candidates could originate from any social class. In consequence, chiefly ranks would no longer be filled by "traditional" aristocrats and notables or "modernizing" lackeys of the administration. Their powers checked by councillors, their rule would no longer be arbitrary. Finally, the RDA argued, chiefs should be better compensated, rendering less likely their plunder of the local population.[85] According to Tourou Sylla, a prominent female militant from Mamou, the chiefs were not impressed:

> Obviously, the existing chiefs did not want the RDA. They were the rulers. They benefited from what existed. They robbed the poor. They appropriated people's inheritance, leaving nothing for the deceased's wives and children. The RDA said it would abolish these practices.[86]

As the administration made no move to implement reforms, the RDA continued its anti-chief campaign. It was largely because of this focus that the forest region became one of the party's most important rural strongholds. Prior to conquest, forest chiefs had been far less powerful than their counterparts in the Futa Jallon and Upper-Guinea. However, the colonial regime provided them with new, unchecked powers. Hostile toward the government-imposed chiefs and their tyrannical order, forest peoples rallied to the RDA's egalitarian platform.

The party quickly realized the region's political potential. Despite the fact that some canton chiefs had vowed to "physically eject him from their fiefdoms," Mamadou Traoré (alias Ray Autra), a member of the Guinean RDA board of directors, arrived in N'Zérékoré in October 1949 to mobilize for the

party.[87] A Malinke born in the Futa Jallon city of Mamou, an important trad-
ing center at the crossroads of Upper- and Lower-Guinea and the Futa Jallon,
Autra was a classic example of a geographically mobile, "modernizing" elite.
He had completed lower-primary school in Mamou, upper-primary school in
Conakry, and the prestigious teacher training program at William Ponty in
Dakar. As a teacher, he had been posted to Labé circle in the Futa Jallon and
to Beyla and N'Zérékoré circles in the forest region. Having completed two
stints as a teacher in N'Zérékoré, Autra had intimate knowledge of the
region.[88] According to the government, Autra's recruitment campaign in
N'Zérékoré was highly successful. In the wake of his visit, RDA village committees were formed throughout the countryside.[89] Overwhelmed by the
effectiveness of the recruitment drive, the administration urged local authorities "to employ all possible means to destroy the action of the R.D.A."[90]

Meanwhile, the RDA continued its campaign in other venues. In July 1950,
the party attacked Peul "feudalism" in its newspaper *Coup de Bambou.* The
same month, Baba Camara, a member of the Guinean RDA board of directors, traveled by train from Conakry to Kindia (Lower-Guinea), Mamou and
Dabola (Futa Jallon), and Faranah (Upper-Guinea). Besides recruiting new
members, Camara gathered information on recent incidents in Dabola
between the canton chief, Almamy Barry Aguibou, and some of his subjects.[91] Simultaneously, Ray Autra was sent to the Futa Jallon to collect information on other chiefs' activities. The police worried that he would rouse the
population against the almamy and his associates.[92]

In its campaign against chiefly abuses, the RDA focused on the chiefs' continued use of forced labor.[93] The RDA claimed that with the abolition of
forced labor in 1946, rural residents should no longer have to work in the
chiefs' fields, construct and maintain their huts, and perform domestic services without pay. Toward these ends, the RDA actively encouraged the passive resistance campaign already under way in the rural areas.[94]

From the early 1950s, police records are filled with reports of RDA villagers refusing to obey their chiefs' orders. A typical incident took place on
August 11, 1951, in the predominantly RDA village of Ourouyakoré (Ounah
canton, N'Zérékoré circle). The episode began when several men refused to
carry the canton chief's baggage into the bush without being paid in advance.
Insults and blows ensued, during which the chief himself was struck. Among
those present were Mamadou Foromo, assistant secretary of the N'Zérékoré
RDA subsection, and Ibrahima Foromo, an RDA militant and cousin of the
canton chief. Although they did not participate in the brawl, the two RDA
militants were held responsible for it. Ibrahima Foromo was subsequently
sentenced to 10 months in prison.[95]

The RDA's complaints to the local administration fell on deaf ears. Opponents of forced labor thus pressed their case in the higher echelons of the
French government. In 1951, the N'Zérékoré RDA subsection appealed to the

French overseas minister, who was touring the region. The RDA noted that forced labor, while abolished by French law, continued under the chiefs. Moreover, chiefs were abusing other powers—inflicting exorbitant fines in the regulation of disputes and requiring people to give them huge quantities of rice, fish, chicken, eggs, oil, sheep, and cattle.[96] The government refused to take action, stimulating further support for the RDA.

Having failed in its attempts to reform the chieftaincy, the RDA increasingly pursued another strategy: neglect. It urged local populations to bypass the chiefs, disregarding their authority. In October 1951, the military police charged that the RDA was establishing alternative authority structures in the rural areas, circumventing village and canton chiefs. RDA village committees were collecting taxes and usurping other chiefly functions. According to the military police, "The installation of village committees is being tirelessly pursued, resulting in certain frictions with the village chiefs who want, at all cost, to conserve their authority."[97]

CHIEFS AGAINST THE RDA

In its struggle against the RDA, the colonial administration generally found loyal allies in the canton and village chiefs, who eagerly accused the party of anti-French sedition. Chiefs provided their superiors with the names of "subversive" RDA and trade union leaders. At the behest of circle commandants, they ordered their henchmen to beat and chain up RDA partisans.[98] Claiming that the circle commandants "don't want the RDA," canton chiefs prohibited RDA militants from entering their territory and forbade their subjects to join the party.[99] In their attempts to undermine the RDA, chiefs intervened in territorial and legislative elections. They barred RDA members from registering to vote, intimidated voters, refused to distribute RDA ballots, and falsified election results.[100]

Anti-RDA sentiment was particularly strong among the chiefs of the Futa Jallon, where Peul aristocrats held sway and the descendants of free men dominated the descendants of slaves.[101] The chiefs jealously guarded their power from Western-educated "modernizers," particularly those without traditional claims to status and position. In his annual report for 1949, the Mamou circle commandant described the loyalty of these canton chiefs:

> The chiefs are always with us, if not by sentiment, at least by interest, because they very much value their position and know they are poorly regarded by the *évolués, demi-évolués,* and other jealous parties, some of whom do not hesitate to attack them in an underhanded manner. Also, the chiefs seek our protection, which we don't begrudge them. . . . They are indispensable to us.[102]

Although to a lesser extent than the Peul, the Malinke of Upper-Guinea also lived in a hierarchical society. Kankan and its environs were dominated by two rival families, the Tourés and the Kabas.[103] The intense hostility of the Kaba family toward the RDA stemmed in part from the party's association with Sékou Touré and, by extension, his maternal ancestor Samori Touré, the Malinke empire builder who dominated Upper-Guinea in the late nineteenth century. The RDA made much of Sékou Touré's ancestry and his connection to this primary resister to French conquest. His rivals, in turn, emphasized the bloody nature of Samori's conquests and the enslavement of those he captured.[104] One Kaba ancestor, Chief Daye Kaba, was a defeated rival of Samori's who was returned to power on the heels of French troops.[105]

While much of the Kaba family was hostile to the RDA, there were some exceptions. Feuding within the family resulted in some members aligning themselves with the Tourés. One such member was Lamine Kaba, who had long been associated with the Tourés through his allegiance to the *grand chérif* of Kankan, Fanta Mady, one of the most revered Muslim teachers in the savannah region. Fanta Mady's father, Karamoko Boubacar Sidiki Chérif, had been Samori Touré's spiritual guide and religious teacher. Fanta Mady himself had studied with one of Samori's sons. Not only was Lamine Kaba a loyal disciple of the *grand chérif,* he had attended the founding congress of the RDA in Bamako, presided over the RDA in Kankan after his return from exile, and "adopted" Sékou Touré as a son.[106]

Lamine Kaba, however, was an aberration. Many Kabas of Kankan, along with other chiefs and notables, were willing to collaborate with the government against the RDA. During the armistice day festivities on November 11, 1949, the Kankan circle commandant and police superintendent assembled the canton and village chiefs, African civil servants, and principal notables of the region. Deriding the RDA as an anti-French movement, the officials advised all members or sympathizers to sever their ties to the party.[107] Some months later, Ansa Kaba, chief of Karfamoriah village (Kankan circle), gathered his subjects on the mosque square. The chief and his entourage warned that the circle commandant had ordered all RDA members to resign and turn in their party cards. Twelve family heads did so.[108] In 1951, the commander of Kankan's police brigade reported that the village chiefs remained intensely hostile to the RDA.[109]

Three years later, the hostility had not abated. In October 1954, canton chief Alpha Amadou Kaba convoked a meeting of some 1,300 people, including the most influential notables and RDA members from Kankan and its environs. In his diatribe against the RDA, the chief avowed, "This land is ours. We will never allow individuals imbued with unhealthy ideas, contrary to the customs of the country and to the precepts of the French administration, to come and provoke troubles and division." The French had come to the area peacefully, invited by our forefathers, he claimed. Together, they had defeated the "bloodthirsty" Almamy Samori Touré. The French had delivered our fore-fathers from captivity, the chief declared, and now assured the country's con-tinued evolution:

> Today . . . gathered around the French flag, we must recognize in this gen-erous France, our father, our mother, and our material and moral support. It would be ungrateful, from our part, to hamper the action of the good French administration. We must avoid as much as possible anything that can sepa-rate us from France.
>
> It is for this reason that today, I have assembled you around me, to ask you all, out of respect for tradition, to abandon the RDA. This movement, which has implanted itself in Kankan and in the cantons, tends to radically falsify the road to liberty, equality, and fraternity that generous France has traced for us.

Chief Kaba concluded by imploring all "who call themselves sons of this country" to prove their wisdom by abandoning the RDA forever.[110]

Chiefly animosity toward the RDA was not limited to the Futa Jallon and Upper-Guinea. The forest region was another hotbed of anti-RDA sentiment. While chiefs in the former areas strove to protect deeply rooted social hierar-chies, in the forest region they attempted to safeguard status and privilege recently acquired from the colonial regime. Their power base threatened by widespread hostility to their rule, forest chiefs responded by cracking down. Canton chiefs, circle guards, village notables, and other government agents employed every possible means to suppress the RDA. In 1951, Ray Autra charged that they were threatening RDA militants, confiscating their member-ship cards, and arresting them on trumped-up charges. The canton chiefs instituted penalties—payment of cattle, sheep, or fines of 1,000 to 5,000 francs—for each card they seized. With prospects for personal profit, the campaign to commandeer membership cards took off. By the party's esti-mate, thousands of cards were expropriated. The task was facilitated when the circle commandant seized RDA membership lists, which he provided to all the chiefs. By March 1951, RDA recruitment in N'Zérékoré had ceased. The political movement was paralyzed.[111]

Acting on behalf of the party's board of directors, Madéïra Kéïta submitted a letter of complaint. Since the legislative elections of June 17, 1951, Kéïta charged, governmental repression had intensified in those circles where peo-ple had voted heavily for the RDA. In the forest region, inhabitants of Beyla and Guéckédou circles had been subjected to a new regime of forced labor. In N'Zérékoré, the situation was one of veritable terror. Avowing that they were following the circle commandants' orders, canton chiefs had prohibited all RDA leaders from entering their territories, menacing them with strong pun-ishments—including death—if they violated the ban.[112]

Matters came to a head in 1954, not only in the forest region, but throughout the country. An RDA victory in the legislative elections of June 27 had been denied through massive electoral fraud perpetrated by European officials and colonial chiefs. Despite overwhelming evidence to the contrary, the government claimed that Barry Diawadou, rather than Sékou Touré, had been elected deputy to the French National Assembly.[113] Barry Diawadou, a William Ponty graduate and government clerk, was the son of Almamy Barry Aguibou, the staunchly anti-RDA Dabola canton chief.[114] The fraudulent elections forced the RDA to recognize that it could not capture the rural areas as long as the chieftaincy remained intact.

REFORM OR ABOLITION: THE ESCALATION OF CIVIL DISOBEDIENCE

Until 1954, the RDA had urged that the institution of the colonial chieftaincy be reformed. In the aftermath of the rigged elections, the RDA began to agitate for its abolition.[115] From June 1954, the RDA openly incited people to rebel against the chiefs, adopting methods more radical than passive resistance.[116]

In early November 1954, a number of anti-chief actions took place in the Lower-Guinea circles of Boffa and Forécariah, where village chiefs and their houses were stoned.[117] In the case of Boffa, the authorities charged, the Counibale village chief left his home to attend a reception for the French overseas minister. While he was away, RDA militants went to his home and insulted his wife. A few days later, eight youths returned and attacked her. The following day, the village chief himself was attacked, stripped, beaten, and publicly humiliated by a crowd of men, women, and children. Harnessing the power of religious ritual, villagers smeared the chief's face with flour, conducted fictive sacrifices, and read the Koran over his "corpse." His house was then ransacked.[118] In his year-end report for 1954, the governor noted, with remarkably little sympathy,

> In the bush, the R.D.A. pursues its campaign against the exactions of the chiefs. Faced with the amplitude of popular reprobation, notably in the coastal circles, the chiefs have realized that they represent no one but themselves, and that they are only rich as a result of the credit and luster lent to them by the Administration.

The governor concluded that the position of the chiefs was in real jeopardy, unless they could adapt to the new political situation.[119]

During 1955, the RDA campaign against the chiefs intensified. Throughout Guinea, canton chiefs were denounced and attacked and their homes were burned.[120] From June 1954 through the end of 1955, Siguiri circle (Upper-Guinea) was the focus of intense political agitation characterized by violent

diatribes against the village and canton chiefs.[121] In the forest region, a band
of military veterans in Beyla circle, recruited by an ex–sergeant-major who
was president of the Simandougou RDA subsection, waylaid circle guards
who were helping the village chiefs collect taxes. They disarmed, bound, and
locked the guards in a hut, temporarily thwarting tax collection.[122] The RDA's
message struck a responsive chord in the forest circle of Guéckédou as well.
According to the governor,

> The political situation of the circle underwent a painful modification in
> 1955 under the effect of R.D.A. propaganda. Until then, the canton chiefs
> faced no serious opposition; the organization of a democratic party put an
> end to these "happy times." In consequence, the chiefs are no longer lis-
> tened to and intrigues are being hatched against them.[123]

In Lower-Guinea, anti-chief activity continued unabated. June 1955 witnessed numerous attacks on the chiefs in Boffa circle. In one instance, the
wife of the Tugnifili canton chief threw a wash basin at the head of an RDA
woman who had insulted her. In retaliation, RDA demonstrators attacked the
chief's compound, insulted him, and pelted his home with sticks and rocks.[124]
In Dubréka circle, anti-chief incidents escalated not only in the major population centers but in the most isolated hamlets as well. "The R.D.A. is practically the master in all the villages and the authority of the chiefs is in
complete decline," the governor warned. He concluded that the only chief
who had conserved a modicum of authority until 1955 was David Sylla, chief
of Labaya canton. However, his authority had been demolished completely
after bloody incidents in Tondon in February 1955, when he personally killed
the wife of the local RDA president.[125] Forécariah circle was also marked by
"the ascendancy of the R.D.A. . . . equally . . . by the loss of authority of the
customary chiefs." According to the governor, the Morébayah Kaback canton
chief, opposed since his nomination in 1951, "has lost all authority, and the
islands of Kaback and of Kakossa, as well as the regions of Coké and
Morébayah are essentially off-limits to him."[126]

Similar troubles were reported in the very heart of the Futa Jallon. The governor observed that it was "indisputable that in the central subdivision of
Labé, the R.D.A. occupies a strong position, with the single exception of the
canton of Lelouma, which has remained almost totally obedient to the B.A.G.
[Bloc Africain de Guinée]," the party of Barry Diawadou. In the southern
regions of the subdivision, near the cities of Pita and Dalaba, the Démocratie
Socialiste de Guinée (DSG) had a following. However, the governor pointed
out, the Socialists "often marched hand in hand with the R.D.A., the hostility
to the chieftaincy having constituted a common electoral platform."[127]

A turnabout was also seen in the Futa subdivision of Mali. Until the commencement of the 1954 legislative election campaign, this region was consid-

ered to be "the exclusive domain" of Barry Diawadou. However, the electoral results changed that judgment. Although they had been established only recently, the local RDA subsections succeeded in attracting numerous adherents. Similarly, in the Tougué subdivision, the RDA was gradually winning over the Western-educated Peul, who had long opposed the monopoly of the "traditional" chiefs.[128]

The RDA's success in the Futa Jallon was due largely to its appeal to the descendants of slaves and other low-status residents who harbored deep animosity toward the powerful chiefs. The RDA's outspoken opposition to the chieftaincy and the slave system that supported it, together with its promotion of an egalitarian social order, resonated strongly in the former slave villages. Although the ancestors of some residents had been sold into slavery by Samori Touré's agents, the RDA deflected potential hostility toward his descendant by convincing them that, "If Samory Touré can make you slaves, Sékou Touré can make you free." During the legislative elections of 1951, 1954, and 1956, most of the RDA votes in the Futa Jallon came from the former slave villages.[129]

CONCLUSION

Rural resistance to the colonial chieftaincy, rooted in the exigencies of the war effort, predated RDA mobilization in the countryside. Like military veterans and urban workers, peasants had long-standing grievances that were articulated and channeled, but not initiated, by the RDA. Taking its cue from rural activists, the party encouraged civil disobedience—refusal to obey orders, render taxes, and supply unpaid labor to the chiefs. Until 1954, the RDA focused on exposing unjust practices, ousting abusive chiefs, and democratizing the institution. However, the chiefs saw no possibility for compromise. Their wealth, power, and authority were undermined by the RDA's democratic, egalitarian message. The chiefs struck back, harassing RDA militants and perpetrating electoral fraud that prevented RDA victories. The rigged elections of 1954 were a turning point. Defeated by fraud in the face of burgeoning grassroots support, the RDA recognized that its efforts in the rural areas would be seriously obstructed as long as the chiefs remained. Charging that the institution of the canton chieftaincy was rotten to the core, the RDA began a prolonged campaign for its abolition.

Peasants who resisted the chiefs included men and women from a wide range of ethnic groups in all regions of Guinea. Often they were led by military veterans who had returned to their rural homes with a new sense of confidence, entitlement, and need to prove themselves as men. Peasants were an integral part of the ethnic, class, and gender alliance that the RDA mobilized for the nationalist cause. In the next phase of the struggle, they would be joined by urban women, the majority of whom were nonliterate.

5

WOMEN TAKE THE LEAD: FEMALE EMANCIPATION AND THE NATIONALIST MOVEMENT, 1949–1954

While continuing its campaign among peasants in the rural areas, the RDA turned its attention to another constituency previously neglected by nationalist leaders. Women had not participated in the founding of the Guinean RDA. They were not mobilized on a large scale until after the 1953 general strike, during which they had played a decisive role in sustaining striking workers and their families. Recognizing women's critical contribution to the strike's success, the RDA began a concerted effort to mobilize women into the nationalist movement. It was the RDA's identification of women as an untapped resource and its ability to attract them that gave it an edge over other political parties. "You must know that women brought about independence. It was really the women," claimed RDA activist Aissatou N'Diaye.[1]

If the RDA's ultimate triumph was due to its ability to form a broad-based ethnic, class, and gender alliance, women were crucial participants in this project. Women joined the nationalist struggle as members of ethnic groups and socioeconomic classes. Susu, Malinke, and Peul women, and those from the small ethnic groups of the forest region flocked to the RDA. Women of slave descent and from low-caste artisan families were attracted to the party's egalitarian message. Peasant women, who had resisted the chiefs, and urban women in the informal sector, who had supported striking workers, found common cause in the broader political struggle. Among the tiny group of Western-educated women, a small contingent, notably teachers and mid-wives, joined the RDA women's committees. However, ethnicity, class, and colonial oppression affected women differently than they did men. Because these experiences are gendered, women also joined the nationalist struggle as women.

The RDA made explicit appeals to women as women. Focusing on issues that women considered important, it emphasized those that underscored women's primary social roles as mothers and sustainers of their families. Promoting improvements in health, sanitation, education, and workers' benefits that included family allowances, the party grew strong by addressing women's preexisting grievances and identifying solutions for them. Like military veterans, trade unionists, and peasants, women thus determined many of the basic claims on the nationalist agenda and helped to shape the nationalist movement from the bottom up.

Equally important was the RDA's public recognition of women as crucial players in the nationalist struggle. Praising women for their dynamic role and opening doors for them as other parties shut them out, the RDA invited women to mobilize families, friends, and even strangers through preexisting social and cultural organizations and, eventually, the women's wing of the RDA.[2] The opportunity to engage in new activities and establish alternative identities was an attractive proposition for many women. They relished their prominent roles and enhanced status.

If women helped to define the RDA's program and objectives, they also had a decisive influence on its methods. Most Guinean women were not literate and thus were largely beyond the reach of party tracts and newspapers. Women therefore devised new, more appropriate methods of communication. They composed songs and slogans to communicate among themselves, with the party leadership, and to interpret the leaders' messages in terms they found meaningful. They designed and wore uniforms, sporting party symbols and colors. They employed preexisting cultural practices and worked through indigenous women's organizations for new, explicitly political ends. Women, more than any other popular group, transformed the methods the party used to mobilize.

As women were thrust to the forefront of the movement, assuming roles never before even contemplated, they were confronted by deeply entrenched gender biases. Although they had entered the struggle to conserve their roles as mothers and family guardians, their activism in the public arena forced them to challenge gender norms. Increasingly, women addressed mixed audiences, attended late-night meetings, traveled without escorts, and left their husbands and children for prolonged periods. Their emancipation generated serious tensions within households and dissension within the party.

While party leaders preached female emancipation, male response at the household level was not always positive. Some informants claimed that men supported their wives' political involvement; others referred to intense domestic struggles. The violation of the most entrenched gender norms, those pertaining to spousal relations and obligations, was rarely tolerated, resulting in tremendous tension and upheaval. Women's liberation in the domestic arena, while sometimes achieved, was neither widespread nor permanent.

Women's emancipation in Guinea was but a brief interlude; gender-role changes were ephemeral. Opposition within the male-dominated party and the lack of an independent women's organization were contributing factors. So, too, were women's own desires. After independence, most women chose to translate their newfound status into traditional terms: pilgrimages to Mecca, many children and grandchildren, and the dignified behavior befitting older Muslim women. They had challenged male authority in their youth, when men were not manly enough to do the jobs required of them. In the end, however, women wanted men to be men and women to be women. In this regard, they were in accord with their male counterparts.

THE ABSENCE OF WOMEN IN THE EARLY YEARS

While many men ignored women during the struggle's early phase or opposed their political involvement, some in the male leadership lamented their initial absence. As early as 1948, Madéïra Kéïta, secretary-general of the Guinean RDA, proclaimed in a public meeting, "We also ask for the assistance of all the women's groups. . . . We must make contact with the women; they could be very useful to us."[3] The following year, Léon Maka, accompanied by his wife, Mira Baldé, attended the first congress of the Soudanese RDA as part of an official Guinean delegation. The couple was struck by elite women's active involvement in party activities and the fact that they all wore national, as opposed to Western, dress. In Guinea, Maka recalled, educated women—the teachers and midwives—distinguished themselves from the masses of women by imitating European fashions.[4]

Upon his return to Conakry, Maka gave a public briefing in which he highlighted the political participation of elite Soudanese women. "I gave a long speech in which I spoke at length about the women," he recalled. "I saw teachers and midwives mingling with men to promote the work of the party. They had a great deal of responsibility in the party. I said that we should also make use of women in our activities."[5]

Maka's concerns were echoed in the interterritorial organization. In late 1949, Gabriel d'Arboussier, secretary-general of the interterritorial RDA, toured Guinea to rally support for the incipient political movement. Concerned that there had been no effort to organize women, d'Arboussier instructed the local leaders to institute a women's committee. On December 6, 1949, at a private meeting in Amara Soumah's courtyard, d'Arboussier and other male leaders established a national women's committee, which, within a week, included some 100 members.[6] That same day, at a public meeting attended by some 1,000 people, a new bureau of the Conakry RDA subsection was elected. For the first time it included a woman, Jeanne Martin, a widowed school teacher.[7]

The new women's committee was led by Western-educated elites who were far from representative of the majority of Guinean women. Some clearly were chosen because of their marital affiliation; most were the wives of prominent RDA leaders. The new women's committee was led by Nankoria Kourouma (Mme. Madéïra Kéïta), Jeanne Martin (Mme. Veuve Mohamed Camara), Sarata Diané (Mme. Moussa Touré), and Mariama Kourouma. The first three women were teachers and the wives (or widow) of civil servants; the last, a midwife, was unmarried. By the early 1950s, three of these women had left Guinea, some when their husbands were transferred due to their political activities. Nankoria Kourouma went first to Dahomey and subsequently to the French Soudan. Jeanne Martin moved to Senegal, and Sarata Diané to the Ivory Coast.[8] The early attempt to incorporate women thus ended in failure.

After the Guinean RDA's second party congress in 1950, the territorial board of directors again ordered militants to form women's committees in the interior and to involve women in popular mobilization. Women were to use every occasion to mobilize—marriages, baptisms, circumcisions, and sacrifices. Despite these directives, few women joined the party.[9] Many were thwarted by their husbands, who believed that women's involvement in politics was unseemly. If they joined any formal grouping, most preferred to join cultural, mutual aid, or ethnic organizations in which men and women were segregated by sex.[10]

On the coast, women joined associations such as *kabila* and *muso sere* (Malinke), *mamaya* (Susu), and *laba* (Peul), which grouped women according to age or kinship and provided mutual aid in times of hardship or celebration. These associations also served social and community-building functions by organizing dances and ceremonies for marriages, baptisms, initiations, and funerals. They provided a separate space for women to dance and enjoy themselves without the hindrance of male authority.[11] Women also joined regionally based ethnic associations that had subsections in various towns and neighborhoods. The ethnic associations were equipped with women's auxiliaries that performed functions similar to those of the cultural and mutual aid associations.[12]

THE RDA COURTS THE WOMEN

The turning point for women came in the aftermath of the federation-wide general strike of 1953. Nonelite women had been critical in sustaining the strike through material assistance and community mobilization. Recognizing women's political potential, the male RDA leadership made a conscious effort to capture their loyalty and recruit them into the nationalist movement. Sékou Touré was particularly savvy in this regard. Thus, women interviewed decades later frequently credited him personally with the party initiatives that benefited women.[13] They often used the RDA party symbol, *syli*, or elephant, to denote the person of Sékou Touré rather than the party as a whole.[14]

The appeal of the party—and Sékou Touré—to Guinean women was not lost on the government. In March 1955, H. Pruvost, the secretary of state for Overseas France, remarked that the Guinean RDA was "conducting a vigorous combat for women's emancipation." Sékou Touré, as the party's uncontested leader, had thus become "the idol of Susu and Malinke women," especially in Lower-Guinea, where women had become a force "with whom we henceforth must reckon."[15]

Acknowledging the power inherent in women's social relations and the relevance of their cultural associations, male RDA leaders supported women's use of these resources in mobilizing their families and communities. Although marriages, baptisms, initiations, and funerals continued to be organized under the auspices of various women's associations, from the early 1950s RDA women used such occasions to recruit new members.[16] Néné Diallo recalled that many of the mutual aid societies and the ethnic associations' women's auxiliaries were transformed into veritable organs of the RDA.[17]

When women first joined the RDA, they were not intent upon violating socially constructed gender roles or toppling male authority structures. They were proud to be the bearers of children, sustainers of the family, and guardians of the social order. They were spurred to action when colonial policies threatened their ability to fulfill these roles. Relying on long-standing practices of female solidarity and collective action, they challenged the forces that prevented them from carrying out their duties. Temma Kaplan refers to this form of consciousness as "female." In contrast, women imbued with "feminist" consciousness challenge established gender roles, particularly those that perpetuate female inferiority and prevent women from exercising "full rights and powers" in the broader society.[18] For RDA women, the latter form of consciousness evolved as their struggle unfolded.[19]

While other parties ignored women or resisted their political participation, the RDA actively courted them by targeting issues of particular concern to them. In keeping with women's established gender roles, the RDA promoted health, sanitation, and educational services that affected the well-being of women and their families. It advocated the building of health clinics, hospitals, maternity facilities, and schools in both the urban and rural areas, and demanded paid maternity leave and increased educational opportunities for girls as well as boys.[20] The RDA championed policies that promoted larger food rations and higher prices and better distribution for agricultural products, many of which were produced by women. The party fostered the construction of markets and roads, increasing the prospects of commerce for women and for the rural population in general. It favored increased use of products and technologies that lessened the burden of women's labor.[21] All of these proposals held a tremendous appeal for women.

Health and Hygiene

Health care and public hygiene were burning issues for African women. Colonial health services focused primarily on the army, the colonial administration, and European settlers—seriously neglecting the African majority. Government hygiene services, established almost exclusively in the urban areas, were intended to protect the health of the European population. Schemes for improved urban sanitation often entailed strict racial segregation and the forced removal of African populations deemed too close to European residential areas. Unless their illnesses also threatened the health of Europeans, little attention or resources were devoted to African health care.[22]

From the outset, the RDA's male leadership articulated demands that promoted family health. As early as 1947, male leaders urged that the unhygienic conditions in Conakry be ameliorated. In August, the RDA passed a motion imploring the local public health, hygiene, and road services to dispose of the mountains of garbage lining the streets. At a public meeting in December, Ray Autra claimed that nothing had been done to ameliorate the situation. Decrying the unhygienic conditions in the capital city, he charged that the piles of garbage served as breeding grounds for flies and vultures. The stagnant ponds were propagating mosquitoes. Because there were no urinals, people relieved themselves behind the mango trees. "The seashore is the dumping-ground of the city," he lamented. "Littered with garbage and dead animals, the stench is terrible. Ballay Hospital is infested with spiders and rats. These conditions threaten the lives of the population."[23]

If sanitary conditions were intolerable, provisions for African health care were appalling. In 1947, Guinea had only 1 hospital—Ballay Hospital in Conakry—1 institution for convalescents, 26 maternity wards, and 29 dispensaries.[24] Rural infirmaries and dispensaries generally were staffed by underqualified personnel.[25] In 1950, Guinea had only 12 fully qualified (European) doctors, 4 of whom were based in Conakry. Two of these worked almost exclusively with the European population. The other two functioned primarily as administrators, directing Ballay Hospital and the government health services. Apart from the fully qualified European doctors, there were 37 African assistant doctors, 4 of whom were based in the capital city, and 10 special nurses who made home visits. The rest of the territory, with an African population nearing 2.5 million, was served by 8 fully qualified doctors and 33 assistant doctors. There were no dentists in the whole territory.[26]

Throughout the late 1940s and 1950s, the Guinean RDA urged the government to address African health concerns. Specifically, the party called for the creation of a network of medical and sanitary services to fight malnutrition and related illnesses and to wipe out yellow fever, leprosy, and other endemic diseases. In order to decrease the rate of infant and child mortality, the RDA demanded the construction of dispensaries, infirmaries, and maternity wards; free medication and medical care; increased availability of prenatal consultations; and the promotion of health education throughout the territory. It called for the training and employment of more doctors, midwives, and African nurses, and the establishment of nursing schools in Guinea.[27]

RDA regional subsections also attempted to speak to women's concerns. However, they tended to view those concerns more narrowly, focusing almost exclusively on pregnancy and birth-related matters. Invariably male dominated, the subsections echoed prevailing gender norms and values. In November 1954, for instance, the Mamou subsection discussed the woeful inadequacy of a single eight-bed maternity facility, intended to serve a city of some 10,000 inhabitants. Because of insufficient space, pre- and postnatal consultations were performed in the open air, in good weather and bad. Mamou's new hospital, which served the whole district, had only 16 beds. The Mamou subsection thus passed a resolution calling for the construction of new facilities in order to rectify the pitiful health conditions "which seriously jeopardize the lives of our women, our children, and our sick."[28]

In the same vein, the RDA subsection in Dinguiraye petitioned the colonial administration for a midwife to be posted to the local maternity facility. The male doctor was overburdened by the assumption of a midwife's tasks as well as his own. Moreover, "the presence of the doctor during the birth process (rather than a midwife) constitutes an affront to the modesty of the women of the city," the male leadership wrote.[29]

While some female-oriented initiatives may have been conceived of and presented to the women by male party leaders, others were clearly taken by women themselves, particularly once they had been mobilized into party structures in the mid-1950s. In late 1954/early 1955, for instance, a group of women from the Kaporo suburb of Conakry wrote to Guinea's director of public health. In their letter, reprinted in *La Liberté,* they elaborated upon the difficulties they faced due to the lack of a medical clinic in Kaporo. Because few could afford the cost of transport, they wrote, women in need of medical attention were forced to walk 15 to 20 kilometers to the nearest facility in suburban Dixinn. This included pregnant women, who were required to make the trip weekly, wait all day on empty stomachs for their turn at the clinic, then make the return trip on foot. The authors petitioned the director of public health to build a clinic in Kaporo and to staff it with a qualified nurse and midwives so that the whole population, but especially pregnant women, "who produce children for the good of society," could be assured of adequate treatment.[30]

Education

If women were attentive to their children's health, they were equally concerned about their education—their passport to success in the new society. As early as 1947, the Kankan RDA subsection organized a fund-raising drive to build a neighborhood school.[31] The following year, the Kindia subsection urged the government to replace the old round huts that had served as local schools with solid square (i.e., modern) structures.[32] By the 1950s, the RDA was regularly demanding the construction of more primary schools, permitting a greater number of children—both boys and girls—to attend. The party also requested better teacher training facilities and more technical colleges.[33] Concern for their children's education was followed by demands for more adult education, embracing women as well as men. The suggested curricula included the rudiments of French, theoretical and practical training in agriculture, animal husbandry, hygiene, child care, and housekeeping.[34] All of these party initiatives were extremely attractive to women.

Urban Food Supply and Women's Labor

Urban food supply was another central issue for women. The rations attached to workers' wages were woefully inadequate, making it extremely difficult for women to feed their families. At the December 1947 meeting in Conakry, Sékou Touré addressed some of these concerns. In August 1947, the RDA had requested that workers' rice rations be raised to 15 kilograms per month, he noted. The government's response had been to reduce rice rations to 10 kilos per month.[35] It was not until 1953 that workers' monthly rice rations were increased to 15 kilos, a result of the general strike spearheaded by RDA-dominated trade unions. Significantly, the new agreement stipulated that the rice be white. Women favored white rice because it was already hulled and thus did not have to be pounded with heavy pestles. The provision of white rice lessened women's heavy work burden. While the increased rice ration had been demanded by male party leaders since 1947, it is likely that women initiated the demand for hulled (white) rice.[36]

Women were also inconvenienced by the fact that rice could not be sold freely. In 1947, the RDA noted that in Conakry, only three to four stores were authorized to sell rice, resulting in long lines and delays. The party asked that the number of approved merchants be augmented—or that rice circulate

Photo 5.1   Market women selling fruit, Conakry. (CAOM)

freely. Although its arguments were to no avail, the RDA demonstrated its support for women's concerns.[37]

Agricultural Prices and Distribution

In its early appeals to urban women, the RDA decried artificially inflated food prices. In 1947, Sékou Touré challenged Conakry's mayor to explain the rising cost of rice, whose price was regulated by the government. The mayor responded that high prices, as well as government-controlled distribution, were intended to stimulate peasant production. Sékou Touré responded that production should be stimulated by increasing the amount of cultivable land available to the rural population and by reserving rice for the local market, rather than exporting it to France.[38]

By the early 1950s, the RDA was singing a different tune. As it made inroads into the rural areas, the party petitioned the government to raise the prices of local agricultural products, ensuring African peasants a fair price for their labor.[39] It requested that rural producers be permitted to sell their rice wherever they chose, rather than be restricted to their own locality.[40] Such a program obviously appealed to rural women, who, in many parts of Guinea, were the primary agricultural producers. However, it conflicted with the needs of urban women, who had to feed their families with meager resources. Caught between the opposing interests of two important constituencies, the party attempted to alleviate urban women's concerns by focusing on increased rations and the greater availability of foodstuffs.

Markets and Roads

Promoting the interests of both rural agricultural producers and urban market women, the RDA advocated the construction and maintenance of markets and connecting roads.[41] The party's efforts on behalf of market women were particularly effective. In 1948, the RDA successfully challenged a regulation that forced the Labé and Kindia markets to close early on Sundays—not only a costly inconvenience, but an affront to the predominantly Muslim population.[42] Two years later, in response to popular demand, the RDA constructed an unofficial market in the coastal town of Manéah.[43] That same year, the party complained that despite the high taxes paid by market women, the Conakry market was in a deplorable state. Repairs and improvements were never made.[44] Not long thereafter, an association of market women, organized by Sékou Touré, began to agitate for a diminution of market taxes.[45] In 1955, the RDA succeeded in eliminating altogether the taxes imposed on (predominantly female) merchants who sold their goods from market tables.[46]

Photo 5.2   Market women selling their wares, Conakry, 1954. (CAOM)

Taxes

The RDA's demand for decreased taxation was popular in all quarters. In tandem with its appeal for a general diminution of taxes on the populace, the party called for increased levies on commercial enterprises. The revenue so raised should be used to benefit the African population.[47] Moreover, to compensate for any resulting deficit, a new tax should be imposed on alcoholic beverages, potentially leading to reduced consumption. Concerning this secondary benefit, RDA members decried the debilitating effects of liquor, which damaged Africans' minds and morals, rendered them susceptible to exploitation, and turned them from the Islamic path.[48] Women most likely applauded this stance. For cultural reasons, they were far less likely than men to drink. Moreover, a decline in male alcohol consumption meant more money for their families and diminished domestic violence.

Water Taps and Firewood

When the RDA promoted white rice rations, it strove to lessen women's work burden while ensuring their families' proper nutrition. When it advocated the construction of public water taps on Conakry street corners, it targeted women's health as well as labor concerns. In terms of health, the party demanded that the government do more to secure an adequate supply of potable water.[49] It decried the scarcity of public water taps in the urban centers and called upon the administration to increase the number.[50] At the December 1947 meeting in Conakry, Ray Autra lamented, "Women fight one another to get access to a single water pump from which a thin stream of water trickles." This intolerable situation prevailed in a territory called "the reservoir of French West Africa."[51]

In terms of labor, plentiful water taps meant that women and girls would not have to walk long distances with buckets of water balanced on their heads. Nearby sources of water would free young girls from onerous domestic chores, enabling more of them to attend school. According to RDA militant Fatou Kéïta,

> One day, Sékou Touré met the women and said the women's work should be alleviated. They should not be carrying water on their heads, going long distances to look for firewood. . . . This was when the party introduced water taps in the compounds and on the street corners.[52]

The provision of firewood, the primary cooking fuel, was another burden women faced on a daily basis. To lighten their load, the party encouraged women to produce and use longer-burning charcoal. Moreover, at the party's initiative, Kéïta claimed, "The trains began to bring wood in their empty cars when they came to town; women no longer had to go long distances to find it." Whether or not these developments were, in fact, the result of party action, it is significant that Guinean women perceived them to be so.[53]

Equality and Respect

While early party initiatives generally bolstered established gender norms, RDA women also experienced an expansion of their commonly accepted roles. Among the male leaders, Sékou Touré was notorious for pushing the boundaries. In an appeal to women, he remarked, "The parties that fight the RDA have forgotten the women, ignoring the fact that the law that governs the world was made by God himself, and not for men only. God, in making this law, wanted men and women to be equal on earth." In France, he continued, women were among the deputies, councillors, and mayors. They were elected for their abilities and their accomplishments. Such should also be the case in Guinea.[54]

If women were to be liberated in the public sphere, they must first be emancipated in their homes. According to RDA militant Bocar Biro Barry, Sékou Touré urged women to reject their husbands' complete domination of their lives. Decrying the practice of female seclusion, he told them, "'You must be able to go to the market yourselves. You must be able to accompany your children to school. Everything that men do, you also must be able to do.'"[55]

Women eagerly embraced these new attitudes, frequently venturing into unexplored territory. Increasingly, they gave public speeches. Before that time, Fatou Diarra recalled, "Women did not speak in front of men. They did not stand up in the man's world to speak."[56] However, in March 1955, Gnamakoron Kaba rose at an RDA meeting in Kankan and addressed the crowd. "I am only a woman," she said,

> No woman of Kankan has yet spoken here in this public meeting. Before the arrival of the RDA, women did not have the right to speak in an assembly of men! Today, thank God, thanks to the RDA, I will speak to this tribunal like the men. The woman has become the equal of the man.[57]

In the Futa Jallon, which was dominated by the religiously conservative and socially hierarchical Peul, aristocratic women dared not speak to their husbands while standing. Nor could they speak in public. Thus, it was left to Tourou Sylla, a lower-class Malinke cloth dyer, to do the unthinkable in addressing mixed crowds of men and women. Even more scandalous, she brazenly stood on the tabletops to ensure that her anticolonial message carried to the farthest reaches of the assemblies. This was considered absolutely shocking, Bocar Biro Barry reminisced.[58]

Other barriers were broken by lower-class Peul women outside the Futa Jallon. In 1955, Néné Diallo, a Conakry-based cloth dyer with no formal schooling, was included in an official RDA delegation that campaigned in Boké (Lower-Guinea). That was the first time she stood at a podium and spoke in public, she recalled. "Previously, women would not accept such an offer—to stand at a podium and talk. But that day, Allah gave me the strength, and things came about as if Allah had created me to talk in public."[59]

In interviews conducted many years later, RDA women claimed that they were shown a degree of respect in the party that they did not experience elsewhere. They were invited to speak at public meetings; to share their grievances; to mobilize not only their families and neighbors but also total strangers in towns, villages, and hamlets across the country. According to Fatou Kéïta, an unschooled Susu seamstress, before the transformations brought about by the party,

Women were slaves. Wherever there were more than two men, women were not allowed to speak. It was Sékou Touré who brought about that change. The Socialists and the BAG did not allow women to speak, but the RDA did. The other parties acted out of jealousy. They said that households would be split, that women would divorce their husbands if they were allowed to enter party politics. But women were clear that their involvement in politics was a good thing. And most went to the RDA. They thought that sending their daughters to school was a good thing, and many began sending their daughters to school.[60]

Néné Diallo echoed these sentiments: "We were all equal in the RDA, women and men. For women, when you worked you reaped the fruits for yourself, regardless of status and wealth. That is why we liked the RDA."[61]

THE AFTERMATH OF THE 1953 GENERAL STRIKE

The 1953 general strike was a turning point not only for the RDA but for women within the nationalist movement. The critical role of nonelite women was widely acknowledged, and female activists were actively recruited to the nationalist cause. Sékou Touré, in particular, made much of women's power, using images, anecdotes, and parables that appealed to the largely nonliterate population. According to Sékou Touré, "The women are the fire of the RDA. When we want to make a knife we need iron, water and fire. The knife is Africa. We are the blacksmiths. We must use fire to make our knife. Our fire is our women. Our women mold us, carry us."[62]

Having failed to build a movement based on the tiny cadre of elite women, the RDA shifted its focus to the nonliterate majority. The first territorial congress of RDA women, convened on July 31, 1954, included all the presidents of the urban neighborhoods' women's committees but not their rural counterparts. The urban bias was probably due to financial constraints and transportation difficulties, rather than an exclusionary agenda. At the conclusion of the congress, the participants put forth demands that echoed those championed by male leaders in the late 1940s and early 1950s. The women called upon the government to construct new schools in order to augment the number of children enrolled, increase the number of public water taps, build new maternity wards, decrease market taxes, and apply the articles of the Overseas Labor Code that concerned women and children.[63] The latter included family allowances, central to women's demands during the 1953 general strike.[64]

At the first women's congress, a new territorial women's committee was established, replacing the defunct committee formed in 1949. The presidents of the urban neighborhoods' women's committees elected the territorial board, including the new territorial president, Mafory Bangoura, a cloth dyer and seamstress without formal schooling.[65] Notably absent from the 1954 board were the officers of the first RDA women's committee—Western-educated elites, most of whom had left Guinea following the expulsion of their civil servant husbands during the anti-RDA repression of the late 1940s and early 1950s.[66] The urban-based board was charged with coordinating and supervising the activities of all the women's committees in the territory.[67]

In the aftermath of the June 1954 legislative elections and the July women's congress, local RDA women's committees were established throughout the territory.[68] Delegations of RDA women and men crisscrossed the interior, establishing women's committees linked to RDA neighborhood and village committees and regional subsections.[69] By August, there were an estimated 6,000 female RDA members in Lower-Guinea, 4,800 of whom resided in Conakry.[70] In September, Abdoulaye Diallo, a Guinean trade unionist based in the French Soudan, was impressed enough to remark that while the RDA was strong in the French Soudan, "the women were not as well organized as in Guinea"—a marked contrast to the Makas' observations in 1949.[71]

Women's involvement continued to grow. In October 1954, Sékou Touré proclaimed that "the women have constituted a vast movement that is worrying our adversaries." They were the force behind many of the newly created neighborhood and village committees and the expanded membership drives.[72] Mamadou Bela Doumbouya echoed these sentiments: "The women thus brought their contribution. Everywhere, they participated in this renaissance of the party. . . . And women found themselves in all the subsections and committees. . . . They participated at all levels."[73] From 1954 on, Mira Baldé recalled, all RDA actions and official delegations included both women and men.[74]

NEW METHODS OF MOBILIZATION:
HOW WOMEN WORKED

If women left a strong imprint on the RDA's program and objectives, their impact on its mobilizing methods was equally notable. In Tanganyika, the production of nationalism was "women's work" par excellence, Geiger writes. "Women activists evoked, created and performed" nationalism through their songs and dances.[75] Similarly, in Guinea, women sang and danced the message of independence. Oral transmission of information was crucial to the success of the RDA, which targeted the large mass of Guineans who had little or no formal education. According to Guinean scholar Idiatou Camara, women were considered to be the best sloganeers; as traditional storytellers and singers, they were the practiced creators of ideas, images, and phrases that appealed to the nonelite population.[76]

Like the women of coastal Nigeria, Guinean women used long-established kinship and market networks to convey antigovernment information.[77] The women's "bush telegraph" was highly effective. "From the markets to the public water taps, from the train station to the taxi stands, information was transmitted along a chain," Camara writes. At their habitual meeting places, women popularized the slogans, demands, and grievances of the party.[78] The public water taps and markets were especially important for this purpose. According to Fatou Kéïta,

> The women congregated there and discussed where to go next. . . . News circulated fast in both places. If a woman went to get water, she stayed until the next person came and told her the news. The new arrival would wait and tell the next person, etc. This is how [RDA] news was spread.[79]

While information circulated rapidly through informal channels, women also institutionalized the flow of information. As market women joined the RDA, they took advantage of preexisting market structures. Urban markets were divided into sections, each devoted to a particular type of product. The female vendors organized themselves into associations, defined by the products they sold. Thus, associations of sellers of fruits, vegetables, spices, and fish presided over the various market sections, fixing prices, enforcing the rules and regulations of the market, and generally defending the interests of their members. Each section was presided over by a female leader, chosen by the women who sold that product.[80]

During the nationalist struggle, it was the market leaders who disseminated political information to the women in their sections. According to RDA activist Mabalo Sakho, the section leaders were the only ones authorized to circulate the morning news.[81] Once the sellers had received the news, they conveyed it to their customers, who spread the word at their next stop. Since women

Photo 5.3   Market women crossing the Milo River with their produce, before the construction of the bridge, Kankan, November 1949. Photographer, M. G. Barachet. *(La Documentation Française)*

bought salt from one seller, tomatoes from another, leaves from another, and fish from another, the news spread rapidly through the market.[82]

The use of song was an essential educational and mobilizing tool for women, many of whom were not literate and therefore could not read the party tracts and newspapers. Women composed songs to communicate with their peers and to transmit messages up and down the chain of command. They used songs to convey information among themselves, to direct their own messages to the elites, and to interpret elite messages in terms meaningful to themselves. "Everything was with a song," recalled Néné Diallo. "There were countless songs. . . . Day after day, songs were made up. Everyone sang songs. We repeated the songs of others as they did ours. . . . There was not any one person singing the songs. There were many singers."[83] Fatou Kéïta concurred: "The women composed these songs. They did it spontaneously. There was not one author. When somebody found a song, they sang it. The next person heard it and sang it, and so on. It spread like that."[84] Fatou Diarra, another former militant, remembered,

> Women went to the markets every day. . . . If there was a new song, all the women learned it and sang it in the taxis, teaching one another. When there

was an event, the leader went to the market with the song to teach it to the other women.

After the 1954 elections, women sang at the markets that the colonial authorities had rigged the elections. "You women who go up, You women who go down. The other party has stolen our votes, Stolen the votes of *Syli*." All the women sang this song, so by the time they heard the election results, they already knew that they had been cheated, that the election had been rigged.[85]

The women who sang at the market performed in teams. When the police came, they fled, as political activities in the marketplace were officially prohibited.[86]

RDA women's songs praised the party, ridiculed the opposition, and commented on recent political events. Sexually charged lyrics, aimed at reticent men, were intended to mock rivals and shame laggards, as well as to mobilize RDA followers. Publicly disgracing hesitant husbands, women were quick to humiliate such men through songs of ridicule that questioned their manhood.[87] Although their political content was new, songs that ridiculed the virility of their male targets were in keeping with long-standing practices among Susu women. Historically, Susu women had used sexually explicit

Photo 5.4 Market women selling their wares near the Milo River bridge, Kankan, 1950. Photographer, M. G. Barachet. *(La Documentation Française)*

songs and dances to publicly humiliate and sanction men who had abused their wives.[88]

Even women who violated female gender norms generally accepted those applicable to men. Embracing ideals that associated masculinity with bravery and self-assertion, RDA women's songs frequently accused men of "behaving like women"—that is, of being cowardly and timid. They scorned those who were unwilling to stand up and fight. According to Kadiatou Meunier, contemptuous women proclaimed, "I don't want to be married to a woman like me, a man who is a coward."[89] In other songs, women contrasted Guinea's ineffectual male population with the virile RDA leader:

> Sékou Touré wears the pants
> He is a handsome man
> There is no other man who
> Dares stand in his way
> Wear your pants, Handsome!

This song taunted reticent men, asserting that they were not big enough for Sékou Touré's trousers, and warned his opponents that their efforts were futile.[90]

Some songs went further in their admonitions: if men were afraid of repression, they should give their trousers to the women who would wear them in their stead.[91] Women who sang these songs firmly believed that men should wear the pants in the family. Courage and initiative were not considered to be womanly traits; women assumed them only if men would not.[92]

Other songs were more graphic in insulting the manhood of those who failed to support the RDA or who joined rival parties. Between April and June 1955, police reports indicate that groups of RDA militants roamed the streets of Conakry singing the praises of "Governor Sékou Touré" and casting aspersions on his chief rival, Barry Diawadou, whose election as deputy they refused to recognize. Each day groups of women, organized by neighborhood, paraded before the home of Sékou Touré singing political songs. Then they marched in formation across the city, carrying banners and singing songs in which Barry Diawadou was derided as being uncircumcised—a mere boy rather than a real man.[93] One account records the following lyrics:

> Barry Diawadou left Conakry
> To go to Upper-Guinea
> Because he found
> That *Syli* is always in the lead
> Barry was slapped like a dog
> The penis of Barry
> Is circumcised this time![94]

Even more grave than insulting a man's genitals was the denigration of his father's. In the following song, a double insult was intended. Barry Diawadou's father, Almamy Barry Aguibou, was the powerful Dabola canton chief and an important collaborator of the colonial regime. Having helped to perpetuate the electoral fraud that resulted in his son's election to the French National Assembly, the chief was held accountable for sending him to France.[95] Hence, the women sang:

> Barry Diawadou's father's penis
> The saboteur's father's penis
> Barry Diawadou left Conakry
> He went to France
> There he found his father's circumcision
> Sékou Touré is always in the lead![96]

Through their songs, women were public purveyors of information. However, government repression and retaliation by rival parties forced much of women's work underground. Néné Diallo discussed the clandestine nature of women's meetings during that period:

> You had to go inside the house to meet, by groups of two or three. The RDA was not yet strong. . . . But since the women had chosen Sékou, they had chosen him for good. . . . Because when we make up our minds, we are not easily swayed. We were beaten, sworn at. We did not quit. Some were sent to jail. We remained steadfast in our support for him.[97]

Because of the crackdown, other critical tasks, including the sale and distribution of illicit party membership cards, were performed covertly. According to Aissatou N'Diaye,

> Women launched the membership drives. . . . We had our first meeting in Lengebunji, a neighborhood in Boulbinet [Conakry]. Membership cards were distributed there. . . . Well, I took my cards. I was given two assistants. Every other day I would go out with one of them. Their role was to take down the names of new members. . . . We mobilized lots of women.[98]

Fearing retribution by rival parties, Fatou Kéïta recalled, small groups of women canvassed neighborhoods where they were well known.[99] Women had to work cautiously, concealing the cards from both government authorities and opposition party members. Aissatou N'Diaye observed:

> The cards were hidden in their head scarves. The women would roll the cards into their scarves and put the scarves under their arm pits. Over this,

they wore big *boubous.* They went to compounds where they knew there could be Socialists and BAG members present, as well as RDA. The person selling the cards would lift her arms and *boubou* so that people would know she had something under her arm pit. RDA people knew what that meant. Then they would ask her into the house and buy their cards.[100]

On other occasions, the women strolled through hospital wards, visiting patients, nurses, and office workers. Operating according to code, they flashed 100 franc notes, indicating that they had RDA cards to sell. If a customer wanted a card, the seller casually slipped it under papers scattered on the table, and the customer gave her a 100 franc note in return. "We didn't know how to write, to compose a membership list. But the number of cards we sold indicated the number of members who joined each day," Mamayimbe Bangoura explained.[101]

Besides selling membership cards, RDA women performed a variety of other tasks. They sold party newspapers, including *Le Phare de Guinée, Coup de Bambou,* and *La Liberté.* They distributed party tracts, posted meeting announcements, and popularized party slogans. Because the RDA was forced to work clandestinely, the members toiled at night, traversing the town with pots of starch paste, posting their leaflets on baobab and mango trees.[102] They served as security guards, warning of attacks by members of rival organizations. Seated behind platters of fruit at roadside stands, female vendors kept all-night vigils at party headquarters and at the home of Sékou Touré. They acted as sentinels during secret meetings, signaling the participants to disperse as soon as they spied police vans.[103]

Women gathered intelligence, observing neighborhood activities and informing party leaders of imminent actions against the RDA—by the government or by opposition parties. According to Idiatou Camara, RDA women

> penetrated into the courtyards, pretending to take embers to the kitchen, and listened to the conversations. Or, in the seamstresses' workshops, at the popular hairdressers', during the ceremonies of marriage, baptism, circumcision, and funerals, they listened to everything and made note of all tendentious turns and unusual movements.

Stationed in hospitals, at the marketplaces, taxi stands, and public water taps, women collected data and reported to the RDA neighborhood officials. Mamayimbe Bangoura was so adept at slipping into enemy territory to ferret out information that she was called *"Nyari,"* or "Cat," out of respect for her stealth and agility.[104]

Women played important roles when RDA men were imprisoned. Market women took up collections to support the prisoners' families.[105] Inmates' wives smuggled party newspapers and letters into the prisons when they brought their husbands' meals. They informed party officials about prison conditions and conveyed messages from their husbands.[106] Even the police admitted that the inmates in Conakry's civil prison were in permanent contact with the RDA through intermediaries, including visitors and wardens, who transmitted correspondence.[107]

Initially, RDA women used simple methods to penetrate prison security. During family visits, they slipped letters and newspapers to the prisoners or passed information orally. When these techniques were discovered, they buried letters and clippings in the platters of rice they brought to feed their husbands. Exposed again, they stuffed messages into aspirin bottles and inserted them into large pieces of fish smothered in sauce. The scraps they carried home concealed the same bottles, now bearing their husbands' replies.[108]

During periods of political violence, women's Red Cross committees were established in all the RDA subsections. Every Sunday, committee members visited the injured, provided them with letters and newspapers, and informed them of the latest political developments. In Conakry, the Red Cross committee was led by Mafory Bangoura, whose residence was transformed into a hospital for the injured.[109]

While the nature of women's participation often reinforced established gender norms, Fatou Diarra emphasized the ways in which it also challenged male primacy:

> Women struggled in their own ways. They will say that they cooked for
> RDA meetings; that was their contribution to the struggle according to the
> traditional division of labor. But they challenged their husbands. They pro-
> tected them, hid them from the authorities. The women informed them
> when there was danger and hid them. During the campaign before the 1954
> elections, women teachers hid RDA militants under the benches in the
> classrooms. This empowered women, the act of protecting men. They
> struggled because the struggle promised to help them out of slavery. My
> grandmother [Oumou Cissé, a Mamou activist] will tell you glowingly of
> this power—of protecting big men, cooking for them, etc.[110]

STRETCHING THE LIMITS OF GENDER NORMS: WOMEN'S SHOCK TROOPS

While women's explicitly political roles were, for the most part, unprecedented, many were logical extensions of their preexisting caretaking functions. Others evolved from culturally acceptable ways for women to redress their grievances. In 1954, during the upheaval surrounding the general strike and legislative election campaign, a new institution emerged that stretched the limits of gender norms. Beleaguered by brawls with opposing political parties, RDA women organized "shock troops" in the large urban centers. Daring and physically aggressive, traits typically associated with male warriors, the all-woman brigades took punitive action against rival party members.[111] RDA women fought with their hands and with clubs, attacking men and women alike. Sometimes, mimicking male garb, they wore belts.[112] Many proudly assumed noms de guerre. Mahawa Touré, for instance, was dubbed *"Pagailleur,"* or "Promoter of Disorder." N'Youla Doumbouya, noted for her derring-do, was called "Montgomery, Eighth Army," after General Bernard Law Montgomery, who commanded the British Eighth Army in its successful North African campaigns during World War II.[113]

While the phenomenon of politicized female street fighters was new, women's assumption of male gender roles was not. Historically, temporary transformations had occurred in times of crisis. In the forest region, for instance, women took collective action against men who abused their wives and did not respond to lesser sanctions. Dressed as men ready for war and armed with sharp knives they called "penis cutters," women surrounded the offending parties' homes and pounded on the buildings with large clubs. No man dared to show his face publicly until the women had completed their action.[114]

This precolonial gender practice and its extension to the political realm under colonial rule bears a striking resemblance to that of Igbo women in southeastern Nigeria. There, Judith Van Allen notes, "making war" or "sitting on a man" was women's "ultimate sanction." If a man perpetually abused his wife, broke market rules, or allowed his livestock to devour women's crops, village women converged on his compound, singing songs that expressed their grievances and insulted him with sexually explicit lyrics that questioned his virility. They hammered his hut with their pestles, sometimes even tearing off the roof. [115] Women who took the unusual step of "making war" typically dressed as men. Donning short loincloths, they wore ornamentation and carried implements that connoted war. They painted their faces with charcoal or ashes, wrapped their heads in ferns, and carried sticks sheathed in palm fronds intended to call forth the powers of female ancestral spirits.[116]

These deeply rooted gender sanctions were transformed in 1929, when thousands of Igbo women "made war" on government-appointed chiefs who, they believed, were about to impose taxes on them. Dancing, chanting, and singing insults, these women, dressed as male warriors, demanded the chiefs' symbolic caps of office. Although applied to a new circumstance, this act of war was, Van Allen contends, "an extension of their traditional method for settling grievances with men who had acted badly toward them."[117]

In Conakry, the first women's shock troops were led by Mafory Bangoura. Members included Mahawa Touré, N'Youla Doumbouya, Nabya Haidara, Khady Bangoura, Aissata Bangoura, and Néné Soumah. At night, this women's brigade policed the neighborhood of Sandervalia, where Sékou Touré lived surrounded by members of opposing parties. Eventually, women's brigades were organized in all the principal neighborhoods of Conakry—Sandervalia, Boulbinet, Coronthie—and included the most active female members of the RDA.[118] Their primary opponents were members of the BAG, an ethnically based party founded in 1954 in order to more effectively counter RDA influence. In its defense of the status quo, the BAG was supported by the Peul aristocracy, the colonial administration, collaborating chiefs, and the most highly educated of the Western-educated elites, who coveted the crumbs of privilege thrown to them by the colonial regime.[119]

The most famous of the RDA's women warriors was Nabya Haidara, whose mother was Susu and father was Lebanese. Haidara was particularly notorious for her brazen violation of gender norms, epitomizing the man-like woman who cowed insipid men. Her female admirers referred to her as a "man in a wrapper" or a "man who had been given the wrong sex."[120] Still legendary some four decades later, Haidara's escapades, whether tall tale or fact, were eagerly recounted by her supporters. According to Idiatou Camara, Haidara dressed as a man and fought with a saber. When she was arrested, the police were said to have found some 30 sabers in her house, each engraved with her initials.[121] On another occasion, Léon Maka recalled, Haidara and her female followers stormed the civil prison in Conakry, where Sékou Touré was being held. The women caused such havoc that the police commissioner quickly released the party leader, Maka claimed.[122] In another incident, Aissatou N'Di- aye remembered, an RDA rival aimed his gun at a crowd of RDA supporters outside his window. Nabya Haidara "jumped into the air, grabbed the gun, and brought the man down," she said. The man was wounded in the fray.[123]

Considered to be dangerous perpetrators of disorder, the women's shock troops were heavily scrutinized by the government. Many members were arrested and imprisoned. On April 12, 1955, *La Liberté* published a list of RDA militants whose arrests had been demanded by rival parties. All of the women's shock troops were included. A few days later, Nabya Haidara, Mahawa Touré, Khady Bangoura, Nnady Soumah, and Sayon Bangoura were arrested and imprisoned. Haidara was eventually sentenced to five months in prison, whereas the other women were sentenced to three.[124]

N'Youla Doumbouya was arrested shortly thereafter. As was her daily cus- tom, she had met Mafory Bangoura and other colleagues at the major inter- section in Sandervalia, where they exchanged information about the preceding night's events. Bangoura urged Doumbouya to quickly prepare her family's dinner—her domestic responsibilities were paramount—and collect her mat and pillow, as the police would soon come for her. Indeed, they did. "My nickname—Montgomery—led the colonial authorities to believe that I was the leader of all the insurrections in Guinea," Doumbouya explained. "As a result, my dossier was transmitted to Dakar." Doumbouya found a number of RDA women already in prison. Some were wounded; some were in chains. Deprived of sleep and adequate food, water, and clothing, the women kept up their morale by singing party songs.[125]

More arrests followed. Mafory Bangoura was a primary target. Disparaged by the police as a former prostitute, Bangoura was dubbed "the terrible woman of the RDA" and "the dangerous amazon of the PDG."[126] In July 1955, Bangoura was arrested, fined 70,000 francs, and sentenced to one year in prison for having transmitted an "anti-French document" to inmates in Conakry's civil prison. As news of her arrest spread through the city, women took to the streets by the hundreds. Brandishing pestles, branches, and stones, they marched to the commissariat, where they blocked traffic and threatened the police, who responded with fire hoses.[127] On August 17, Bangoura was freed on bail, collected by RDA women. She was carried from the commissariat to her home in Sandervalia, accompanied by tam-tams, balafons, and singing and dancing.[128] In February 1956, her sentence and fine were reduced by the court of appeals in Dakar to three months in prison, of which she served only 28 days. The remainder of the sentence was suspended, pending appeal to a higher court.[129]

While grassroots militants applauded the actions of the women's shock troops, Western-educated elites, particularly those in the party's territorial leadership, warned that the women were victims of false consciousness. According to Mamadou Bela Doumbouya, a Mamou-based trade unionist and elite civil servant in the *cadre commun secondaire,* the RDA leadership systematically opposed the shock troops' intimidatory actions. "The party had no interest in recruiting members by force," he claimed.

> The opposition was composed of people who had the same interests as we did, but who did not understand. It was necessary for us to help them understand so that they would join us. These people were not "saboteurs," as they were called [by some RDA militants]. They were not the enemy. It was the circle commandant who was the enemy.[130]

The most colorful and provocative of women's new roles, the shock brigades were not typical of women's work in the nationalist movement. Nonetheless, they became a focal point for male anxiety over events they could no longer control.

THE VIOLATION OF GENDER NORMS:
HOUSEHOLDS IN UPHEAVAL

While the male-dominated RDA leadership criticized the women street fighters, as party leaders, they publicly supported most of the RDA women's other initiatives. Their attitudes did not necessarily trickle down to the grassroots. Many men, RDA and otherwise, resisted women's emancipation, particularly in the Futa Jallon. While women's public roles were circumscribed throughout Guinea, the Futa Jallon was particularly notorious for its religious and social conservatism. In Dinguiraye, an important religious center in the Futa, women lived in seclusion. According to Mira Baldé, "They stayed in their homes. They did not even go to the market."[131] Léon Maka elaborated:

> [Before the nationalist movement] in Dinguiraye, there was never a woman in the street. If by chance a man or a group of men was walking along a path and met a woman, the woman would hasten into the bush, covering her head with a cloth. She would not get up until the men had passed.[132]

Elsewhere in the Futa, Tourou Sylla reminisced, "If men were gathered in a . . . compound and a woman wanted to cross the yard, she would have to bow down when passing."[133]

Thus, it was left to low-status "outsiders" like Tourou Sylla to mobilize women in the Futa Jallon. Her efforts were strongly resisted by the male establishment. As a young woman in the 1950s, Sylla was renowned for her aggressive campaigns against the colonial government and the canton chiefs. A lower-class Malinke woman in a region dominated by religiously conservative, status-conscious Peul aristocrats, Tourou Sylla allegedly took great pleasure in shocking highborn Peul elders by violating the most important social codes. According to Bocar Biro Barry, a male RDA leader and himself a Peul aristocrat, each time there was an RDA mission in the interior of the Futa, Sylla volunteered to go. She always chose to visit the aristocratic families, of which Barry's family was one.[134] In an interview conducted in 1991, Sylla concurred with Barry's assessment. She had indeed journeyed to aristocratic towns and stood on tables to harangue the notables. "I spoke," Sylla recalled. "I pounded sense into their heads—to shame them for their bad deeds, to remind them of all the wrongs they had done to people. I said it while they watched me in broad daylight. I told them that those days were long gone by, Allah willing!"[135]

In the early 1990s, tales of Tourou Sylla's anticolonial, antiaristocratic, and antipatriarchal escapades were still on the lips of aging nationalists across the country. Some of the stories, corroborated by Sylla, are undoubtedly true. In other instances, uneasy men may have concocted tall tales of unseemly behavior simply because Sylla had raised her voice in public. The following story, exemplifying the most extreme violation of gender norms, was eagerly recounted by Bocar Biro Barry, yet denied by Sylla herself.[136]

One day, Barry recalled, Sylla arrived in a village over which his uncle presided as chief. She immediately seated herself in the chiefly hammock—an absolutely unthinkable act for a commoner, particularly a woman. She then proceeded to order the chief to her side and dictated her menu to him. She wanted eggs, beef, chicken, and so forth—all the good things Europeans liked to eat. Finally, she declared that all RDA dues must be collected and submitted before six o'clock that evening. "It was practically a dictate," Barry exclaimed. "It was as if the circle guard had come into the village!"

The chief was thunderstruck. Who was this woman to take such liberties, to give orders to a chief? His wives were even more astonished than he. Who was this woman who did what they did not so much as dare, who took the hammock of their husband, who dictated what she should eat—not to the women, but to the man! How could it be that a woman gave orders to their husband? According to his nephew, the old chief was so disturbed by Sylla's comportment that he could not sleep that night. It was not so much *what* she did, as the fact that a woman had done it. According to Barry, his uncle could have accepted such actions from a European, from another chief, even from a male member of the RDA—but *never* from a woman.

Tourou Sylla disputed the extreme nature of Barry's account. When asked if she had usurped the hammock of the chief and dictated her menu to him, she laughed heartily, and with a glimmer of light in her eyes, denied that she had. "That has sweetened the story slightly," she laughed. "We did not personally sit in a hammock!"[137] Tourou Sylla may have been speaking the truth. Perhaps she never sat in a chiefly hammock. Outraged men may have exaggerated the nature and extent of her activities. However, it is equally possible that *Hadja* Tourou Sylla, a respected older woman who prayed daily at the mosque, was not anxious to reveal all the details of her unconventional past. A woman of lowly origins, her nationalist activities had brought her prominence, which she had translated into traditional terms of respectability. It was hard-won respect that she was not willing to jeopardize lightly. What is certain is that the transformation of gender roles did not occur smoothly. Fatou Kéïta explained: "Men liked the quiet of the colonial times, when their wives followed them. . . . There were no problems. After the party, it took a lot of readjusting. Men had to learn to do some things."[138]

Although the RDA leadership encouraged the rank and file to accept and even encourage women's political activities, a discrepancy between theory and practice remained. While some husbands supported their wives' involvement, many did not.[139] Wife beating, marital breakdown, and the taking of additional, more subservient wives were common responses. "For the husbands it was a shock," recounted Fatou Diarra. "They were not used to seeing their wives outside the home. There were a lot of divorces, or the men married more wives."[140]

While refusing to relinquish their newfound roles, some women conceded the validity of their husbands' complaints. The marriage contract entailed certain mutually agreed upon responsibilities. If wives could no longer fulfill their allotted roles, they were obliged to find surrogates who would. Aissatou N'Diaye noted that her husband readily agreed to her participation in RDA activities "because I had a young woman at home who could do my chores."[141] Because her political work entailed significant national and international travel, Fatou Kéïta reported that she was often unable to perform her wifely duties, which included cooking, childcare, and sexual relations with her husband. To win consent for her political activities, Kéïta found her husband six additional wives to perform the requisite functions in her place. Thus, when Kéïta toured Guinea for three months in 1954, mobilizing for the RDA, she left her husband in good hands. Her cowives took care of him and her children.[142]

Spousal obligations and domestic responsibilities were not the only sticking points. Some men were intensely jealous of their wives' loyalty to another man—Sékou Touré—and their willingness to follow his orders on a moment's notice. Others were concerned about their wives' attendance at late-night meetings that included men as well as women, a situation they associated with sexual promiscuity.[143] Some allowed only their older (postmenopausal) wives to go to such meetings, forbidding their younger (fertile) ones from associating so closely with other men.[144] According to Bocar Biro Barry, "The men said, 'Fine! Since it is now Sékou Touré who is your husband, since it is his orders you are following and not mine, go then. Go marry him!'"[145] Women quickly took up the refrain. Léon Maka recalled a song in which women sang, "Whether you agree or not, I will participate in this movement!" They threw out their husbands' clothes and informed them that they had chosen Sékou Touré.[146]

Concern about women's rapid emancipation was not always confined to the rank and file. At times, even the RDA leadership felt Sékou Touré was bordering on extremism. Barry recalled that male leaders in the party's political bureau said to Sékou Touré, "'Truly, you are going too far. You are tearing households apart. . . . You are inciting women against their husbands.'" Unable to accept their wives' newfound roles, they exclaimed, "'I am a member of the RDA—that is sufficient. My wife and my children need only to stay at home.'" However, Barry continued, "It was there that [Sékou Touré] attacked them. He even attacked members of the political bureau, saying, 'You are reactionaries. If you are of the RDA, you must be of the RDA entirely— that is, you, your wives, and your children.'" Nonetheless, Barry concluded,

> There was something that was not public, but which was in each father, in each married man. He was suspicious when his wife abandoned the house with the children. . . . When [Sékou Touré] was to arrive at noon, by eight o'clock in the morning, all the women were in the streets. They did not do any of their chores. They did not mind the children. They did not know whether they had gone to school or not. The women went into the streets and stayed there until noon, one o'clock, two o'clock in the afternoon, to wait for *that other man*. Upon returning home, the husband had nothing to eat, . . . and there was a scene.[147]

Because of tensions within RDA households, the party quickly gained a reputation as a haven for prostitutes, loose women, and divorcées.[148] Rival political parties and the colonial administration eagerly capitalized on this image, railing against the evil of wifely disobedience. According to a 1954 police report, Kémoko Kouyaté, a member of the RDA's board of directors and a childhood friend of Sékou Touré's, resigned from the RDA, publicly attacking the party's emancipatory policies. "Women who do not follow their husbands are condemned by religion," Kouyaté proclaimed. "A woman who engages in political activities other than her husband's is nothing more than a prostitute."[149] That same year, Fatoumata Traoré, sister of the president of the Siguiri RDA subsection, was beaten bloody by the police because she refused to join her husband, who was active in the BAG.[150]

Members of rival parties peppered the police with allegations concerning the "dubious reputation" of RDA women. The police, for their part, were receptive to the notion that the party constituted "a hotbed of prostitution."[151] When some 40 women in Kankan joined the RDA, the governor of Guinea considered it serious enough to write to the high commissioner in Dakar, noting: "Among them are a number of notorious prostitutes, including: Kéritou Kaba, Kitiba Fanta Cissé—repudiated by her husband, El Hadj N'Faly Kaba—Kiaka Kaba, Diaka Kaba, etc."[152] Clearly, the historic Kaba/Touré rivalry did not affect women in the same way as it did men. Kaba women readily endorsed the RDA.

Despite pressure from husbands, families, and the colonial authorities, women continued to join the RDA. They did so, Néné Diallo explained, because they "had made up [their] minds."[153] Aissatou N'Diaye elaborated:

> When we decided to join the struggle, we told our husbands that if, in the name of Allah and His Envoy, they would forgive us, we would appreciate it. But should they decide to divorce us for our politics, they may go ahead, because we intended to stick with the struggle of the RDA.[154]

Women chronicled their determination in song, asserting that whether their husbands agreed or not, they were going to leave their homes to participate in the nationalist movement:

> Even when the rain pours
> The women are out
> Even when the sun shines
> The women are out
> Oh! How sweet the cause of *Syli*
> Women of Guinea, the cause of *Syli* is sweet
> Let us take the cause of *Syli* to heart.[155]

While some women joined the party openly, others did so in secret. Among the latter was Fatou Diarra, whose civil servant husband was a member of the DSG, a party of highly educated intellectuals who generally disdained the nonliterate masses of the RDA base. Brought into the RDA by other women, Diarra hid her party membership from her husband and stole away to meetings while he was at work. "Women were expected to follow their husbands," she recalled. "But I was RDA—like all the women."[156]

In the hope of avoiding complete marital breakdown, women called upon each other for assistance. Collectively, they accomplished what individuals could not. As Fatou Kéïta recalled,

> The women in the movement organized to support the women who had problems at home. They told them to stick to their guns, that their husbands would follow them sooner or later. The women went to see the husbands and stressed that if their wives turned out to be right [about the RDA] and they had not supported them, they would be very ashamed in the future.[157]

When shame did not suffice, sexual extortion was employed. In one notorious speech, Sékou Touré threatened, "Each morning, each noon, each evening, the women must incite their husbands to join the RDA. If they do not comply, the women only have to refuse themselves to their husbands. The next day, they will be obliged to join the RDA."[158] Speaking in the same vein, RDA women's leader Mafory Bangoura took the floor during a 1954 party meeting in Conakry. According to the police, she invited "RDA women to refuse to have sexual relations with their husbands if they did not join the party. They should not worry; Sékou Touré would provide them with another husband—a real democrat." The audience sang in response,

> We will no longer share the bed
> Of any enemy of *Syli*
> If not our legitimate husband,
> Sékou Touré will choose us
> A husband who is a democrat.[159]

Domestic relations were in turmoil. A woman's refusal to engage in sexual relations with her husband constituted a serious violation of the marital contract—clear grounds for divorce. Some women left husbands who refused to join the party. Others reportedly refused to marry men who could not produce an RDA membership card.[160] It was dramatic, exclaimed Bocar Biro Barry. "I tell you, the RDA infiltrated right into the homes!"[161]

In fact, the RDA had little interest in promoting marital discord or divorce. Rather, party leaders hoped that women's dedication to the struggle would influence their men to join them.[162] According to Bocar Biro Barry, Sékou Touré encouraged women in this endeavor, saying, "'If you are with the RDA, it is up to you to emancipate your husbands.'"[163] Often, it worked. Mira Baldé noted, "There were lots of women who made their husbands stray into the movement. . . . The husbands were not committed at first, but later they followed."[164] Even the tensions caused by women's independence paid off, as jealous husbands, having trailed their wives to late-night meetings, were enticed into the party.[165]

CONCLUSION

Women joined the RDA en masse, with or without their husbands' consent. As Tourou Sylla explained, "Once the sun rises, one cannot help but feel it." People had to move with the times.[166] The process of political mobilization raised women's consciousness, prompting them to take an interest in subjects previously considered off limits. They championed the nationalist cause in public, to audiences that included men as well as women.[167] They challenged a colonial administration that was composed almost exclusively of men and, in the process, learned that they could also defy the authority of their husbands.

While women contested long-standing gender roles during the nationalist movement, these norms were not permanently transformed. After independence, women frequently translated their newly acquired respectability into conventional terms. Tourou Sylla, the fiery rabble-rouser, was, in the early 1990s, a deeply religious *hadja* who dressed in black and prayed daily at the mosque. Likewise, Nabya Haidara, the famous woman street fighter who had gained a reputation as a "man in a wrapper," was dramatically changed by her pilgrimage to Mecca. "You know the pilgrimage is very difficult," explained Aissatou N'Diaye. "One must be clean of some kinds of sins . . . to survive the experience." The implication was that Haidara's activities as a street fighter had been improper, even sinful.[168] N'Youla Doumbouya, another member of the women's shock troops, refused to discuss her unorthodox political activities.[169] Hadja Fatou Kéïta initially agreed to share bawdy songs sung by RDA women to taunt timid or obstructionist men, then abruptly denied knowledge of them, even claiming that such songs did not exist.[170]

The circumstances mitigating against women's postindependence emancipation were strongly rooted in the past and were evident during the nationalist period. For the most part, women themselves accepted the societally designated gender norms that undervalued women's capacities. Like their husbands, they generally believed that men should wear the pants in the family. When their husbands lacked courage and initiative, women followed the lead of another man, Sékou Touré. They donned the trappings of male authority only when their husbands would not. Even the most militant women rarely contested their husbands' right to plural wives, the nature of their marital obligations, or the gender division of labor in the domestic arena. Rather, they violated gender roles in order to create conditions in which they once again could fulfill those same gender roles. They believed that unusual circumstances required abnormal tactics. In the final analysis, during the nationalist period and its aftermath, "female" held sway over "feminist" consciousness.

Although gender roles were not permanently transformed by the nationalist struggle, women made an indelible mark on the movement. They formulated many of its fundamental demands. They created some of its most effective methods. They helped to make the broad-based ethnic, class, and gender alliance a reality. Without the massive participation of Guinean women, the RDA could not have built the grassroots structure so critical to its success. Along with veterans, workers, and peasants, women shaped the RDA from the bottom up.

6

ETHNICITY, CLASS, AND VIOLENCE: INTERNAL DISSENT IN THE RDA, 1955–1956

The RDA's struggle to forge an ethnic, class, and gender alliance was fraught with tensions and marred by setbacks. The mobilization of women revealed a gap between the RDA's progressive message of female emancipation and reality. The endeavor exposed divisions between men, as well as between men and women. While party leaders at the highest echelon promoted female emancipation, local male leaders and men of the rank and file were often adamantly opposed. Even women who violated gender norms frequently did so reluctantly. While some relished their newfound liberation, many believed that men should ultimately reassume society's dominant roles. Women would shoulder male responsibilities only if men failed to fulfill them, and only temporarily.

Tensions over female emancipation were not the only ones that threatened party unity in the mid-1950s. The RDA leadership and rank and file struggled incessantly over issues of ethnic exclusivism and ethnically based political violence. While the party's top echelons promoted the ideology of inclusive nationalism, the reality of regionalism, ethnic chauvinism, and class bias remained strong at the grassroots. Since the fraudulent elections of 1954, RDA membership had grown dramatically, and the party had consolidated its base in both town and country.[1] However, party ranks expanded more rapidly than the leaders' ability to educate the cadre. While RDA leaders remained deeply committed to transethnic nation building, they were often unable to convince the swelling grassroots membership on this point.

Disputes over tactics also threatened to tear the party apart. During the years of repression when the party had no legal means to promote its cause, extralegal maneuvers had become commonplace. By the middle of the decade, the party was no longer the underdog. Massive popular support and a relaxation of government repression had resulted in successive electoral victories. By 1956, the RDA had become the majority party. While the party leadership was ready to join the governing process, preaching adherence to the law and the mainte- nance of order, grassroots militants refused to concede that violent tactics were counterproductive.

Although RDA achievements were marred by escalating political and eth- nic violence, the party met with significant success in 1955 and 1956. In the rural areas, the struggle against the canton chieftaincy escalated as the party focused on abolishing, rather than reforming, the institution. Carrying its anti-chief message into the interior, the party successfully penetrated the last opposition stronghold: the intensely conservative, socially hierarchical Futa Jallon. The RDA's triumph in this bastion of chiefly authority was due largely to its effective mobilization of ethnic outsiders and people of lower class and slave ancestry. These groups had borne the brunt of chiefly imposi- tions and class-based discrimination. They would serve as the backbone of the RDA's electoral successes in the Futa Jallon. The RDA's superior grass- roots organization resulted in extraordinary victories at the polls, which gar- nered two out of three seats in the French National Assembly. However, fissures within the party continued to grow, and underlying conflicts remained unresolved.

ETHNICITY AND CLASS IN THE FUTA JALLON

One of the RDA's primary objectives was to build a nation that transcended ethnic boundaries, bringing people together as Guineans, rather than mem- bers of particular ethnic groups. Yet, party leaders were intensely aware of the potency of ethnic identity. Thus, for reasons of ideology and the practicalities of communication, RDA delegations generally included women and men of diverse ethnic backgrounds. While Susu, Malinke, and Peul militants focused on recruiting members of their own ethnic groups, their participation in mixed delegations sent a message of transethnic national solidarity.

The delegation that campaigned in Boké circle (Lower-Guinea) in 1955 is a case in point. That group included three women, Néné Diallo (Peul), Mafory Bangoura (Susu), and Yombo N'Diaye (Tukulor), as well as Sékou Touré (Malinke).[2] According to Néné Diallo, each woman concentrated on recruiting women of her own ethnic group:

> We were first assigned the role of interpreters, to translate what the leaders said into our respective languages. Mafory spoke Susu. Myself, I spoke Pulaar, because I am Peul. . . . They were very pleased to see that; it meant a lot to the people with whom we spoke.[3]

Leaving her base in Lower-Guinea, Néné Diallo also recruited Peul women in the Futa Jallon. She campaigned in Dinguiraye, an extremely conservative Muslim city—the one-time headquarters of the nineteenth-century Muslim reformer and empire builder El-Hadj Umar b. Said Tall. According to Léon Maka, before the coming of the RDA, one never saw a woman in the streets of Dinguiraye, not even in the marketplace.[4] Mira Baldé recalled, "It was Néné Diallo who brought out the women of Dinguiraye; it was Néné Diallo who made them bloom."[5]

Aissatou N'Diaye was another Conakry militant who rallied Peul women to the party. Of Tukulor ancestry, an ethnic group closely related to the Peul, N'Diaye spoke Susu, Maninka, Pulaar, and Wolof. "Whenever the RDA needed someone to go out and mobilize Peul women," noted her son, Siaka Sylla, "they sent [Aissatou N'Diaye]. She went to the Futa to mobilize women."[6]

While the RDA was frequently characterized as the party of the Susu and Malinke, and the BAG as the party of the Peul, this portrayal is overly simplistic.[7] In Guinea, as elsewhere, class cleavages often masqueraded as ethnic ones, and class solidarity frequently transcended ethnic boundaries. Of the grassroots RDA activists who championed class unity over ethnic exclusiveness, Néné Diallo was exemplary. A Conakry-based cloth dyer whose low-status Peul ancestors came from the Labé area, Diallo recalled that the RDA welcomed everyone. "It treated everyone like family," she said. "That is what I liked. They did not discriminate against the downtrodden or the poor. . . . You know, rich and poor people are not alike. . . . Sékou's group did not have wealth."[8]

Diallo claimed to be among the first Peul women to join the party. Kinship and common ethnicity were irrelevant to her choice, Diallo continued, although such bonds were so strong that she used the terms interchangeably. Diallo joined the party that would help her: the RDA, as personified by Sékou Touré. "The other [parties] did nothing for me," Diallo recalled. Despite their common ethnicity, the Peul aristocrats who led rival parties spurned her, undoubtedly because of her low social status and probable slave origins.[9] "Even if they were my mother, I would not support them," Diallo exclaimed.

> Why were they opposed to Sékou? Sékou worked for us. Allah and his Envoy are my witness. He told us he had no material things to offer, but he stood up for us and respected us. That is why we followed him. Diawadou [the BAG leader] is my kin. Barry III [the DSG leader] is my kin. Although Sékou did not give us anything, he cared for us. . . . Sékou stood up for the victims' rights. When he stood up for [a Peul man who had been killed by a white man], he won the hearts of all Guinean women.[10]

Aissatou N'Diaye also joined the RDA because of its ethnic and class inclusiveness. Although the DSG and the BAG were dominated by Peuls,

they had ignored her—probably due to her lower-class status—until they recognized her successful work on behalf of the RDA. "Why did I decide to join
the RDA?" she queried.

> Look, the Socialists were here. Nobody ever asked me to join them. No one
> came to me and said, "Come and join our party." The BAG was also in
> town. Nobody came to tell me that they had begun a movement that I could
> join. . . .
>
> One cannot join a cause if one has not been invited. On this street where
> I live, this is where Yacine Diallo [the Socialist deputy] stayed when he was
> in town. Nobody from that compound spoke to me about anything. As a
> matter of fact, I fetched water from the tap on their compound. They con-
> cocted all sorts of stories on that compound; they pretended we did not
> exist. I would go to fetch water sometimes and hear Barry Diawadou and
> Yacine Diallo arguing about things. Barry III, the Socialist, had a family
> near my aunt's. They had a huge compound there. Neither he nor his family
> contacted either my aunt or me about what they were doing.
>
> Had these two groups asked us to join them, perhaps I would not have
> listened to anyone else. But they had no consideration for us. Maybe they
> thought I was not a human being. I do not know. Otherwise, before I was
> informed about things, it is likely that I would have gone with the first
> group that contacted me. . . .
>
> After the RDA women's committee was set up under the leadership of
> Mafory, Mafory's group sent for me. Marie Sandé came to see me. She
> explained that they were organizing women and that she hoped I would
> join. She added that many people knew of me and trusted me and that I
> should join them. She told me everything about the RDA. She said it was
> about being ourselves, being free. Marie Sandé said that she was sent to ask
> me, in the name of Allah and His Envoy, to also accept to lead the move-
> ment in my neighborhood. I had just weaned Siaka [my second son]. I
> thought that was fair and agreed to join. That is how I joined. . . .
>
> A month after I began working with the people—and was meeting with
> success—Karim Bangoura, who was BAG, came to see me. He praised me
> for my hard work and suggested that I join his group. I said that it was a bit
> too late, because he never acknowledged me until the [RDA] had come to
> talk to me. I told him that I could not leave the people who had trusted me
> and to whom I had given my word. I added that besides, our side seemed to
> be growing faster, as evidenced by the recent confrontations among the var-
> ious groups in town. I said, "Look at the crowds following the RDA. That's
> where the people are!"[11]

Class was a central issue in the Futa Jallon. While aristocrats dominated the
region politically, people of slave ancestry constituted a significant proportion of its population. In 1905, the official year of emancipation, colonial
administrators estimated that one-half to two-thirds of the Futa's population

was composed of slaves.[12] Out-migration after emancipation, low birth rates, and high death rates resulted in a diminution of the slave and former slave populations. Thus, a 1954–1955 survey indicated that among 852,000 Pulaar speakers in the Futa Jallon, 202,000 (one-quarter) were slaves, former slaves, and their descendants.[13] In slavery, class and ethnicity overlapped. The majority of the slave population had descended from the original Jallonke inhabitants—agriculturalists who had been conquered by the Fulbe-Peul during the Islamic jihads of the eighteenth century—and from war captives imported into the region.[14]

As the RDA penetrated this aristocratic Peul stronghold in 1955, class became a primary focus of the party. People of slave descent were targeted by party organizers. Having borne the brunt of colonial oppression, this population was particularly hostile to the colonial regime and the Peul aristocrats and chiefs who sustained it. A number of factors contributed to their antagonism. People of slave ancestry were disproportionately represented among forced labor and military recruits.[15] Although slavery had been outlawed in 1905, some former slaves still served their erstwhile masters without pay.[16] Social and economic discrimination against freed slaves and their descendants continued unabated.[17]

Labé circle, whose population included a particularly high proportion of former slaves, was rapidly mobilized by the RDA.[18] Slaves constituted 60 percent of the circle's population at the time of emancipation. The figure was still significant in 1953, when one-third of Labé's inhabitants were of slave descent.[19] People of slave ancestry found new status as party leaders and campaigned enthusiastically for the party that had "liberated" them. According to RDA activist Bocar Biro Barry, himself a renegade Peul aristocrat,

> In Labé . . . we took a former slave, a certain Samba Safé. . . . The party used Samba Safé to do violence to the ethic of the Peul civilization. He said to himself, "All these people here are my masters. Now, the party has taken me; it has made me the leader. So, I am going to show them how I am now enfranchised!" This is how the party penetrated the Futa.[20]

Once again, the party's success was due largely to its focus on issues of deep concern to the local population. RDA propaganda denounced class-based discrimination, opposing former slaves with Peul aristocrats on numerous issues. The party challenged the wide-ranging inequality of rights between free Peuls and those of slave descent. In particular, it decried the fact that descendants of slaves had weaker rights to land and other property. They had less access to education and civil service positions—a turnabout from the time when aristocrats boycotted colonial schools. Men of slave descent bore the brunt of military service; they were recruited in times of war, while free Peuls were conscripted in peacetime. Finally, men of slave ancestry were prohibited from marrying free Peul women.[21] The RDA's stand on these issues had widespread appeal among large segments of the Futa's population.

Although the RDA's foothold in the Futa was strongest among those of slave ancestry, other low-status populations eagerly joined the RDA as well. These recruits included "bush" or "cow" Peuls, low status but free people who herded cattle for the aristocratic minority.[22] The RDA made significant inroads among the Jakhanke, a Mande-speaking people closely related to the Malinke, who worked as traders, farmers, and Islamic scholars. Like the Jallonke, the Jakhanke had settled in the Futa prior to Peul arrival.[23]

The RDA also met with success among the ethnically diverse peoples in low-status occupations, notably traders, artisans, and griots. Once again, class and ethnicity intersected. Trading, considered to be of low status, was usually the province of the Malinke, Jakhanke, and Jallonke.[24] Prior to emancipation, artisans were generally slaves and low status but free Peuls, Malinkes, and Jallonkes. After abolition, many former slaves sought work as cloth dyers (women), blacksmiths, weavers, tailors, basket makers, leather workers, copper workers, and butchers, further entrenching the low regard for these crafts.[25] Because blacksmiths, griots, former slaves, and other people of caste lived in separate villages—apart from the Peul aristocracy—they could be mobilized in relative secrecy. The RDA used this residential segregation to its advantage.[26]

Photo 6.1   Male weavers, Labé, Futa Jallon. *(La Documentation Française)*

Police reports and RDA activists confirm the ethnic-, class-, and occupation-based nature of RDA recruits in Labé. In October 1954, the police noted that M'Bemba Diakabi, a master carpenter of the Jakhanke ethnic group, was among the most active RDA militants in Labé circle.[27] In February 1955, the police noted that the RDA was making significant headway among returned war veterans, who were primarily of slave origin.[28] Finally, RDA activist Bocar Biro Barry noted that in Labé, the RDA was particularly strong among the low-status blacksmiths, many of whom were Malinke.[29] The RDA's heavy reliance on non-Peul recruits was mirrored elsewhere in the Futa. For instance, the Gaoual circle commandant noted in August 1955 that the RDA was growing stronger in his circle, particularly in the Youkounkoun subdivision, where the Coniagui people were especially receptive.[30]

Geographically, the RDA took root most readily in the more ethnically diverse regions of the Futa Jallon. According to Bocar Biro Barry, Labé, Mamou, and Dabola were the most cosmopolitan cities in the Futa, and they rapidly became RDA strongholds. The inhabitants of Labé included Peuls, Tukulors, Jallonkes, Jakhankes, and Malinkes. Mamou was located at the crossroads of trade between Upper-Guinea (Malinke), Lower-Guinea (Susu), the Futa Jallon (Peul), and the forest region (Kissi, Loma, Kpelle). Dabola, also situated between regions (Upper-Guinea and the Futa Jallon), claimed a Malinke majority and a Peul minority.[31] In these three cities, Barry noted, the RDA attracted its first followers from among the non-Peul ethnic groups—the original non-Peul inhabitants, including and especially the former slaves, as well as "outsiders" to the region such as Malinkes, forest people, and coastal Susus.[32]

RDA women, like their male counterparts, were heavily recruited from among the non-Peul population. "Who mobilized women in the Futa Jallon?" queried Bocar Biro Barry.

Among the Peul, a woman was not supposed to address her husband while standing upright. She was to address him formally and never to say his name. For a Peul woman to get up on a table and harangue a mixed crowd was shocking. It was not the Peul women who did those things in the Futa Jallon. They would not dare.[33]

In Labé circle, female "outsiders"—Malinkes, Susus, and forest people—rather than Peul women composed the ranks of the RDA women's subsection.[34] In Labé town, most of these "outsiders" lived in the Dowo-Sare neighborhood. The neighborhood's ethnic mix was reflected in its RDA women's committee, where in 1954 the provisional officers, as well as the rank-and-file members, were of Malinke, Susu, and Wolof background. According to the police, "The Peul women have refused to involve themselves in any way in this provisional bureau."[35]

Photo 6.2   Malinke women spinning and dying cloth. (CAOM)

In Mamou, the RDA women were led by Tourou Sylla, a lower-class Malinke woman who was a cloth dyer by trade, a profession Peul aristocrats derided as unclean and fit only for former slaves. Her husband, a dark-skinned Maraka or Soninke, was a former slave and a butcher, another purportedly unclean profession and one of those most disparaged by light-skinned, aristocratic Peul society.[36] According to Bocar Biro Barry,

> The RDA said, among the women it is better to take a Malinke from [the Mamou neighborhood of] Kimbely, not a Peul. She will not be afraid to confront the Peuls, because she is not Peul. She is not bound by the Peul discipline, by the Peul civilization. This is what explains the rise of a woman like Tourou Sylla in Mamou.

While Peul women might have demurred, Sylla actually enjoyed upsetting aristocratic Peul elders by violating social norms.[37]

Tourou Sylla's own recollections offer further insights into the class-based nature of the struggle, the inextricable linkage of gender and class, and Sylla's willingness to challenge Peul aristocrats. In a 1968 interview conducted by R. W. Johnson, Sylla recalled:

> The Party came and I realised I was the slave of a slave. We struggled among the women to awaken their consciousness too. I was often in trouble

with the police because we attacked the wife of the *Commissaire de Police* for not making her husband respect women. We went into the *roundé* (slave villages) and also attacked the chiefs through their wives. We struggled to destroy the chiefs' families by getting a majority of their wives to divorce them for the way they treated the people.[38]

As in Labé, female militants in the Mamou neighborhoods were ethnically diverse. Among the first RDA women activists were Oumou Cissé, Mama Traoré, Aissata Konaté, Yama Diouf, and Fatoumata Horefello, who were Susu, Malinke, Wolof, and Peul.[39] According to Tourou Sylla, "Fatoumata Horefello was Peul. The leader of the Boulbinet women was Malinke. Poudrière's leader was also Malinke. . . . Susu women were leaders, too. . . . You know, most Peuls were with the others, but we had Peul women among us."[40]

The same pattern was repeated in other Futa circles. In Pita circle, the women's committee executive included Fatoumata Fofana, Aissata Camara, Bobo Barry, Maciré Sylla, Yakha Touré, Kadiatou Soumah, Terrin Camara, Nassirou Kéïta, Aissata Sylla, and Fanta Sané. Only Bobo Barry was Peul.[41] The predominance of Malinkes and Susus on the women's committee executive also pertained in Toumania in Télimélé circle. In Dalaba, half the women's committee executive was Peul, while Malinkes, Susus, Jakhankes, and Tukulors made up the rest.[42]

Only after the RDA was well established among the non-Peul residents of the Futa Jallon did it succeed in penetrating the Peul population. Among the Peul, the first to join were the low-status craftsmen and cattle herders. These were followed by the intellectuals—the Western-educated "modernizing" elite. According to Barry, many Peul intellectuals joined the RDA when they were students at the elite federal school École Normale William Ponty. A large number became teachers who, upon their return to Guinea, took the RDA to the villages where they were posted.[43] Police reports corroborate Barry's assessment. Since the legislative elections of June 1954, the police noted, RDA mobilization in Labé circle had resulted in a large number of new members. Civil servants, particularly teachers, were the force behind the recruitment drive.[44]

The identification of party with class was complicated by the fact that profession and class did not always coincide. Peul intellectuals, in particular, straddled class categories. While many came from low-status backgrounds, others were scions of the "traditional" elite.[45] Composed of a handful of wealthy families, rendered exclusive through intermarriage, Peul aristocrats relied heavily on colonial authorities to secure their hold on power.[46] In keeping with their class interests, most "traditional" elites remained loyal to fellow aristocrats—Barry Diawadou (BAG) and Barry III (DSG), in particular.[47] However, intellectuals of aristocratic background were sometimes influenced by their low-born peers. Hence, a small group of Peul aristocrats joined the RDA.

Bocar Biro Barry was a case in point. A Western-educated intellectual, Barry was a graduate of the elite William Ponty school, a teacher, and a trade unionist. He was also a grandson of the Almamy of Timbo, Bokar Biro—a powerful politico-religious leader who resisted French conquest until he was killed in battle in 1896. For nearly two centuries, the Almamy of Timbo had been the most important political and religious leader of the Futa Jallon, ruling over a confederation of nine provinces. After Bokar Biro's death, the French authorities moved his successor from the central location of Timbo to Dabola, on the fringes of the Futa Jallon. The Almamy's status was reduced to that of canton chief—and collaborator with the colonial regime. Throughout the colonial period, the Barry family dominated the political scene in Dabola, working closely with the colonial administration. During the height of RDA activities in the 1950s, Barry Diawadou led the rival BAG and served as a deputy in the French National Assembly. His father, Almamy Barry Aguibou, one of Bokar Biro's successors, was the Dabola canton chief. It was in this context that Bocar Biro Barry broke with his family and class to work with the RDA.[48]

Although unusual, Bocar Biro Barry was not the only Peul aristocrat to turn his back on his class. Even more prominent was Saïfoulaye Diallo, who, in January 1956, was elected to the French National Assembly on the RDA ticket. The son of Alpha Bocar Diallo, a canton chief in Labé circle and a senior member of the Futa chieftaincy, Saïfoulaye was also a grandson of Alfa Yaya Diallo, the chief of Labé province and another early resister to French conquest. An arch rival of Bokar Biro, Alfa Yaya eventually collaborated with the French to defeat him. However, he was, in turn, arrested and deported, dying in exile in 1912. Along with his strong traditionalist credentials, Saïfoulaye Diallo was also a member of the Western-educated elite. Like Bocar Biro Barry, he studied at William Ponty, where he graduated first in his class. A member of the GEC, Diallo attended the RDA's founding congress in Bamako in 1946 and was one of Guinea's earliest RDA activists.[49]

ETHNICITY AND VIOLENCE AT THE GRASSROOTS

Even as the RDA penetrated the Futa Jallon, attracting low-status Peuls as well as ethnic "outsiders," opponents continued to characterize the party as anti-Peul. Asserting that its campaign was against the Peul aristocracy rather than the ethnic group as a whole, the RDA leadership aggressively promoted its platform of transethnic nation building, based on the common experience of colonial oppression. Intellectuals writing for the local party newspaper, *La Liberté,* decried the attempts of RDA adversaries to convince Peuls that the RDA was their enemy. "The RDA defends and will always defend the Peuls, as it does all other Africans," one writer concluded.[50]

While many RDA activists embraced the party's nation-building appeals, others failed to distinguish between their rivals' ideological and ethnic differences. These RDA members, like their antagonists, succumbed to the simplistic view that the RDA was the party of Malinkes and Susus, while the BAG was the party of Peuls. In the ethnically diverse coastal areas, politically inspired violence at the grassroots increasingly took on an ethnic character.

As popular unrest spread, cleavages deepened between the territorial and local RDA leadership and between the territorial leadership and the rank and file. While the territorial board of directors (and its interterritorial counterpart) consistently appealed for calm and urged nonresponse to provocations, local leaders were more tolerant of their constituents' violent reactions. While the territorial leadership constantly appealed to a sense of transethnic national identity, local leaders and their constituents were more likely to perceive differences in ethnic terms. The result was a series of contradictory messages that left the population angry and confused.[51]

Known for employing anecdotes, parables, and imagery to mobilize nonliterate populations, Sékou Touré increasingly used them to comment on the ethnic situation. To one crowd, Sékou Touré proclaimed that human beings differed only superficially: "Man is like water, equal and alike at the beginning. Then some are heated and some are frozen and so they become different. Just change the conditions, heat or freeze, and the original equality is again clear." Turning his attention to the particular situation in Guinea, he continued, "Do you think you are Soussou, Malinke, Bambara? No, you are water and you are equal. At sunset when you pray to God say over and over that each man is a brother, and that all men are equal."[52]

Superficial characteristics such as a name or style of dress were often used to identify a person's ethnic group or nationality, Sékou Touré said. However, if that person were simply to change his name and clothing, he would be classified by another label. Thus, Sékou Touré contended,

> If I wore a grey *boubou* and were called Amadou Guèye and spoke Wolof you would think me Senegalese. If I wore a white cloth and spoke Bambara and were called Mamadou Sissoko you would think me Soudanese. If I wore tan wool and spoke Fulani and were called Diallo Alpha you might think me Soudanese. If I wore khaki trousers and spoke Ewe you would think me Togolese. But I am called Sékou Touré and I am Soussou and I speak Soussou. But I also speak Bambara, and Malinke, and Wolof. . . . I change my clothes and I change my language. The clothes can change and the language can be learned. I am like you; I am a man like you; my race is African.[53]

RDA women, with whom Sékou Touré had such a personalized relationship, were not immune from his criticism. At numerous meetings he chastised women for what party leaders deemed inappropriate songs. One popular song focused on Barry Diawadou's ethnicity rather than his program and insulted all Peuls, not just the RDA rival.[54] Requesting a personal favor, Sékou Touré, beseeched the women,

> Will you do something for me? I know you are angry at Diawadou. Anger makes us stupid. Use the anger against me and so cure your anger. Do not play the song again. Do not dance the song again. Forget the song. The [Peul] is your brother. He is the most oppressed, the saddest, the poorest. Diawadou is not [Peul]. Diawadou is without a country. You are [Peul]. You are all races.[55]

While tensions between the Peul and other ethnic groups attracted the most attention, cross-ethnic strains were not limited to these.[56] In the multiethnic forest region, Malinke men were disproportionately influential. As traders, craftsmen, and religious leaders, they were mobile, literate, and urbanized. They frequently dominated the leadership of RDA subsections and committees.[57] Ethnic divisions existed even among people who spoke a common tongue. The police reported that on the island of Kassa, off the coast of Conakry, there were two competing RDA women's committees—one composed of natives of Kassa, and the other of coastal immigrants: Landumas, Bagas, and Mandegines.[58] Yet all of the women were Susu speakers.

If the RDA leadership and rank and file were divided over the ethnic question, they were also at loggerheads over the issue of violence. By the mid-1950s, the territorial leadership, anxious to establish a working relationship with the colonial administration, was convinced that the maintenance of law and order was necessary for the achievement of its objectives.[59] Local leaders, under pressure from the rank and file, were more apt to call for a tit-for-tat response to provocations.[60]

Guinean youths were among those who most vehemently contested their leaders' pleas for calm. Since its second party congress in October 1950, the Guinean RDA had made a conscious effort to mobilize the territory's young people, establishing separate youth committees at the village and neighborhood levels.[61] In December 1954, the disparate RDA youth committees were brought together in a single organization, the Rassemblement de la Jeunesse Démocratique Africaine (RJDA).[62] The establishment of the RJDA underscored the increasing prominence of youths on the Guinean political scene. In general, the youth were more radical than their elders, impatient with the slow pace of change, and prone to independent action.[63] The large number of restless, unemployed youths clustered in the urban areas was both a boon to the RDA and a challenge.[64]

Conflict between the RDA's territorial leadership and the grassroots was evident from the beginning of 1955. On January 21, 1955, the French National Assembly validated Barry Diawadou's victory in the June 1954 legislative elections, sparking a wave of unrest in Guinea.[65] During the volatile period that followed, the RDA's territorial board of directors urgently appealed for calm. However, at the local level, a divergent sentiment prevailed. At a January 23 youth meeting in Conakry, Fodé Bangoura, a clerk at the city hall, pleaded with party youths to avoid all further provocations. He urged them to report to the police if they were attacked by rivals, rather than taking matters into their own hands. He advised them to calm their wives, who, he said, must stop insulting the new deputy. Police spies reported that Bangoura's words were not universally well received; a few murmurs of disapproval rippled through the crowd.[66]

The furor over the election validation was followed by violent incidents in Tondon, culminating in the killing of RDA militant M'Balia Camara, wife of the local RDA president, by the canton chief David Sylla. Again, the RDA leadership urged party members to respect law and order. On February 18, 1955, the day of Camara's death and burial, the territorial board of directors issued a communiqué urging the population to refrain from violence. The message, reprinted in the March 1 issue of *La Liberté,* was widely circulated.[67]

On March 5, with rural unrest still pervasive, territorial leaders, male and female leaders of the Conakry RDA subsection, and delegates from the interior gathered in the capital city. Sékou Touré enjoined them to preach calm in their areas and to use every means to reestablish order. Bengaly Camara and Sinkoun Kaba were appointed to tour the interior with the same message. The interterritorial RDA's political director, Ouezzin Coulibaly, who had been sent by Houphouët-Boigny to bring the Guinean RDA back into line, warned the assembly, "It is a matter of stopping the masses in their actions. I ask you to do what is necessary toward that end. The methods now employed cannot serve any political party."[68]

That very day, the RDA board of directors' law-and-order message was carried to the Conakry neighborhood of Boulbinet, where a crowd of some 300 people, including 200 women, had assembled. It was Mafory Bangoura herself who urged the crowd to obey the leadership's directives.[69] Three days later, approximately 100 RDA women met in the Conakry suburb of Coléah, at the home of the local women's president, Mabinty Soumah. Soumah explained the directives given by Sékou Touré and Ouezzin Coulibaly during the March 5 meeting. She added, "I, myself, have noted that certain RDA women provoked their neighbor women in non-RDA households. Our role is not that; we must convince our comrades without molesting them."[70]

The governor confirmed that the RDA leaders' appeal for calm and respect for the law was broadly disseminated.[71] Both the governor and Secretary of State Pruvost, head of the government team investigating the unrest, acknowledged that the violence would have been far more serious had it not been for the appeasement efforts of RDA leaders, notably Sékou Touré and

Ouezzin Coulibaly, who urged popular acceptance of the official election results.[72] Numerous government sources, as well as the international press, reported that local RDA leaders and territorial leaders from Conakry attempted to placate the crowds and help restore order following the violence in Tondon.[73]

Although many local leaders followed the territorial directives, not all saw eye to eye with the party's highest echelons. Dissenting leaders often held views that were closer to those of their grassroots constituents. The Kankan subsection was a case in point. On February 27, 1955, at a public meeting attended by some 500 people, local RDA leader Moriba Magassouba warned of plots and rumors against the RDA. Despite the apparent urgency of the situation, he followed the orders of the territorial board of directors, admonishing, "Don't provoke anyone." However, he closed the speech with his own advice:

> But at the same time, always be ready to react against provocateurs! We are ready to defend you, all the way to Paris, against anyone, no matter what his individual importance and his social rank! . . . In conclusion, I ask you one more time to never resign yourselves, but, to the contrary, to react vigorously against provocateurs.

His militant words, welcomed with lively applause, were echoed by Sayon Mady Kaba, another leader of the Kankan subsection. Kaba also warned the populace not to provoke anyone, but noted that people were not precluded from reacting to provocateurs, no matter who they were. "As Magassouba said, we will support you in all circumstances," he concluded.[74]

When the subsection met again on March 6 to promulgate the territorial board of directors' latest appeal for calm, only 150 people were present. Moriba Magassouba executed an unacknowledged about-face that left the audience bewildered:

> As I advised you last week, I ask you again today to remain calm. The board of directors in Conakry sent us a document asking us always to remain calm. If adversaries insult you, wound you, strike you, trample on you—stay calm and never respond to these provocations. Address your complaints first to the board of directors.

A police spy overheard one audience member mutter,

> What is this about? They have always told us here to respond to all of our adversaries' provocations. They told us that we would be defended, all the way to Paris, if need be. The treasury of the party was made for that. Today, they advise us to remain passive before provocations of all sorts. They even threaten us with expulsion from the R.D.A. We do not understand a thing![75]

In spite of their best efforts, the governor noted, RDA leaders had been "overwhelmed by the grassroots militants."[76] Appeals from on high produced little effect.

If the uncontrolled militancy of the masses concerned the RDA's territorial leadership, it caused even greater consternation at the interterritorial level. From July 8–12, 1955, the interterritorial RDA's Coordinating Committee held a congress in Conakry to elaborate its new policy of moderation and collaboration. In choosing Conakry as its venue, the interterritorial party hoped to exert a moderating influence on the Guinean branch. Although it was the supreme governing organ of the interterritorial body, the Coordinating Committee had not met since 1950, when RDA parliamentarians, under pressure from the French government, severed their ties to the PCF. During the 1955 congress, the Coordinating Committee confirmed the parliamentarians' disaffiliation decision, rendering it binding.[77] It further resolved to expel all dissident sections still operating with communist sympathies. Finally, it promoted a policy of détente with the chieftaincy and collaboration with the colonial administration.[78]

To entrench the collaborationist line, the Coordinating Committee sought to reassert control over the Guinean RDA. The co-optation of Sékou Touré was crucial to this endeavor.[79] By the mid-1950s, a veritable personality cult had developed around Sékou Touré. In March 1955, Secretary of State Pruvost acknowledged that Sékou Touré was an "excellent orator, knowing how to reach the crowds. . . . He is the beneficiary of an incontestable prestige and a large audience in Guinea. . . . [He is the] idol of Lower-Guinea . . . and sufficiently popular in Upper-Guinea as in the forest region."[80] Likewise, the governor recognized Sékou Touré's tremendous hold over the local population, noting, "It is undeniable that Sékou Touré was able to show the degree of his personal ascendancy over the mass of Guinean militants on the occasion of demonstrations cleverly carried out and magnificently orchestrated."[81] If the Guinean RDA were to be tamed, the leadership had to be co-opted, and that meant Sékou Touré, first and foremost.

There had been previous attempts to corrupt Sékou Touré. In October 1951, the government had hoped to produce a schism in the French West African trade union movement by enticing Sékou Touré to establish an African trade union federation independent of the French communist–linked CGT.[82] Sékou Touré had not taken the bait. By the mid-1950s, however, Sékou Touré had achieved even greater renown as a nationalist than as a workers' hero.[83] Having risen to prominence through the trade union movement, Sékou Touré had used the workers' struggle as a launching pad for the nationalist one. In 1955, with working class issues securely subordinated to the broader nationalist program, Sékou Touré was prepared to break with his erstwhile allies in the CGT.

At the Coordinating Committee's Conakry congress, Sékou Touré completed his bow to the collaborationist line. Having endorsed the rift between the RDA and the PCF in October 1951, he now proposed the long-awaited break of African unions from the French CGT and the communist-dominated World Federation of Trade Unions.[84] Sékou Touré, once denounced by the government as a "notorious marxist" and a "fierce partisan of the Third International," was now regarded as an *interlocuteur valable*.[85]

In the aftermath of the Conakry congress, orders for moderation, emanating from the interterritorial and territorial leadership, were disseminated throughout the territory. Numerous public and private meetings were organized for this purpose. Interterritorial leaders employed their personal prestige on behalf of the new directives. Houphouët-Boigny visited the local committees in Conakry to champion the new cause.[86] Ouezzin Coulibaly, who had spent the first part of 1955 touring Guinea with Sékou Touré, continued to campaign on behalf of the RDA and its new policy. According to Morgenthau, it was the involvement of these interterritorial leaders, especially Coulibaly, that laid the groundwork for the Guinean RDA's "shift from the tactics and vocabulary of total opposition to those of partial communication with French officials."[87]

Initially, it was not clear whether local leaders and the rank and file would accept the accommodationist stance or derail the new agenda. Activists from across Guinea had come to the capital in droves to attend the interterritorial congress. Some 5,000 people had attended the public session on July 10.[88] With grassroots militants looking over their shoulders, local leaders embraced the new policy only hesitantly.[89] The Mamou RDA subsection was a case in point. At the behest of the territorial leadership, meetings to discuss the new accommodationist policy were held in Mamou on July 15 and 25.[90] On August 1, Pléah Koniba, an assistant doctor and secretary-general of the Mamou subsection, wrote an angry letter to the party's board of directors in Conakry.[91] On behalf of the subsection's bureau, he roundly criticized Sékou Touré's break with the CGT. He accused Sékou Touré of dictatorship within the party, fostering a personality cult, censoring the ideas of party members, holding numerous meetings with the high commissioner without witnesses, and catastrophic management practices. Pléah Koniba and the Mamou subsection demanded a return to collective leadership, the ideal of the party over the myth of the person, criticism and self-criticism within the party, and a trade union movement that was truly combative.[92]

A subsequent letter from the subsection's bureau raised similar concerns. It noted that on August 9, Sékou Touré had sent a circular to the high commissioner without consulting anyone. Written communications between the party and the administration were not the domain of the secretary-general alone, but of the territorial board of directors, the bureau noted. Further, all physical contacts between party leaders and the administration were to include at least three members of the leadership—to guard against corruption and illicit deal making. Yet, Sékou Touré had made many solo trips to Paris and Dakar, using those occasions to meet with government officials. In closing, the Mamou bureau reiterated the need for collective leadership and democratic methods within the party.[93]

Although some militants, such as those in Mamou, initially resisted the new accommodationist policy, by the end of the year the governor sensed victory. The territorial and interterritorial directives of calm and moderation were winning out. For the most part, the RDA was well organized, he wrote. Its adherents were disciplined, and orders were effectively diffused and followed, even in the most remote areas.[94] By the last trimester of 1955, grassroots hostility toward the new policy had "evolved little by little toward trust and collaboration."[95]

THE LEGISLATIVE ELECTIONS OF JANUARY 2, 1956

The ability of party leaders to control the rank and file was not nearly as effective as the governor believed. However, in the face of ongoing grassroots opposition, territorial leaders continued to promote inclusive nationalism as the RDA's ultimate goal. The mark of the party leadership was particularly evident in the legislative elections of January 1956. Recognizing its relative weakness among the Peul population, RDA leaders were determined to field a high-profile Peul candidate who would draw his brethren into the fold. The party first approached Barry III, leader of the severely weakened DSG, and invited him to join Sékou Touré on the RDA ticket. When Barry III rejected the proposition, the RDA turned to Saïfoulaye Diallo, who accepted it. Diallo's early militance on behalf of the RDA, as well as his GEC membership, had attracted the attention of colonial authorities. As a result, he had been transferred from Guinea and posted successively in the French Soudan and Niger.[96] Thus, in 1956, he was virtually unknown on the Guinean political scene. However, he had impeccable "traditional" as well as "modern" credentials.

The RDA made the most of Diallo's aristocratic background. Employing French Revolutionary imagery, *La Liberté* compared Diallo's actions to those of another aristocrat, the Marquis de La Fayette, who "renounced his privileges to join the democratic camp."[97] Like La Fayette in 1789, Diallo was considered by his rivals to be a traitor to his family and class. Putting class interests over family ties, Diallo's family opposed his election in 1956 and backed Barry Diawadou instead.[98]

Paying careful attention to regional, ethnic, and religious concerns, the RDA constructed a diverse list for the three National Assembly seats. Sékou Touré, a Muslim, was a Malinke from Upper-Guinea. Saïfoulaye Diallo, also a Muslim, was a Peul from the Futa Jallon. Joining them on the RDA ticket was Louis Lansana Béavogui, a Christian Loma from the forest region. The RDA did not field a candidate from the fourth geographic region, Lower-

Guinea, home to the Susu population and a major RDA stronghold. Confident of its strength in this area, the RDA concentrated its efforts on the rest of the territory.[99]

The electoral campaign officially began on December 13, 1955.[100] Leaflets signed by Sékou Touré, Saïfoulaye Diallo, and Louis Lansana Béavogui were widely distributed. Stressing the party's ethnic, class, and gender alliance, the leaflets were addressed to peasants, workers, soldiers, veterans, transporters, merchants, artisans, marabouts, and griots; and to men and women of all professions, ethnic groups, and religions. All Guineans were urged to vote en masse for the RDA, which was described as a movement for African emancipation and fraternity between the races and peoples.[101]

Once again, the RDA responded to the concerns of its grassroots constituents. It routinely presented itself as the liberator—responsible for the abolition of forced labor and other injustices. It credited itself with the implementation of the Overseas Labor Code, which ensured that workers and their families would receive just benefits. It supported rural cultivators in their demands for lower tax rates, reform of the SIP, and the parceling out of forest land. Identifying itself with the emancipation of the African people, the party promised even greater accomplishments in the future. The governor reported that the RDA's rhetoric was extremely powerful and "raise[d] the enthusiasm of the crowds."[102]

Popular fervor resulted in a highly successful voter registration campaign orchestrated by the RDA. With a large number of new members, the majority of whom were nonliterate, the party embarked on a program of civic instruction.[103] RDA cadres, including students and teachers on Christmas vacation, carefully tutored new adherents in voting formalities. They provided local leaders with circulars concerning voting regulations and established evening courses for officials who would man the polling stations. Finally, the party subsidized civil servants who had taken vacation without pay to mobilize for the RDA.[104] Even the governor grudgingly acknowledged the party's accomplishments. "It seems that the masses, especially in the bush, are beginning to interest themselves in electoral problems," he observed. "The flood of male and female voters, generally illiterate, understood the sense of the elections," he admitted, noting that "the education of the voting masses" was largely due to the work of the RDA.[105]

While mass meetings were held in the towns, the electoral campaign in the rural areas took shape primarily through the actions of RDA cells.[106] There was no formal campaigning in the RDA strongholds of Conakry and Beyla, the latter represented by Sékou Touré in the Territorial Assembly. Instead, Conakry-based cadres were urged to travel to their ancestral villages and mobilize the people there. Conakry women were charged with organizing the coastal areas, while men from Lower-Guinea were sent to the Futa Jallon.[107]

Thus, women as well as men explained the voting procedures and carried the party program to all the urban neighborhoods, rural villages, and hamlets.[108]

Once again, the party benefited from its broad-based class alliance. Teachers, trade unionists, and mobile populations such as Malinke traders and nurses involved in vaccination campaigns were particularly effective at mobilizing the masses.[109] Traders and transporters lent their vehicles to facilitate work in the rural areas. Local party officials provided food and lodging, as well as oil and gasoline, to large numbers of visiting cadres.[110] The RDA youth wing raised funds through dances and other social events.[111] Local women's committees arranged publicity and organized dances that attracted all the women of the area, as well as high-level RDA leaders from the capital.[112]

The party's grassroots campaign was enormously successful. Election day witnessed a massive outpouring of support for the RDA, which won 61.7 percent of the votes. The BAG came in second with 26 percent. The DSG trailed with 9.8 percent, while other parties took the remainder.[113] So overwhelming was its victory that the RDA only narrowly missed winning all three National Assembly seats.[114] In the end, Barry Diawadou managed to retain his seat, while the other two went to RDA candidates Sékou Touré and Saïfoulaye Diallo.[115]

RESUMPTION OF VIOLENCE AT THE GRASSROOTS

Throughout most of the territory, the RDA victory was celebrated without incident. According to the governor, this turn of events was largely due to "the good will and the sincere efforts of the R.D.A. leaders," who took their new responsibilities seriously. By telegram, letter, emissary, and direct intervention on the ground, members of the RDA board of directors spread the word and enforced the order that people should remain calm and respect the law. The party leadership was anxious to demonstrate that it could handle the responsibilities of victory and maintain the order necessary to govern.[116]

Once again, this broad-brushed portrayal did not capture the diversity of responses on the ground. In the interior of the territory, some RDA cells flagrantly disregarded the board of directors' orders. Although scattered incidents occurred throughout the territory, the most serious were in Lower-Guinea, where homes were burned and plantations destroyed.[117] While party leaders condemned the violence and property destruction, it was clear that they had little control over the rank and file in these areas. The governor observed:

> The ensemble of these incidents prove the difficulty with which the instructions for calm and objectivity, sent out by the leaders . . . of the RDA, are accepted at the base. The prevalence of calm or agitation will be the mea-

sure of their internal authority over their militants and the exact reflection
of the latter's political maturity.[118]

The RDA leadership made a determined effort to reassert control. In February 1956, a delegation from the capital was sent to the village of Boola in
Beyla circle. Representing the territorial leadership, Bengaly Camara warned
local RDA leaders that the party would abandon those who provoked violent
incidents.[119] Numerous circulars were also sent to local committees in the
interior, hailing the political maturity of the local population—as well as the
political neutrality of the administration in the recent elections. The circulars
warned militants to remain vigilant. Agents of rival parties hoped to lead them
astray. To thwart these plans, they should shun agitation and disorder and
refuse to respond to provocations. RDA circulars also instructed party members to change their attitudes toward colonial authorities, avoiding violence
and acerbic criticism. According to the governor, "This work of educating the
masses, recommended by the party, these appeals to calm have been taken up
in the course of numerous meetings" in Mamou, Kankan, and Labé before
thousands of people (in total).[120]

Although party leaders disavowed those who promoted violence and
unrest, and most militants heeded their warnings, street fighters continued to
garner strong grassroots support. In his monthly report, the governor noted
the divergence between the official instructions of party leaders and their
application at the local level. In Kankan, for instance, where RDA victory cel-
ebrations had "degenerated into brawls or aggressions," some militants complained that preaching calm when spirits were still hot was to show weakness.
The party must not renounce the courage, combative attitude, and methods
that had permitted it to oppose colonial oppression successfully, these partisans said.[121]

The colonial administration, which had recently treated all RDA members
as dangerous radicals, now championed the territorial leaders as moderates
searching for an acceptable modus vivendi with the administration. "It must
be underscored that the R.D.A. is a vast society open to all, whites and blacks,
in all brotherhood," wrote the governor. The problem, he continued, was that
territorial leaders were unable to filter their accommodationist attitude to the
grassroots—either to the local leadership or the rank and file. The result was
an extremely confusing and contradictory situation. Alongside territorial
leaders' efforts to create a climate of peace and confidence, the governor
claimed, one found vehement attacks against the administration and white
people in general. These sentiments were articulated in antigovernment, anti-
French slogans that were widely circulated in 1954–1956.[122]

The ambivalent position of local leaders further confounded the situation.
Their approach varied with their audience. When speaking to well-informed
évolués, local leaders were relatively reserved and "prudent," the governor

reported. In contrast, they applied no brakes when addressing the "more primitive and more malleable" populations of the interior. In such cases, their "demagoguery" was extremely virulent, he claimed. Kankan RDA leaders, including longtime agitator and subsection president Lamine Kaba, were a case in point. They directly challenged French authority with the slogan "The rule of the whites is over!"[123] Similarly, in Beyla circle, the president of the Simandougou subsection was Sékou "François" Camara, a former sergeant-major who campaigned vociferously against the French and the canton chiefs.[124]

THE STRUGGLE FOR NATIONAL UNITY

While ethnic rivalries, thinly disguised as party differences, continued to plague the grassroots, RDA territorial leaders persevered in their attempts to build a multiethnic nation. In July 1956, Saïfoulaye Diallo told a crowd of 4,000 in Kindia that during his victory tour of Guinea, he had been welcomed everywhere with enthusiasm. This spirited reception had proven that the RDA was not racist—that it was not only a party of Susus, Malinkes, and forest people—for people had come in huge numbers to acclaim a Peul.[125] In Mamou, Diallo addressed a crowd of 1,000 in Pulaar, vigorously opposing the struggle between ethnic groups, while Mouctar Dia, speaking in Susu, vehemently criticized the BAG.[126] In August 1956, Deputy Diallo toured the territory, covering 7,300 kilometers in Upper- and Lower-Guinea, the Futa Jallon, and the forest region. Everywhere, he preached the message of unity. In Conakry, he addressed a crowd of 2,000 in French, his remarks translated into Susu. "Our adversaries say that the Susus don't want the Peuls," he exclaimed. "That is false. The people are opposed to the B.A.G. and its harmful policies—not to the Peuls."[127]

Sékou Touré pursued this theme in September, when he addressed a Conakry crowd of some 2,000 people. Initially speaking in French—for the benefit of non-Susu elites and the colonial administration—his remarks were translated into Susu for the general populace. He then spoke exclusively in Susu. He exhorted the people not to consider family ties (ethnicity) in the upcoming municipal elections. Rather, the voters should simply clear out rotten elected officials and replace them with true democrats.[128]

Despite these appeals from on high, in Conakry and its suburbs, the period preceding the November 18 municipal council elections was punctuated by a series of violent ethnic incidents. Throughout the month of September and in early October, unruly mobs engaged in an orgy of violence.[129] In the most serious incidents, which occurred between September 29 and October 5, seven people were killed and hundreds injured. The dead included six Peuls and one Susu, the latter a BAG member.[130]

Since an estimated 80 percent of Conakry's population supported the RDA, BAG and DSG partisans were the most frequent targets of attack. According to a commonly reported scenario, RDA militants stopped passers-by, demanded to see their RDA party cards, and beat those who could not produce them. Quarrels between members of rival political parties rapidly degenerated into ethnic conflicts between Susus (predominantly RDA) and Peuls (mostly BAG and DSG). Susus began to systematically target Peuls, whether or not their party affiliation was known.[131]

On October 4, after reaching an accord, RDA, BAG, and DSG leaders toured the city and its suburbs in jeeps equipped with loudspeakers, urging their followers to desist from all violence.[132] Addressing a public meeting a few days later, Sékou Touré told Susus not to chase Peuls from their homes, because racial hatred risked provoking divisions in the heart of the party. He announced the opening of a fund to aid RDA members, both Susus and Peuls, who had been injured or whose homes had been pillaged during the latest incidents.[133]

Violence between Susus and Peuls in Conakry had repercussions elsewhere in the territory, particularly in the Futa Jallon. Because many Peuls who had settled in Lower-Guinea continued to view the Futa as their home, the chiefs and notables of the region remained their reference points. Desperately seeking an end to the violence, the RDA board of directors sent a delegation including Saïfoulaye Diallo to the Futa Jallon to negotiate with the notables.[134]

Meanwhile, in Conakry, Sékou Touré continued to preach inclusive nationalism, stressing the common oppression of all Guineans. Informing a crowd of some 1,200 that their deputy had gone to the Futa, he noted: "The R.D.A. is the party of the Peuls. . . . If I tell you that the RDA is the party of the Peuls, it is because it is in the Futa that the pressure of the customary chiefs is felt the most." He reminded the crowd that "Saïfoulaye" in Arabic meant "saber," and that Saïfoulaye Diallo was the knife that would cut the cords binding the Peuls who were oppressed by the chiefs.[135] Addressing another Conakry crowd of 3,000, Sékou Touré reiterated that the RDA was not racist. In the RDA "we do not have Peuls, Malinkes, or Susus, etc. . . . but Africans." He carefully drew distinctions between Europeans, some of whom were potential allies. There were bad ones, with whom the BAG was working, he said. However, there were also good ones. "We must join with the good ones in the anticolonial struggle," he declared.[136]

Despite attempts by RDA leaders to unite all people as Guineans, ethnic tensions, always close to the surface, exploded repeatedly. In order to minimize ethnically motivated jealousies, a number of strategies were employed. First, ethnic balance was maintained within the territorial leadership. The four highest ranking leaders were members of ethnic groups from Guinea's four geographical regions: Sékou Touré was a Malinke from Upper-Guinea; Saïfoulaye Diallo was a Peul from the Futa Jallon; Louis Lansana Béavogui was a Loma from the forest region; and Bengaly Camara was a Susu from Lower-Guinea.[137] Second, to promote national rather than ethnic identity, the RDA had begun to disband all ethnic and regional committees within the party. By 1956, most local committees were organized exclusively on neighborhood or village, rather than ethnic or regional, bases. In Conakry, where many neighborhoods were ethnically mixed, ethnically diverse local committees were common.[138] Finally, RDA leaders refused to acknowledge publicly a person's ethnic group, claiming that everyone was a Guinean. According to Morgenthau, "Their very rigidity on this principle showed there was a problem."[139]

Pleas for transethnic solidarity were common themes in RDA publications. Writing in *La Liberté* shortly after the 1956 Conakry riots, RDA stalwart Moriba Magassouba implored,

> Our Peul brothers must know that there exists no age-old racial hatred between them and the Susus. They must know that in the current world, there are but two races; that which dominates and exploits in an inhuman fashion and that is composed of the national and international trusts, and that which is unremittingly dominated and exploited, composed of all the colonized peoples . . . Peuls and Susus.

The Peul, Susu, Malinke, Loma, Kpelle, Kissi, Coniagui, Baga, and Landuma people of Guinea were all brothers, subjected to the same regime of exploitation and daily humiliation, he argued. Divisions between them were provoked by the colonialists, who were afraid of the unity of all Guineans.[140]

Tibou Tounkara elaborated upon this theme. With *La Liberté* as his vehicle, he decried attempts to rally people on the basis of ethnicity or region. The RDA opposed these manipulative divide-and-rule tactics, which were employed by rivals to bolster their own influence. Throughout the previous decade, the RDA had vehemently resisted all ethnic or regional chauvinism and sought the unity of all Africans around a program of economic, social, and political emancipation.[141]

The prevalence of such articles is proof that ethnic cleavages within the Guinean population were a serious problem and that party leaders took the problem seriously. However, the articles also demonstrate the ease with which some leaders cast the blame elsewhere. The people's false consciousness was due to the manipulations of the colonialists and the divide-and-rule tactics of rival parties rather than the failure of RDA leaders to adequately educate the masses. The struggle to build an inclusive nation would continue through the remainder of the colonial period, and RDA successes would continue to be tarnished by ethnic violence.

CONCLUSION

The years 1955 and 1956 were pivotal for the RDA. Membership rolls grew dramatically, and the party consolidated its base. Rivals in the political arena and chiefs in the rural areas were severely weakened. The party's strug-

gle to build an ethnic, class, and gender alliance to bring about African emancipation seemed within reach. However, RDA achievements were undermined by escalating political and ethnic violence. Moreover, the party's rise
to power brought renewed dissension within the ranks. While territorial leaders attempted to build an inclusive national party, regional and ethnic chauvinism, compounded by class bias, continued at the grassroots. Local leaders
and activists, accustomed to their oppositional role, clashed with territorial
leaders who now shouldered the responsibilities of governing.

Since its overwhelming victory in the January 1956 legislative elections,
the RDA effectively had become part of the governing system. In light of the
party's new duties, respect for law and order was clearly in its interest. While
territorial leaders recognized January 1956 as a turning point, with legal
routes to representation now opened, local activists, having gained strength
through struggle and opposition, continued to employ old methods. Having
experienced years of repression and the obstruction of all legal means of
expressing their views, local militants were not convinced that the tide had
turned. According to the governor, they were neither inclined to work within
the law, nor to respect the programs defined by the RDA's interterritorial
Coordinating Committee.[142]

Like the rank and file, local party leaders were less responsive than territorial ones to the changed political situation. Many had begun their careers as
trade union activists and belonged to a long tradition of permanent opposition
to an established political and economic system. They had difficulty grap-
pling with the new circumstances, the fact that they were now part of the system and could not continue wholly to oppose it.[143]

Territorial leaders exacerbated the problem by refusing to publicly acknowledge indiscipline or dissension within the ranks. Some leaders blamed the ethnic violence on the divide-and-rule tactics of the colonialists.[144] Others
claimed that opposition parties had been paid to sow discord between Susus
and Peuls within the RDA.[145] Sékou Touré faulted outsiders, contending that
Peuls from Pita, who were sympathetic to the BAG, had been brought to
Conakry to provoke problems.[146] In the aftermath of a spate of bloody incidents in Conakry, the RDA board of directors sent a circular to all subsections,
charging that agents provocateurs were infiltrating RDA ranks with the intent
of goading militants into violent confrontations.[147]

Whatever its public face, the RDA board of directors was clearly concerned
about the breakdown of law and order—and its members' responsibility for it.
The board constantly reiterated the need to maintain the peace, without which
the RDA program could not be implemented. It warned RDA members not to
respond to provocations, whatever the source. "The tranquility that we preach
should be understood and explained at all echelons, and each militant should
anticipate and quash agitation," the leaders proclaimed.[148]

As the decade progressed, the gulf between the territorial leadership and the grassroots grew wider. The new system of local self-government, established in 1956 and 1957, would highlight the opposing interests of the leadership and the rank and file. As Guinea moved toward independence in 1958, it was the masses, rather than the leaders, who gained the upper hand. Shaping their movement from the bottom up, grassroots activists pushed the leaders sharply to the Left, decrying the limitations of local autonomy and championing the goal of immediate independence.

7

INDEPENDENCE NOW: THE RESURGENCE OF THE LEFT AND THE MOVE TOWARD INDEPENDENCE, 1956–1958

By the mid-1950s, the French empire was under attack on several fronts, most seriously in Indochina and North Africa. Again, France embarked upon a program of imperial reform. In sub-Saharan Africa, France established a system of local self-government, which in Guinea was quickly dominated by the RDA. In another wave of electoral victories, the RDA gained control of nearly all Guinea's major municipalities (November 1956) and swept away virtually all opposition in the Territorial Assembly (March 1957). Despite these successes, the party continued to be fraught by divisions, many of which were exacerbated by the RDA's rise to power and its leaders' contested determination to "rule responsibly." Once again, the party's ability to sustain a heterogeneous ethnic, class, and gender alliance was threatened.

Class, like ethnicity and violence, was a major source of tension between territorial leaders and the grassroots. The RDA leadership was composed primarily of lower-level civil servants—members of the Western-educated "modernizing" elite. Apart from this relatively small group, the party had focused its early appeals on the nonliterate majority of the population—peasants, unskilled workers, and women in the informal sector. Emphasizing the exploitative nature of the colonial system, it had targeted chiefs, notables, and European-owned enterprises. Thus, in the initial phase, the nationalist and class struggles had been virtually interchangeable. Nationalism was essentially a battle between the haves and the have nots. As the RDA gained power through mass mobilization and successive electoral victories, it attempted to broaden its base. Those previously considered class enemies were increasingly seen as potential recruits, particularly as the now governing party sought to fill technical and bureaucratic positions with "qualified" personnel. The rank and file cried foul, considering this move a betrayal of RDA principles.

Intergenerational tensions also grew more pronounced. Among the Western-educated elite, elders, wooed by government positions, were increasingly willing to work within the system. Students, especially the most privileged who had received French university diplomas, were less willing to compromise on principle. Having been exposed to Marxist and Pan-African ideals in France, these young men (and they were men) returned to Guinea as committed Leftists. They disparaged their elders, who seemed willing to accept crumbs from the French table rather than demanding the whole loaf. Young members of the teachers' union joined with students and other youths to push the party to a more radical stance.

In the September 1958 referendum, the people of Guinea, under the RDA banner, decisively rejected the constitutional project that laid the groundwork for the Fifth French Republic. Decrying it as a formula for junior partnership in a French-dominated community, grassroots activists had converged on the capital city and demanded that the party disavow the project. Resisting the appeals of interterritorial RDA leaders and critiquing their own leaders' conservatism, local-level actors promoted an alternative nationalist agenda. Led by trade unionists, students, and the party's women's and youth wings, the populace pushed the Guinean RDA to endorse a "No" vote. When Guinea opted for immediate independence in September 1958, it was the only French territory to do so. In the end, the leaders followed the masses, just as they had in the beginning.

LOCAL SELF-GOVERNMENT AND AFRICAN AUTONOMY

More than a decade after France began to reform imperialism in order to save it, the National Assembly granted limited self-government to the overseas territories. Paris conceded some control in order to forestall complete independence. Buffeted by the humiliating French defeat in Vietnam (1954), violent confrontations resulting in the independence of Morocco and Tunisia (1956), an escalating war in Algeria, and widespread grassroots mobilization elsewhere, the National Assembly recognized that concessions were essential.[1] The result was a new legal framework, or *loi-cadre,* enacted on June 23, 1956, which authorized the French government to implement a series of legal reforms in the overseas territories.[2]

Under *loi-cadre,* the overseas territories were retained within the frame-work of a unitary French Republic. As such, they continued to fall under the jurisdiction of the French constitution. However, the conduct of territorial affairs was decentralized and, to some extent, democratized. Some powers previously exercised by the appointed governor, high commissioner, and overseas minister, as well as the elected Grand Council in Dakar, were trans-ferred to elected governments in each territory.[3] Before the implementation of *loi-cadre,* territorial assemblies were primarily consultative rather than delib-erative bodies. The new legal framework granted the assemblies legislative powers in a number of areas, including territorial services, public works, land, conservation, agriculture, fisheries, and most mineral rights. The assemblies also gained responsibility for health, primary and secondary education, coop-eratives, urbanization, and the codification of indigenous law.[4]

Loi-cadre also established elected cabinets, or councils of government, that served as territorial executive bodies. Composed of 6 to 12 ministers, each council was overseen by the governor of the territory, who also served as the council president. The position of vice president was filled by the chief minis-ter. While the ministers were elected by the territorial assembly, the governor, a holdover from the old imperialism, was appointed by the French government.[5]

Just as it democratized some local government structures, *loi-cadre* democ-ratized the franchise, instituting universal suffrage for adult citizens of both sexes within a single electoral college. The last vestiges of the discriminatory two-tiered electoral system were abolished. The single electoral college, already in place in French West Africa for National Assembly and municipal elections, was instituted for all bodies, including territorial assemblies, circle (district) councils, and the Council of the Republic—the second chamber of the French parliament.[6]

Despite these moves toward democratization, imperial control remained strong. The governor, who continued as the territory's chief executive, still enjoyed substantial prerogatives. He was in charge of foreign affairs, defense, the fiscal and monetary system, and economic, social, and cultural develop-ment. He oversaw the council of government and could request that the terri-torial assembly reconsider its decisions and that the French government nullify those of the territorial assembly and council of government.[7]

The *loi-cadre* system fell short of independence in other ways as well. Met-ropolitan France preserved its dominant position in the overseas territories. The French parliament retained ultimate power over all legislation. State pub-lic services, as opposed to territorial ones, were still financed and controlled by Paris. The powerful circle commandants, appointed by the governor, were included within the framework of state public services and thus were not sub-ject to territorial control. Finally, the French government retained the power to dissolve African assemblies and to invalidate their decisions.[8]

Despite these shortcomings, *loi-cadre* was generally viewed by territorial political leaders as a progressive development. Before 1957, independence, as opposed to local political autonomy, was not on the mainstream African political agenda.[9] While segments of the student and youth movements had been agitating for immediate independence since 1956, the territorial leadership had merely used this pressure to extract more modest goals concerning local autonomy.[10] As late as December 1956, Sékou Touré had extolled the virtues of the Franco-African union, declaring that the future of France was inseparable from that of the people overseas and leading a crowd in the cheer "Long live Franco-African Fraternity!"[11]

While territorial leaders were anxious to benefit from colonial reforms, local leaders, under growing pressure from the grassroots, became more militant in their demands. Increasingly, they made reference to French departure and the end of colonial rule. In March 1957, for instance, RDA leaders in Siguiri inspired a crowd with the notion that Guinea, like France, would acquire its liberty after a revolution. "We want to be independent," the leaders cried. "The French have done nothing for us. They are in Africa uniquely for their own interests—not for ours. As soon as we have [African] ministers, we will show the bad French the door and replace them with those who please us."[12] Such ideas, emanating from the grassroots, increasingly infiltrated all levels of political discourse.

THE RDA'S RISE TO POWER

In an attempt to mollify African discontent, the imperial power had begun to democratize local government even before the enactment of *loi-cadre*. The law of November 18, 1955, instituted partially self-governing and fully self-governing municipalities in French West and Equatorial Africa. In both cases, elected municipal councils replaced commissions appointed by the governor. In each fully self-governing municipality, municipal councillors elected the mayor from among their members. Affairs previously under the authority of colonial officials thus devolved to elected municipal councils and mayors. In each partially self-governing municipality, the mayor was, as before, the European circle commandant. However, an assistant mayor, elected by the municipal council from among its members, was authorized to stand in for the mayor when absent. Five Guinean municipalities were designated as fully self-governing, while nine others were designated as partially self-governing.[13]

The municipal council elections of November 18, 1956, were the first to be held under the new universal suffrage law.[14] Mobilization by the RDA in the months preceding the elections led to a massive increase in the number of registered voters.[15] The extraordinary turnout on election day overwhelmingly benefited the RDA. In the five fully self-governing municipalities, 70 percent of the registered voters cast their ballots; 85 percent favored the RDA. In the nine partially self-governing municipalities, 66 percent of the registered electorate went to the polls, giving the RDA 63 percent of the vote.[16] Overall, the RDA won 243 of 327 municipal council seats, the position of mayor in all five fully self-governing municipalities, and the position of assistant mayor in eight of the nine partially self-governing ones.[17]

The March 1957 elections for the Territorial Assembly, the first territory-wide elections under the universal suffrage law, served as the second major testing ground for *loi-cadre*.[18] With significant new powers to run local affairs, the Territorial Assembly was far more important than previously. Moreover, the party winning the elections would dominate not only the legislative body but also the newly created executive body whose ministers would be elected by the Territorial Assembly.[19]

The RDA winning streak continued in landslide proportions. In the territorial elections of March 1957, the RDA won 75 percent of the vote, acquiring 56 of the 60 seats in the Territorial Assembly.[20] With the assembly firmly under RDA control, the first *loi-cadre* government was formed on May 14, 1957. Sékou Touré was elected vice president of the Council of Government, while Saïfoulaye Diallo was elected president of the Territorial Assembly.[21] Although the French governor remained Guinea's chief executive, the RDA had greater control over the organs of state than ever before. By the end of 1957, the party controlled two-thirds of Guinea's National Assembly seats, 74 percent of the municipal council seats, and 93 percent of the mayoral and assistant mayoral positions in the urban areas. All the ministers of the *loi-cadre* government and 57 out of 60 representatives in the Territorial Assembly were RDA, a member of the opposition having joined the party in September.[22]

With the formation of the *loi-cadre* government, the party rapidly consolidated its power, implementing significant reforms within the first several months.[23] The RDA government replaced the hated SIP with peasant-run cooperatives. It abolished appointed councils of notables in favor of district and village councils elected by universal suffrage.[24] Most notably, the *loi-cadre* government suppressed the despised institution of the canton chieftaincy.[25]

The canton chieftaincy's abolition was preceded by a high-level conference in July 1957, during which the Council of Government and the circle commandants discussed the pros and cons of the institution.[26] Rather than focusing on the abuses of the chiefs, as they had in the past, RDA leaders emphasized the chieftaincy's redundancy. They contended that the new system of semiautonomous government had rendered the colonial institution obsolete. For their part, the circle commandants, longtime champions of the chieftaincy, admitted that the canton chiefs no longer had effective powers and thus were no longer useful to the administration. Their functions now assumed by elected councils, the chiefs simply consumed a major portion of the local budget.[27] In the words of the governor, "We all know that the chieftaincy has terminated its role."[28]

In December 1957, two decrees issued by the Council of Government divested the canton chiefs of their powers. The decree of December 11, 1957, abolished the 26 "customary" tribunals that had provided the canton chiefs with judicial power.[29] This was followed by the decree of December 31, 1957, which officially abolished the institution of the canton chieftaincy.[30] Once again, RDA leaders had been propelled into action by a groundswell of opposition at the grassroots. While the RDA government had taken charge of the situation, the chieftaincy's abolition was, in the words of Suret-Canale, "the end result of a profound popular movement . . . the legal consecration of a popular revolution."[31]

Pushed upon the leadership by the rank and file, the decree of December 31, 1957, had enormous political ramifications. Throughout the 1950s, the chiefs had used their influence to manipulate elections to the detriment of the RDA. Rabidly hostile to the RDA, and with significant coercive powers at the local level, the chiefs, had they survived, may well have forced a different outcome to the September 1958 referendum.[32]

STRUGGLES OVER RACE, CLASS, ETHNICITY, AND REGION

Success exacerbated long-standing tensions within the party. While disputes over ethnicity and region continued to plague the RDA, issues of race and class increasingly came to the fore. In electoral contests, rank-and-file activists who had paid their dues in the struggle were increasingly sidelined by "qualified" candidates who had not. Among the most highly educated and privileged Guineans, "qualified" professionals were generally members of rival parties that were closely linked to the colonial administration. Others were Europeans or members of the mixed-race community. Thus, in many instances, race and class overlapped.

In preparation for the November 1956 municipal council elections, RDA leaders again attempted to broaden the party's base. Stressing the need for unity in the struggle against colonialism, territorial leaders called for an expansive alliance that welcomed candidates of all races, classes, ethnicities, and regions. Toward this end, they recommended the construction of "unity tickets" composed of candidates without regard to party affiliation.[33]

Despite party calls for grassroots participation, the diversity requirements were clearly imposed from the top down. To ensure the representation of women, Europeans, and "qualified" candidates, the RDA's territorial board of directors determined the shape and, to some extent, the composition of the local tickets. In Conakry, for instance, the board resolved that the RDA neighborhood committees would select 20 municipal council candidates. The women of Conakry would choose one. Eight seats would be reserved for Europeans, who would designate their own candidates. To ensure that at least some candidates were chosen for their professional qualifications rather than race, region, ethnicity, gender, or family ties, the board would select four professionals without regard to party affiliation.[34]

Recognizing the value of Europeans' skills and influence in the *loi-cadre* government—and hoping to thwart the development of an anti-RDA bloc—the territorial leadership avidly sought European candidates. Although RDA leaders claimed that they would work only with progressive whites, they seemed willing to stretch the definition when necessary.[35] In Conakry, for instance, BAG vice president Soriba Touré was stunned to learn that the RDA was courting establishment whites on BAG turf. At both the Chamber of Commerce and the Chamber of Agriculture and Industry, Soriba Touré found that Sékou Touré had preceded him, requesting that these institutions designate representatives for the RDA tickets.[36]

Race, class, and ethnicity were not the only divisive issues. In Kindia, the issue was regional rather than ethnic particularism. Citizens were hostile to the candidacy of individuals who, while Susu, were not natives of Kindia. Impatiently, Sékou Touré reminded his supporters that "what matters is not the place of birth, but the place of residence. A person does not have to be a native of the city to represent it well."[37] Sékou Touré's attempts at popular education failed to put the issue to rest. Following the municipal council elections, N'Famara Kéïta, a newly elected councillor, was chosen by his peers to serve as mayor. A number of citizens rejected this choice because Kéïta hailed from the village of Molota in Kindia circle, rather than the town itself. Once again, Sékou Touré endeavored to show the citizens the errors of their ways: "It is shameful to say that the mayor of Kindia is a native of Molota and not of your city, and as a result, should not occupy this place. According to this reasoning, the municipal council should have designated Sékou Fofana, who is a native of Kindia." According to a police spy, Sékou Touré's words sparked murmurs in the crowd, because Sékou Fofana was a BAG stalwart.[38]

Similar episodes transpired in Kankan, where critics complained that the subsection's secretary-general was not a Kankan native yet was a candidate in the municipal council elections.[39] Once again, Sékou Touré personally took the citizenry to task. On October 31, he addressed a crowd of some 1,000 people, indicating his concern. "I am upset by what is happening in Kankan," he said.

People want to make the elections a family affair. The citizens of Kankan are asleep. Our conferences have taught them nothing. The municipal elections have nothing to do with families—Kaba, Touré, Diané, etc. Of the 50 municipal councillors in Abidjan, only eight were originally from there. This is the spirit of the RDA. We Africans want to manage our own affairs.

This is the goal of the RDA. We do not see ethnicity or family or clan—only blacks. Your board of directors will establish slates of capable people—even whites—but good whites only.[40]

While combating ethnic and regional exclusivism, the RDA leadership also pushed hard on the gender front. Speaking to an RDA rally in November, Sékou Touré noted that 10 years previously, women were not present at political meetings. In 1956, however, no husband could prevent his wife from attending RDA functions. In previous elections, few women could vote; in November 1956, all men and women age 21 and over were eligible to be electors.[41] In the past, there were no female candidates. However, in the municipal council elections of November 1956, the RDA had included a woman among the candidates in each of Guinea's municipalities.[42] Contrasting the RDA's philosophy with that of its rivals, Sékou Touré noted:

We will be happy in the next Territorial Assembly to see women seated by our side. The Barry Diawadous, the Karim Bangouras can be sure that women will have seats in the Territorial Assembly. When our adversaries see women in the Territorial Assembly, in the Assembly of the French Union, they will know that the RDA has triumphed.[43]

In its attempt to create balanced tickets that accurately reflected the diversity of the urban populations, the RDA leadership's efforts were often misunderstood—or simply rejected—by the rank and file. They were also ridiculed by rival parties. If RDA militants felt that their party's slates included too many professionals without activist credentials, rival parties claimed that the RDA had too few. Although the RDA's municipal council slate for Conakry included a doctor, a lawyer, and a Martiniquan civil servant working at the Ministry of Finance, the BAG claimed that RDA candidates were not from the educated elite.[44] At one public meeting, Barry Diawadou derided the RDA candidates as a collection of uneducated nobodies and street fighters: "Note the absence of African intellectuals on the RDA tickets! Apart from a handful, the rest are unknowns, shock elements—and it is to them that one is going to entrust the interests of Conakry!"[45] The BAG organ, *La République,* cast aspersions on Sékou Touré's own intellectual formation, calling him the "victim" of his poor education. Afraid of being eclipsed by intellectuals who were better educated than he, the author charged, Sékou Touré surrounded himself with poorly educated yes-men.[46]

Rival parties not only mocked the professional qualifications of RDA candidates, they also ridiculed the party's attempts to promote ethnic and regional diversity. In Mamou, the DSG and BAG attempted to generate controversy by criticizing the municipal council candidacy of Saïfoulaye Diallo. Although he was a Peul from the Futa Jallon, he was a "stranger" to Mamou, they said.[47] Similarly, BAG leader Soriba Touré pointed to the plethora of "outsiders" on the RDA's Conakry tickets. While the heads of all the BAG tickets were Baga or Susu, Sékou Touré, a Malinke, headed the RDA slate in Boulbinet, the first Baga village in Conakry. According to Soriba Touré, there was not a single Baga on the RDA ticket for that preeminently Baga neighborhood. Barry Diawadou took up the refrain. "Conakry is, above all, Susu and Baga country," he asserted. "There are no representatives of these ethnic groups on Sékou Touré's tickets. He is mocking the Susus!" Without a hint of irony, Amara Soumah then passed the microphone to Mamadou Aribot, who translated Barry Diawadou's speech into Susu, presumably from French or his native Pulaar. Outside the BAG meeting, Susu market women, evidently RDA loyalists, sang "saboteurs" and "*Syli, Syli,*" as the crowd dispersed.[48]

In an attempt to calm RDA partisans who were angered by their adversaries' ridicule, Sékou Touré queried, "Have the BAG and DSG been as democratic as the RDA, letting their neighborhood committees establish their own tickets? Certainly not! So, if in your presence, ill is spoken of RDA tickets, let them speak. Do not respond. There is no possible comparison between them and us."[49] While the establishment of RDA slates was not purely the product of local initiative, the process was, in fact, more democratic than that of rival parties. In Kankan, for instance, rank-and-file BAG partisans had no role in candidate selection. Neighborhood chiefs and notables, as well as family heads, suggested desirable candidates to the BAG leadership, which then composed the party tickets.[50]

Unable to face the reality of a half-raised consciousness and incomplete political education, the RDA leadership blamed increasing dissension within the ranks on agents provocateurs. In anticipation of the March 1957 territorial elections, the board of directors sent a circular to all Guinean subsections. The circular warned partisans that RDA adversaries were attempting to destroy the party from within. Toward this end, they were manipulating RDA militants, inciting ethnic chauvinism, racism, and regionalism. In Dubréka, Boké, and Boffa, they had organized Associations of Natives of various regions. "Our political maturity should serve as a weapon to stem these injurious political maneuvers, to realize the unity, fraternity, and honesty necessary for the rapid emancipation of our people," the leadership warned. "All those who participate in racist, ethnically chauvinistic or regionalist movements will be expelled from the RDA. Their names will be published in *La Liberté.*"[51]

The territorial elections, like those at the municipal level, served as a testing ground for the leadership's ideals. The RDA board of directors proposed a process for candidate selection that permitted territorial leaders to check any irresponsible impulses from the grassroots. For the 60 contested seats, 37 candidates would be selected by the RDA subsections. The remaining 23 would be designated by the RDA board of directors, which would ensure representation of all strata of the population, including Europeans, Lebano-Syrians, and people of mixed ancestry. Eight of the 23 seats would be reserved for these groups, whose skills and qualities would be needed as *loi-cadre* was applied, Sékou Touré explained.[52]

At the RDA territorial conference in February 1957, the board's proposal was hotly debated. Among the most ardent opponents was Ismaël Touré, Sékou Touré's brother, who vehemently objected to the inclusion of Europeans on the RDA slate. Sékou Touré accused his brother of racism and reminded him that the RDA deputies in Paris had made a deal. In order to garner support in the National Assembly for a single college system in all elections, as well as a greater number of seats in the Territorial Assembly, the RDA had promised that Europeans would be included on the RDA ticket. The RDA was bound by its promise; thus, there would be eight Europeans on the RDA slate. Moreover, Sékou Touré continued, it was in the RDA's interest to sponsor European, Lebano-Syrian, and Caribbean candidates in the local assemblies. The RDA needed the support of their constituencies during this period of major reform. Finally, Sékou Touré concluded, even if they betrayed the RDA's trust, what could eight councillors do against 52?[53]

As Sékou and Ismaël Touré battled out their differences, most of the delegates appeared to side with Ismaël. Police spies reported that loud whistling interrupted the discussion. Sékou Touré invited the hecklers to step up to the podium to elaborate their arguments. No one came forward. The debate continued. Some critics contended that eight representatives were too many for a European population of approximately 5,000. In some circles, they noted, 70,000 Africans were represented by only two councillors.[54] Again, Sékou Touré donned the cap of political educator. "The R.D.A. is not a knife that divides, but a needle that sews [together]," he admonished. He reminded the delegates of the services rendered by particular Europeans. He cautioned that they must distinguish between reactionary Europeans, who mobilized African lackeys against the RDA, and progressive ones, who sought to aid their African brothers. The elimination of all European representation would only supply ammunition to reactionary forces to be used against the RDA, he warned.[55] In the end, the category "European" was expanded to include all people of mixed racial ancestry and Martiniquans of all races.[56]

Once the matter of European representation was settled, another sticky point was raised. Having built his party from the ranks of the nonliterate, who were ridiculed by the educated elites, Sékou Touré now asked those uneducated stalwarts to step aside—for the good of the country. He insisted that "qualified" candidates be sought, those with the education and skills necessary to fulfill the new responsibilities of self-government. It would be ill advised to allow 60 illiterates to occupy the seats of the Territorial Assembly, he cautioned.[57]

Local RDA leaders conveyed the conference resolutions to their respective populations—with the appropriate warnings. At a public meeting in Kankan, Assistant Mayor Moussa Diakité noted,

> You know that the RDA calls its members together each time an important decision is to be made. At the February conference, the RDA outlined the principles according to which candidates will be chosen. They will not be chosen according to whether they are a relative or a friend . . . but only according to their ability. If someone opposes the slates chosen by the subsection and the board of directors, they will be expelled from the party.[58]

Skills and ability, rather than past activity or party loyalty, would be the fundamental criteria for selection. The need for discipline was paramount; grassroots activists would obey territorial directives—or face the consequences.

Pleas for unity and political maturity were made at countless RDA rallies. At public meetings and on the pages of *La Liberté,* Sékou Touré vigorously denounced regionalism.[59] In Kindia, he informed a crowd that their subsection would select one candidate, while the RDA board of directors would choose the second. "The RDA will proceed in this manner in all the circles, because the RDA is against racism," he said.

> We are against racial and ethnic prejudice. We are for qualified people, whether they be European, Senegalese, Peul, or Bambara. Some of you say you will not vote for the RDA ticket because a European is on it. This reasoning is stupid. European lawyers have defended the RDA very well. We accepted their assistance then.[60]

Sékou Touré made similar claims in Boké, where residents were critical of the candidacy of Moustapha Camara. A teacher posted to Boké and president of the RDA subsection, Camara had been derided as a "foreigner." Once again, Sékou Touré stressed that the RDA opposed regionalism. In Africa, no African was a foreigner, he continued. Qualified people, like good wood, could be employed everywhere. Moustapha Camara, the "foreigner," was the one who had set the course for the RDA in Boké circle and opened the eyes of the population.[61] In Boké, the territorial leadership also made good on its threats of punishment; two residents who had formed dissident slates were expelled from the party.[62]

Despite the efforts of RDA leaders, many party members continued to prize ethnic and regional identity over national identity. Generational and gender hierarchies continued to prevail. The RDA was, in some ways, a victim of its own success. The party's rapid increase in membership during the legislative and municipal council campaigns had resulted in large numbers of new, predominantly rural members who had not embraced RDA positions. Local particularisms, especially ethnic favoritism, were difficult to eradicate, the police observed. It would be difficult to convince the rural population to vote for "foreigners" since each region wanted to elect its own men, whether or not they were capable or qualified.[63] If political education had not kept pace in the countryside, the urban areas were also subject to divisive tendencies. In Conakry, elders and notables, sidelined from candidacy in both the municipal and territorial elections, were disgruntled that the young, who should be following, were leading. Residents of the suburbs and city center, old and young alike, were angry that "foreigners" from other regions, rather than Susus and Bagas from their neighborhoods, had been selected as their candidates by the RDA.[64]

The RDA's rapidly swelling ranks were only part of the problem. Long-time militants had their own disputes with party leaders. Having struggled for many years at great cost to themselves, unschooled activists, like their Western-educated leaders, hoped to benefit from the new system of local government. Aspiring to leadership positions, they were unwilling to step aside to make way for more "qualified" candidates. What the leadership considered to be words of wisdom, grassroots militants considered betrayal.

Local activists' complaints were grounded in reality. According to the police, the most militant RDA cadres included very few "qualified" individuals. Many hopefuls from among their ranks had been rejected as ill suited for the tasks at hand. The BAG, in contrast, had a plethora of educated members. When the RDA leadership attempted to include some of them on RDA tickets, party militants cried foul. They would not accept the inclusion of BAG "saboteurs" on RDA slates—especially if they replaced loyal but illiterate RDA members.[65]

In the end, the RDA Territorial Assembly slate included dozens of "qualified" candidates. Among the 60 candidates were 14 teachers; 8 clerks and accountants; 7 assistant doctors and veterinarians; 5 heads of administrative services; 5 nurses; 3 canton chiefs; 3 trade unionists; 2 merchants; 2 military veterans; 2 engineers; 2 notables; 1 industrialist; 1 lawyer; 1 tax inspector; 1 artist; 1 transporter; 1 master workman; and 1 cultivator, who was most representative of the party's membership. The RDA board of directors had been responsible for selecting 8 Europeans and 15 Africans. However, it had found only four willing and acceptable whites, including a lawyer who had frequently defended RDA detainees. Thus, it counted as European two candidates of mixed race, a Martiniquan, and a Senegalese whose French citizenship had perhaps predated the Lamine Guèye Law of 1946.[66]

FRANCE MOVES RIGHT, GUINEA MOVES LEFT

Although internal divisions hampered its nation-building project, the RDA had achieved a critical mass and momentum that continued to drive it forward. While issues of race, class, ethnicity, and region continued to plague the party at the grassroots, in 1957 and 1958 the biggest schisms occurred between radical elements who denounced the compromises of the *loi-cadre* government and those who had acquired positions of power.[67] The politics of position frequently coincided with generation, as younger elements reproached their elders for their conservatism and quiescence.[68] Local leaders, in close proximity to the grassroots, tended to be more radical than those with territorial responsibility.[69]

As the RDA government moved toward a centrist policy of accommodation, dissident elements continued to push to the Left, appealing to the RDA's original power base. Autonomous trade unionists such as railway workers and teachers, as well as students and other youths, were among the most vocal critics of the new policy of "constructive collaboration." On numerous occasions, they harshly and publicly condemned the RDA leadership and the new government it had formed.[70] Shortly after the establishment of the *loi-cadre* government in May 1957, students, teachers, and railway workers—the nucleus of left-wing resistance to the RDA leadership—held their annual congresses. All were critical of the compromises made by the RDA government. Charging that the leadership had betrayed the people, the students demanded immediate independence. The autonomous railway workers' union, in turn, condemned the increasing subordination of the trade union movement to RDA control.[71] According to the police, these revolutionary sentiments reflected the views of local RDA leaders, as well as followers, in the interior. Subsection leaders in the forest had generally adopted a proindependence position; so had Upper-Guinea leaders Lansana Diané and Moriba Magassouba. Again, the gulf between territorial and local leaders seemed to be widening.[72]

Propelled by growing criticisms from students, youths, trade unionists, and the grassroots, the Guinean RDA moved incrementally to the Left. During its third party congress, held on January 23–26, 1958, a number of RDA leaders proclaimed that the reforms of *loi-cadre* were insufficient. They put forth new demands for complete internal autonomy, including the removal of the governor as the president of the Council of Government and his replacement with an elected African leader.[73] Continuing to value membership in the French Union, however, the party refrained from demanding independence. It simply asserted that the relationship between France and the overseas territories had to be reestablished on a more equitable basis.[74]

Although the Guinean RDA had moved to the Left, it had not moved quickly enough. Dissension within the party provided an opportunity for its opponents, who tried to outflank it on the Left. In February 1958, anti-RDA forces coalesced in the interterritorial Parti du Regroupement Africain (PRA). The PRA brought together all the political parties of French West Africa—with the exception of the RDA.[75] Forming a united front at both the interterritorial and territorial levels, the PRA's principal message was a systematic critique of the RDA and its compromises with the French government. Adopting a more radical stance than the RDA, most of the PRA's constituent elements affirmed that the African territories had an inalienable right to independence.[76]

The PRA's Guinean branch, the Union Progressiste Guinéenne, was formed in April 1958. A union of the BAG and the DSG, it was dominated by Western-educated Peul elites, including Barry Diawadou and Barry III.[77] Deprived of its chiefly base and rejected by the masses, the BAG had been all but defeated by the RDA. Although it had long supported Guinea's most conservative elements, the BAG saw the writing on the wall. With popular opinion more radical than the RDA's territorial leadership, the BAG qua PRA would attempt to capture this disgruntled constituency.

While Guinea was coping with internal struggles, a political crisis in France dramatically altered the political context in which the parties were operating. Since 1954, France had been engaged in a brutal war against an independence movement in Algeria, where 1.5 million French people of metropolitan origin lived among 8 million Africans. The target of French repression was the Front de Libération Nationale (FLN) and its supporters—alleged and real—in the civilian population.[78] The Battle of Algiers, which took place from January to October 1957, was particularly bloody. The French established tight control over the civilian population by recruiting informers, collaborators, and auxiliary forces, and systematically using torture to discover and destroy rebel cells. By the end of the operation, all the local FLN leaders were either dead or in prison.[79]

In the spring of 1958, bloody battles along the Algerian-Tunisian border, which resulted in many civilian deaths, brought international opprobrium to France.[80] The French public was deeply divided over the Algerian question, resulting in tremendous economic and political instability.[81] As successive French governments tried and failed to resolve the Algerian crisis, General Charles de Gaulle prepared to step into the breach.[82] Associated with French glory and patriotism, de Gaulle was popular among many segments of the population. Numerous appeals had been made for his return from retirement.[83] On May 26, 1958, de Gaulle suggested to the ineffectual prime minister that he step aside and make room for Charles de Gaulle.[84] As he moved to fill the power vacuum, de Gaulle demanded substantial new powers and an immediate revision of the constitution.[85]

THE NEW CONSTITUTION AND THE FIFTH REPUBLIC

Determined to reassert control over the French empire, de Gaulle proposed a constitution that would eliminate many of the liberal reforms of postwar imperialism. According to de Gaulle's draft constitution, the French Community would replace the French Union. The Community would be subordinate to the French Republic, which would retain the most important powers. The Republic, primarily through its president, would determine common foreign, economic, and defense policies for the French Community. France would also oversee justice, higher education, telecommunications, and transportation within the Community.[86] The Republic and Community would be led by a strong president with little check on his powers.[87]

Under the 1958 constitution, Africans would be granted an even smaller role in the making of common policies than they had in 1946. They would no longer have representation in the National Assembly. The Council of the Republic and the Assembly of the French Union would disappear.[88] The work of *loi-cadre* would be completed through the balkanization of the French African federations. Both French West Africa and French Equatorial Africa would be dissolved, and with them, the Grand Councils that brought together Africans from all of the territories. It was hoped that the dissolution of the federations would forestall moves toward independence. With diverse resources and a population of more than 20 million people, French West Africa might seek independence as a nation-state. However, the eight small territories that comprised the federation might be dissuaded from following such a course if they were forced to accept independence as discrete, possibly nonviable entities.[89]

Africans had little role in drafting the 1958 constitution. While a few hand-picked African deputies had participated in an advisory committee that commented on the draft, the constitution had been written without consulting the councils of government, territorial assemblies, and political movements in the various territories.[90] Millions of Africans would be permitted merely to vote "Yes" or "No" to a constitution that broke up the African federations and ruled out independence—then or in the future.[91]

In June 1958, as the constitution was being drafted in Paris, the Guinean RDA held another territory-wide congress. The resulting party resolutions, pushed through by young radicals, indicated a growing cleavage between the Guinean RDA and the interterritorial leadership, which generally favored the new constitution. The Guinean RDA called for the strengthening of *loi-cadre* provisions that would result in the complete internal autonomy of the overseas territories. Further, all territories in French sub-Saharan Africa should be accorded the right to independence as part of the larger federations of French West and Equatorial Africa. A federal executive elected by members of the Grand Council should be established to oversee all interterritorial services. A proposed federal state, responsible for foreign and economic affairs, defense, and higher education, would remove further powers from the French Republic's control.[92]

The question of independence, immediately or in the future, dominated all political discussions. At its July 25–27, 1958, interterritorial congress, the

PRA's elder statesmen, like those of the RDA, were outflanked by young radicals. No longer satisfied with a principled right to independence, to be achieved at some future date, young Leftists pushed through a resolution in favor of immediate independence on the basis of a united federation of French West Africa. Once sovereign and independent, the federation would decide whether or not to freely associate with France. The interterritorial PRA thus opted to reject the proposed constitution, calling for a "No" vote in the September 28 referendum.[93]

Despite its dissatisfaction with the draft constitution, the Guinean RDA, unlike the PRA, did not call for a "No" vote. In July 1958, it continued to champion association with France and hold out hope that the necessary constitutional revisions would be made. In *La Liberté,* Sékou Touré pleaded that self-determination and continued association with France were not mutually exclusive. Together with France, the overseas territories hoped to form a large federation of autonomous, politically equal states joined together by mutual consent. The territories' "exercise of their right to self-determination" should not be confused "with any desire to separate themselves from France," Sékou Touré contended. To the contrary, the African people, their political organizations, and trade unions were conscious of the economic and cultural roles France could continue to play. However, the constitution as it stood was not sufficient. It did not provide for a "true community," because the one envisioned would not be established on the basis of free consent by sovereign peoples. Such a community was totally unacceptable.[94]

Rather than compromise, de Gaulle proposed to punish those who opposed the constitution's basic tenets. The general posed two stark alternatives: adherence to the French Community, as described in the draft constitution, through a "Yes" vote, or secession from France through a "No" vote.[95] Openly threatening those territories considering independence, de Gaulle declared,

> It is well understood, and I understand it, one can desire secession. [Secession] imposes duties. It carries dangers. Independence has its burdens. The referendum will ascertain if the idea of secession carries the day. *But one cannot conceive of an independent territory and a France that continues to aid it. The [independent] government will bear the consequences, economic and otherwise, that are entailed in the manifestation of such a will.*[96]

De Gaulle had drawn the line. Any declaration of independence would be taken as a personal affront, with cause for retribution.

GENERAL DE GAULLE COMES TO AFRICA

During the month of August 1958, General de Gaulle toured French West and Equatorial Africa to rally support for his constitutional project.[97] On

August 24, the day before his arrival in Guinea, he proclaimed that he had accepted two alterations to the text. First, if a territory voted "Yes" in the referendum, choosing to join the French Community, it could still, at some point in the future, vote for independence "without risk or peril." Such a vote, unlike a "No" vote in the referendum, would not be considered "secession," although upon attaining independence the state would cease to be a member of the Community. Second, territories would be permitted to join the Community individually or in groups. However, de Gaulle refused to accede to the demand that the territorial groupings be institutionalized in the constitution as, for instance, French West Africa or French Equatorial Africa. Their formation—or lack thereof—would be left to the initiative of the various territorial assemblies. Moreover, he stood firm that there would be no federal executive.[98]

Photo 7.1 General de Gaulle greeted by a crowd on his arrival in Conakry, August 1958. (AFP/Getty Images)

The following day, Sékou Touré addressed the Guinean Territorial Assembly, which had convened to receive the French leader.[99] Sékou Touré reiterated the need for further revisions to the proposed constitution. The Guinean people would not vote in favor of the constitution unless it proclaimed "the right to independence and the juridical equality of peoples associated [with France]." The people must have the right to self-determination and to dissolve the union with France if they so chose. Absent such rights, the Community would constitute an arbitrary construction imposed upon future generations.[100] Sékou Touré concluded with a flourish:

> We will not renounce and we will never renounce our legitimate and natural right to independence. . . . We prefer poverty in liberty to riches in slavery. . . .
>
> We wish to be free citizens of our African states, members of the Franco-African Community. In effect, the French Republic, within the Franco-African association, will be an element, as all the African states will equally be elements, of this grand multinational community composed of free and equal states.[101]

De Gaulle refused to negotiate further. The constitution would stand as it was: Guinea could take it or leave it. Responding to the Guinean leader, de Gaulle declared:

> France is proposing this Community; no one is bound to adhere to it. There has been talk of independence; I say more loudly here than elsewhere that independence is at Guinea's disposal. She can take it, she can take it on the 28th of September by saying "No" to the proposition that has been made to her and in this case I guarantee that the *métropole* will create no obstacles. [The *métropole*] will, of course, draw inferences from it, but it will put up no obstacles.[102]

Although de Gaulle presumed that the die was cast, it was not. The general assumed that Sékou Touré's speech meant that he personally favored a "No" vote in the referendum and that an overwhelming Guinean vote against the constitution would result. However, Sékou Touré's speech did not point to a definitive position regarding the referendum. Moreover, the leader's personal position was not necessarily that of the party as a whole. The Guinean RDA was due to hold a territorial conference on September 14. It was there that a final decision on the constitution would be made and the position for or against would be determined.[103]

THE MOVE TOWARD INDEPENDENCE

As de Gaulle dug in his heels, the interterritorial RDA joined him in a push from the Right. With the exception of Guinea, all of the party's territorial branches had weighed in for a "Yes" vote.[104] While the interterritorial RDA pushed for accommodation on French terms, African trade unions, youth and student organizations, and the PRA pushed Guinea in the other direction. By September 1958, all of these elements had called for rejection of the constitution.[105] On September 10–11, the Guinean RDA's youth and women's wings paved the way for the territorial branch by endorsing a "No" vote.[106] Meanwhile, nationalist forces on the ground coalesced. In early September, the Guinean PRA proposed collaboration with the Guinean RDA.[107] The elusive quest for African unity seemed within reach.

On September 14, the Guinean RDA held the territory-wide conference that would determine its final disposition on the constitution. Some 680 leaders from RDA subsections, neighborhood and village committees, and the youth wing assembled in the capital to determine, according to a democratic procedure, the party's final position.[108] Pressing the Guinean branch to tow the line, the interterritorial RDA sent high-level representatives to argue its case.[109] Bocar Biro Barry remembered the conference, which was held in the neighborhood of Boulbinet:

> It was there that things were played out. That was the day fixed for the national conference to decide if one must vote "Yes" or "No." It was there that [interterritorial RDA president] Houphouët sent a delegation—to plead with Sékou to vote "Yes." He wanted all the territories of the RDA—Conakry, Bamako, Niamey, Abidjan, Cotonou—to vote "Yes" to please General de Gaulle. Afterwards, one would see about independence.
>
> So, this delegation arrived here at the airport at ten o'clock in the morning. They went to the [Territorial Assembly] building. The conference of Boulbinet was at the port of Boulbinet—there where the people fish. There was an old hangar there—a place where they smoked the fish. That is where they held the conference.

An activist in the teachers' union as well as the left-wing of the RDA, Barry remembered the surprising outcome of the interterritorial delegation's meeting with Sékou Touré:

> Sékou went into a meeting with Houphouët's delegation—from ten o'clock until one o'clock. We were in the conference room. We waited for Sékou's order to vote "Yes"—to not follow the teachers, because we were teachers; to not follow the youth, to vote "Yes." He had accepted it. Until September 14, he was for the "Yes."
>
> He arrived at the [territorial] conference after the delegation's departure. We, the young people, the teachers' union—we were in the room, impatient. We said to ourselves, "The delegation of Houphouët is there. It is to corrupt Sékou. If he ever accepts to vote 'Yes,' we will liquidate him." That was whispered amongst ourselves in the conference room. All the secretaries-general were there—it was a national conference for which all the

political leaders had been called to Conakry. All the subsections were led by teachers. There was an overwhelming majority of teachers, of young people. The youth of Guinea and [the university students' organization] were there. We were there, side by side with the trade unions and the youth movements. All of us, we were for the "No."

He arrived toward one o'clock. It was hot. Everyone was irritable. He arrived in the room. As soon as he entered, everyone cried, "No!" I still remember as if it were today. Everyone cried, "NO, NO, NO, NO, NO!" We were all sure that he had been led astray by Houphouët's delegation. He arrived. He sat down, calmly at first. The people continued to cry, "NO, NO, NO, NO, NO, NO!" He rose. He began to speak. The conference lasted five minutes. Because he was a great maneuverer, a great opportunist, he saw which way the wind was blowing, and he said to himself, "If I say the other thing, they are going to liquidate me." So, he said, "The 28th of September, we must vote. What will be the vote of the Parti Démocratique de Guinée?" The people cried, "NO, NO, NO, NO, NO, NO!" There we were. He saw that the atmosphere was for the "No." It was at this moment that he changed sides.

. . . The teachers' union, the youth movement, and the students could have cast Sékou Touré aside. . . . It was that that frightened Sékou.[110]

Thus, it was not until September 14, two weeks before the referendum, that Sékou Touré came out definitively for a "No" vote. He reached this decision only after much debate—and under immense pressure from trade unionists, students, and youths. The teachers' union, with its relatively young membership, the students' organizations, and the youth movement, whose membership overlapped with both teachers and students, were the driving force behind the "No" vote. According to Bocar Biro Barry, these groups forced Sékou Touré to break from the official position of the interterritorial RDA.[111]

Addressing the jubilant throng, Sékou Touré took up the refrain and urged a "No" vote. "Comrades," Sékou Touré proclaimed,

We have declared unanimously to the Representative of France that we pre-fer poverty in liberty to riches in slavery. . . . We will vote "No" to a com-munity that is no more than the French Union rebaptized—the old merchandise with a new label. We will vote "No" to inequality.

A "No" vote would end French colonialism and permit independent African nations to create a truly egalitarian, fraternal association with France, Sékou Touré argued. That evening the territorial conference unanimously approved a resolution in favor of immediate independence.[112]

On September 16, Guinea's Council of Government issued a communiqué announcing the formation of a proindependence united front that included the

Photo 7.2   Sékou Touré, president of newly independent Guinea, October 6, 1958. (AFP/Getty Images)

RDA, PRA, youth and military veterans' associations, and the majority of Guinea's trade unions. Despite the wavering of some veterans, their associations officially returned to the nationalist fold.[113] The next day, the Guinean RDA and PRA issued a joint communiqué inviting all militants—male and female, African and European—to campaign for a "No" vote in the referendum.[114] The Guinean PRA then dissolved itself, and its members joined the Guinean RDA, which then included 43 subsections and 4,300 local committees.[115] In the final drive for national independence, the cracks in Guinean unity were papered over, at least temporarily.

CONCLUSION

On September 28, 1958, French citizens throughout the empire went to the polls to vote for or against the constitution that would serve as the foundation of the Fifth Republic.[116] In Guinea, with the canton chieftaincy eliminated, there was no counterauthority to the RDA in the countryside.[117] Victory for the RDA position, once more determined by the party's grassroots, was essentially assured.

Voter turnout in Guinea was extremely high; 85 percent of the registered voters cast their ballots, overwhelmingly rejecting the new constitutional project. Of the total, 1,136,324 (94 percent) voted "No," and 56,981 (4.7 percent) voted "Yes."[118] Guinea alone rejected membership in the French Community. In every other French sub-Saharan African territory, the constitution was approved by an equally staggering majority. In the referendum's aftermath, the federation of French West Africa was dissolved, and the interterritorial RDA disintegrated. Guinea was independent, but isolated.[119]

CONCLUSION

The RDA was not the only political party on the scene in postwar Guinea. However, it was the only one able to mobilize an ethnic, class, and gender alliance strong enough to effectively challenge the colonial system. This broad-based alliance embraced a progressive political tradition of inclusive nationalism, combating the divisive tendencies of regionalism, ethnic chauvinism, class bias, and male domination. While some of these ideas were derived from European models, others were the product of African experience, both precolonial and colonial. European models were not simply transplanted onto African soil.

The RDA's strength lay in its solid grassroots foundation. In the rural areas, military veterans, largely of peasant origin, and male and female peasants shaped the contours of the party. In the urban areas, male trade unionists, both nonliterate and Western-educated, and women in the informal sector were the dominant influences on the party's methods and agenda. Critical to the RDA's success was the fact that these groups had already mobilized themselves. Articulating their grievances and embracing their causes, the RDA drew them into the nationalist struggle, profiting from their organization and momentum.

The political movement that resulted in Guinea's independence was primarily a movement of the masses, shaped from the bottom up rather than the top down. While Western-educated elites held most of the high-level positions, they followed the masses' lead on many fronts. Latching onto the grievances of veterans, workers, peasants, and women, the party channeled their energies into an explicitly anticolonial and nationalist movement. Thus, it was the grievances of the vast nonliterate majority that determined the nationalist agenda and their energies that fueled the movement. Although the elites supplied many of the particulars, the fundamental demands emanated from the party's rank and file. If grassroots activists determined many of the basic claims on the nationalist agenda, they also influenced it in other ways. Rejecting certain aspects of their leaders' vision, they struggled over gender, ethnicity, class, and political violence. Incompatible imaginings of the nation resulted in strains and rifts that threatened the movement's existence.

Grassroots activists not only inspired the party's political agenda, they also left a strong imprint on its methods. Indigenous histories, practices, and beliefs had a major impact on the way in which nationalism was produced in Guinea. Religious and cultural imagery were employed, and preexisting organizations were used to promote the nationalist agenda. While party tracts and newspapers were read by the small class of Western-educated elite, the vast majority of Guinea's populace was not literate. In order to transmit their ideas to the party leadership and to communicate the party's message more broadly, men and women invented new methods of communication. Women, especially, composed songs and slogans that were widely disseminated. They wore party uniforms, colors, and symbols that proudly announced their identity and affiliation. Thus, both the message and the methods were constructed from the bottom up.

Although the nationalist movement blossomed in the postwar period, its roots lay deep in Guinea's past. It was the shared history of this heterogeneous people that permitted the idea of the nation to emerge. In the precolonial period, many Guineans were bound by common economic and political structures and by religion. After conquest, they were joined together by their shared experience of colonialism. In defining the Guinean nation, however, the experience of war was decisive. World War II brought new hardships and opportunities that politicized peasants in the rural areas and African soldiers abroad. Forced labor and crop production, enforced by the colonial chieftaincy, fell heavily on both women and men. The war effort stimulated widespread rural resistance. In its aftermath, challenges to chiefly authority became a constant in the countryside. Military veterans, who had fought side by side with Frenchmen, were both proud of their contributions to French liberation and chagrined by their poor postwar treatment. Searching for justice and new ways to assert their manhood, aggrieved veterans frequently led peasant resistance to the colonial chiefs. These grassroots struggles culminated in the abolition of the canton chieftaincy, which in turn assured the RDA's triumph in the rural areas.

If the struggles of peasants and veterans often overlapped, so, too, did those of veterans and trade unionists. Both groups challenged France to live up to its postwar claims of reformed imperialism. Making French assimilationist rhetoric their own, they demanded an end to discriminatory treatment. While veterans agitated for equal pensions and other benefits, workers demanded family allowances, wages, and workweeks commensurate with those of their metropolitan counterparts. Their economic demands rooted in political principle, trade unionists were a critical RDA constituency. When veterans' claims were satisfied in the mid-1950s, most retreated from the political scene. Trade unionists, in contrast, moved to the forefront of the nationalist struggle, consistently pushing the party to the Left.

Urban women supported male workers in their demands. Although their own involvement in wage employment was extremely limited, urban women contributed to their families' maintenance through informal sector activities. Even so, they generally supported the notion of the male breadwinner, expecting that their children would benefit from their fathers' improved wages, rations, and family allowances. Through connections to female farmers in the rural areas and through market networks and other informal sector activities, urban women sustained striking workers and their families. Having mobilized themselves in support of their husbands and families, women in turn were courted by the RDA.

When they bridged the gap between the labor and nationalist movements, Guinean women were not in pursuit of female emancipation. Rather, they joined the nationalist struggle to improve their families' lives. In the harsh postwar climate of scarcity and inflation, they agitated for more sanitary living conditions, better health care, and greater access to education. Only as they fought for these benefits did women begin to challenge the gender roles that circumscribed their political involvement. These challenges brought dissension within the ranks and the first of many fissures in the ethnic, class, and gender alliance that was the RDA.

Women's emancipation was a major source of division within the party. While the territorial leadership extolled the virtues of female participation in the nationalist struggle, many male activists remained unconvinced. Even women were ambivalent about their newfound roles. Like their male counterparts, many women considered their abandonment of female gender roles to be a short-term necessity in abnormal times. After independence, women as well as men expected to return to the status quo ante.

While ethnic, class, and gender diversity were the party's strengths, they were also the source of its weakness. Ethnic and class cleavages, along with tensions over women's roles, were papered over rather than bridged or destroyed. Regular eruptions of ethnically based political violence threatened to tear the party apart. Ethnic and class conflict created divisions between the party leadership and the rank and file, the former castigating the latter for its flawed political consciousness. Local leaders, torn between the demands of their territorial superiors and their grassroots constituencies, vacillated from one end of the spectrum to the other, generally siding with local militants.

The RDA's success resulted in new fractures. As electoral victories gave the RDA control of the major municipalities and the Territorial Assembly, party leaders acquired a new interest in the maintenance of law and order. Violence, particularly ethnically motivated violence, would no longer be tolerated. Grassroots militants, however, were disinclined to renounce tactics that had served them well in the past. Likewise, as the party took on the challenges of self-government, territorial leaders attempted to broaden its base. Embracing Europeans, Lebano-Syrians, and Western-educated elites who had previously cast their lot with the colonial system, RDA leaders asserted that self-rule required "qualified" personnel with diverse technical skills. Party loyalty and past militance were no longer sufficient qualifications for government office. Not surprisingly, the largely nonliterate rank and file vehemently contested this claim.

By 1957, it seemed as if the territorial leadership had wrested control of the party from the militants who had been the foundation of its earlier success. However, in 1958, a new alliance of rank-and-file members, including both Western-educated and nonliterate cadres, pushed the party to a more radical stance. Trade unionists, students, and other youths criticized the *loi-cadre* government from the Left, claiming that the RDA had made unacceptable compromises with the colonial administration. When confronted by a new constitution that destroyed the African federations and enshrined junior partnership with France, these groups endorsed immediate independence instead. As momentum for independence gathered at the grassroots, the RDA's territorial leadership had little choice but to follow. When it called for a "No" vote in the September 1958 referendum, rejecting the new constitution and membership in the French Community, the RDA board of directors was simply trailing the masses as it had done previously. The resounding "No" that resulted in Guinea's independence was the culmination of nationalist mobilization from the bottom up.

NOTES

INTRODUCTION

1.   "Les Résultats du Scrutin," *La Liberté,* 4 October 1958, p. 5; Sidiki Kobélé Kéïta, *Le P.D.G.: Artisan de l'Indépendance Nationale en Guinée (1947–1958)* (Conakry: I.N.R.D.G., Bibliothèque Nationale, 1978), 2:147–149; Lansiné Kaba, *Le "Non" de la Guinée à De Gaulle,* vol. 1 of *Afrique Contemporaine* (Paris: Éditions Chaka, 1989), pp. 161–162, 168; Patrick Manning, *Francophone Sub-Saharan Africa, 1880–1985* (New York: Cambridge University Press, 1988), pp. 148–149.

2.   Pierre Kipré, *Le Congrès de Bamako ou La Naissance du RDA en 1946,* vol. 3 of *Afrique Contemporaine* (Paris: Éditions Chaka, 1989), pp. 135, 137–138, 162.

3.   Interview with Bocar Biro Barry, Camayenne, Conakry, 21 January 1991; AG, AM-1339, Idiatou Camara, "La Contribution de la Femme de Guinée à la Lutte de Libération Nationale (1945–1958)" (Mémoire de Fin d'Études Supérieures, IPGAN, Conakry, 1979), p. 42; Siba N. Grovogui, personal communication, 1988.

4.   Gnan Félix Mathos, "Le R.D.A. et l'Intellectuel," *La Liberté,* 25 January 1955, p. 4.

5.   For Europe, see E. J. Hobsbawm, *The Age of Revolution: Europe, 1789–1848* (London: Weidenfeld and Nicolson, 1962), pp. 135–136; Ernest Gellner, *Nations and Nationalism* (Ithaca, N.Y.: Cornell University Press, 1983), pp. 63, 89; Benedict Anderson, *Imagined Communities: Reflections on the Origin and Spread of Nationalism,* 2nd ed. (New York: Verso, 1991), pp. 36–40, 116.

6.   Susan Geiger, *TANU Women: Gender and Culture in the Making of Tanganyikan Nationalism, 1955–1965* (Portsmouth, N.H.: Heinemann; Oxford: James Currey, 1997), p. 14.

7.   These ideas have been elaborated upon in Elizabeth Schmidt, "Top Down or Bottom Up?: Nationalist Mobilization Reconsidered, with Special Reference to Guinea (French West Africa)," under consideration by the *American Historical Review.*

8.   See, for instance, James S. Coleman, "Nationalism in Tropical Africa," *American Political Science Review* 48, no. 2 (June 1954): pp. 404–426; Thomas Hodgkin, *Nationalism in Colonial Africa* (New York: New York University Press, 1957); James S. Coleman, *Nigeria: Background to Nationalism* (Berkeley: University of California Press, 1958);

Jacob F. Ajayi, "The Place of African History and Culture in the Process of Nation-Building in Africa South of the Sahara," *Journal of Negro Education* 30, no. 3 (1960): pp. 206–213; David Apter, *Ghana in Transition* (Princeton, N.J.: Princeton University Press, 1963); Robert I. Rotberg, *The Rise of Nationalism in Central Africa: The Making of Malawi and Zambia, 1873–1964* (Cambridge, Mass.: Harvard University Press, 1965); Carl G. Rosberg and John Nottingham, *The Myth of "Mau Mau": Nationalism in Kenya* (Stanford, Calif.: Hoover Institution Press, 1966).

9.   John Lonsdale, "Some Origins of Nationalism in East Africa," *Journal of African History* 9, no. 1 (1968): p. 146.

10.   John Lonsdale, "The Emergence of African Nations: A Historiographical Analysis," *African Affairs* 67, no. 266 (1968): p. 25.

11.   Lonsdale, "Origins of Nationalism," pp. 140–141, 146.

12.   Susan Geiger, "Tanganyikan Nationalism as 'Women's Work': Life Histories, Collective Biography and Changing Historiography," *Journal of African History* 37, no. 3 (1996): pp. 468–469.

Similarly, Benedict Anderson argues that nationalism "has to be understood by aligning it, not with self-consciously held political ideologies, but with the large cultural systems that preceded it, out of which—as well as against which—it came into being." Anderson, *Imagined Communities,* p. 12.

13.   See, for instance, Janet M. Bujra, "Women 'Entrepreneurs' of Early Nairobi," *Canadian Journal of African Studies* 9, no. 2 (1975): pp. 213–234; Margaret Jean Hay, "Luo Women and Economic Change during the Colonial Period," in *Women in Africa: Studies in Social and Economic Change,* ed. Nancy J. Hafkin and Edna G. Bay (Stanford, Calif.: Stanford University Press, 1976), pp. 87–109; George Chauncey Jr., "The Locus of Reproduction: Women's Labour in the Zambian Copperbelt, 1927–1953," *Journal of Southern African Studies* 7, no. 2 (April 1981): pp. 135–164; Elias Mandala, "Peasant Cotton Agriculture, Gender and Inter-Generational Relationships: The Lower Tchiri (Shire) Valley of Malawi, 1906–1940," *African Studies Review* 25, nos. 2/3 (June/September 1982): pp. 27–44; Marcia Wright, "Technology, Marriage and Women's Work in the History of Maize-Growers in Mazabuka, Zambia: A Reconnaissance," *Journal of Southern African Studies* 10, no. 1 (October 1983): pp. 71–85; Luise White, "A Colonial State and an African Petty Bourgeoisie: Prostitution, Property, and Class Struggle in Nairobi, 1936–1940," in *Struggle for the City: Migrant Labor, Capital, and the State in Urban Africa,* ed. Frederick Cooper (Beverly Hills, Calif.: Sage Publications, 1983), pp. 167–194; Luise White, *The Comforts of Home: Prostitution in Colonial Nairobi* (Chicago: University of Chicago Press, 1990); Jane L. Parpart, "The Household and the Mine Shaft: Gender and Class Struggles on the Zambian Copperbelt, 1926–64," *Journal of Southern African Studies* 13, no. 1 (October 1986): pp. 36–56; Elizabeth Schmidt, *Peasants, Traders, and Wives: Shona Women in the History of Zimbabwe, 1870–1939* (Portsmouth, N.H.: Heinemann; London: James Currey, 1992); Lisa A. Lindsay, "Domesticity and Difference: Male Breadwinners, Working Women, and Colonial Citizenship in the 1945 Nigerian General Strike," *American Historical Review* 104, no. 3 (June 1999): pp. 783–812.

14.   See, for instance, LaRay Denzer, "Towards a Study of the History of West African Women's Participation in Nationalist Politics: The Early Phase, 1935–1950," *Africana Research Bulletin* 6, no. 4 (1976): pp. 65–85; LaRay Denzer, "Constance A. Cummings-John of Sierra Leone: Her Early Political Career," *Tarikh* 7, no. 1 (1981): pp. 20–32; LaRay Denzer, "Women in Freetown Politics, 1914–61: A Preliminary Study," *Africa* 57, no. 4 (1987): pp. 439–456. For more recent scholarship in this vein, see Jane Turrittin,

"Aoua Kéita and the Nascent Women's Movement in the French Soudan," *African Studies Review* 36, no. 1 (April 1993): pp. 59–89.

15. See Susan Geiger, "Anti-Colonial Protest in Africa: A Female Strategy Reconsidered," *Heresies* 9, no. 3 (1980): pp. 22–25; Susan Geiger, "Women in Nationalist Struggle: TANU Activists in Dar es Salaam," *International Journal of African Historical Studies* 20, no. 1 (1987): pp. 1–26; Susan Geiger, "Women and African Nationalism," *Journal of Women's History* 2, no. 1 (1990): pp. 227–244; Geiger, "Tanganyikan Nationalism," pp. 465–478; Geiger, *TANU Women;* Susan Geiger, "Engendering and Gendering African Nationalism: Rethinking the Case of Tanganyika (Tanzania)," *Social Identities* 5, no. 3 (1999): pp. 331–343; Cheryl Johnson, "Madam Alimotu Pelewura and the Lagos Market Women," *Tarikh* 7, no. 1 (1981): pp. 1–10; Cheryl Johnson, "Grassroots Organizing: Women in Anti-Colonial Activity in Southwestern Nigeria," *African Studies Review* 25, no. 2 (September 1982): pp. 137–157; Cheryl Johnson-Odim and Nina Emma Mba, *For Women and the Nation: Funmilayo Ransome-Kuti of Nigeria* (Urbana: University of Illinois Press, 1997); Nina Emma Mba, *Nigerian Women Mobilized: Women's Political Activity in Southern Nigeria, 1900-1965,* Research Series, no. 48 (Berkeley: Institute of International Studies, University of California, 1982); Cora Ann Presley, *Kikuyu Women, the Mau Mau Rebellion, and Social Change in Kenya* (Boulder, Colo.: Westview, 1992); Timothy Scarnecchia, "Poor Women and Nationalist Politics: Alliances and Fissures in the Formation of a Nationalist Political Movement in Salisbury, Rhodesia, 1950–6," *Journal of African History* 37, no. 2 (1996): pp. 283–310; Elizabeth Schmidt, " 'Emancipate Your Husbands!': Women and Nationalism in Guinea, 1953–1958," in *Women in African Colonial Histories,* ed. Jean Allman, Susan Geiger, and Nakanyike Musisi (Bloomington: Indiana University Press, 2002), pp. 282–304; Cherryl Walker, *Women and Resistance in South Africa* (London: Onyx Press, 1982).

16. Geiger, *TANU Women,* p. 14.

17. See Ruth Schachter Morgenthau, *Political Parties in French-Speaking West Africa* (Oxford: Clarendon Press, 1964), pp. 219–254; Jean Suret-Canale, *La République de Guinée* (Paris: Éditions Sociales, 1970), pp. 141–146, 159–172; Claude Rivière, *Guinea: The Mobilization of a People,* trans. Virginia Thompson and Richard Adloff (Ithaca, N.Y.: Cornell University Press, 1977), pp. 51–82.

18. Sidiki Kobélé Kéïta, *P.D.G.* Unfortunately, Kéïta's two-volume work has not been widely circulated outside of Guinea.

19. See, for instance, Margarita Dobert, "Civic and Political Participation of Women in French-Speaking West Africa" (Ph.D. diss., George Washington University, 1970).

20. Idiatou Camara, "Contribution de la Femme."

21. See Anderson, *Imagined Communities,* p. 12.

22. Henley refers to this phenomenon as "integrative," as opposed to "inclusive," nationalism, which he contrasts with "exclusive" nationalism. David E. F. Henley, "Ethno-geographic Integration and Exclusion in Anticolonial Nationalism: Indonesia and Indochina," *Comparative Studies in Society and History* 37, no. 2 (April 1995): pp. 286, 289–290.

23. See Morgenthau, *Political Parties;* Suret-Canale, *République;* Rivière, *Guinea.*

24. See Hobsbawm, *Age of Revolution.*

25. See Myron Echenberg, *Colonial Conscripts: The Tirailleurs Sénégalais in French West Africa, 1857–1960* (Portsmouth, N.H.: Heinemann; London: James Currey, 1991); Myron Echenberg, " 'Morts Pour La France': The African Soldier in France during the Second World War," *Journal of African History* 26, no. 4 (1985): pp. 363–380; Myron

Echenberg, "Tragedy at Thiaroye: The Senegalese Soldiers' Uprising of 1944," in *African Labor History,* ed. Peter C. W. Gutkind, Robin Cohen, and Jean Copans (Beverly Hills, Calif.: Sage Publications, 1978), pp. 109–128; Nancy Ellen Lawler, *Soldiers of Misfortune: Ivoirien Tirailleurs of World War II* (Athens: Ohio University Press, 1992).

26.   Echenberg, "Tragedy at Thiaroye," p. 124; Echenberg, *Colonial Conscripts,* pp. 104, 152.

27.   Frederick Cooper, *Decolonization and African Society: The Labor Question in French and British Africa* (New York: Cambridge University Press, 1996), pp. 178, 290.

28.   See Cooper, *Decolonization.*

29.   Agitation against government-appointed chiefs and other forms of rural resistance were by no means unique to Guinea. A pioneer in this field of investigation, Allen Isaacman has explored forced crop cultivation—and the role of chiefs in that process—as a spur to resistance in colonial Mozambique. Similarly, Beinart and Bundy have investigated peasant resistance, including actions against the chiefs, in South Africa. See Allen Isaacman, et al., " 'Cotton Is the Mother of Poverty': Peasant Resistance to Forced Cotton Production in Mozambique, 1938–1961," *International Journal of African Historical Studies* 13 (1980): pp. 581–615; Allen Isaacman, "Chiefs, Rural Differentiation and Peasant Protest: The Mozambican Forced Cotton Regime, 1938–61," *African Economic History* 14 (1985): pp. 15–56; Allen Isaacman, "Peasants and Rural Social Protest in Africa," *African Studies Review* 33 (1990): pp. 1–120; Allen Isaacman, "Coercion, Paternalism and the Labor Process: The Mozambican Cotton Regime, 1938–1961," *Journal of Southern African Studies* 18, no. 3 (1992): pp. 487–526; Allen Isaacman, *Cotton Is the Mother of Poverty: Peasants, Work, and Rural Struggle in Colonial Mozambique, 1938–1961* (Portsmouth, N.H.: Heinemann; London: James Currey, 1996), pp. 174–181, 205–237; William Beinart and Colin Bundy, "State Intervention and Rural Resistance: The Transkei, 1900–1965," in *Peasants in Africa: Historical and Contemporary Perspectives,* ed. Martin Klein (Beverly Hills, Calif.: Sage Publications, 1980), pp. 270–315; William Beinart and Colin Bundy, *Hidden Struggles in Rural South Africa: Politics and Popular Movements in the Transkei and Eastern Cape, 1890–1930* (Berkeley: University of California Press, 1987).

30.   Unless otherwise indicated, all translations from French language sources are the author's.

31.   Suret-Canale, *République,* pp. 172–173; Sidiki Kobélé Kéïta, *P.D.G.,* 2:149; Morgenthau, *Political Parties,* p. 253.

32.   All interviews were conducted by the author, in collaboration with Siba N. Grovogui. Those conducted in French were transcribed and translated by the author. Those conducted in Susu and Malinke were transcribed and translated by Siba N. Grovogui.

33.   See Susan Geiger, "The Concept of Nationalism Revisited (Again): Culture and Politics in Tanzanian Women's Life Histories" (paper presented at the Annual Meeting of the African Studies Association, Denver, Colo., 21 November 1987); Popular Memory Group, "Popular Memory: Theory, Politics, Method," in *Making Histories: Studies in History-Writing and Politics,* ed. Richard Johnson, Gregor McLennan, Bill Schwarz, and David Sutton (Minneapolis: University of Minnesota Press, 1982), pp. 211–212, 223.

As Prasenjit Duara notes, "if the past is shaped by the present, the present is also shaped by the past as inheritance, and the most fertile questions lie in understanding how this dialectic is articulated with the contest over the significance of national history." Prasenjit Duara, "Historicizing National Identity, or Who Imagines What and When," in *Becoming National: A Reader,* ed. Geoff Eley and Ronald Grigor Suny (New York: Oxford University Press, 1996), p. 161.

CHAPTER 1: HISTORY, CULTURE, AND WAR: THE ROOTS OF GUINEAN NATIONALISM, 1939–1947

1.   See E. J. Hobsbawm, *The Age of Revolution: Europe, 1789–1848* (London: Weidenfeld and Nicolson, 1962). Also see Elizabeth Schmidt, "Top Down or Bottom Up?: Nationalist Mobilization Reconsidered, with Special Reference to Guinea (French West Africa)," under consideration by the *American Historical Review.*

2.   Benedict Anderson, *Imagined Communities: Reflections on the Origin and Spread of Nationalism,* 2nd ed. (New York: Verso, 1991), pp. 6–7. Also see Anthony D. Smith, *State and Nation in the Third World: The Western State and African Nationalism* (New York: St. Martin's Press, 1983), p. 6.

3.   Miroslav Hroch, "From National Movement to the Fully-Formed Nation: The Nation-Building Process in Europe," in *Becoming National: A Reader,* ed. Geoff Eley and Ronald Grigor Suny (New York: Oxford University Press, 1996), p. 61; Miroslav Hroch, *Social Preconditions of National Revival in Europe: A Comparative Analysis of the Social Composition of Patriotic Groups among the Smaller European Nations,* trans. Ben Fowkes (Cambridge: Cambridge University Press, 1985), pp. 4–5. Also see E. J. Hobsbawm, *Nations and Nationalism since 1780: Program, Myth, Reality,* 2nd ed. (Cambridge: Cambridge University Press, 1992), p. 87.

4.   See interview with Néné Diallo, Conakry, 11 April 1991.

5.   Walter Rodney, "Jihad and Social Revolution in Futa Djalon in the Eighteenth Century," *Journal of the Historical Society of Nigeria* 4, no. 2 (June 1968): pp. 269–274.

The Malinke (Mandinka/Mandinga/Mandingo) are part of the greater Mande social formation. Their language is called Maninka. The Fulbe are sometimes referred to as "Fulani," a Hausa term, or "Fula," a Mande term. In Guinea, the Fulbe are divided into Tukulor, originally from the Futa Toro (Senegal), and Peul, from the Futa Jallon (Guinea). The term "Peul" is a French corruption of the word "Pullo" ("Fulbe" in the plural), which is the term used by the people to describe themselves. The language of the Fulbe is Fulfulde; that of the Peul is Pulaar. See Andrew F. Clark, *From Frontier to Backwater: Economy and Society in the Upper Senegal Valley (West Africa), 1850–1920* (Lanham, Md.: University Press of America, 1999), pp. 41, 44–47; Jacques Richard-Molard, *Afrique Occidentale Française* (Paris: Éditions Berger-Levrault, 1952), p. 93.

6.   Rodney, "Jihad," pp. 269–284.

7.   Umar Tall's mid-nineteenth-century empire extended eastward from French military bases on the Lower Senegal River to the ancient city of Timbuktu on the Niger River. His capital, Dinguiraye, was in the Futa Jallon. Some decades later, Samori Touré built an empire that included Upper-Guinea and the forest region and extended eastward to modern Ghana. See Rodney, "Jihad," pp. 269–284; A. S. Kanya-Forstner, "Mali-Tukulor," in *West African Resistance: The Military Response to Colonial Occupation,* ed. Michael Crowder (New York: Africana Publishing Corp., 1971), pp. 53–79; A. S. Kanya-Forstner, *The Conquest of the Western Sudan: A Study in French Military Imperialism* (Cambridge: Cambridge University Press, 1969); David Robinson, *The Holy War of Umar Tal: The Western Sudan in the Mid-Nineteenth Century* (Oxford: Oxford University Press, 1985); Yves Person, "Guinea-Samori," trans. Joan White, in *West African Resistance,* pp. 111–143; Yves Person, *Samori: Une Révolution Dyula,* 3 vols. (Dakar, Senegal: IFAN, 1968–1975); Daniel R. Headrick, *The Tools of Empire: Technology and European Imperialism in the Nineteenth Century* (New York: Oxford University Press, 1981), pp. 119–120; Philip Curtin, Steven Feierman, Leonard Thompson, and Jan Vansina, *African History: From Earliest Times to Independence,* 2nd ed. (New York: Longman, 1995), pp. 343–351.

8.   Hobsbawm, *Nations and Nationalism,* p. 73; Duara makes similar claims for pre-modern China, India, and Japan. See Prasenjit Duara, "Historicizing National Identity, or Who Imagines What and When," in *Becoming National,* p. 152.

9.   Ruth Schachter Morgenthau, *Political Parties in French-Speaking West Africa* (Oxford: Clarendon Press, 1964), p. 234.

10.   Ibid., p. 235.

11.   Interviews with Léon Maka, Sangoyah, Conakry, 20 February 1991; Joseph Montlouis, Coléah, Conakry, 28 February 1991; Siba N. Grovogui, personal communication, 1991.

12.   Anderson, *Imagined Communities,* pp. 52–53, 113–114. Also see Smith, *State and Nation,* preface.

13.   "General Act of the Conference of Berlin (1885)," in *Colonial Rule in Africa: Readings from Primary Sources,* ed. Bruce Fetter (Madison: University of Wisconsin Press, 1979), p. 38. Also see Hobsbawm, *Nations and Nationalism,* p. 137; Smith, *State and Nation,* p. 27; Hugh Seton-Watson, *Nations and States: An Enquiry into the Origins of Nations and the Politics of Nationalism* (Boulder, Colo.: Westview Press, 1977), p. 339.

14.   Hobsbawm, *Nations and Nationalism,* p. 138. Also see Smith, *State and Nation,* p. 27.

15.   See Karl W. Deutsch, *Nationalism and Social Communication: An Inquiry into the Foundations of Nationality,* 2nd ed. (Cambridge, Mass.: M.I.T. Press, 1966), p. 97; John Breuilly, *Nationalism and the State,* 2nd ed. (Chicago: University of Chicago Press, 1994), p. 6; Hobsbawm, *Nations and Nationalism,* pp. 20, 33, 63; Hroch, "National Movement," p. 61; Anthony D. Smith, "The Origins of Nations," in *Becoming National,* pp. 107, 113, 116; Geoff Eley and Ronald Grigor Suny, "Introduction: From the Moment of Social History to the Work of Cultural Representation," in *Becoming National,* pp. 8, 22.

16.   For a more general discussion of these issues, see Hobsbawm, *Nations and Nationalism,* pp. 136–137.

17.   ANS, 2G44/30, Guinée Française, Gouverneur, "Rapport sur le Travail et la Main d'Oeuvre de la Guinée Française Pendant l'Année 1944," Conakry; Myron Echenberg, *Colonial Conscripts: The Tirailleurs Sénégalais in French West Africa, 1857–1960* (Portsmouth, N.H.: Heinemann; London: James Currey, 1991), pp. 50–54, 83–84; Nancy Ellen Lawler, *Soldiers of Misfortune: Ivoirien Tirailleurs of World War II* (Athens: Ohio University Press, 1992), p. 24; Morgenthau, *Political Parties,* p. 400; Virginia Thompson and Richard Adloff, *French West Africa* (New York: Greenwood Press, 1969), p. 227.

18.   Lawler, *Soldiers,* p. 27; Echenberg, *Colonial Conscripts,* p. 88.

19.   ANS, 2G42/22, Guinée Française, "Rapport Politique Annuel, 1942"; 2G43/19, Guinée Française, "Rapport Politique Annuel, 1943"; 2G47/22, Guinée Française, "Rapport Politique Annuel, 1947," #271/APA; 17G573, "Rapport Général d'Activité 1947–1950," présenté par Mamadou Madéïra Kéïta, Secrétaire Général du P.D.G. au Premier Congrès Territorial du Parti Démocratique de Guinée (Section Guinéenne du Rassemblement Démocratique Africain), Conakry, 15–18 October 1950. Also see Morgenthau, *Political Parties,* p. 2; Sidiki Kobélé Kéïta, *Le P.D.G.: Artisan de l'Indépendance Nationale en Guinée (1947–1958)* (Conakry: I.N.R.D.G., Bibliothèque Nationale, 1978), 1:143; Babacar Fall, *Le Travail Forcé en Afrique-Occidentale Française (1900–1945)* (Paris: Éditions Karthala, 1993), chapter 5.

20.   ANS, 2G43/25, Guinée Française, Gouverneur, "Rapport sur le Travail et la Main d'Oeuvre de la Guinée Française Pendant l'Année 1943," Conakry, 24 July 1944, #994/IT; Fall, *Travail Forcé,* pp. 157–159.

21.   ANS, 2G41/21, Guinée Française, "Rapport Politique Annuel, 1941"; Sidiki Kobélé Kéïta, *P.D.G.,* 1:96.

22. ANS, 2G42/22, "Rapport Politique Annuel, 1942"; 2G43/19, "Rapport Politique Annuel, 1943"; 2G47/22, "Rapport Politique Annuel, 1947."

23. ANS, 2G45/21, Guinée Française, Gouverneur, "Rapport sur le Travail et la Main d'Oeuvre de la Guinée Française Pendant l'Année 1945," Conakry, 2 August 1946, #208/IT.

24. Echenberg, *Colonial Conscripts,* p. 88; Myron Echenberg, " 'Morts Pour La France': The African Soldier in France during the Second World War," *Journal of African History* 26, no. 4 (1985): p. 365; ANS, 17G573, "Rapport Général d'Activité 1947–1950," P.D.G., 15–18 October 1950.

25. Echenberg, *Colonial Conscripts,* p. 84; Thompson and Adloff, *French West Africa,* p. 227.

26. Echenberg, *Colonial Conscripts,* p. 88; Lawler, *Soldiers,* pp. 34, 65.
For comparison with the King's African Rifles in British East Africa, see Timothy H. Parsons, *The African Rank-and-File: Social Implications of Colonial Military Service in the King's African Rifles, 1902–1964* (Portsmouth, N.H.: Heinemann; Oxford: James Currey, 1999), pp. 2, 25–35.

27. Lawler, *Soldiers,* pp. 75, 77, 79, 80–81, 88, 109. Also see Echenberg, *Colonial Conscripts,* pp. 88, 94; Echenberg, "Morts Pour la France," pp. 369, 377.
Joe Lunn makes similar claims concerning Senegalese soldiers recruited during World War I. See Joe Lunn, *Memoirs of the Maelstrom: A Senegalese Oral History of the First World War* (Portsmouth, N.H.: Heinemann; Oxford: James Currey, 1999), pp. 6, 120–121, 138–140, 143–146.

28. Echenberg, *Colonial Conscripts,* p. 91; Echenberg, "Morts Pour la France," p. 368; Lawler, *Soldiers,* pp. 76, 80, 87, 99; Smith, *State and Nation,* p. 48. For World War I, see Lunn, *Memoirs of the Maelstrom,* pp. 140, 146, 161, 164–166.

29. Lawler, *Soldiers,* pp. 68–69, 72–75; Echenberg, "Morts Pour la France," pp. 366–368, 377. Also see Parsons, *African Rank-and-File,* p. 232. For World War I, see Lunn, *Memoirs of the Maelstrom,* pp. 147, 157, 161, 163, 166–178, 184 n. 68, 185 n. 76.

30. Echenberg, *Colonial Conscripts,* p. 101; Echenberg, "Morts Pour la France," pp. 376, 378. Also see Parsons, *African Rank-and-File,* pp. 231–233, 243–244. For World War I, see Lunn, *Memoirs of the Maelstrom,* pp. 6, 111, 147, 157, 176–179, 187–189, 212, 226.

31. Charles de Gaulle, *The War Memoirs of Charles de Gaulle: Unity, 1942–1944* (New York: Simon and Schuster, 1959), p. 206; Charles de Gaulle, *Memoirs of Hope: Renewal and Endeavor,* trans. Terence Kilmartin (New York: Simon and Schuster, 1971), p. 11.

32. Frederick Cooper, *Decolonization and African Society: The Labor Question in French and British Africa* (New York: Cambridge University Press, 1996), p. 159; Richard-Molard, *Afrique,* pp. 165–168.

33. ANS, 2G43/19, "Rapport Politique Annuel, 1943"; Thompson and Adloff, *French West Africa,* p. 29.

34. ANS, 2G41/21, "Rapport Politique Annuel, 1941"; 2G43/19, "Rapport Politique Annuel, 1943"; Jean Suret-Canale, *French Colonialism in Tropical Africa, 1900–1945,* trans. Till Gottheiner (New York: Pica Press, 1971), pp. 462, 477, 481–482; Jean Suret-Canale, *La République de Guinée* (Paris: Éditions Sociales, 1970), p. 106; Jean Suret-Canale, "La Fin de la Chefferie en Guinée," *Journal of African History* 7, no. 3 (1966): pp. 472–475; Fall, *Travail Forcé,* pp. 270–271; Morgenthau, *Political Parties,* p. 8; Sidiki Kobélé Kéïta, *P.D.G.,* 1:101, 144–145; Thompson and Adloff, *French West Africa,* pp. 314, 316, 386, 388, 390.

35.   René Pleven, commissioner for the colonies, and Pierre Cournarie, governor-general of French West Africa, quoted in Cooper, *Decolonization,* p. 159. Also see Charles de Gaulle, *War Memoirs: The Call to Honour, 1940–1942* (New York: The Viking Press, 1955), p. 100; Suret-Canale, *French Colonialism,* p. 476; Suret-Canale, "Fin de la Chefferie," p. 472; Sidiki Kobélé Kéïta, *P.D.G.,* 1:144–145; Richard-Molard, *Afrique,* p. 166.

36.   Lawler, *Soldiers,* p. 207.

37.   ANS, 2G43/19, "Rapport Politique Annuel, 1943."

38.   Ibid.; Thompson and Adloff, *French West Africa,* p. 29.

39.   Suret-Canale, *French Colonialism,* p. 480; Suret-Canale, "Fin de la Chefferie," p. 473; Thompson and Adloff, *French West Africa,* p. 29.

40.   Richard-Molard, *Afrique,* p. 167; Morgenthau, *Political Parties,* p. 9. Also see Suret-Canale, *République,* p. 106; Suret-Canale, *French Colonialism,* pp. 479–480.

41.   Quoted in Suret-Canale, *French Colonialism,* pp. 478–479. Also see Suret-Canale, "Fin de la Chefferie," pp. 472, 475–476.

42.   Richard-Molard, *Afrique,* p. 167; Suret-Canale, *French Colonialism,* pp. 480–481; Suret-Canale, "Fin de la Chefferie," pp. 472–473; Fall, *Travail Forcé,* pp. 55–56.

43.   ANS, 2G46/50, Guinée Française, Inspecteur des Colonies (Pruvost), Mission en Guinée, "Rapport sur La Main d'Oeuvre en Guinée," Conakry, 13 July 1946, #116/C; Richard-Molard, *Afrique,* p. 167; Thompson and Adloff, *French West Africa,* pp. 315, 388.

44.   ANS, 2G41/21, "Rapport Politique Annuel, 1941."

45.   ANS, 2G44/30, "Rapport sur le Travail . . . 1944"; 2G45/21, "Rapport sur le Travail . . . 1945."

For a discussion of manioc (cassava) production and nutritional value, see Jette Bukh, *The Village Woman in Ghana* (Uppsala, Sweden: Scandinavian Institute of African Studies, 1979), pp. 29, 84–88.

46.   Lawler, *Soldiers,* pp. 204–205, 207; Suret-Canale, "Fin de la Chefferie," p. 475.

47.   ANS, 2G41/21, "Rapport Politique Annuel, 1941"; 2G42/22, "Rapport Politique Annuel, 1942"; 2G43/19, "Rapport Politique Annuel, 1943"; 2G43/25, Guinée Française, "Rapport de Tournée Effectuée du 27 Janvier au 9 Février par M. Chopin, Administrateur des Colonies, Inspecteur du Travail, dans les Cercles de Conakry-Kindia-Forécariah," Conakry, 2 April 1943; 2G43/25, "Rapport sur le Travail . . . 1943"; 2G45/21, "Rapport sur le Travail . . . 1945"; Richard-Molard, *Afrique,* p. 167.

48.   ANS, 2G41/21, "Rapport Politique Annuel, 1941." Also see 2G43/25, "Rapport de Tournée . . . ," 2 April 1943.

49.   ANS, 2G44/30, "Rapport sur le Travail . . . 1944"; Suret-Canale, "Fin de la Chefferie," pp. 474–475.

50.   Suret-Canale, *République,* pp. 106–107; Suret-Canale, *French Colonialism,* pp. 472, 477–478; Suret-Canale, "Fin de la Chefferie," pp. 475–476; Morgenthau, *Political Parties,* p. 8; Sidiki Kobélé Kéïta, *P.D.G.,* 1:101; Lawler, *Soldiers,* pp. 204, 213; Cooper, *Decolonization,* pp. 146–147; AG, AM-1339, Idiatou Camara, "La Contribution de la Femme de Guinée à la Lutte de Libération Nationale (1945–1958)" (Mémoire de Fin d'Études Supérieures, IPGAN, Conakry, 1979), p. 29.

51.   ANS, 2G43/19, "Rapport Politique Annuel, 1943"; 2G44/30, "Rapport sur le Travail . . . 1944"; 2G45/21, "Rapport sur le Travail . . . 1945"; Suret-Canale, *French Colonialism,* p. 472; Suret-Canale, "Fin de la Chefferie," pp. 474–475; Cooper, *Decolonization,* pp. 149, 152.

52.   Kouroussa Archives, Political Reports, 25 August 1942, quoted in Suret-Canale, *French Colonialism,* p. 472. Also see Sidiki Kobélé Kéïta, *P.D.G.,* 1:99.

53. ANS, 2G41/21, "Rapport Politique Annuel, 1941"; 2G43/19, "Rapport Politique Annuel, 1943"; 2G46/50, "Rapport sur La Main d'Oeuvre en Guinée," 13 July 1946; Suret-Canale, *French Colonialism,* pp. 477–479; Suret-Canale, "Fin de la Chefferie," pp. 473–474; Fall, *Travail Forcé,* pp. 270–271.

54. ANS, 2G43/19, "Rapport Politique Annuel, 1943."

55. Richard-Molard, *Afrique,* p. 167. Also see Suret-Canale, *French Colonialism,* p. 479; Suret-Canale, "Fin de la Chefferie," pp. 473–474.

56. AG, 1E38, Guinée Française, Cercle de Gaoual, Subdivision Centrale, "Rapport Politique Annuel, Année 1948"; Sidiki Kobélé Kéïta, *P.D.G.,* 1:144; Suret-Canale, "Fin de la Chefferie," pp. 474–475.

57. ANS, 2G43/19, "Rapport Politique Annuel, 1943."

58. Suret-Canale, *French Colonialism,* pp. 483–484, 490 n. 49; Suret-Canale, "Fin de la Chefferie," pp. 474–475.

59. ANS, 2G43/25, "Rapport de Tournée . . . ," 2 April 1943; 2G46/50, "Rapport sur La Main d'Oeuvre en Guinée," 13 July 1946; 2G46/50, Guinée Française, Inspecteur du Travail, "Rapport Annuel du Travail, 1946," Conakry, 15 February 1947, #66/IT.GV.

60. ANS, 2G43/25, "Rapport sur le Travail . . . 1943."

61. ANS, 2G43/19, "Rapport Politique Annuel, 1943." Also see 2G41/21, "Rapport Politique Annuel, 1941."

62. ANS, 2G43/19, "Rapport Politique Annuel, 1943."

63. ANS, 2G41/21, "Rapport Politique Annuel, 1941." Also see 2G42/22, "Rapport Politique Annuel, 1942."

64. ANS, 2G46/22, Guinée Française, "Rapport Politique Annuel, 1946," #284/APA; 2G47/22, "Rapport Politique Annuel, 1947."

65. ANS, 2G43/19, "Rapport Politique Annuel, 1943."

66. ANS, 2G45/105, AOF, Dakar, "Exposé Sommaire de la Situation Politique de l'Afrique Occidentale Française et du Togo Pendant le Mois de Février 1945," 30 April 1945.
In his contemporary account, Richard-Molard describes the burden of the war effort as unprecedented in its intensity, and sanctions for the failure to fulfill impossible demands as draconian in character. See Richard-Molard, *Afrique,* pp. 166–167.

67. ANS, 2G45/105, AOF, Dakar, "Exposé Sommaire de la Situation Politique de l'Afrique Occidentale Française et du Togo au 30 Mai 1945," 26 June 1945. Also see 2G45/105, "Situation Politique de l'AOF . . . Mois de Février 1945."

68. Cooper, *Decolonization,* pp. 178, 290. Also see Catherine Coquery-Vidrovitch, "Nationalité et Citoyenneté en Afrique Occidentale Français[e]: Originaires et Citoyens dans Le Sénégal Colonial," *Journal of African History* 42, no. 2 (2001): pp. 285–286, 296, 304–305; Tony Chafer, *The End of Empire in French West Africa: France's Successful Decolonization?* (New York: Berg, 2002), pp. 74–76, 90, 94–103, 109, 111, 119, 157, 188.

69. Cooper, *Decolonization,* pp. 229, 286, 292. For a more general treatment of this theme, see Partha Chatterjee, *The Nation and Its Fragments: Colonial and Postcolonial Histories* (Princeton, N.J.: Princeton University Press, 1993), pp. 10, 26.

70. John D. Hargreaves, *Decolonization in Africa,* 2nd ed. (New York: Longman, 1996), pp. 59–60.

71. "The Atlantic Charter, Joint Declaration by the President and the Prime Minister, Declaration of Principles, Known as the Atlantic Charter," 14 August 1941, U.S.-U.K., 55 Stat. app. 1603. http://www1.umn.edu/humanrts/education/FDRjointdec.html

72. "Declaration by United Nations," 1 January 1942. http://www.ibiblio.org/pha/policy/1942/420101a.html

73.   Hargreaves, *Decolonization,* pp. 59–60, 68; Suret-Canale, *French Colonialism,* p. 485; Chafer, *End of Empire,* p. 91; James S. Coleman, *Nigeria: Background to National-ism* (Berkeley: University of California Press, 1958), pp. 231–233; Thomas Hodgkin, *Nationalism in Colonial Africa* (New York: New York University Press, 1957), pp. 19, 32–33, 142.

74.   Suret-Canale, *French Colonialism,* pp. 484–486; Hargreaves, *Decolonization,* pp. 68, 86–87; Chafer, *End of Empire,* p. 85; Smith, *State and Nation,* pp. 48–49; de Gaulle, *War Memoirs: Unity,* pp. 205–209.

75.   Suret-Canale, *French Colonialism,* pp. 484–485; Patrick Manning, *Francophone Sub-Saharan Africa, 1880–1985* (New York: Cambridge University Press, 1988), p. 141; de Gaulle, *War Memoirs: Unity,* pp. 207–209; de Gaulle, *Memoirs of Hope,* p. 12.

76.   Morgenthau, *Political Parties,* p. 37; Suret-Canale, *French Colonialism,* p. 486; Hargreaves, *Decolonization,* p. 69.

77.   Suret-Canale, *French Colonialism,* pp. 485, 487. Also see "Recommendations Adopted by the Brazzaville Conference," in *Colonial Rule in Africa,* p. 169.

78.   "Brazzaville Recommendations," p. 169; Morgenthau, *Political Parties,* pp. 38–40; Manning, *Francophone,* p. 141.

79.   "Brazzaville Recommendations," p. 170; B. Ameillon, *La Guinée: Bilan d'une Indépendance,* Cahiers Libres, nos. 58–59 (Paris: François Maspero, 1964), p. 19.

80.   "Brazzaville Recommendations," pp. 170–173; Hodgkin, *Nationalism,* p. 35; Har-greaves, *Decolonization,* p. 69; Manning, *Francophone,* p. 141; Suret-Canale, *French Colonialism,* pp. 381–382, 487; Morgenthau, *Political Parties,* p. 39; Sidiki Kobélé Kéïta, *P.D.G.,* 1:73.

81.   Morgenthau, *Political Parties,* pp. 40–41, 55; Coquery-Vidrovitch, "Nationalité," pp. 286, 297 n. 53, 304.

82.   Morgenthau, *Political Parties,* p. 28; Manning, *Francophone,* p. 141.

83.   Ordinance of August 22, 1945, quoted in Morgenthau, *Political Parties,* p. 30. Also see Sidiki Kobélé Kéïta, *P.D.G.,* 1:157; Hargreaves, *Decolonization,* p. 86.

84.   Morgenthau, *Political Parties,* p. 40; Hargreaves, *Decolonization,* pp. 85–86; Manning, *Francophone,* p. 142.

85.   CAOM, Carton 2181, dos. 6, "Note sur la Guinée," 6 May 1958; Morgenthau, *Political Parties,* pp. 396, 400, 412; Sidiki Kobélé Kéïta, *P.D.G.,* 1:157, 182, 191; Thomp-son and Adloff, *French West Africa,* p. 555.

86.   Jean-Pierre Rioux, *The Fourth Republic, 1944–1958,* trans. Godfrey Rogers (New York: Cambridge University Press, 1987), pp. 100–101; de Gaulle, *War Memoirs: Unity,* pp. 159–160, 164, 169–170, 186, 205, 286–287, 327, 357; Charles de Gaulle, *The War Memoirs of Charles de Gaulle: Salvation, 1944–1946* (New York: Simon and Schuster, 1960), pp. 10–11, 48, 113, 270–272, 307.

87.   Rioux, *Fourth Republic,* pp. 100–101. Also see de Gaulle, *War Memoirs: Salva-tion,* pp. 319–320.

88.   Manning, *Francophone,* p. 142; Hargreaves, *Decolonization,* pp. 86–87; Morgen-thau, *Political Parties,* pp. 41–43, 85, 379–381, 396–397. Relevant excerpts of the April 1946 Constitution can be found in Morgenthau, pp. 379–381.

89.   Morgenthau, *Political Parties,* pp. 44, 396–397; Rioux, *Fourth Republic,* p. 101; Edward Mortimer, *France and the Africans, 1944–1960: A Political History* (New York: Walker, 1969), pp. 81–82.

90.   "Brazzaville Recommendations," pp. 170–172.

91.   ANS, 2G46/22 "Rapport Politique Annuel, 1946"; Hodgkin, *Nationalism,* p. 36; Hargreaves, *Decolonization,* pp. 69, 87; Thompson and Adloff, *French West Africa,* p. 34;

Morgenthau, *Political Parties,* p. 43; Pierre Kipré, *Le Congrès de Bamako ou La Naissance du RDA en 1946,* vol. 3 of *Afrique Contemporaine* (Paris: Éditions Chaka, 1989), pp. 53–54.

92. Morgenthau, *Political Parties,* p. 43.

93. Ibid., pp. 46–47; Kipré, *Congrès,* p. 83; Rioux, *Fourth Republic,* p. 101.

94. Rioux, *Fourth Republic,* pp. 102–103; Manning, *Francophone,* p. 142; Morgenthau, *Political Parties,* pp. 43–48, 86–87; Kipré, *Congrès,* pp. 55, 83–84. Relevant excerpts of what would become the October 1946 Constitution can be found in Morgenthau, pp. 382–385.

95. "Constitution of the French Republic of 28 October 1946," as quoted in Morgenthau, *Political Parties,* pp. 384–385.

96. Mortimer, *France and the Africans,* pp. 39, 101–102; Morgenthau, *Political Parties,* pp. 43, 43 n. 2, 49–50; Articles 80–82 of the "October Constitution," as quoted in Morgenthau, pp. 384–385; Kipré, *Congrès,* p. 62; Chafer, *End of Empire,* pp. 64, 115 n. 40. By distinguishing between those who lived according to French civil and African customary law, France justified its policy of granting disparate political rights to those of French and African origin. See Coquery-Vidrovitch, "Nationalité," pp. 285, 290–292, 296–297, 299–301, 303.

97. Thompson and Adloff, *French West Africa,* p. 46.

98. Morgenthau, *Political Parties,* pp. 48–50, 53, 87, 382–385; Kipré, *Congrès,* pp. 62–63; Sidiki Kobélé Kéïta, *P.D.G.,* 1:84.

99. Hargreaves, *Decolonization,* p. 88; Morgenthau, *Political Parties,* pp. 43, 50, 51, 53, 56, 394, 396, 400; Thompson and Adloff, *French West Africa,* pp. 45, 55; Mortimer, *France and the Africans,* pp. 173, 174 n. 1.

100. Rioux, *Fourth Republic,* p. 106; Hargreaves, *Decolonization,* p. 87; Morgenthau, *Political Parties,* pp. 54, 87, 397–398.

101. Manning, *Francophone,* p. 142; Kipré, *Congrès,* pp. 63, 65, 67, 79.

102. Kipré, *Congrès,* pp. 63, 65, 86–87, 89–90; Manning, *Francophone,* p. 142; Hargreaves, *Decolonization,* p. 99; Morgenthau, *Political Parties,* pp. 88–89.

103. Morgenthau, *Political Parties,* pp. 225, 418; Sidiki Kobélé Kéïta, *P.D.G.,* 1:169.

104. Sidiki Kobélé Kéïta, *P.D.G.,* 1:170–172, 186.

105. Kipré, *Congrès,* p. 111; Ameillon, *Guinée,* pp. 49, 51; Sidiki Kobélé Kéïta, *P.D.G.,* 1:179, 186–187; Sidiki Kobélé Kéïta, *Ahmed Sékou Touré: L'Homme du 28 Septembre 1958,* 2nd ed. (Conakry: I.N.R.D.G., Bibliothèque Nationale, 1977), pp. 29, 41; interview with Joseph Montlouis, Coléah, Conakry, 6 March 1991; AG, 1E41, Guinée Française, Services de Police, Conakry, "Renseignements A/S Réunion Tenue sous l'Initiative du Comité du Rassemblement Démocratique Africain de Bamako," 15 October 1946; ANS, 17G573, Section Locale du R.D.A. à Conakry, 9 July 1947.

106. Manning, *Francophone,* pp. 142–143; Hargreaves, *Decolonization,* p. 99; Kipré, *Congrès,* p. 135; Sidiki Kobélé Kéïta, *P.D.G.,* 1:187.

107. Chafer, *End of Empire,* pp. 75–76, 109.

108. Kipré, *Congrès,* pp. 137–138, 160–162, 164–169; Hodgkin, *Nationalism,* pp. 145–146; Sidiki Kobélé Kéïta, *P.D.G.,* 1:188. The RDA's position was in keeping with the United Nations Charter, signed in June 1945. The UN Charter stresses that "relations among nations" should be "based on respect for the principle of equal rights and self-determination of peoples." Furthermore, the United Nations will promote "universal respect for, and observance of, human rights and fundamental freedoms for all without distinction as to race, sex, language, or religion." Chapter I, Article 1 and Chapter IX, Article 55, "Charter of the United Nations," San Fran-

cisco, 26 June 1945. http://www.un.org/aboutun/charter/chapter1.htm; http://www.un.org/aboutun/charter/chapter9.htm

109. Manning, *Francophone,* pp. 142–143; Morgenthau, *Political Parties,* p. 90.

110. Sidiki Kobélé Kéïta, *P.D.G.,* 1:172, 190; Suret-Canale, *République,* p. 144; Suret-Canale, "Fin de la Chefferie," p. 477; Morgenthau, *Political Parties,* pp. 220, 223–224.

111. AG, 1E41, "Renseignements A/S Réunion . . . RDA," 15 October 1946.

112. Montlouis, interview, 6 March 1991; Morgenthau, *Political Parties,* p. 418.

113. Sidiki Kobélé Kéïta, *P.D.G.,* 1:194; Suret-Canale, *République,* p. 144; Idiatou Camara, "Contribution de la Femme," p. 33; CRDA, P.D.G., Secrétaire Général, "Circulaire," Conakry, 15 June 1947.

114. Idiatou Camara, "Contribution de la Femme," p. 33.

115. CRDA, "Statuts de la Section de Guinée du R.D.A.," adoptés à Conakry, 14 June 1947; P.D.G., "Circulaire," 15 June 1947; AG, 5B49, Guinée Française, Inspecteur des Affaires Administratives, pour le Gouverneur, Conakry, à Consul de France au Liberia, l'Agent Consulaire à Bissao, l'Agent Consulaire à Freetown, 5 July 1948, #383/APA; Sidiki Kobélé Kéïta, *P.D.G.,* 1:194.

116. ANS, 17G573, Section Locale du R.D.A. . . . , 9 July 1947; 17G573, Guinée Française, Chef du Service de la Sûreté, Conakry, à Inspecteur Général de la Sûreté en A.O.F., Dakar, 5 November 1948, #11762/64 PS; Sidiki Kobélé Kéïta, *P.D.G.,* 1:194–196.

117. ANS, 17G573, Guinée Française, Services de Police, Conakry, "Renseignements *Objet:* Groupements Politiques en Guinée," 13 July 1947. Also see 17G573, Guinée Française, Services de Police, Conakry, "Renseignements A/S Deputé Yacine Diallo et Association Gilbert Vieillard," 15 March 1947; 17G573, Guinée Française, Services de Police, Conakry, "Renseignements A/S Section R.D.A. Kindia," 1 July 1947, 504 A. #575 G.

For overlapping GEC/RDA membership, see ANS, 17G573, Guinée Française, Services de Police, Conakry, "Renseignements *Objet:* Constitution de Nouveaux Groupements Politiques," 10 March 1947; 17G573, Section Locale du R.D.A. . . . , 9 July 1947.

118. AG, 1E41, Madéïra Kéïta, Secrétaire Général du R.D.A., Section de Guinée, Conakry, à Gouverneur de la Guinée Française, 30 June 1947: "Declaration d'Association" ; 1E41, Secrétaire Général du R.D.A., S/Section de Macenta, à Commandant de Cercle, Macenta, 5 August 1947; Sidiki Kobélé Kéïta, *P.D.G.,* 1:197.

119. ANS, 17G573, Sûreté, Conakry, à Sûreté, Dakar, 5 November 1948; Doudou Guèye, "Notre Volonté d'Union," *Le Phare de Guinée,* 15 October 1947, p. 1.

120. Sidiki Kobélé Kéïta, *P.D.G.,* 1:197.

Gabriel d'Arboussier, a native of the French Soudan and a resident of Senegal, had recently been elected to represent the Ivory Coast in the Assembly of the French Union. ANS, 21G91, "Assemblée de l'Union Française, Liste des Conseillers Elus" (dated after 13 January 1947); Georges Chaffard, *Les Carnets Secrets de la Décolonisation* (Paris: Calmann-Lévy, 1965), 1:103–104.

A police report noted the registration of the Guinean section of the RDA "after a long stay in Conakry" by Gabriel d'Arboussier. ANS, 17G573, Police, " . . . Groupements Politiques en Guinée," 13 July 1947. Also see 17G573, Guinée Française, Assistant de Police *Sidibé* Soulé, Kankan, à Commissaire de Police du Cercle de Kankan, 24 June 1947; 17G573, "Revue Trimestrielle de la Guinée, 4ème Trimestre 1947"; 17G573, "Rapport Général d'Activité 1947–1950," P.D.G., 15–18 October 1950; CRDA, P.D.G., "Circulaire," 15 June 1947.

121. ANS, 17G573, "Revue Trimestrielle . . . 4ème Trimestre 1947"; 17G573, Guinée Française, Services de Police, Conakry, "Renseignements A/S Nouveaux Groupements Politiques," 10 November 1947.

CHAPTER 2: *LIBERTÉ, ÉGALITÉ, FRATERNITÉ:* MILITARY VETERANS AND THE POSTWAR NATIONALIST MOVEMENT, 1940–1955

1. Nancy Ellen Lawler, *Soldiers of Misfortune: Ivoirien Tirailleurs of World War II* (Athens: Ohio University Press, 1992), pp. 93–94, 118; Myron Echenberg, *Colonial Conscripts: The Tirailleurs Sénégalais in French West Africa, 1857–1960* (Portsmouth, N.H.: Heinemann; London: James Currey, 1991), pp. 88, 193 n. 40.

2. Lawler, *Soldiers,* pp. 94–114; Echenberg, *Colonial Conscripts,* pp. 88, 96, 97, 193 n. 40; Myron Echenberg, " 'Morts Pour La France': The African Soldier in France during the Second World War," *Journal of African History* 26, no. 4 (1985): pp. 367–372.

3. Lawler, *Soldiers,* pp. 102, 104, 105, 107–108; Echenberg, *Colonial Conscripts,* pp. 87, 96–97; Echenberg, "Morts Pour la France," p. 372; Myron Echenberg, "Tragedy at Thiaroye: The Senegalese Soldiers' Uprising of 1944," in *African Labor History,* ed. Peter C. W. Gutkind, Robin Cohen, and Jean Copans (Beverly Hills, Calif.: Sage Publications, 1978), p. 113.

4. Lawler, *Soldiers,* pp. 104, 108; Echenberg, *Colonial Conscripts,* p. 97; Echenberg, "Morts Pour la France," p. 372; Echenberg, "Tragedy at Thiaroye," p. 113.

5. Lawler, *Soldiers,* pp. 98, 102, 113; Echenberg, "Morts Pour la France," p. 372; Echenberg, "Tragedy at Thiaroye," pp. 110, 113.

6. Lawler, *Soldiers,* p. 93; Alistair Horne, *To Lose a Battle: France 1940* (Boston: Little, Brown, 1969), p. 583; Charles de Gaulle, *War Memoirs: The Call to Honour, 1940–1942* (New York: Viking Press, 1955), pp. 83–84, 88–94.

7. Lawler, *Soldiers,* pp. 149, 154–155, 168, 171–178; Echenberg, *Colonial Conscripts,* pp. 87–88, 98; Echenberg, "Morts Pour la France," pp. 364, 374; Jean Suret-Canale, *French Colonialism in Tropical Africa, 1900–1945,* trans. Till Gottheiner (New York: Pica Press, 1971), p. 469; Charles de Gaulle, *The War Memoirs of Charles de Gaulle: Unity, 1942–1944* (New York: Simon and Schuster, 1959), pp. 67, 110–111, 152, 322–323; Charles de Gaulle, *The War Memoirs of Charles de Gaulle: Salvation, 1944–1946* (New York: Simon and Schuster, 1960), pp. 11–13, 36, 151–152.

8. Lawler, *Soldiers,* pp. 78, 80–81, 88, 109, 178–182, 187–188, 191; Echenberg, *Colonial Conscripts,* pp. 92–94, 98–99; Echenberg, "Morts Pour la France," pp. 373–374, 379; de Gaulle, *War Memoirs: Unity,* pp. 158–160, 164, 169–170, 186, 205, 241, 286–287, 291–292, 295, 323, 327, 332–333, 342, 348, 351, 356–357; de Gaulle, *War Memoirs: Salvation,* pp. 10–11, 12–15, 18, 24, 31, 36, 114.

9. de Gaulle, *War Memoirs: Honour,* pp. 106–107, 111, 132, 136; de Gaulle, *War Memoirs: Unity,* pp. 35, 110–112, 164, 205–206, 208, 277, 322; de Gaulle, *War Memoirs: Salvation,* pp. 32, 36, 38.

10. Lawler, *Soldiers,* pp. 193–194, 196; Echenberg, *Colonial Conscripts,* pp. 97–99; Echenberg, "Morts Pour la France," pp. 373–374; Echenberg, "Tragedy at Thiaroye," pp. 113–114.

11. Quoted in Lawler, *Soldiers,* p. 194; de Gaulle, *War Memoirs: Unity,* pp. 126, 168, 207.

12. For an in-depth discussion of these incidents, see Echenberg, "Tragedy at Thiaroye," pp. 109–128; Echenberg, *Colonial Conscripts,* pp. 100–104; Echenberg, "Morts Pour la France," p. 375; Lawler, *Soldiers,* pp. 194–200.

13. Echenberg, "Tragedy at Thiaroye," pp. 109–110, 116–117; Echenberg, *Colonial Conscripts,* pp. 100–101; Echenberg, "Morts Pour la France," pp. 375–376; Lawler, *Soldiers,* p. 194.

14. Echenberg, *Colonial Conscripts,* pp. 128, 159; Lawler, *Soldiers,* p. 239.

15. Echenberg, *Colonial Conscripts,* p. 128; Lawler, *Soldiers,* p. 240.

16. For a discussion of these issues among veterans in the French Soudan, see Gregory Mann, "Old Soldiers, Young Men: Masculinity, Islam, and Military Veterans in Late 1950s Soudan Français (Mali)," in *Men and Masculinities in Modern Africa,* ed. Lisa A. Lindsay and Stephan F. Miescher (Portsmouth, N.H.: Heinemann, 2003), pp. 74–75. Also see Jean Suret-Canale, *La République de Guinée* (Paris: Éditions Sociales, 1970), pp. 136–137; Suret-Canale, *French Colonialism,* pp. 374–375, 377, 384, 388; Echenberg, *Colonial Conscripts,* pp. 11–19.

For a comparison with the King's African Rifles in British East Africa, see Timothy H. Parsons, *The African Rank-and-File: Social Implications of Colonial Military Service in the King's African Rifles, 1902–1964* (Portsmouth, N.H.: Heinemann; Oxford: James Currey, 1999), pp. 1, 4–6, 224–225, 231–260. For Senegalese veterans after World War I, see Joe Lunn, *Memoirs of the Maelstrom: A Senegalese Oral History of the First World War* (Portsmouth, N.H.: Heinemann; Oxford: James Currey, 1999), pp. 191–192, 214.

17. Mann, "Old Soldiers," pp. 73–74; Echenberg, *Colonial Conscripts,* pp. 11–19; Martin Klein, *Slavery and Colonial Rule in French West Africa* (New York: Cambridge University Press, 1998), pp. 216–217, 251; interview with Ibrahima Fofana, Lansanaya, Conakry, 5 May 1991. Also see Lunn, *Memoirs of the Maelstrom,* pp. 209, 212, 226.

18. Mann, "Old Soldiers," pp. 74–76; Echenberg, *Colonial Conscripts,* pp. 136, 138; Stephan F. Miescher and Lisa A. Lindsay, "Introduction: Men and Masculinities in Modern African History," in *Men and Masculinities,* pp. 7–11. Also see Lunn, *Memoirs of the Maelstrom,* pp. 191–192.

For a discussion of adult, senior, and "big man" status, and their evolution in the colonial environment, see Lisa A. Lindsay, " 'No Need . . . to Think of Home?': Masculinity and Domestic Life on the Nigerian Railway, c. 1940–61," *Journal of African History* 39, no. 3 (1998): pp. 446, 448–449, 454, 457–458, 460–462, 465; Lisa A. Lindsay, *Working with Gender: Wage Labor and Social Change in Southwestern Nigeria, 1930–1964* (Portsmouth, N.H.: Heinemann, 2003), pp. 36, 41–43, 45, 134; Lisa A. Lindsay, "Money, Marriage, and Masculinity on the Colonial Nigerian Railway," in *Men and Masculinities,* pp. 140–141; Carolyn A. Brown, "A 'Man' in the Village is a 'Boy' in the Workplace: Colonial Racism, Worker Militance, and Igbo Notions of Masculinity in the Nigerian Coal Industry, 1930–1945," in *Men and Masculinities,* pp. 161–162, 167; Pashington Obeng, "Gendered Nationalism: Forms of Masculinity in Modern Asante of Ghana," in *Men and Masculinities,* pp. 193, 201–203, 206.

19. Suret-Canale, *République,* p. 137. Also see Klein, *Slavery and Colonial Rule,* pp. 216–219; interview with Léon Maka, Sangoyah, Conakry, 25 February 1991; Ibrahima Fofana, interview, 5 May 1991.

20. See Miescher and Lindsay, "Introduction," p. 10.

21. Echenberg, *Colonial Conscripts,* pp. 149, 155; Lawler, *Soldiers,* p. 214. Also see Parsons, *African Rank-and-File,* pp. 225, 231, 235–236, 252, 260; Lunn, *Memoirs of the Maelstrom,* pp. 196–199, 225.

22. ANS, 2G47/121, Guinée Française, Affaires Politiques et Administratives, "Revues Trimestrielles des Événements, 1er Trimestre 1947," 17 June 1947, #143 APA; 2G47/121, Guinée Française, Affaires Politiques et Administratives, "Revues Trimestrielles des Événements, 2ème Trimestre 1947," 11 October 1947, #273 APA; 2G47/121, Guinée Française, Affaires Politiques et Administratives, "Revues Trimestrielles des Événements, 3ème

Trimestre 1947," 5 December 1947, #389 APA; 2G47/22, Guinée Française, Gouverneur, "Rapport Politique Annuel, 1947," #271/APA; Echenberg, *Colonial Conscripts,* p. 133.

23.   Echenberg, *Colonial Conscripts,* pp. 133–136, 138; Lawler, *Soldiers,* p. 217; Virginia Thompson and Richard Adloff, *French West Africa* (New York: Greenwood Press, 1969), p. 229.

24.   Echenberg, *Colonial Conscripts,* p. 155. Also see Parsons, *African Rank-and-File,* pp. 225, 260.

25.   Echenberg, *Colonial Conscripts,* pp. 139–140.

26.   Ibid., pp. 134–135, 138; Lawler, *Soldiers,* p. 217; ANS, 2G47/121, "Revues Trimestrielles . . . 3ème Trimestre 1947"; 2G47/22, "Rapport Politique Annuel, 1947."

27.   ANS, 21G116, Guinée Française, Service de la Sûreté, Conakry, "Renseignements *Objet:* Réaction des Militaires Indigènes Devant les Élections," ca. 1946.

28.   In June 1947, as a result of tremendous political pressure, the French government granted a general amnesty to those convicted and imprisoned during the Thiaroye uprising. By that time, however, 5 of the 34 prisoners had died in captivity. Echenberg, "Tragedy at Thiaroye," pp. 115–117, 123; Echenberg, *Colonial Conscripts,* pp. 101, 141–142, 147–148; Echenberg, "Morts Pour la France," pp. 376–377; Lawler, *Soldiers,* p. 204; ANS, 17G573, Gendarmerie, A.O.F., "En Guinée Française," 12 September 1951, #174/4.

29.   AG, 1E42, Guinée Française, Commissariat de Police, Kankan, "Renseignements, Situation des Anciens Combattants," 22 May 1950, #518/PS/I; Echenberg, "Tragedy at Thiaroye," p. 124; Echenberg, *Colonial Conscripts,* pp. 104, 152; Thompson and Adloff, *French West Africa,* pp. 227–228. Also see Lunn, *Memoirs of the Maelstrom,* pp. 6, 188, 194, 224–226.

30.   ANS, 21G116, Sûreté, "Réaction des Militaires Indigènes Devant les Élections," ca. 1946; AG, 1E37, Guinée Française, Cercle de Beyla, "Rapport Politique Annuel, Année 1947"; 5B49, Guinée Française, Gouverneur, Conakry, à Procureur de la République, Conakry, 10 May 1948, #247/APA; 5B49, Guinée Française, Inspecteur des Affaires Administratives, pour le Gouverneur, Conakry, à Procureur de la République, Conakry, 24 August 1948, #548/APA; 1E38, Guinée Française, Cercle de Kouroussa, "Rapport Politique Annuel, Année 1948"; 1E39, Guinée Française, Cercle de Kouroussa, "Rapport Politique Annuel, Année 1949"; Echenberg, *Colonial Conscripts,* pp. 103, 144; Echenberg, "Tragedy at Thiaroye," p. 119; Echenberg, "Morts Pour la France," p. 378; Lawler, *Soldiers,* p. 197.

31.   Echenberg, *Colonial Conscripts,* pp. 128, 160.

32.   Ibid., pp. 140, 145, 149; Ruth Schachter Morgenthau, *Political Parties in French-Speaking West Africa* (Oxford: Clarendon Press, 1964), p. 401.

33.   Echenberg, *Colonial Conscripts,* pp. 15, 18, 75–76; Klein, *Slavery and Colonial Rule,* pp. 216–217, 251; Ibrahima Fofana, interview, 5 May 1991.

34.   Echenberg, *Colonial Conscripts,* p. 91; Echenberg, "Morts Pour la France," pp. 366–368, 377; Philip Curtin, Steven Feierman, Leonard Thompson, and Jan Vansina, *African History: From Earliest Times to Independence,* 2nd ed. (New York: Longman, 1995), pp. 444–445; Anthony D. Smith, *State and Nation in the Third World: The Western State and African Nationalism* (New York: St. Martin's Press, 1983), p. 48; John Breuilly, *Nationalism and the State,* 2nd ed. (Chicago: University of Chicago Press, 1994), p. 20. For World War I, see Lunn, *Memoirs of the Maelstrom,* pp. 140, 146–147, 157, 161, 163–178, 184 n. 68, 185 n. 76.

35.   Echenberg, "Tragedy at Thiaroye," p. 118; Echenberg, *Colonial Conscripts,* pp. 91, 143; Echenberg, "Morts Pour la France," pp. 377–378; Lawler, *Soldiers,* pp. 68–69,

73–75, 188, 192–193. For World War I, see Lunn, *Memoirs of the Maelstrom,* pp. 6, 111, 147, 157, 176–179, 187–189, 212, 226.

36. ANS, 2G41/21, Guinée Française, "Rapport Politique Annuel, 1941"; 2G45/105, AOF, Dakar, "Rapport sur la Situation Politique de l'Afrique Occidentale Française et du Togo au 30 Juin 1945," July 1945; 2G45/105, AOF, Dakar, "Rapport Sur la Situation Politique de l'Afrique Occidentale Française et du Togo au 31 Juillet 1945"; Echenberg, *Colonial Conscripts,* pp. 103, 143; Echenberg, "Tragedy at Thiaroye," p. 119; Echenberg, "Morts Pour la France," p. 378; Lawler, *Soldiers,* p. 197.

37. ANS, 2G47/121, "Revues Trimestrielles . . . 2ème Trimestre 1947"; 2G47/121, "Revues Trimestrielles . . . 3ème Trimestre 1947"; Echenberg, *Colonial Conscripts,* p. 102; Echenberg, "Morts Pour la France," p. 377.

38. Echenberg, *Colonial Conscripts,* pp. 103–104; Echenberg, "Tragedy at Thiaroye," pp. 118–119, 124; Echenberg, "Morts Pour la France," pp. 377, 379.

39. Echenberg, *Colonial Conscripts,* pp. 129–131.

40. ANS, 2G47/121, "Revues Trimestrielles . . . 2ème Trimestre 1947"; 2G47/22, "Rapport Politique Annuel, 1947."

41. Echenberg, *Colonial Conscripts,* pp. 130–131.

42. Ibid., pp. 131, 133.

43. ANS, 2G47/121, "Revues Trimestrielles . . . 1er Trimestre 1947"; 2G47/121, "Revues Trimestrielles . . . 2ème Trimestre 1947."

44. Echenberg, *Colonial Conscripts,* pp. 132, 201 n. 32.

45. ANS, 2G45/105, AOF, Dakar, "Exposé Sommaire de la Situation Politique de l'Afrique Occidentale Française et du Togo Pendant le Mois de Janvier 1945," 28 March 1945; Echenberg, *Colonial Conscripts,* pp. 102, 104, 142, 147–148, 152; Echenberg, "Tragedy at Thiaroye," pp. 118, 121–122, 124; Echenberg, "Morts Pour la France," p. 379; Lawler, *Soldiers,* pp. 72–73; Thompson and Adloff, *French West Africa,* pp. 227–228.

46. ANS, 2G45/105, AOF, "Situation Politique de l'AOF . . . Mois de Janvier 1945"; Echenberg, *Colonial Conscripts,* pp. 102, 104, 142, 147–148, 152; Echenberg, "Tragedy at Thiaroye," pp. 118, 121–122, 124; Echenberg, "Morts Pour la France," p. 379; Lawler, *Soldiers,* pp. 72–73.

47. Echenberg, *Colonial Conscripts,* pp. 136, 153; Thompson and Adloff, *French West Africa,* pp. 227–228.

48. For labor's embrace of French universalism, see Frederick Cooper, *Decolonization and African Society: The Labor Question in French and British Africa* (New York: Cambridge University Press, 1996), pp. 178, 184, 290.

49. ANS, 21G101, Gouverneur du Sénégal, "Rapport Politique, 4ème Trimestre, 1949." Also see 2G45/105, AOF, "Situation Politique de l'AOF . . . Mois de Janvier 1945."

50. AG, 5B43, Gouverneur Général, Dakar, à Gouverneur de la Guinée Française, Conakry, 7 July 1947, #352/AP.2.

51. Echenberg, *Colonial Conscripts,* p. 159; Sidiki Kobélé Kéïta, *Le P.D.G.: Artisan de l'Indépendance Nationale en Guinée (1947–1958)* (Conakry: I.N.R.D.G., Bibliothèque Nationale, 1978), 1:122.

52. AG, 5B43, Guinée Française, Gouverneur, Conakry, à Gouverneur Général, Dakar, 22 February 1947, #37/BM. Also see ANS, 2G47/121, "Revues Trimestrielles . . . 1er Trimestre 1947"; 2G47/121, "Revues Trimestrielles . . . 2ème Trimestre 1947"; 2G47/22, "Rapport Politique Annuel, 1947."

53. AG, 2Z5, "Association des Anciens Combattants et Amicale des Anciens Combattants de la Guinée Française, 1920–1947"; 2Z5, 504/2, "Renseignements," 3 March 1947,

#148/C; 5B47, "Statuts de l'Association des Anciens Combattants et Anciens Militaires Africains de la Guinée," Conakry, ca. 12 March 1947. Also see 2G56/138, Guinée Française, Gouverneur, "Rapport Politique Mensuel, Mai 1956," 11 June 1956, #260/APA.

54. AG, 2Z5, 504/2, "Renseignements," 12 March 1947, #177/C/PS.

55. AG, 2Z5, 504/2, "Renseignements," 3 March 1947.

56. AG, 5B43, Guinée Française, Gouverneur, Conakry, à Intendant Général, Chef de Service de l'Intendance des Troupes du Groupe de l'A.O.F., Dakar, 10 March 1947, #43/BM.

57. AG, 5B43, Guinée Française, Gouverneur, Conakry, à Gouverneur Général, Dakar, 21 June 1947, #155/APA; Suret-Canale, *République,* p. 107.

58. AG, 5B43, Gouverneur à Gouverneur Général, 21 June 1947; AG, 5B43, Gouverneur Général à Gouverneur, Guinée Française, 7 July 1947.

59. Kaba was an unsuccessful candidate for the First Constituent Assembly in October 1945, the Second Constituent Assembly in June 1946, the National Assembly in November 1946, and Guinea's General Council in December 1946.
AG, 5B43, Guinée Française, Gouverneur, Conakry, à Gouverneur Général, Dakar, 18 January 1947; 5B43, Guinée Française, Services de Police, "Renseignements A/S Affaire Lamine Caba, Chef du P.R.S.G.," 7 February 1947; 5B43, Guinée Française, Chef de la Sûreté, Conakry, à Secrétaire Général à la Présidence de la République et de l'Union Française, Conakry, 28 March 1947; Morgenthau, *Political Parties,* p. 223; Sidiki Kobélé Kéïta, *P.D.G.,* 1:165, 182, 191.

60. AG, 5B43, Gouverneur à Gouverneur Général, 18 January 1947; 5B43, Guinée Française, Gouverneur, Conakry, à Gouverneur Général, Dakar, 11 March 1947, #44; Sidiki Kobélé Kéïta, *P.D.G.,* 1:160, 164–165, 173.

61. AG, 5B43, Gouverneur à Gouverneur Général, 18 January 1947; 5B43, Chef de la Sûreté à Secrétaire Général à la Présidence, 28 March 1947; 5B43, Guinée Française, Commissariat de Police, Kankan, "Retour à Kankan du 'Laministe' Mory-Oulin Caba," ca. 9 April 1947.

62. Mann, "Old Soldiers," pp. 69–72.

63. Ibid., pp. 73–76. Also see Lunn, *Memoirs of the Maelstrom,* pp. 191–192.

64. Mann, "Old Soldiers," pp. 71–72, 77, 80–81; Miescher and Lindsay, "Introduction," p. 11.

65. AG, 5B43, Guinée Française, Services de Police, "Renseignements A/S Lamine Kaba et Chériff Kankan," 26 February 1947; Morgenthau, *Political Parties,* p. 236; Sidiki Kobélé Kéïta, *P.D.G.,* 1:165.

66. AG, 5B43, Gouverneur à Gouverneur Général, 18 January 1947.

67. Jean Suret-Canale, "La Fin de la Chefferie en Guinée," *Journal of African History* 7, no. 3 (1966): p. 478.

68. AG, 5B43, Gouverneur à Gouverneur Général, 18 January 1947; 5B43, Gouverneur à Gouverneur Général, 11 March 1947; 5B47, Guinée Française, Gouverneur, Conakry, à Procureur de la République, Affaires Politiques et Administratives, 20 December 1947, #852/APA; 1E37, Beyla, "Rapport Politique Annuel, 1947"; ANS, 2G47/22, "Rapport Politique Annuel, 1947."

69. ANS, 2G46/22, Guinée Française, Rapport Politique Annuel, 1946, #284/APA; 2G47/121, "Revues Trimestrielles . . . 1er Trimestre 1947"; 2G47/22, "Rapport Politique Annuel, 1947"; AG, 5B43, Gouverneur à Gouverneur Général, 11 March 1947; 5B43, Guinée Française, Commissariat de Police, Kankan, "Arrivée du Gouverneur Général à Kankan le 28 Mars [1947]," ca. 9 April 1947; 1E37, Beyla, "Rapport Politique Annuel, 1947."

70.   AG, 1E37, Beyla, "Rapport Politique Annuel, 1947." For veterans' resistance to chiefly authority in other areas, see 1E38, Guinée Française, Cercle de N'Zérékoré, "Rapport Politique Annuel, Année 1948"; 1E38, Guinée Française, Cercle de Macenta, "Rapport Politique Annuel, Année 1948"; 1E38, Guinée Française, Cercle de Labé, Subdivision de Tougué, "Rapport Politique Annuel, Année 1948"; 1E39, Guinée Française, Cercle de Labé, "Rapport Politique Annuel, Année 1949"; ANS, 17G573, Gendarmerie, "En Guinée Française," 12 September 1951.

71.   ANS, 2G47/121, "Revues Trimestrielles . . . 1er Trimestre 1947"; 2G47/121, "Revues Trimestrielles . . . 2ème Trimestre 1947"; 2G47/121, "Revues Trimestrielles . . . 3ème Trimestre 1947"; 2G47/22, "Rapport Politique Annuel, 1947"; Morgenthau, *Political Parties,* pp. 27–28; Lawler, *Soldiers,* p. 214. For a general discussion of this trend, see Breuilly, *Nationalism and the State,* p. 20.

72.   AG, 1E38, N'Zérékoré, "Rapport Politique Annuel, 1948."

73.   AG, 1E38, Macenta, "Rapport Politique Annuel, 1948."

74.   AG, 5B49, Gouverneur à Procureur de la République, 10 May 1948; 1E38, Kouroussa, "Rapport Politique Annuel, 1948"; 1E39, Kouroussa, "Rapport Politique Annuel, 1949."

75.   AG, 5B49, Inspecteur des Affaires Administratives à Procureur de la République, 24 August 1948.

76.   AG, 1E38, Labé, Subdivision de Tougué, "Rapport Politique Annuel, 1948." Also see ANS, 17G586, Guinée Française, Services de Police, Labé, "Renseignements *Objet:* Situation Politique à Labé dans la Première Quinzaine de Novembre 1954," 23 November 1954, #2999/1180, C/PS.2.

77.   AG, 1E39, Labé, "Rapport Politique Annuel, 1949."

78.   AG, 5B43, Police, Kankan, "Arrivée du Gouverneur Général à Kankan le 28 Mars [1947]."

79.   Ibid.

80.   AG, 5B43, Guinée Française, Commissariat de Police, Kankan, "Mouvement des 'Laministes'," 9 April 1947.

81.   AG, 5B43, Guinée Française, Assistant de Police en Mission à Kankan, à Chef de la Sûreté, Conakry, 9 April 1947. Also see Echenberg, "Tragedy at Thiaroye," p. 119.

82.   AG, 5B43, Guinée Française, Commissaire de Police, Kankan, à Chef du Service de la Sûreté, Kankan, 8 April 1947, #200.

One of the veterans' grievances was the French policy instituted in 1944 of confiscating returning soldiers' weapons and uniforms. See Lawler, *Soldiers,* pp. 198–199.

83.   AG, 5B43, Gouverneur à Gouverneur Général, 18 January 1947; 5B43, Gouverneur à Gouverneur Général, 21 June 1947; 5B43, Gouverneur Général, Dakar, à Gouverneur, Conakry, 25 November, 1947, #730 AP/2; 5B49, Guinée Française, Gouverneur, Conakry, à Gouverneur Général, Dakar, 14 December 1948, #366/APA.

84.   AG, 5B43, Guinée Française, Gouverneur, Conakry, à Gouverneur Général, Dakar, 29 October 1947, #311/APA; AG, 1E38, Guinée Française, Cercle de Kankan, "Rapport Politique Annuel, Année 1948"; ANS, 2G47/121, "Revues Trimestrielles . . . 3ème Trimestre 1947."

85.   AG, 5B49, Guinée Française, Gouverneur, Conakry, à Commandants de Cercle: Kankan, Siguiri, Beyla, Kissidougou, Kouroussa, 16 April 1948, #205/APA.

86.   AG, 1E38, Kankan, "Rapport Politique Annuel, 1948."

87.   AG, 1E42, Police, Kankan, "Situation des Anciens Combattants," 22 May 1950; 2G56/138, "Rapport Politique Mensuel, Mai 1956."

88.   AG, 1E42, Police, Kankan, "Situation des Anciens Combattants," 22 May 1950.

89. ANS, 17G573, Guinée Française, Services de Police, "Renseignements de Kankan, A/S Passage de Ray Autra (R.D.A.)," 29 November 1949, #2428/73, C/PS. Also see 17G573, Gouvernement Général de l'A.O.F., Cabinet, Bureau Technique de Liaison et de Coordination, "Note de Renseignements *Objet:* Activité de la Sous-Section R.D.A. de Kankan," 25 November 1949, #738, CAB/LC/DK.

90. AG, 1E42, Police, Kankan, "Situation des Anciens Combattants," 22 May 1950.

91. AG, 5B43, Guinée Française, Services de Police, "Renseignements A/S Réunion Publique Organisée à Kindia, le 6 Avril 1947 par le R.D.A.," ca. 7 April 1947, #320/C; 2Z5, 504/2, "Renseignements," 3 March 1947.

92. Sidiki Kobélé Kéïta, *P.D.G.,* 1:139–140, 196. Also see Smith, *State and Nation,* pp. 48–49.

93. ANS, 17G573, Guinée Française, Services de Police, Conakry, "Renseignements A/S Section R.D.A. Kindia," 1 July 1947, 504 A. #575 G.

94. ANS, 17G573, Guinée Française, Services de Police, "Renseignements A/S Réunion Publique Organisée à Kindia le 1er Février par le R.D.A.," 2 February 1948, #159/55 C; 17G573, Guinée Française, Services de Police, "Renseignements de Kankan, A/S Passage Léon Maka, Militant R.D.A.," 13 October 1949, #2048, C/PS/I; Sidiki Kobélé Kéïta, *P.D.G.,* 1:122; Echenberg, *Colonial Conscripts,* pp. 151–153; Lawler, *Soldiers,* pp. 217, 220.

95. ANS, 17G573, Police, "Kankan, A/S Passage Léon Maka," 13 October 1949.

96. ANS, 17G573, Guinée Française, Services de Police, Labé, "Renseignements *Objet:* Activité du R.D.A.," 11 May 1948; 17G573, Guinée Française, Services de Police, Conakry, "Renseignements *Objet:* Groupements Politiques," 10 June 1948; 17G573, Guinée Française, Services de Police, "Renseignements A/S Activité Politique," 18 July 1951, #1040/490, C/PS.2.

For later developments, see 17G573, Gendarmerie Nationale, Détachement de l'A.O.F./Togo, Service des Recherches, Diffusion et Fichier, Dakar, "Note de Renseignements *Objet:* Activité Politique de Deux Militaires Africains de l'Escale Aérienne de Labé," 17 July 1950, #200/4R; 17G573, Gendarmerie Nationale, Détachement de l'A.O.F./Togo, Service des Recherches, Diffusion et Fichier, Dakar, "Note de Renseignements *Objet:* Activité Politique des Militaires Africains de l'Escale Aérienne de Labé," 22 July 1950, #207/4R; 17G573, Secrétaire Général, Direction Générale de l'Intérieur, Service des Affaires Politiques, Dakar, à Gouverneur de la Guinée Française, Conakry, 31 July 1950, #2961, INT/AP.2; 17G586, Guinée Française, Services de Police, Labé, "Renseignements *Objet:* Position des A.C. de Labé," 23 November 1954, #3001/1182, C/PS.2.

97. ANS, 17G573, Guinée Française, Services de Police, Kissidougou, "Renseignements *Objet:* Groupements Politiques," 13 January 1948; 2G55/152, Guinée Française, Gouverneur, "Rapport Politique pour l'Année 1955," #281/APA; Echenberg, *Colonial Conscripts,* pp. 143, 151, 157–158.

98. "Justice aux Anciens Combattants," *Réveil,* 13 May 1948. On the powers of the Assembly of the French Union, see Morgenthau, *Political Parties,* p. 383.

99. "Justice"; Thompson and Adloff, *French West Africa,* pp. 227–228.

100. Echenberg, *Colonial Conscripts,* p. 152.

101. AG, 1E42, Guinée Française, Commissariat de Police, Kankan, "Rapport Mensuel, Mois de Mars 1950."

102. AG, 1E39, Guinée Française, Cercle de N'Zérékoré, "Rapport Politique Annuel, Année 1949."

103. ANS, 17G573, Gendarmerie, "En Guinée Française," 12 September 1951.

The General Council became the Territorial Assembly in 1952. See Morgenthau, *Political Parties,* pp. 56–57; Sidiki Kobélé Kéïta, *P.D.G.,* 1:134 n. 6.

104. Lawler, *Soldiers,* pp. 200, 210–212, 216–217.

105. Maka, interview, 25 February 1991. Also see ANS, 2G55/151, Guinée Française, Gouverneur, Conakry, à Haut Commissaire, Dakar, "Revue des Événements du 4ème Trimestre 1955," February 1956, #131/APA; B. Ameillon, *La Guinée: Bilan d'une Indépendance,* Cahiers Libres nos. 58–59 (Paris: François Maspero, 1964), p. 22.

106. Maka, interview, 25 February 1991.

107. AG, 1E38, Kankan, "Rapport Politique Annuel, 1948."

108. AG, 5B43, Gouverneur à Gouverneur Général, 11 March 1947.

109. AG, 5B43, Gouverneur Général, Dakar, à Gouverneurs des Colonies du Groupe, 16 September 1947, #406/AP.2. Also ANS, 2G45/105, AOF, Dakar, "Exposé Sommaire de la Situation Politique de l'Afrique Occidentale Française et du Togo au 30 Mai 1945," 26 June 1945; Echenberg, *Colonial Conscripts,* pp. 103, 144; Echenberg, "Tragedy at Thiaroye," p. 119; Lawler, *Soldiers,* p. 197.

110. Echenberg, *Colonial Conscripts,* pp. 159–160; Lawler, *Soldiers,* pp. 241–242; Thompson and Adloff, *French West Africa,* pp. 228–229.

111. Echenberg, *Colonial Conscripts,* pp. 136, 147, 153; Lawler, *Soldiers,* p. 196; "Justice."

112. Sidiki Kobélé Kéïta, *P.D.G.,* 1:121–122.

113. Echenberg, *Colonial Conscripts,* pp. 157, 208 n. 81; Thompson and Adloff, *French West Africa,* p. 229.

114. Echenberg, *Colonial Conscripts,* pp. 147–148, 155, 159–162; Thompson and Adloff, *French West Africa,* p. 229.

115. Echenberg, *Colonial Conscripts,* pp. 147–148, 155, 159–162. For a similar trend in British East Africa, see Parsons, *African Rank-and-File,* pp. 225, 231, 256–257, 260.

116. ANS, 2G55/152, "Rapport Politique Annuel, 1955." Also see Echenberg, *Colonial Conscripts,* p. 162.

117. ANS, 2G55/151, "Revue des Événements du 4ème Trimestre 1955."

CHAPTER 3: THE UNIVERSAL WORKER: ORGANIZED LABOR AND NATIONALIST MOBILIZATION, 1946–1953

1. Frederick Cooper, *Decolonization and African Society: The Labor Question in French and British Africa* (New York: Cambridge University Press, 1996), pp. 229, 286, 292. Also see Catherine Coquery-Vidrovitch, "Nationalité et Citoyenneté en Afrique Occidentale Français[e]: Originaires et Citoyens dans Le Sénégal Colonial," *Journal of African History* 42, no. 2 (2001): pp. 285–286, 296, 304–305; Partha Chatterjee, *The Nation and Its Fragments: Colonial and Postcolonial Histories* (Princeton, N.J.: Princeton University Press, 1993), pp. 10, 26.

2. Jean Suret-Canale, "The French West African Railway Workers' Strike, 1947–1948," in *African Labor History,* ed. Peter C. W. Gutkind, Robin Cohen, and Jean Copans (Beverly Hills, Calif.: Sage Publications, 1978), p. 129.

3. ANS, 2G45/21, Guinée Française, Gouverneur, "Rapport sur le Travail et la Main d'Oeuvre de la Guinée Française Pendant l'Année 1945," Conakry, 2 August 1946, #208/IT; 2G46/50, Guinée Française, Inspecteur du Travail, "Rapport Annuel du Travail, 1946," Conakry, 15 February 1947, #66/IT.GV; 2G46/50, Guinée Française, Inspecteur

des Colonies (Pruvost), Mission en Guinée, "Rapport sur La Main d'Oeuvre en Guinée," Conakry, 13 July 1946, #116/C.

4.   ANS, 2G45/21, "Rapport sur le Travail . . . 1945."

5.   ANS, 2G46/50, "Rapport Annuel du Travail, 1946"; 2G46/50, "Rapport sur La Main d'Oeuvre en Guinée . . . ," 13 July 1946.

6.   ANS, 2G46/50, "Rapport Annuel du Travail, 1946"; Cooper, *Decolonization,* p. 280.

7.   ANS, 2G46/50, "Rapport sur La Main d'Oeuvre en Guinée . . . ," 13 July 1946. Also see Virginia Thompson and Richard Adloff, *French West Africa* (New York: Greenwood Press, 1969), p. 492.

8.   ANS, 2G46/50, "Rapport Annuel du Travail, 1946."

9.   Ibid.

10.   Ruth Schachter Morgenthau, *Political Parties in French-Speaking West Africa* (Oxford: Clarendon Press, 1964), p. 28; Thomas Hodgkin, *Nationalism in Colonial Africa* (New York: New York University Press, 1957), p. 129; Patrick Manning, *Francophone Sub-Saharan Africa, 1880–1985* (New York: Cambridge University Press, 1988), p. 141; Sidiki Kobélé Kéïta, *Le P.D.G.: Artisan de l'Indépendance Nationale en Guinée (1947–1958)* (Conakry: I.N.R.D.G., Bibliothèque Nationale, 1978), 1:175–176; Cooper, *Decolonization,* pp. 227–228; Frederick Cooper, " 'Our Strike': Equality, Anticolonial Politics and the 1947–48 Railway Strike in French West Africa," *Journal of African History* 37, no. 1 (1996): pp. 88–89.

11.   AG, 2Z27, "Syndicat Professionnel des Agents et Sous-Agents Indigènes du Service des Transmissions de la Guinée Française," Conakry, 18 March 1945; Sidiki Kobélé Kéïta, *Ahmed Sékou Touré: L'Homme du 28 Septembre 1958,* 2nd ed. (Conakry: I.N.R.D.G., Bibliothèque Nationale, 1977), p. 41; Sidiki Kobélé Kéïta, *P.D.G.,* 1:176–177; interviews with Joseph Montlouis (assistant secretary-general, PTT workers' union), Coléah, Conakry, 3 and 6 March 1991.

12.   AG, 2Z27, "Syndicat Professionnel . . . Service des Transmissions . . . ," 18 March 1945; personal archives of Joseph Montlouis, letter from Secrétaire Général, Syndicat Professionnel des Agents et Sous-Agents Indigènes du Service des Transmissions de la Guinée Française, à Chef du Groupe Postal de la Guinée Française, Conakry, 30 July 1945; interview with Léon Maka, Sangoyah, Conakry, 20 February 1991; Montlouis, interview, 28 February 1991.

13.   Personal archives of Joseph Montlouis, Réunion des Membres du Comité Provisoire du Syndicat Postal de Guinée, tenue chez Joseph Montlouis, Conakry, 7 January 1945; Montlouis, interview, 28 February, 3 and 6 March 1991.

14.   Montlouis, interview, 3 March 1991. Also see AG, 1E41, Gouverneur Général de l'A.O.F., "Notice de Renseignements Concernant Mr. Sékou Touré, Élections Législatives du 2 Janvier 1956"; Jean Suret-Canale, *La République de Guinée* (Paris: Éditions Sociales, 1970), p. 147; Sidiki Kobélé Kéïta, *Ahmed Sékou Touré: L'Homme et son Combat Anti-Colonial (1922–1958)* (Conakry: Éditions S.K.K., 1998), p. 29; B. Ameillon, *La Guinée: Bilan d'une Indépendance,* Cahiers Libres, nos. 58–59 (Paris: François Maspero, 1964), p. 49.

15.   Sidiki Kobélé Kéïta, *P.D.G.,* 1:176–177; Cooper, *Decolonization,* pp. 228–229; Maka, interview, 20 February 1991; Montlouis, interview, 3 March 1991.

16.   Montlouis, interview, 3 March 1991.

Decrees permitting freedom of association and the right to hold meetings were issued in March and April 1946. These paved the way for the establishment of political parties in French West Africa. See Thompson and Adloff, *French West Africa,* p. 34; Tony Chafer,

The End of Empire in French West Africa: France's Successful Decolonization? (New York: Berg, 2002), p. 55.

17. Personal archives of Joseph Montlouis, "Revendications d'Ordre Général Accordé à l'Employé un Traitement qui lui Permettre de Vivre Décemment," n.d.; Maka, interview, 20 February 1991; Sidiki Kobélé Kéïta, *P.D.G.,* 1:177–178; Cooper, *Decolonization,* pp. 228–229.

18. AG, 2Z27, "Syndicat Professionnel . . . Service des Transmissions . . . ," 18 March 1945; Maka, interview, 20 February 1991; Sidiki Kobélé Kéïta, *P.D.G.,* 1:178.

19. Sidiki Kobélé Kéïta, *P.D.G.,* 1:180; Suret-Canale, *République,* p. 147; Jean Suret-Canale, *French Colonialism in Tropical Africa, 1900–1945,* trans. Till Gottheiner (New York: Pica Press, 1971), p. 388.

20. Suret-Canale, "Railway Workers," p. 131; Cooper, "Our Strike," p. 88.

21. Hodgkin, *Nationalism,* p. 129; Suret-Canale, "Railway Workers," pp. 132–133; Cooper, *Decolonization,* p. 242; Cooper, "Our Strike," pp. 88–89; James A. Jones, *Industrial Labor in the Colonial World: Workers of the Chemin de Fer Dakar-Niger, 1881–1963* (Portsmouth, N.H.: Heinemann, 2002), p. 55; interviews with Adama Diop, Conakry, 14 and 18 March 1991.

22. Jones, *Industrial Labor,* p. 55.

For the trade unions' subsequent move toward autonomy, see ANS, 21G215, Union des Syndicats Sénégal-Mauritanie, Confédération Générale des Travailleurs Africains (C.G.T.A.), Kaolack, "Appel à tous les Travailleurs Africains," 12 November 1955; 21G215, Sûreté du Sénégal, "Renseignements sur la Scission au sein de l'Union Territoriale des Syndicats C.G.T.K. Sénégal-Mauritanie," 15 November 1955, #1916 C/Su; 2G55/152, Guinée Française, Gouverneur, "Rapport Politique pour l'Année 1955," #281/APA; 2G56/138, Guinée Française, Gouverneur, "Rapport Politique Mensuel, Février 1956"; 179K432, Sékou Touré, Secrétaire Général, et Mamady Kaba, 1er Secrétaire, Union des Syndicats Confédérés de Guinée, Conakry, à Inspecteur Général du Travail, Conakry, 9 May 1956; Morgenthau, *Political Parties,* pp. 108–109, 241–242; Cooper, *Decolonization,* pp. 407–408; Sidiki Kobélé Kéïta, *P.D.G.,* 2:119–121; Jean Meynaud and Anisse Salah Bey, *Trade Unionism in Africa: A Study of Its Growth and Orientation,* trans. Angela Brench (London: Methuen, 1967), pp. 58–59.

23. Diop, interview, 14 March 1991; Adama Diop, "Le Syndicat des Cheminots Africains de la Région Conakry-Niger Proteste contre l'Arrestation de *Diané* Yayé, *Touré* Faciné et Mamby *Diawara,*" part I, *Réveil,* 15 April 1948, p. 4; Cooper, "Our Strike," p. 87.

24. Diop, interview, 14 March 1991.

25. Diop, interview, 14 and 18 March 1991; Cooper, "Our Strike," pp. 85–87, 115 n. 128; Cooper, *Decolonization,* p. 242; Jones, *Industrial Labor,* p. 55; Suret-Canale, *République,* p. 147.

A member of the Syndicat des Cheminots from 1947 to 1956, Diop was secretary-general of the Guinean branch during the 1947–1948 strike. Originally from Senegal, with a diploma from an *école primaire supérieure,* he had been posted to Guinea as a member of the relatively elite railway staff system. Representing the Guinean railway workers, Diop was a signatory to the protocol that ended the 1947–1948 railway strike.

26. Suret-Canale, "Railway Workers," p. 132; Cooper, *Decolonization,* pp. 242–243; Cooper, "Our Strike," pp. 82, 87, 89–90.

Although they may have worked on the railways for years and acquired numerous skills, the vast majority of African workers were considered auxiliaries outside the staff system. As such, they lacked the job security and benefits enjoyed by regular workers. Their diminished status saved the railway management a considerable sum.

For similar demands among Sudanese railway workers, see Ahmad Alawad Sikainga, *"City of Steel and Fire": A Social History of Atbara, Sudan's Railway Town, 1906–1984* (Portsmouth, N.H.: Heinemann; Oxford: James Currey, 2002), pp. 103–105, 108, 112.

27. ANS, 26K365, Inspecteur Général du Travail, Dakar, à Haut Commissaire, Dakar, 10 October 1947, #140/C; 179K457, Inspection Générale du Travail de l'A.O.F., "Différend Collectif du Travail entre la Régie des Chemins de Fer de l'A.O.F. et son Personnel Africain," 24 January 1948, #16/C/IGT/AOF; Suret-Canale, "Railway Workers," pp. 129, 132; Cooper, *Decolonization,* pp. 242–243; Cooper, "Our Strike," pp. 90–91.

28. ANS, 26K365, "Motion Votée à l'Unanimité par le Comité Fédéral des Syndicats des Cheminots Africains de l'A.O.F.," Thiès, 1 September 1947; 26K365, Direction de la Sûreté Générale, Dakar, "Compte-Rendu Réunion Tenue aux Ateliers du D.N. A/S Revendications des Employés du D.N.," 11 September 1947, #4066; 26K379, Haut Commissaire, Dakar, à Ministre, FOM, Paris, 8 October 1947, #680 AP; 26K365, Inspecteur Général du Travail à Haut Commissaire, 10 October 1947; 26K365, Gendarmerie Nationale, Détachement de l'A.O.F.-Togo, Section du Soudan, "Rapport du Capitaine Pontjean, Commandant la Section de Gendarmerie de Bamako," Bamako, 11 October 1947, #158/4; 179K457, Inspection Générale du Travail, "Différend Collectif du Travail . . . ," 24 January 1948; Suret-Canale, "Railway Workers," pp. 135–136; Cooper, *Decolonization,* p. 243; Cooper, "Our Strike," p. 91.

29. ANS, 26K365, "Motion Votée à l'Unanimité . . . ," 1 September 1947; 26K365, Sûreté Générale, " . . . Revendications des Employés du D.N.," 11 September 1947; 26K365, Inspecteur Général du Travail à Haut Commissaire, 10 October 1947; 179K457, Inspection Générale du Travail, "Différend Collectif du Travail . . . ," 24 January 1948; Suret-Canale, "Railway Workers," p. 136; Cooper, "Our Strike," p. 92; Cooper, *Decolonization,* pp. 242–243; Sidiki Kobélé Kéïta, *P.D.G.,* 1:251–252.

For similar claims in colonial Nigeria, see Lisa A. Lindsay, "Domesticity and Difference: Male Breadwinners, Working Women, and Colonial Citizenship in the 1945 Nigerian General Strike," *American Historical Review* 104, no. 3 (June 1999): pp. 794, 802. For the Sudan, see Sikainga, *City of Steel and Fire,* pp. 103, 108.

30. ANS, 179K457, Guinée Française, Service de la Sûreté, Conakry, "Renseignements A/S Activité du Syndicat des Ouvriers du Conakry-Niger," 12 September 1947, #255/C.

31. AG, 5B47, Guinée Française, Gouverneur, Conakry, à Administrateurs de Cercle, "Sécurité Intérieure du Territoire," 23 September 1947, #643/APA.

32. Suret-Canale, "Railway Workers," pp. 137, 152 n. 5, 6. The figures for the ports and wharves are for 1946.

33. ANS, 26K365, Gendarmerie Nationale, Détachement de l'A.O.F.-Togo, Section de Conakry, Colonie de la Guinée, "Rapport du Lieutenant Berge, Commandant la Section," Conakry, 11 October 1947, #152/4; 26K379, Haut Commissaire, Dakar, à Ministre, FOM, Paris, 11 October 1947, #701 AP; 179K457, "Quelques Jours d'Économie Guinnéene," *La Guinée Française,* 20 November 1947; 179K457, Direction Fédérale de la Régie des Chemins de Fer de l'A.O.F., "Situations des Effectifs de la Régie des Chemins de Fer au 2 Janvier 1948"; 179K457, Inspection Générale du Travail, "Différend Collectif du Travail . . . ," 24 January 1948; AG, 5B49, Guinée Française, Gouverneur, Conakry, à Haut Commissaire, Dakar, "Revue des Événements du 4ème Trimestre 1947," 17 February 1948, #35/APA; Suret-Canale, "Railway Workers," pp. 129, 137, 152 n. 5, 6; Cooper, *Decolonization,* pp. 241, 243; Cooper, "Our Strike," pp. 81, 93.

34. ANS, 179K457, Inspecteur du Travail de la Guinée Française, Conakry, à Inspecteur Général du Travail de l'A.O.F., Dakar, 19 November 1947, #34/C/IT/Gu;

26K365, Gendarmerie Nationale, "Rapport du Lieutenant Berge . . . ," Conakry, 11 October 1947; AG, 5B49, "Revue des Événements du 4ème Trimestre 1947."

35. ANS, 179K457, Inspection Générale du Travail, "Différend Collectif du Travail . . . ," 24 January 1948; 26K365, Sénégal, Service de la Sûreté, Thiès, "Renseignements," 25 October 1947; 26K365, A. Ferrey, "Sentence Surarbitrale," (Différend entre la Régie des Chemins de Fer de l'Afrique Occidentale Française, d'une part, et la Fédération des Syndicats des Cheminots Africains de l'Afrique Occidentale Française, d'autre part), Dakar, 20 October 1947. Also see Cooper, "Our Strike," p. 108.

36. ANS, 179K457, Inspecteur du Travail de la Guinée Française, Conakry, à Inspecteur Général du Travail de l'A.O.F., Dakar, 26 November 1947, #578/IT.Gu (includes "Quelques Jours d'Économie Guinéenne," *La Guinée Française,* 15 November 1947); Suret-Canale, "Railway Workers," pp. 129–131, 143, 146, 148–149.

37. ANS, 179K457, Inspection Générale du Travail, "Différend Collectif du Travail . . . ," 24 January 1948; Suret-Canale, "Railway Workers," p. 148; Cooper, *Decolonization,* p. 244; Cooper, "Our Strike," p. 96.

38. Suret-Canale, *République,* p. 111; Suret-Canale, "Railway Workers," p. 131; Diop, interview, 14 March 1991.

39. AG, 5B47, Guinée Française, Gouverneur, Conakry, à Ministre, FOM, Paris, 25 October 1947, #711/APA.

40. ANS, 179K457, Guinée Française, Service de la Sûreté, Conakry, "Renseignements A/S Production," 10 November 1947; 179K457, Inspecteur du Travail à Inspecteur Général du Travail, 19 November 1947; 179K457, Inspecteur du Travail à Inspecteur Général du Travail, 26 November 1947; 179K457, "Quelques Jours d'Économie Guinéenne," *La Guinée Française,* 21 November 1947, p. 2; AG, 5B47, Gouverneur à Ministre, FOM, 25 October 1947; 5B49, "Revue des Événements du 4ème Trimestre 1947"; AG, 1E38, Guinée Française, Cercle de Kankan, "Rapport Politique Annuel, Année 1948"; Diop, interview, 18 March 1991; Suret-Canale, *République,* pp. 90, 115–116; Suret-Canale, "Railway Workers," pp. 130, 149.

41. ANS, 179K457, Direction Fédérale . . . Chemins de Fer, " . . . Effectifs . . . des Chemins de Fer au 2 Janvier 1948"; 179K457, Inspection Générale du Travail, "Différend Collectif du Travail . . . ," 24 January 1948; Morgenthau, *Political Parties,* p. 177; Suret-Canale, "Railway Workers," pp. 142, 147–148; Cooper, "Our Strike," pp. 99–100, 102, 106, 108–109.

42. ANS, 179K457, Inspecteur du Travail à Inspecteur Général du Travail, 19 November 1947; Sidiki Kobélé Kéïta, *P.D.G.,* 1:252.

43. ANS, 26K379, Haut Commissaire à Ministre, FOM, 8 October 1947; 26K379, Haut Commissaire, Dakar, à Ministre, FOM, Paris, 21 December 1947, #895 AP/4T; 179K457, Inspection Générale du Travail, "Différend Collectif du Travail . . . ," 24 January 1948; Suret-Canale, "Railway Workers," pp. 136, 138.

44. ANS, 179K457, Inspecteur du Travail à Inspecteur Général du Travail, 19 November 1947; Suret-Canale, "Railway Workers," p. 138; Cooper, "Our Strike," p. 105.

45. ANS, 179K457, Inspecteur du Travail à Inspecteur Général du Travail, 19 November 1947; 26K379, Haut Commissaire, Dakar, à Ministre, FOM, Paris, 21 November 1947, #795 AP; 26K379, Procureur de la République, Dakar, à Procureur Général, Dakar, 8 January 1948, #15/PG; 26K379, Secrétaire Général, pour le Haut Commissaire, Dakar, à Ministre, FOM, Paris, 8 January 1948, #16 AP/4T; 179K457, Inspection Générale du Travail, "Différend Collectif du Travail . . . ," 24 January 1948; AG, 5B43, Haut Commissaire, Dakar, à Gouverneurs des Colonies, Directeur Fédéral de la Régie des Chemins

de Fer, 21 November 1947, #109/CM.3; Diop, interview, 14 March 1991; interview with Louis Marquis Camara, Conakry, 27 March 1991; Suret-Canale, "Railway Workers," pp. 138–141; Cooper, "Our Strike," pp. 105–107.

46. ANS, 179K457, Inspecteur du Travail à Inspecteur Général du Travail, 19 November 1947; 26K379, "Le Trafic du C.F.C.N. va Reprendre; Les Spécialistes du Génie Militaire sont à Conakry," *La Guinée Française,* 21 November 1947, p. 2; 26K379, "Quelques Jours d'Économie Guinéenne," *La Guinée Française,* 20 and 21 November 1947; AG, 5B49, "Revue des Événements du 4ème Trimestre 1947."

47. Cooper, "Our Strike," pp. 106–107.

48. Diop, interview, 18 March 1991. Diop's view was seconded by Louis Marquis Camara, 27 March 1991.

49. ANS, 26K386, Télégramme Arrivée, Haut Commissaire, Dakar. Envoyé par Affaires Courantes, Conakry, 10 January 1948, #15; 26K379, Guinée Française, Services de Police, "Renseignements A/S Interruption de Trafic de Chemin de Fer," 15 January 1948; Diop, interview, 18 March 1991; Adama Diop, personal notebooks; Sidiki Kobélé Kéïta, *P.D.G.,* 1:253.

50. ANS, 26K386, Gendarmerie Nationale, Détachement de l'A.O.F. et du Togo, Section de Conakry, Territoire de la Guinée, "Rapport du Lieutenant Berge, Commandant la Section de Conakry, sur Tentatives de Sabotage sur la Ligne de Chemin de Fer Conakry-Niger," Conakry, 15 January 1948; 26K386, Télégramme Départ, Affaires Courantes, Conakry, à FOM, Paris, 15 January 1948, #AP/6; AG, 5B49, Guinée Française, Secrétaire Général chargé de l'expédition des Affaires Courantes à Gouverneur, Conakry, 27 January 1948, #53/APA; 1K37, Télégramme Départ, Haut Commissaire, Dakar, à Gouverneur, Guinée Française, Conakry, 22 March 1948, #148; 1K37, Télégramme Arrivée, Haut Commissaire, Dakar. Envoyé par Gouverneur, Guinée Française, Conakry, 27 March 1948, #80; Diop, interview, 18 March 1991; Diop, personal notebooks; Sidiki Kobélé Kéïta, *P.D.G.,* 1:253.

51. ANS, 26K386, Télégramme Arrivée, Haut Commissaire, Dakar. Envoyé par Gouverneur, Guinée Française, Conakry, 9 April 1948, #96; 26K386, Télégramme Arrivée, Haut Commissaire, Dakar. Envoyé par Gouverneur, Guinée Française, Conakry, 14 April 1948, #100; AG, 5B49, Affaires Courantes à Gouverneur, 27 January 1948.

52. Adama Diop, "Syndicat des Cheminots Africains . . . Proteste contre l'Arresta-tion . . . ," part I, *Réveil,* 15 April 1948, p. 4; ANS, 26K386, Gendarmerie Nationale, " . . . Tentatives de Sabotage sur la Ligne de Chemin de Fer Conakry-Niger," 15 January 1948.

53. Cooper, "Our Strike," pp. 88, 92, 107.

54. Ibid., pp. 92, 107, 115.

55. Ibid., p. 115; Cooper, *Decolonization,* p. 242.

56. ANS, 179K457, Direction de la Sûreté Générale, Dakar, à Inspecteur Général du Travail, Dakar, "Notice de Renseignements A/S Grève C.F.C.N. du 10 Octobre 1947," 28 September 1947, #4403.

For the use of imperial languages as nationalist vernaculars, see Benedict Anderson, *Imagined Communities: Reflections on the Origin and Spread of Nationalism,* 2nd ed. (New York: Verso, 1991), pp. 113, 133–134, 138.

57. ANS, 26K365, Sûreté, Thiès, "Renseignements" 25 October 1947. Also see Cooper, "Our Strike," p. 107; Suret-Canale, "Railway Workers," p. 137; Ibrahima Sarr, "Démenti à la Réaction, Syndicat des Cheminots Africains, Circulaire à tous les Cama-rades," *Réveil,* 20 November 1947, p. 1.

58.   Adama Diop, "Le Syndicat des Cheminots Africains de la Région Conakry-Niger Proteste contre l'Arrestation de *Diané* Yayé, *Touré* Faciné et Mamby *Diawara*," part II, *Réveil,* 19 April 1948, p. 4.

59.   Cooper, "Our Strike," pp. 107–108.

60.   Diop, interview, 14 and 18 March 1991.

61.   ANS, 26K365, Guinée Française, Service de la Sûreté, Conakry, à Gouverneur, Guinée Française, Conakry, 8 November 1947, #1256/163, C/PS/I; 26K379/179K457, Guinée Française, Services de Police, Kankan, "Renseignements," 17 January 1948.

62.   ANS, 179K457, Guinée Française, Service de la Sûreté, Conakry, "Renseigne-ments A/S Grève Cheminots," 27 November 1947, #1379/212/C.

63.   ANS, 179K457, Sûreté, " . . . Grève Cheminots," 27 November 1947; Morgen-thau, *Political Parties,* pp. 59, 86; Jean-Pierre Rioux, *The Fourth Republic, 1944–1958,* trans. Godfrey Rogers (New York: Cambridge University Press, 1987), pp. 104–106; Charles de Gaulle, *The War Memoirs of Charles de Gaulle: Salvation, 1944–1946* (New York: Simon and Schuster, 1960), p. 328; Charles de Gaulle, *Memoirs of Hope: Renewal and Endeavor,* trans. Terence Kilmartin (New York: Simon and Schuster, 1971), pp. 15–16.

64.   ANS, 179K457, Inspection Générale du Travail, "Différend Collectif du Tra-vail . . . ," 24 January 1948. Also see Cooper, "Our Strike," pp. 96–97.

65.   Suret-Canale, "Railway Workers," pp. 147–148; Cooper, *Decolonization,* pp. 241, 244, 247; Cooper, "Our Strike," pp. 82, 93–97, 103, 108; Jones, *Industrial Labor,* p. 61.

For a striking exception to this generalization, see the report of the inspector general of labor: ANS, 179K457, Inspection Générale du Travail, "Différend Collectif du Travail . . . ," 24 January 1948.

For a fictionalized account of the French West African railway workers' strike and the crucial role of the community in sustaining it, see Ousmane Sembene's classic novel, *God's Bits of Wood,* trans. Francis Price (Portsmouth, N.H.: Heinemann, 1986). For similar trends during the 1945 general strike in Nigeria, see Lindsay, "Domesticity and Differ-ence," pp. 795–800. For the 1947 and 1948 Sudanese railway strikes, see Sikainga, *City of Steel and Fire,* pp. 97, 106, 107, 109.

66.   Cooper, "Our Strike," pp. 95–96. Also see Sembene, *God's Bits of Wood.*

For urban market women's links to rural producers in colonial Ghana, see Claire C. Robertson, *Sharing the Same Bowl: A Socioeconomic History of Women and Class in Accra, Ghana* (Bloomington: Indiana University Press, 1984), pp. 80–97; Gracia Clark, *Onions Are My Husband: Survival and Accumulation by West African Market Women* (Chicago: University of Chicago Press, 1994), pp. 319, 321, 323, 327.

For the role of Nigerian market women in supporting striking workers, see Lindsay, "Domesticity and Difference," pp. 783, 787–788, 795–800, 810; Lisa A. Lindsay, *Working with Gender: Wage Labor and Social Change in Southwestern Nigeria, 1930–1964* (Portsmouth, N.H.: Heinemann, 2003), pp. 22, 105, 173, 192; Cheryl Johnson, "Madam Alimotu Pelewura and the Lagos Market Women," *Tarikh* 7, no. 1 (1981): p. 9; Cheryl Johnson, "Grassroots Organizing: Women in Anti-Colonial Activity in Southwestern Nige-ria," *African Studies Review* 25, no. 2 (September 1982): p. 143; Judith Van Allen, " 'Aba Riots' or Igbo 'Women's War'?: Ideology, Stratification, and the Invisibility of Women," in *Women in Africa: Studies in Social and Economic Change,* ed. Nancy J. Hafkin and Edna G. Bay (Stanford, Calif.: Stanford University Press, 1976), pp. 72–73.

For women's support of Sudanese railway workers' strikes, see Sikainga, *City of Steel and Fire,* p. 109.

67.   ANS, 179K457, "Le Chemin de Fer Conakry-Niger en Grève," *Marchés Coloni-aux,* 18 October 1947 (typed extract); 26K379/179K457, Guinée Française, Services de

Police, "Renseignements A/S Ravitaillement," 10 November 1947; 179K457, Inspecteur du Travail à Inspecteur Général du Travail, 19 November 1947; AG, 5B49, "Revue des Événements du 4ème Trimestre 1947"; AG, 1E38, Kankan, "Rapport Politique Annuel, 1948."

68. See Montlouis, interview, 3 March 1991; ANS, 26K386/179K457, Guinée Française, Service de la Sûreté, Conakry, "Renseignements A/S Grève du Chemin de Fer," 10 February 1948, #63/C; 26K386, Télégramme Arrivée, Haut Commissaire, 9 April 1948; 26K386, Télégramme Arrivée, Haut Commissaire, 14 April 1948; 26K386, Procureur Général, Dakar, à Procureur de la République, Conakry, 20 April 1948, #2322 P/G; 26K386, Juge d'Instruction, Conakry, à Procureur de la République, Conakry, 7 May 1948, #256/11–48; AG, 5B49, Affaires Courantes à Gouverneur, 27 January 1948.

69. ANS, 26K379/179K457, Guinée Française, Services de Police, Coyah, "Renseignements A/S Grève des Cheminots," 20 December 1947. Also see 26K379, Guinée Française, Services de Police, "Renseignements A/S Grèves," 10 November 1947; 26K379, C.G.T., Union Régionale Syndicale de Guinée, "Motion," Conakry, 18 November 1947; Cooper, "Our Strike," p. 95.

70. ANS, 26K365, Sûreté, Thiès, "Renseignements," 25 October 1947; Suret-Canale, "Railway Workers," pp. 138, 147–148; Cooper, "Our Strike," pp. 94–96; Cooper, *Decolonization,* pp. 241, 244.

71. ANS, 26K379, Police, " . . . Grèves," 10 November 1947.

72. ANS, 26K379/179K457, Police, Coyah, " . . . Grève des Cheminots," 20 December 1947.

Like the African community, the colonial administration was aware that the railway workers' struggle was being "followed with an attentive eye by other categories of workers." See ANS, 179K457, Inspection Générale du Travail, "Différend Collectif du Travail . . . ," 24 January 1948.

73. AG, 5B49, "Revue des Événements du 4ème Trimestre 1947"; Suret-Canale, "Railway Workers," pp. 144–147.

74. ANS, 179K457, Soudan, Service de la Sûreté, Bamako, "Renseignements: Réunion de la Commission Exécutive des Syndicats du Soudan," 17 November 1947, #1148/CF/SU; 26K379, C.G.T., "Motion," Conakry, 18 November 1947; 179K457, Inspecteur du Travail à Inspecteur Général du Travail, 19 November 1947; Suret-Canale, "Railway Workers," pp. 144–147; Cooper, "Our Strike," pp. 96–97; Cooper, *Decolonization,* p. 244. Also see "La Solidarité des Travailleurs s'Affirme," *Réveil,* 4 December 1947, p. 1; AG, 5B49, "Revue des Événements du 4ème Trimestre 1947," 17 February 1948.

75. ANS, 179K457, Inspection Générale du Travail, "Différend Collectif du Travail . . . ," 24 January 1948. For the return to work on March 19, 1948, see Suret-Canale, "Railway Workers," pp. 129, 149; Cooper, "Our Strike," p. 111; Cooper, *Decolonization,* p. 247.

76. ANS, 179K457, Inspecteur du Travail à Inspecteur Général du Travail, 19 November 1947.

77. Diop, interview, 14 March 1991.

78. ANS, 179K457, Inspection Générale du Travail, "Différend Collectif du Travail . . . ," 24 January 1948; Suret-Canale, "Railway Workers," pp. 149–150; Cooper, "Our Strike," pp. 109–114; Cooper, *Decolonization,* p. 247; Diop, interview, 18 March 1991.

79. ANS, 179K457, Inspection Générale du Travail, "Différend Collectif du Travail . . . ," 24 January 1948; Suret-Canale, "Railway Workers," p. 150; Cooper, "Our Strike," pp. 109–114; Cooper, *Decolonization,* p. 247; Diop, interview, 18 March 1991.

80. Diop, interview, 18 March 1991; Cooper, "Our Strike," p. 113.

81. ANS, 17G573, "Rapport Général d'Activité 1947–1950," présenté par Mamadou Madéïra Kéïta, Secrétaire Général du P.D.G. au Premier Congrès Territorial du Parti Démocratique de Guinée (Section Guinéenne du Rassemblement Démocratique Africain), Conakry, 15–18 October 1950; 17G573, Karamoko Diafodé Kéïta, Prison Civile de Kankan, à Groupe Parlementaire R.D.A., Paris, 3 January 1951; interview with Mamadou Bela Doumbouya, Camayenne, Conakry, 26 January 1991; Morgenthau, *Political Parties,* pp. 60–61, 63, 90–91, 101; Sidiki Kobélé Kéïta, *P.D.G.,* 1:129, 233. Also see Elizabeth Schmidt, "Cold War and Decolonization in Guinea, 1946–1958," unpublished book manuscript.

82. ANS, 17G573, Guinée Française, Services de Police, "Renseignements A/S Activités R.D.A.," 1 June 1949, #517, C/PS.

83. Cooper, *Decolonization,* pp. 281–282; Frederick Cooper, "From Free Labor to Family Allowances: Labor and African Society in Colonial Discourse," *American Ethnologist* 16, no. 4 (November 1989): p. 755; Frederick Cooper, "Industrial Man Goes to Africa," in *Men and Masculinities in Modern Africa,* ed. Lisa A. Lindsay and Stephan F. Miescher (Portsmouth, N.H.: Heinemann, 2003), pp. 133–134.

84. Cooper, *Decolonization,* pp. 287, 303.

85. ANS, 1K44, Inspection Territoriale du Travail de la Guinée Française, "Décision de la Commission Mixte Locale du 1er Juillet 1950 fixant les Salaires des Travailleurs du Batiment et de l'Industrie de la Guinée Française"; 17G271, Gouverneur, Conakry, à Haut Commissaire, Dakar, "A/S Activité Syndicale," 25 February 1952, #85/APA; 17G529, Guinée Française, "Liste des Organisations Professionnelles," 1952; Sidiki Kobélé Kéïta, *P.D.G.,* 1:256–257.

Some of Guinea's richest bauxite and iron mines are found along the Atlantic Coast—in Boké, Conakry, and on the Iles de Loos. The coastal region and adjacent islands were among the few areas penetrated by Christian missionaries. Suret-Canale, *République,* pp. 118, 121–122; Suret-Canale, *French Colonialism,* p. 372.

86. ANS, 1K44, Inspecteur Général du Travail, Dakar, "Note Schématique Concernant la Grève des 9 et 10 Juin 1950 à Conakry," 12 June 1950, #108/C IGT/AOF.

87. ANS, 1K44, Comité Intersyndical, C.F.T.C., C.G.T., Conakry, "Motion," 31 May 1950; 1K44, Comité Intersyndical, C.F.T.C., C.G.T., Conakry, "Travailleurs Guinéens: L'Union dans L'Action," 31 May 1950; 1K44, C.F.T.C., C.G.T., "Camarades Travailleurs," Conakry, 10 June 1950; 1K44, Inspecteur Général du Travail, Dakar, "Rapport: Fixation du Salaire Minimum en Guinée et Grève des 9 et 10 Juin 1950," 19 June 1950, #113/C IGT/AOF; 1K44, Inspecteur Général du Travail, Dakar, "Rapport: Le Salaire Minimum en Guinée et les Conditions de Résorption des Séquelles de la Grève des 9 et 10 Juin 1950," 21 August 1950, #145/C IGT/AOF.

88. ANS, 1K44, Comité Intersyndical, ". . . L'Union dans L'Action," 31 May 1950. Also see Sidiki Kobélé Kéïta, *P.D.G.,* 1:254.

89. ANS, 1K44, Comité Intersyndical, ". . . L'Union dans L'Action," 31 May 1950. Also see Claude Rivière, *Guinea: The Mobilization of a People,* trans. Virginia Thompson and Richard Adloff (Ithaca, N.Y.: Cornell University Press, 1977), p. 56.

90. ANS, 1K44, Télégramme Arrivée, Haut Commissaire, Dakar. Envoyé par Gouverneur, Guinée Française, Conakry, 11 June 1950, #44.

91. ANS, 1K44, Inspecteur Général du Travail, ". . . Salaire Minimum . . . et Grève des 9 et 10 Juin 1950," 19 June 1950; 1K44, Les Unions des Syndicats Confédérés C.F.T.C. et C.G.T. de Guinée, à Haut Commissaire, Dakar, 4 July 1950; 1K44, Inspecteur Général du Travail, ". . . Salaire Minimum . . . et . . . la Grève des 9 et 10 Juin 1950," 21 August 1950; Sidiki Kobélé Kéïta, *P.D.G.,* 1:263.

92. ANS, 1K44, Inspecteur Général du Travail, " . . . Salaire Minimum . . . et Grève des 9 et 10 Juin 1950," 19 June 1950; 1K44, Inspection Territoriale du Travail, "Décision . . . du 1er Juillet 1950 . . . "; 1K44, Inspection Territoriale du Travail de la Guinée Française, "Décision de la Commission Mixte Locale portant Avenant de la Convention Collective du 12 Novembre 1947 intéressant les Chauffeurs d'Automobiles de la Guinée," ca. 3 August 1950; 1K44, Inspecteur Général du Travail, " . . . Salaire Minimum . . . et . . . la Grève des 9 et 10 Juin 1950," 21 August 1950.

93. Sidiki Kobélé Kéïta, *P.D.G.*, 1:263. Also see AG, 1F20, Guinée Française, Services de Police, "Renseignements A/S Réunion de la Commission Consultative du Travail, 13 Décembre 1951," 14 December 1951, #2263/1333, C/PS.2; 1F20, Guinée Française, Services de Police et de la Sûreté, "Procès Verbal de la Réunion de la Commission Consultative du Travail Relative au Minimum Vital du Manoeuvre Non-Spécialisé à Conakry," 2 January 1952; 1F20, Guinée Française, Inspecteur Territorial du Travail, Conakry, à Gouverneur, Conakry, "Rapport de Présentation des Avis de la Commission Consultative en Matière de Minimum Vital du Travailleur Non-Spécialisé," 28 January 1952, #18, IT/GU.

94. ANS, 1K44, Framoï Bérété (président), pour la Commission Permanente, Conseil Général de la Guinée Française, Conakry, à Haut Commissaire, Dakar, 26 June 1950, #177/CG.

95. ANS, 1K44, Haut Commissaire, Dakar, à FOM, Paris, 16 June 1950, #300–301.

96. ANS, 1K44, Inspecteur Général du Travail, " . . . Salaire Minimum . . . et Grève des 9 et 10 Juin 1950," 19 June 1950.

97. ANS, 1K44, Inspecteur Général du Travail, " . . . Salaire Minimum . . . et . . . la Grève des 9 et 10 Juin 1950," 21 August 1950.

98. Ibid.

99. ANS, 1K44, Inspecteur Général du Travail, " . . . Salaire Minimum . . . et Grève des 9 et 10 Juin 1950," 19 June 1950.

100. Ibid.

101. Ibid.

102. ANS, 1K44, Inspecteur Général du Travail, " . . . Salaire Minimum . . . et . . . la Grève des 9 et 10 Juin 1950," 21 August 1950.

103. ANS, 1K44, Conseil Général, Conakry, à Haut Commissaire, 26 June 1950.

104. ANS, 1K44, Inspecteur Général du Travail, " . . . Salaire Minimum . . . et . . . la Grève des 9 et 10 Juin 1950," 21 August 1950; Morgenthau, *Political Parties,* pp. 224–225. Founded in 1949, the Comité d'Entente Guinéenne was financed by several large French trading companies and supported by ethnic associations, wealthy African planters, chiefs, and notables. AG, 1E41, Guinée Française, Services de Police, "Renseignements A/S Comité de Rénovation de Basse Guinée et Opposition R.D.A.," 17 August 1949, #796/C/PS; Sidiki Kobélé Kéïta, *P.D.G.*, 1:210–211; Rivière, *Guinea,* pp. 66–67. Also see Thomas Hodgkin, *African Political Parties: An Introductory Guide* (Gloucester, Mass.: Peter Smith, 1971), p. 72.

105. ANS, 1K44, Conseil Général, Conakry, à Haut Commissaire, 26 June 1950.

106. ANS, 1K44, Inspecteur Général du Travail, " . . . Salaire Minimum . . . et . . . la Grève des 9 et 10 Juin 1950," 21 August 1950.

107. Cooper, *Decolonization,* p. 280. Also see comments of Mamadou Konaté in ANS, 1K44, Mamadou Konaté, "Cinglant Démenti aux Valets des Colonialistes de Conakry," extraits de *Réveil,* 14 August 1950.

108. Cooper, *Decolonization,* pp. 280–281; Cooper, "Free Labor," p. 754.

109. Cooper, *Decolonization,* pp. 286, 292; Cooper, "Free Labor," p. 754.

110. Cooper, *Decolonization,* p. 293; Sidiki Kobélé Kéïta, *P.D.G.,* 1:266.

111. Sidiki Kobélé Kéïta, *P.D.G.,* 1:266–267.

112. Cooper, *Decolonization,* p. 293; Sidiki Kobélé Kéïta, *P.D.G.,* 1:268–269.

113. Cooper, *Decolonization,* p. 293; Sidiki Kobélé Kéïta, *P.D.G.,* 1:269; Morgenthau, *Political Parties,* p. 228.

114. Cooper, *Decolonization,* p. 303; Sidiki Kobélé Kéïta, *P.D.G.,* 1:257, 269; Morgenthau, *Political Parties,* p. 228; Sidiki Kobélé Kéïta, *Ahmed Sékou Touré: 28 Septembre,* p. 45; Jones, *Industrial Labor,* pp. 66, 115 n. 54; Edward Mortimer, *France and the Africans, 1944–1960: A Political History* (New York: Walker, 1969), p. 180.

115. Cooper, *Decolonization,* pp. 303–304; Sidiki Kobélé Kéïta, *P.D.G.,* 1:269.

116. AG, 1F20, JS/LL, #7235, "Nouvelles de l'Union Française," *West Africa,* 22 November 1952 (retyped article); Cooper, *Decolonization,* pp. 303–304; Cooper, "Our Strike," p. 117.

117. AG, 1F20, JS/LL, #7235, "Nouvelles de l'Union Française."

118. AG, 1E42, Guinée Française, Gendarmerie Nationale, Commandant la Brigade de Mamou, "Rapport sur une Grève des Employés de Divers Services à Mamou," ca. 3 November 1952, #7/4.

119. Quoted in Sidiki Kobélé Kéïta, *P.D.G.,* 1:273.

120. Cooper, *Decolonization,* pp. 293–294, 303–305; Cooper, "Industrial Man," p. 133. For similar claims by Nigerian trade unionists, see Lindsay, "Domesticity and Difference," pp. 786–787, 790, 794, 802–812; Lisa A. Lindsay, "Money, Marriage, and Masculinity on the Colonial Nigerian Railway," in *Men and Masculinities,* pp. 148–149; Lindsay, *Working with Gender,* pp. 4, 22, 105, 117, 125, 140, 173, 203; Carolyn A. Brown, "A 'Man' in the Village is a 'Boy' in the Workplace: Colonial Racism, Worker Militance, and Igbo Notions of Masculinity in the Nigerian Coal Industry, 1930–1945," in *Men and Masculinities,* pp. 158, 168.

121. Morgenthau, *Political Parties,* p. 228; Sidiki Kobélé Kéïta, *P.D.G.,* 1:273–274; Cooper, *Decolonization,* p. 294.

122. Sidiki Kobélé Kéïta, *P.D.G.,* 1:274; Cooper, *Decolonization,* pp. 295–296, 313–314, 319; Cooper, "Free Labor," pp. 754–755; Cooper, "Industrial Man," p. 129.

123. Cooper, "Industrial Man," p. 129.

124. Cooper, *Decolonization,* pp. 282, 296–297, 303; Cooper, "Free Labor," pp. 754–755; Sidiki Kobélé Kéïta, *P.D.G.,* 1:276–277; Morgenthau, *Political Parties,* p. 228; Rivière, *Guinea,* p. 56.

125. Cooper, *Decolonization,* pp. 178, 296, 298.

126. Ibid., p. 297.

127. For an extensive discussion of the debate over family allowances, see Cooper, *Decolonization,* pp. 281–282, 284–285, 300–305; Cooper, "Free Labor," pp. 755–756; Cooper, "Industrial Man," pp. 133–134.

For a similar debate in Nigeria, see Lindsay, "Domesticity and Difference," pp. 783–784, 786–788, 794, 802–812; Lindsay, "Money," pp. 147–151; Lindsay, *Working with Gender,* pp. 22, 55–56, 59, 68–69, 72, 107, 117, 125, 134, 140, 173, 185, 197, 203; Lisa A. Lindsay, " 'No Need . . . to Think of Home'?: Masculinity and Domestic Life on the Nigerian Railway, c. 1940–61," *Journal of African History* 39, no. 3 (1998): p. 453; Brown, "Man in the Village," pp. 169–170.

128. Sidiki Kobélé Kéïta, *P.D.G.,* 1:278.

129. Morgenthau, *Political Parties,* p. 228; Sidiki Kobélé Kéïta, *P.D.G.,* 1:279–281.

130. Morgenthau, *Political Parties,* p. 228; Sidiki Kobélé Kéïta, *P.D.G.,* 1:278.

131. Morgenthau, *Political Parties,* p. 229; Sidiki Kobélé Kéïta, *P.D.G.,* 1:308.

132. ANS, 17G277, Télégramme Arrivée, Haut Commissaire, Dakar. Envoyé par Gouverneur, Guinée Française, Conakry, 8 September 1953, #180–182; 17G277, Télégramme Arrivée, Haut Commissaire, Dakar. Envoyé par Gouverneur, Guinée Française, Conakry, 24 September 1953, #211–212.

133. ANS, 17G277, Télégramme Arrivée, Haut Commissaire, 8 September 1953; Morgenthau, *Political Parties,* pp. 228–229; Sidiki Kobélé Kéïta, *P.D.G.,* 1:280–281, 283–284; Cooper, *Decolonization,* pp. 307–308; Cooper, "Our Strike," p. 117.

134. ANS, 17G277, Télégramme Arrivée, Haut Commissaire, 8 September 1953.

135. Morgenthau, *Political Parties,* p. 229; Sidiki Kobélé Kéïta, *P.D.G.,* 1:284; Cooper, *Decolonization,* p. 308.

136. ANS, 17G277, Télégramme Arrivée, Haut Commissaire, Dakar. Envoyé par Gouverneur, Guinée Française, Conakry, 21 September 1953, #205; 17G277, Télégramme Arrivée, Haut Commissaire, Dakar. Envoyé par Gouverneur, Guinée Française, Conakry, 22 September 1953, #207; 17G277, Télégramme Arrivée, Haut Commissaire, Dakar. Envoyé par Gouverneur, Guinée Française, Conakry, 25 September 1953, #215–216.

137. ANS, 2G53/187, Guinée Française, Secrétaire Général, "Revues Trimestrielles des Événements, 3ème Trimestre 1953," 12 September 1953, #862/APA; Rivière, *Guinea,* p. 57.

138. AG, 5B43, Guinée Française, Commissariat de Police, Kankan, "Retour à Kankan du 'Laministe' Mory-Oulin Caba," ca. 9 April 1947; ANS, 2G46/22, Guinée Française, "Rapport Politique Annuel, 1946," #284/APA; 2G47/121, Guinée Française, Affaires Politiques et Administratives, "Revues Trimestrielles des Événements, 1er Trimestre 1947," 17 June 1947, #143 APA; 5B49, Guinée Française, Inspecteur des Affaires Administratives, pour le Gouverneur, Conakry, à l'Agent Consulaire de France, Bathurst (Gambie), 5 July 1948, #382/APA; 1E38, Guinée Française, Cercle de N'Zérékoré, "Rapport Politique Annuel, Année 1948"; ANS, 17G573, Guinée Française, Services de Police, "Renseignements A/S Réunion des Membres du R.D.A. réunis en Assemblée Générale tenue au Cinéma 'Rialto' le 12 Septembre 1948," 13 September 1948, #KE/978/3.

139. Sidiki Kobélé Kéïta, *P.D.G.,* 1:93, 307–309, 311.

140. ANS, 17G277, Télégramme Arrivée, Haut Commissaire, Dakar. Envoyé par Gouverneur, Guinée Française, Conakry, 20 October 1953, #276–277. Also see 17G277, Télégramme Arrivée, Haut Commissaire, Dakar. Envoyé par Gouverneur, Guinée Française, Conakry, 19 October 1953, #274; 17G277, Télégramme Arrivée, Haut Commissaire, Dakar. Envoyé par Gouverneur, Guinée Française, Conakry, 22 October 1953, #278–279; 17G277, Guinée Française, Services de Police, "Renseignements *Objet:* La Grève à Conakry," 26 October 1953, #2224/1192, C/PS.2; 17G277, Guinée Française, Services de Police, "Renseignements *Objet:* La Grève à Conakry," 26 October 1953, #2228/1194, C/PS.2; 17G277, Guinée Française, Services de Police, "Renseignements *Objet:* La Grève à Conakry," 27 October 1953, #2245/1206, C/PS.2.

141. ANS, 17G277, Police, " . . . Grève à Conakry," 26 October 1953, #2224/1192, C/PS.2; 17G277, Police, " . . . Grève à Conakry," 26 October 1953, #2228/1194, C/PS.2.

142. ANS, 17G277, Police, " . . . Grève à Conakry," 26 October 1953, #2228/1194, C/PS.2.

143. ANS, 17G277, Télégramme Arrivée, Haut Commissaire, Dakar. Envoyé par Gouverneur, Guinée Française, Conakry, 29 October 1953, #293–294.

144. Morgenthau, *Political Parties,* pp. 235–236, 324. For the *chérif's* earlier opposition to the RDA, see ANS, 17G573, Gouvernement Général de l'A.O.F., Cabinet, Bureau

Technique de Liaison et de Coordination, "Note de Renseignements *Objet:* Activité Politique et Sociale en Guinée pendant le Mois de Décembre 1949," 15 January 1950, #141, CAB/LC/DK.

145. ANS, 17G277, Télégramme Arrivée, Haut Commissaire, Dakar. Envoyé par Gouverneur, Guinée Française, Conakry, 28 October 1953, #290–291; 17G277, Télégramme Arrivée, Haut Commissaire, Dakar. Envoyé par Gouverneur, Guinée Française, Conakry, 3 November 1953, #300–303.

146. ANS, 17G277, Télégramme Arrivée, Haut Commissaire, 22 October 1953; 17G277, Télégramme Arrivée, Haut Commissaire, Dakar. Envoyé par Gouverneur, Guinée Française, Conakry, 24 October 1953, #280–282; 17G277, Police, " . . . Grève à Conakry," 27 October 1953; 17G277, Télégramme Arrivée, Haut Commissaire, 28 October 1953; 17G277, Télégramme Arrivée, Haut Commissaire, 29 October 1953.

For the impact of the second Lamine Guèye Law on African civil servants, see Cooper, *Decolonization,* pp. 281–282; Cooper, "Free Labor," p. 755; Cooper, "Industrial Man," pp. 133–134.

147. ANS, 17G277, Police, " . . . Grève à Conakry," 26 October 1953, #2224/1192, C/PS.2.

148. Morgenthau, *Political Parties,* p. 229.

149. ANS, 2G53/189, Guinée Française, Gendarmerie Nationale, Détachement de l'A.O.F.-Togo, Compagnie de la Guinée, "Fiche sur la Situation du Territoire de la Guinée au Cours du 4ème Trimestre 1953," Conakry, 31 December 1953, #182/4.

150. Morgenthau, *Political Parties,* pp. 224, 349.

151. ANS, 17G277, Télégramme Arrivée, Haut Commissaire, 3 November 1953. Also see 17G277, Télégramme Arrivée, Haut Commissaire, 24 October 1953; 17G277, Police, " . . . Grève à Conakry," 26 October 1953, #2224/1192, C/PS.2.

152. ANS, 17G277, Guinée Française, Services de Police, "Renseignements *Objet:* La Grève à Conakry," 16 November 1953, #2392/1277, C/PS.2.

153. Ibid. Also see 17G277, Télégramme Départ, Haut Commissaire, Dakar, à Gouverneur, Guinée Française, Conakry, 9 November 1953, #148; 17G277, Télégramme Départ, Haut Commissaire, Dakar, à Ministre, FOM, Paris, 10 November 1953, #378–379; 17G277, Télégramme Départ, Haut Commissaire, Dakar, à Gouverneur, Guinée Française, Conakry, ca. 11 November 1953 (Réponse son #321).

For a discussion of similar tactics by the colonial government in Nigeria and African reaction, see Lindsay, "Domesticity and Difference," pp. 788–794; Cheryl Johnson, "Madam Alimotu Pelewura," pp. 6–9; Cheryl Johnson, "Grassroots Organizing," pp. 141–143; Nina Emma Mba, *Nigerian Women Mobilized: Women's Political Activity in Southern Nigeria, 1900–1965,* Research Series, no. 48 (Berkeley: Institute of International Studies, University of California, 1982), pp. 226–231.

154. ANS, 17G277, Télégramme Arrivée, Haut Commissaire, Dakar. Envoyé par Gouverneur, Guinée Française, Conakry, 14 October 1953, #269–270; 17G277, Télégramme Arrivée, Haut Commissaire, 3 November 1953; 17G277, Télégramme Départ, Haut Commissaire, Dakar, à Gouverneur, Guinée Française, Conakry, 5 November 1953, #142; 17G277, Télégramme Arrivée, Haut Commissaire, Dakar. Envoyé par Gouverneur, Guinée Française, Conakry, 7 November 1953, #306–307; 17G277, Télégramme Arrivée, Haut Commissaire, Dakar. Envoyé par Gouverneur, Guinée Française, Conakry, 7 November 1953, #308–310; 17G277, Télégramme Arrivée, Haut Commissaire, Dakar. Envoyé par Gouverneur, Guinée Française, Conakry, 9 November 1953, #316–318; 17G277, Guinée Française, Services de Police, "Renseignements *Objet:* La Grève à Conakry," 10 November 1953, #2356/1264, C/PS.2; 17G277, Télégramme Arrivée, Haut Commissaire, Dakar.

Envoyé par Gouverneur, Guinée Française, Conakry, 12 November 1953, #325–327; 17G277, Télégramme Départ, Haut Commissaire, Dakar, à Gouverneur, Guinée Française, Conakry, 12 November 1953, #155; 17G277, Télégramme-Lettre, Gouverneur, Guinée Française, Conakry, à Haut Commissaire, Dakar, 13 November 1953, #469; 17G277, Police, " . . . Grève à Conakry," 16 November 1953.

155. ANS, 17G529, Climat Social AOF, "La Campagne de Baisse," 20 November 1953, #263.

156. Quoted in Cooper, *Decolonization,* pp. 307–308. Also see ANS, 17G277, Télégramme Arrivée, Haut Commissaire, Dakar. Envoyé par Gouverneur, Guinée Française, Conakry, 21 November 1953, #348–350.

157. ANS, 17G529, Télégramme Départ, Gouverneur Général, Dakar, à Ministre, FOM, Paris, 20 November 1953, #424–426. Also see Cooper, *Decolonization,* p. 309.

158. Quoted in Cooper, *Decolonization,* p. 309.

159. See Ibid., pp. 93, 100–104.

For a similar debate in Nigeria, see Lindsay, "Domesticity and Difference," pp. 786, 802–812.

160. ANS, 17G277, Télégramme Départ, Haut Commissaire, Dakar, à Ministre, FOM, Paris, 25 November 1953, #428; Cooper, *Decolonization,* pp. 309, 566 n. 137; Morgenthau, *Political Parties,* p. 229; Sidiki Kobélé Kéïta, *P.D.G.,* 1:285.

161. ANS, 2G53/189, Gendarmerie Nationale, " . . . Situation . . . de la Guinée . . . 4ème Trimestre 1953"; Cooper, *Decolonization,* p. 310.

162. Cooper, *Decolonization,* p. 310; Morgenthau, *Political Parties,* p. 229; Sidiki Kobélé Kéïta, *P.D.G.,* 1:285.

163. ANS, 17G529, Télégramme Arrivée, Gouverneur Général, Dakar. Envoyé par Gouverneur, Guinée Française, Conakry, 16 December 1953, #385–387.

164. Morgenthau, *Political Parties,* p. 229.

165. Interview with Fatou Kéïta, Km 43, Conakry, 7 April 1991.

166. Ibid.; Cooper, *Decolonization,* pp. 317–318, 320; Cooper, "Free Labor," p. 756; Cooper, "Industrial Man," pp. 134–135.

167. ANS, 17G529, Télégramme Arrivée, Gouverneur Général, 6 December 1953.

168. ANS, 17G529, Télégramme Départ, Gouverneur Général, Dakar, à Ministre, FOM, Paris, 25 November 1953, #429–432.

169. Morgenthau, *Political Parties,* p. 229; Margarita Dobert, "Civic and Political Participation of Women in French-Speaking West Africa" (Ph.D. diss., George Washington University, 1970), pp. 77–78.

170. Ahmed Sékou Touré, *L'Afrique et la Révolution* (Geneva: Imprimerie en Suisse, 1966), 13:60.

171. Interview with Kadiatou Meunier [pseud.], Minière, Conakry, 18 January 1991. For similar attitudes among Nigerian women, see Lindsay, "Domesticity and Difference," p. 801; Lindsay, *Working with Gender,* pp. 110–111.

172. Interview with Néné Diallo, Conakry, 11 April 1991.

173. Fatou Kéïta, interview, 7 April 1991. Also see Meunier, interview, 18 January 1991; interview with Fatou Diarra, Lansanaya, Conakry, 17 March 1991.

174. Siba N. Grovogui, personal communication, 1988.

For a more general discussion of this point, see Claire C. Robertson, *Trouble Showed the Way: Women, Men, and Trade in the Nairobi Area, 1890–1990* (Bloomington: Indiana University Press, 1997), p. 65.

175. See Lindsay, "Domesticity and Difference," pp. 784, 786–803, 810; Lindsay, *Working with Gender,* pp. 4–5, 22, 43–44, 72, 105–107, 110–111, 114, 117, 119, 125, 173,

203–204; Lindsay, "Money," pp. 139, 142–145, 147, 150; Lindsay, "No Need," pp. 449–453, 465–466. Also see Cooper, *Decolonization*, p. 319.

176. Diallo, interview, 11 April 1991.

177. Interview with Tourou Sylla, Kimbely, Mamou, 30 May 1991; Fatou Kéïta, interview, 7 April 1991; interview with Bocar Biro Barry, Camayenne, Conakry, 29 January 1991; AG, AM-1339, Idiatou Camara, "La Contribution de la Femme de Guinée à la Lutte de Libération Nationale (1945–1958)" (Mémoire de Fin d'Études Supérieures, IPGAN, Conakry, 1979), pp. 71–72; Sidiki Kobélé Kéïta, *P.D.G.*, 1:345.

178. Fatou Kéïta, interview, 7 April 1991.

179. Interview with Sidiki Kobélé Kéïta, Donka, Conakry, 20 October 1990; Meunier, interview, 18 January 1991; interview with Mamadou Bela Doumbouya, Camayenne, Conakry, 26 January 1991; interview with Ibrahima Fofana, Lansanaya, Conakry, 17 March 1991; Tourou Sylla, interview, 30 May 1991.

180. Tourou Sylla, interview, 30 May 1991.

181. Ahmed Sékou Touré, *L'Afrique*, p. 60; Dobert, "Civic and Political Participation," p. 78; Morgenthau, *Political Parties*, p. 229; Sidiki Kobélé Kéïta, *P.D.G.*, 1:290; CRDA, Claude Gérard, "Incidents en Guinée Française, 1954–1955," *Afrique Informations*, 15 March–1 April 1955, p. 11.

182. Fatou Diarra, interview, 17 March 1991; Diallo, interview, 11 April 1991; interview with Namankoumba Kouyaté, Conakry, 31 January 1991; Maka, interview, 20 February 1991; Sidiki Kobélé Kéïta, *P.D.G.*, 1:290.

183. Interview with Mamady Kaba, Donka, Conakry, 15 January 1991; Meunier, interview, 18 January 1991; Maka, interview, 20 February 1991; Ibrahima Fofana, interview, 17 March 1991; Fatou Diarra, interview, 17 March 1991; Louis Marquis Camara, interview, 27 March 1991; Diallo, interview, 11 April 1991; Tourou Sylla, interview, 30 May 1991; Sidiki Kobélé Kéïta, *P.D.G.*, 1:346; Sidiki Kobélé Kéïta, *Ahmed Sékou Touré: 28 Septembre*, p. 46; Idiatou Camara, "Contribution de la Femme," p. 72.

184. Kouyaté, interview, 31 January 1991; Montlouis, interview, 3 March 1991; Dobert, "Civic and Political Participation," p. 78.

185. Fatou Kéïta, interview, 7 April 1991.

186. Interview with Louis Marquis Camara, interview, 27 March 1991. Also see interview with Tiguidanké Diakhaby, Donka, Conakry, 12 January 1991.

187. Fatou Kéïta, interview, 7 April 1991.

For a discussion of manioc (cassava) as a low-nutrition famine food, see Jette Bukh, *The Village Woman in Ghana* (Uppsala, Sweden: Scandinavian Institute of African Studies, 1979), pp. 84–88.

188. Fatou Kéïta, interview, 7 April 1991.

189. Ibrahima Fofana, interview, 17 March 1991.

190. Interview with Aissatou N'Diaye, Kaloum, Sandervalia, Conakry, 8 April 1991.

Syli is the Susu word for "elephant." It was the symbol of the RDA, and by extension, for Sékou Touré personally.

191. ANS, 17G586, Guinée Française, Services de Police, "Renseignements *Objet*: Réunion Publique R.D.A. à Conakry et ses Suites," 8 September 1954, #2606/942, C/PS.2; 17G586, Guinée Française, Commissaire Central de la Ville de Conakry, "Manifestation sur la Voie Publique," 13 September 1954, #1317/SP.

192. N'Diaye, interview, 8 April 1991. N'Diaye describes *bakutui*, the very loose, full pants worn by men in the Futa Jallon.

193. Diallo, interview, 11 April 1991.

194. Ibid.

195. ANS, 17G277, Télégramme Arrivée, Haut Commissaire, 7 November 1953; 17G277, Télégramme Arrivée, Haut Commissaire, 9 November 1953; 17G277, Police, " . . . Grève à Conakry," 10 November 1953.

196. Dobert, "Civic and Political Participation," p. 78.

197. Morgenthau, *Political Parties,* p. 229.

198. Ibrahima Fofana, interview, 17 March 1991.

199. Meunier, interview, 18 January 1991. Also see Maka, interview, 20 February 1991.

200. Sidiki Kobélé Kéïta, *P.D.G.,* 1:345; Sidiki Kobélé Kéïta, *Ahmed Sékou Touré: 28 Septembre,* p. 47; Idiatou Camara, "Contribution de la Femme," p. 127.

201. N'Diaye, interview, 8 April 1991. Also see Barry, interview, 29 January 1991.

202. Maka, interview, 20 February 1991.

203. N'Diaye, interview, 8 April 1991.

204. Fatou Kéïta, interview, 7 April 1991.

205. N'Diaye, interview, 8 April 1991.

206. Idiatou Camara, "Contribution de la Femme," pp. 71–72; Mamady Kaba, interview, 15 January 1991.

207. Fatou Kéïta, interview, 7 April 1991.

208. Idiatou Camara, "Contribution de la Femme," pp. 71–72; Mamady Kaba, interview, 15 January 1991. For similar sentiments expressed by RDA women in the French Soudan, see Jane Turrittin, "Aoua Kéita and the Nascent Women's Movement in the French Soudan," *African Studies Review* 36, no. 1 (April 1993): p. 72.

209. N'Diaye, interview, 8 April 1991. Also see Doumbouya, interview, 26 January 1991; Barry, interview, 29 January 1991; Sidiki Kobélé Kéïta, *P.D.G.,* 1:339.

210. N'Diaye, interview, 8 April 1991.

211. Fatou Kéïta, interview, 7 and 28 April 1991.

212. Diallo, interview, 11 April 1991.

213. For French West Africa, Kenya, and the Gold Coast, see Cooper, *Decolonization,* pp. 228–260; Frederick Cooper, *On the African Waterfront: Urban Disorder and the Transformation of Work in Colonial Mombasa* (New Haven, Conn.: Yale University Press, 1987), pp. 42–113. For Nigeria, see Lindsay, "Domesticity and Difference," pp. 783–812. For the Sudan, see Sikainga, *City of Steel and Fire,* pp. 97–122. For South Africa, see Dan O'Meara, "The 1946 African Mine Workers' Strike and the Political Economy of South Africa," *Journal of Commonwealth and Comparative Politics* 13, no. 1 (March 1975): pp. 146–173; T. Dunbar Moodie, "The Moral Economy of the Black Miners' Strike of 1946," *Journal of Southern African Studies* 13, no. 1 (October 1986): pp. 1–35. For Northern Rhodesia, see Michael Burawoy, *The Colour of Class on the Copper Mines: From African Advancement to Zambianization,* Zambian Papers, no. 7 (Lusaka, Zambia: University of Zambia, Institute for African Studies, 1972), pp. 13–22. For Southern Rhodesia, see Ian Phimister, *An Economic and Social History of Zimbabwe, 1890–1948: Capital Accumulation and Class Struggle* (New York: Longman, 1988), pp. 263–274; Ian Phimister, *Wangi Kolia: Coal, Capital and Labour in Colonial Zimbabwe, 1894–1954* (Harare, Zimbabwe: Baobab Books; Johannesburg, South Africa: Witwatersrand University Press, 1994), pp. 99–108.

214. Cooper, "Our Strike," p. 11. For a comparison with postal workers' and veterans' demands, see Cooper, *Decolonization,* pp. 228–229; Myron Echenberg, "Tragedy at Thiaroye: The Senegalese Soldiers' Uprising of 1944," in *African Labor History,* ed.

Peter C. W. Gutkind, Robin Cohen, and Jean Copans (Beverly Hills, Calif.: Sage Publications, 1978), p. 124; Myron Echenberg, " 'Morts Pour La France': The African Soldier in France during the Second World War," *Journal of African History* 26, no. 4 (1985): p. 379; Myron Echenberg, *Colonial Conscripts: The Tirailleurs Sénégalais in French West Africa, 1857–1960* (Portsmouth, N.H.: Heinemann; London: James Currey, 1991), pp. 104, 152.

CHAPTER 4: RURAL REVOLT: POPULAR RESISTANCE TO THE COLONIAL CHIEFTAINCY, 1946–1956

1. ANS, 2G41/21, Guinée Française, "Rapport Politique Annuel, 1941"; 2G42/22, Guinée Française, "Rapport Politique Annuel, 1942"; 2G47/121, Guinée Française, Affaires Politiques et Administratives, "Revues Trimestrielles des Événements, 3ème Trimestre 1947," 5 December 1947, #389 APA; Jean Suret-Canale, *La République de Guinée* (Paris: Éditions Sociales, 1970), pp. 95, 137; Jean Suret-Canale, *French Colonialism in Tropical Africa, 1900–1945,* trans. Till Gottheiner (New York: Pica Press, 1971), pp. 80, 322–323, 325, 341–342; Jean Suret-Canale, "La Fin de la Chefferie en Guinée," *Journal of African History* 7, no. 3 (1966): pp. 462, 467, 470; Martin Klein, *Slavery and Colonial Rule in French West Africa* (New York: Cambridge University Press, 1998), pp. 212–213; Sidiki Kobélé Kéïta, *Le P.D.G.: Artisan de l'Indépendance Nationale en Guinée (1947–1958)* (Conakry: I.N.R.D.G., Bibliothèque Nationale, 1978), 1:87–88, 99–102; Mahmood Mamdani, *Citizen and Subject: Contemporary Africa and the Legacy of Late Colonialism* (Princeton, N.J.: Princeton University Press, 1996), pp. 22–23, 33, 39–61.

2. ANS, 2G41/21, "Rapport Politique Annuel, 1941"; 2G46/50, Guinée Française, Inspecteur des Colonies (Pruvost), Mission en Guinée, "Rapport sur La Main d'Oeuvre en Guinée," Conakry, 13 July 1946, #116/C; AG, 1E39, Guinée Française, Cercle de N'Zérékoré, "Rapport Politique Annuel, Année 1949"; Suret-Canale, *République,* pp. 95, 97–98, 108, 138–139; Suret-Canale, *French Colonialism,* pp. 80, 345–346; Sidiki Kobélé Kéïta, *P.D.G.,* 1:87–88, 99–102; Myron Echenberg, *Colonial Conscripts: The Tirailleurs Sénégalais in French West Africa, 1857–1960* (Portsmouth, N.H.: Heinemann; London: James Currey, 1991), p. 84.

3. AG, 5B47, Guinée Française, Gouverneur, Conakry, à Administrateurs de Cercle et Chefs de Subdivision, 3 July 1947, #442/APA; 5B49, Guinée Française, Gouverneur, Conakry, à Commandant de Cercle, Boffa, 5 June 1948, #322/APA.

4. Suret-Canale, *République,* p. 97; Suret-Canale, *French Colonialism,* p. 324; Sidiki Kobélé Kéïta, *P.D.G.,* 1:87–88.

5. Suret-Canale, *République,* pp. 325, 346. For the revocation of village chiefs, see AG, 1E39, Guinée Française, Cercle de Kouroussa, "Rapport Politique Annuel, Année 1949."

6. Suret-Canale, *République,* p. 95; Suret-Canale, *French Colonialism,* p. 324; Sidiki Kobélé Kéïta, *P.D.G.,* 1:88.

7. Suret-Canale, *French Colonialism,* p. 346. Also see Mamdani, *Citizen and Subject,* pp. 54–55, 58.

8. ANS, 2G53/189, Guinée Française, Gendarmerie Nationale, Détachement de l'A.O.F.-Togo, Compagnie de la Guinée, "Fiche sur la Situation du Territoire de la Guinée au Cours du 4ème Trimestre 1953," Conakry, 31 December 1953, #182/4; Suret-Canale, *French Colonialism,* pp. 345–347; Sidiki Kobélé Kéïta, *P.D.G.,* 1:329.

9. AG, 5B49, Guinée Française, Inspecteur des Affaires Administratives, pour le Gouverneur, Conakry, à Commandant de Cercle, Beyla, 24 June 1948, #364/APA. Also see 5B49, Guinée Française, Secrétaire Général, pour le Gouverneur, Conakry, à Commandant de Cercle, Kankan, 28 October 1948, #769/APA.

10. AG, 5B49, Guinée Française, Gouverneur, Conakry, à Tous Cercles et Subdivisions, 16 August 1948, #520/APA.

11. AG, 5B49, Guinée Française, Gouverneur, Conakry, à Chef de Subdivision, Mali, Cercle de Labé, 16 August 1948, #514/APA. Also see ANS, 17G573, Guinée Française, Services de Police, Conakry, "Renseignements A/S Réunion Générale du R.D.A.," 15 September 1948, #KE/989/5.

12. ANS, 2G41/21, Guinée Française, "Rapport Politique Annuel, 1941." Also see Mamdani, *Citizen and Subject,* pp. 56–57.

13. AG, 1E42, Guinée Française, "Renseignements," Cercle de Kankan, 26 January 1945, #66/C/APAN/31/1/46; 1E37, Guinée Française, Cercle de Gaoual, Subdivision Centrale, "Rapport Politique Annuel, Année 1947"; ANS, 2G46/50, "Rapport sur La Main d'Oeuvre en Guinée," 13 July 1946; Suret-Canale, *République,* pp. 96–98, 138–139; Suret-Canale, *French Colonialism,* pp. 80, 327; Suret-Canale, "Fin de la Chefferie," pp. 464, 479–480; Sidiki Kobélé Kéïta, *P.D.G.,* 1:101–102, 331; Babacar Fall, *Le Travail Forcé en Afrique-Occidentale Française (1900–1945)* (Paris: Éditions Karthala, 1993), p. 279.

For discussion of a similar regime in Mozambique, see Allen Isaacman, *Cotton Is the Mother of Poverty: Peasants, Work, and Rural Struggle in Colonial Mozambique, 1938–1961* (Portsmouth, N.H.: Heinemann; London: James Currey, 1996), pp. 174–181.

According to the terms of the *indigénat,* subjects who refused to fulfill their "customary" duties could be imprisoned from six days to three months and fined from 16 to 500 francs. ANS, 2G46/50, "Rapport sur La Main d'Oeuvre en Guinée," 13 July 1946; Sidiki Kobélé Kéïta, *P.D.G.,* 1:102.

14. ANS, 17G573, Guinée Française, Services de Police, "Renseignements A/S Activités du R.D.A. à Kankan," 31 March 1950, #291/165, C/PS; Suret-Canale, *French Colonialism,* p. 327; Suret-Canale, "Fin de la Chefferie," pp. 479–480.

15. ANS, 2G46/50, "Rapport sur La Main d'Oeuvre en Guinée," 13 July 1946.

16. Suret-Canale, *French Colonialism,* pp. 80, 324.

17. Suret-Canale, *République,* p. 80. Also see Mamdani, *Citizen and Subject,* pp. 40, 42–47, 53–54.

18. Suret-Canale, *République,* p. 137; Suret-Canale, "Fin de la Chefferie," p. 462; Suret-Canale, *French Colonialism,* pp. 79–80, 322–325; Sidiki Kobélé Kéïta, *P.D.G.,* 1:87, 90; Ruth Schachter Morgenthau, *Political Parties in French-Speaking West Africa* (Oxford: Clarendon Press, 1964), p. 7.

19. Suret-Canale, *République,* p. 97.

20. Philip Curtin, Steven Feierman, Leonard Thompson, and Jan Vansina, *African History: From Earliest Times to Independence,* 2nd ed. (New York: Longman, 1995), p. 444; Anthony D. Smith, *State and Nation in the Third World: The Western State and African Nationalism* (New York: St. Martin's Press, 1983), pp. 48–49.

21. Interview with Léon Maka, Sangoyah, Conakry, 20 February 1991.

22. Morgenthau, *Political Parties,* p. 9. During the war, the forest town of N'Zérékoré, for instance, was notorious for its smuggling operations into Liberia.

23. ANS, 2G46/22, Guinée Française, "Rapport Politique Annuel, 1946," #284/ APA.

24. See, for instance, ANS, 2G41/21, "Rapport Politique Annuel, 1941"; 2G46/22, "Rapport Politique Annuel, 1946"; 2G47/121, Guinée Française, Affaires Politiques et

Administratives, "Revues Trimestrielles des Événements, 1er Trimestre 1947," 17 June 1947, #143 APA; Suret-Canale, *République,* p. 139.

25. ANS, 2G47/22, Guinée Française, "Rapport Politique Annuel, 1947," #271/APA.

26. Sidiki Kobélé Kéïta, *P.D.G.,* 1:332; Suret-Canale, "Fin de la Chefferie," pp. 479–480; Léon Maka, "Le R.D.A. et Certaines Pratiques Coutumières," *La Liberté,* 1 March 1955, p. 2.

27. AG, 1E38, Guinée Française, Cercle de Gaoual, Subdivision Centrale, "Rapport Politique Annuel, Année 1948." The circle commandant included wives on the list of the chief's possessions.

28. AG, 1E39, Guinée Française, Cercle de Pita, "Rapport Politique Annuel, Année 1949."

29. ANS, 2G41/21, "Rapport Politique Annuel, 1941"; AG, 1E39, N'Zérékoré, "Rapport Politique Annuel, 1949"; Suret-Canale, *République,* p. 137; Suret-Canale, *French Colonialism,* pp. 77, 80, 324; Suret-Canale, "Fin de la Chefferie," p. 462.

30. See, for instance, AG, 1E38, Gaoual, "Rapport Politique Annuel, 1948."

Although the government had created a class of Western-educated elites to serve its needs, it maintained a profound ambivalence toward these *evolués.* Government officials desperately desired chiefs who could understand, speak, and write French. Yet, they found illiterate chiefs to be more malleable and dependent and less likely to be influenced by the RDA and other inappropriate organizations. Thus, they felt a certain responsibility for their illiterate charges. In Boké, for instance, the circle commandant wrote that the chiefs and notables were of "incontestable loyalty" to the administration. They counted on the administration to "protect their customs, their authority, and their traditions against the action of the *evolués.*" AG, 1E38, Guinée Française, Cercle de Boké, "Rapport Politique Annuel, Année 1948"; 1E38, Guinée Française, Cercle de Macenta, "Rapport Politique Annuel, Année 1948."

31. Suret-Canale, *French Colonialism,* pp. 341, 374–375, 377, 381, 384, 388, 393 n. 30, 31; Suret-Canale, *République,* pp. 136–137; Sidiki Kobélé Kéïta, *P.D.G.,* 1:73. For enrollment statistics, see ANS, 2G41/21, "Rapport Politique Annuel, 1941"; 2G42/22, "Rapport Politique Annuel, 1942"; 2G43/19, Guinée Française, "Rapport Politique Annuel, 1943."

32. Suret-Canale, *République,* pp. 136–137; Suret-Canale, *French Colonialism,* p. 388; Klein, *Slavery and Colonial Rule,* p. 251; Siba N. Grovogui, personal communication, 24 October 1991.

The Jallonke inhabitants of the Futa Jallon were conquered and enslaved during the Peul jihads of the eighteenth and nineteenth centuries. See Suret-Canale, "Fin de la Chefferie," pp. 464–465; Klein, *Slavery and Colonial Rule,* p. 45; Walter Rodney, "Jihad and Social Revolution in Futa Djalon in the Eighteenth Century," *Journal of the Historical Society of Nigeria* 4, no. 2 (June 1968): pp. 269–284.

33. Echenberg, *Colonial Conscripts,* pp. 15, 18; Klein, *Slavery and Colonial Rule,* pp. 216–217, 251.

34. Interview with Ibrahima Fofana, Lansanaya, Conakry, 5 May 1991.

35. Suret-Canale, *République,* pp. 136–137; Suret-Canale, *French Colonialism,* pp. 374–375, 377, 384, 388. Also see Echenberg, *Colonial Conscripts,* pp. 11–19.

36. Suret-Canale, *République,* pp. 136–137; Suret-Canale, *French Colonialism,* pp. 374–375, 377, 384, 388; Echenberg, *Colonial Conscripts,* pp. 11–19; Klein, *Slavery and Colonial Rule,* pp. 216–219, 251; Maka, interview, 25 February 1991; Ibrahima Fofana, interview, 5 May 1991.

For a discussion of these issues in the French Soudan, see Gregory Mann, "Old Soldiers, Young Men: Masculinity, Islam, and Military Veterans in Late 1950s Soudan Français (Mali)," in *Men and Masculinities in Modern Africa,* ed. Lisa A. Lindsay and Stephan F. Miescher (Portsmouth, N.H.: Heinemann, 2003), pp. 73–75. For British East Africa, see Timothy H. Parsons, *The African Rank-and-File: Social Implications of Colonial Military Service in the King's African Rifles, 1902–1964* (Portsmouth, N.H.: Heinemann; Oxford: James Currey, 1999), pp. 236, 252.

37.   Ibrahima Fofana, interview, 5 May 1991.

38.   AG, 1E38, Gaoual, "Rapport Politique Annuel, 1948."

39.   Quoted in B. Ameillon, *La Guinée: Bilan d'une Indépendance,* Cahiers Libres nos. 58–59 (Paris: François Maspero, 1964), pp. 17–18. Also see AG, 5B43, Guinée Française, Commissariat de Police, Kankan, "Retour à Kankan du 'Laministe' Mory-Oulin Caba," ca. 9 April 1947; ANS, 2G46/22, "Rapport Politique Annuel, 1946"; 2G47/121, "Revues Trimestrielles des Événements, 1er Trimestre 1947."

40.   Ibrahima Fofana, interview, 5 May 1991.

41.   See, for instance, Echenberg, *Colonial Conscripts,* p. 133.

42.   ANS, 2G47/121, "Revues Trimestrielles des Événements, 1er Trimestre 1947"; Suret-Canale, *French Colonialism,* pp. 79, 323–324; Suret-Canale, "Fin de la Chefferie," pp. 470–471; Suret-Canale, *République,* p. 138.

43.   ANS, 2G46/22, "Rapport Politique Annuel, 1946"; 2G47/22, "Rapport Politique Annuel, 1947"; 2G47/121, "Revues Trimestrielles des Événements, 1er Trimestre 1947"; 2G47/121, Guinée Française, Affaires Politiques et Administratives, "Revues Trimestrielles des Événements, 2ème Trimestre 1947," 11 October 1947, #273 APA.

44.   AG, 1E39, Guinée Française, Cercle de Macenta, "Rapport Politique Annuel, Année 1949."

45.   Ibid.

46.   For elaboration on the origins and forms of peasant protest against rural authorities, see Allen Isaacman et al., " 'Cotton Is the Mother of Poverty': Peasant Resistance to Forced Cotton Production in Mozambique, 1938–1961," *International Journal of African Historical Studies* 13 (1980): pp. 581–615; Allen Isaacman, "Chiefs, Rural Differentiation and Peasant Protest: The Mozambican Forced Cotton Regime, 1938–61," *African Economic History* 14 (1985): pp. 15–56; Allen Isaacman, "Peasants and Rural Social Protest in Africa," *African Studies Review* 33 (1990): pp. 1–120; Allen Isaacman, "Coercion, Paternalism and the Labor Process: The Mozambican Cotton Regime, 1938–1961," *Journal of Southern African Studies* 18, no. 3 (1992): pp. 487–526; Isaacman, *Cotton Is the Mother of Poverty,* pp. 205–237; William Beinart and Colin Bundy, "State Intervention and Rural Resistance: The Transkei, 1900–1965," in *Peasants in Africa: Historical and Contemporary Perspectives,* ed. Martin Klein (Beverly Hills, Calif.: Sage Publications, 1980), pp. 270–315; William Beinart and Colin Bundy, *Hidden Struggles in Rural South Africa: Politics and Popular Movements in the Transkei and Eastern Cape, 1890–1930* (Berkeley: University of California Press, 1987); James C. Scott, *Weapons of the Weak: Everyday Forms of Peasant Resistance* (New Haven, Conn.: Yale University Press, 1985).

47.   The superintendent of police, as quoted in Sidiki Kobélé Kéïta, *P.D.G.,* 1:173.

48.   AG, 1E38, Boké, "Rapport Politique Annuel, 1948."

49.   AG, 1E37, Guinée Française, Cercle de Macenta, "Rapport Politique Annuel, Année 1947."

50.   AG, 1E38, Macenta, "Rapport Politique Annuel, 1948."

A similar situation existed in the Macenta canton of Kononkoro-Malinké, where a former government clerk presided as chief, and in the Beyla canton of Simandougou. 1E38, Macenta, "Rapport Politique Annuel, 1948"; 1E39, Guinée Française, Cercle de Beyla, "Rapport Politique Annuel, Année 1949."

51. AG, 1E37, Macenta, "Rapport Politique Annuel, 1947."

52. AG, 1E39, N'Zérékoré, "Rapport Politique Annuel, 1949."

53. AG, 5B47, Guinée Française, Gouverneur, Conakry, à Administrateur de Cercle, Forécariah, 25 January 1947, #69/APA; 5B47, Guinée Française, Gouverneur, Conakry, Ordre de Mission, 15 March 1947, #195/APA.

54. AG, 1E39, Kouroussa, "Rapport Politique Annuel, 1949."

55. AG, 5B43, Guinée Française, Commissariat de Police, Kankan, "Mouvement des 'Laministes'," 9 April 1947. Also see ANS, 2G46/22, "Rapport Politique Annuel, 1946"; 2G47/121, "Revues Trimestrielles des Événements, 1er Trimestre 1947"; 2G47/22, "Rapport Politique Annuel, 1947"; 2G47/121, Guinée Française, Affaires Politiques et Administratives, "Revues Trimestrielles des Événements, 4ème Trimestre 1947," 17 February 1948, #35 APA.

56. ANS, 2G46/22, "Rapport Politique Annuel, 1946"; 2G47/121, "Revues Trimestrielles des Événements, 1er Trimestre 1947"; 2G47/22, "Rapport Politique Annuel, 1947"; AG, 5B43, Guinée Française, Gouverneur, Conakry, à Gouverneur Général, Dakar, 11 March 1947, #44; 5B43, Guinée Française, Commissariat de Police, Kankan, "Arrivée du Gouverneur Général à Kankan le 28 Mars [1947]," ca. 9 April 1947; 1E37, Guinée Française, Cercle de Beyla, "Rapport Politique Annuel, Année 1947."

57. AG, 1E38, Macenta, "Rapport Politique Annuel, 1948"; 1E39, Macenta, "Rapport Politique Annuel, 1949."

58. AG, 1E37, Beyla, "Rapport Politique Annuel, 1947." Also see ANS, 2G46/22, "Rapport Politique Annuel, 1946"; 2G47/121, "Revues Trimestrielles des Événements, 1er Trimestre 1947"; 2G47/22, "Rapport Politique Annuel, 1947."

59. AG, 1E38, Guinée Française, Cercle de Beyla, "Rapport Politique Annuel, Année 1948."

60. ANS, 2G46/22, "Rapport Politique Annuel, 1946."

61. ANS, 2G47/22, "Rapport Politique Annuel, 1947."

62. ANS, 2G47/121, "Revues Trimestrielles des Événements, 3ème Trimestre 1947."

63. ANS, 2G46/50, "Rapport sur La Main d'Oeuvre en Guinée," 13 July 1946; Fall, *Travail Forcé,* pp. 279, 303; Virginia Thompson and Richard Adloff, *French West Africa* (New York: Greenwood Press, 1969), pp. 230, 492.

64. ANS, 2G46/50, "Rapport sur La Main d'Oeuvre en Guinée," 13 July 1946.

65. ANS, 2G46/22, "Rapport Politique Annuel, 1946"; AG, 1E38, Macenta, "Rapport Politique Annuel, 1948."

66. ANS, 2G46/22, "Rapport Politique Annuel, 1946."

67. ANS, 2G46/50, "Rapport sur La Main d'Oeuvre en Guinée," 13 July 1946. Also see 2G43/25, Guinée Française, "Rapport de Tournée Effectuée du 27 Janvier au 9 Février par M. Chopin, Administrateur des Colonies, Inspecteur du Travail, dans les Cercles de Conakry-Kindia-Forécariah," Conakry, 2 April 1943; Sidiki Kobélé Kéïta, *P.D.G.,* 1:102.

68. AG, 1E38, Macenta, "Rapport Politique Annuel, 1948"; 1E38, Guinée Française, Cercle de Kankan, "Rapport Politique Annuel, Année 1948"; Suret-Canale, "Fin de la Chefferie," p. 475; Sidiki Kobélé Kéïta, *P.D.G.,* 1:116; Jacques Richard-Molard, *Afrique Occidentale Française* (Paris: Éditions Berger-Levrault, 1952): p. 156.

69. ANS, 2G53/187, Guinée Française, Secrétaire Général, "Revues Trimestrielles des Événements, 1ère Trimestre 1953," 11 March 1953, #108/APA; Suret-Canale, *French Colonialism*, p. 347; Sidiki Kobélé Kéïta, *P.D.G.*, 1:329.

70. Sidiki Kobélé Kéïta, *P.D.G.*, 1:329.

71. Maka, interview, 25 February 1991; ANS, 2G55/151, Guinée Française, Gouverneur, Conakry, à Haut Commissaire, Dakar, "Revue des Événements du 4ème Trimestre 1955," February 1956, #131/APA. Also see Ameillon, *Guinée*, p. 22.

72. AG, 1E38, Boké, "Rapport Politique Annuel, 1948."

73. AG, 1E39, Guinée Française, Cercle de Boffa, "Rapport Politique Annuel, Année 1949." Also see 1E39, Beyla, "Rapport Politique Annuel, 1949."

74. AG, 5B43, Guinée Française, Gouverneur, Conakry, à Gouverneur Général, Dakar, 18 January 1947.

75. AG, 5B43, Guinée Française, Services de Police, "Renseignements A/S Impôt 1947," 26 February 1947, #139/C.

76. AG, 5B43, Guinée Française, Gouverneur, Conakry, à Gouverneur Général, Dakar, 29 October 1947, #311/APA.

77. AG, 5B47, Guinée Française, Gouverneur, Conakry, à Administrateur de Cercle, Macenta, 20 March 1947, #211/APA; 5B47, Guinée Française, Gouverneur, Conakry, à Administrateurs de Cercle et Chefs de Subdivision, 20 September 1947, #628/APA.

78. AG, 5B47, Gouverneur à Administrateurs de Cercle et Chefs de Subdivision, 20 September 1947.

79. ANS, 2G55/152, Guinée Française, Gouverneur, "Rapport Politique pour l'Année 1955," #281/APA.

80. Maka, interview, 20 February 1991. Also see Suret-Canale, "Fin de la Chefferie," p. 481; Mamdani, *Citizen and Subject,* pp. 24, 290.

81. Excerpt from the interterritorial RDA's *Réveil,* 10 October 1949, quoted in Suret-Canale, "Fin de la Chefferie," p. 476.

82. CAOM, Carton 2143, dos. 9, Sékou Touré, Dakar, à Félix Houphouët-Boigny, Dakar, 20 May 1955; Sidiki Kobélé Kéïta, *P.D.G.,* 1:332.

83. Interviews with Bocar Biro Barry, Camayenne, Conakry, 21 and 29 January 1991; Ibrahima Fofana, interview, 5 May 1991.
For similar dynamics in colonial Ghana, see Jean Marie Allman, *The Quills of the Porcupine: Asante Nationalism in an Emergent Ghana* (Madison: University of Wisconsin Press, 1993), pp. 28–36; Richard Rathbone, *Nkrumah and the Chiefs: The Politics of Chieftaincy in Ghana, 1951–60* (Athens: Ohio University Press, 2000); Pashington Obeng, "Gendered Nationalism: Forms of Masculinity in Modern Asante of Ghana," in *Men and Masculinities,* pp. 192, 201–202, 205–206; Stephan F. Miescher and Lisa A. Lindsay, "Introduction: Men and Masculinities in Modern African History," in *Men and Masculinities,* pp. 12, 17–18.

84. Interview with Aissatou N'Diaye, Kaloum, Sandervalia, Conakry, 8 April 1991.

85. ANS, 17G573, Guinée Française, Service de la Sûreté, Kankan, "Compte-Rendu de Réunion," 1 December 1947, #1454/240 C; 17G573, Guinée Française, Services de Police, "Renseignements A/S Réunion Publique Organisée à Kindia le 1er Février par le R.D.A.," 2 February 1948, #159/55 C; Sidiki Kobélé Kéïta, *P.D.G.,* 1:239, 334.
At its First Party Congress (October 15–18, 1950), the Guinean RDA called for the "democratization of the chieftaincy with the free election of chiefs, sufficiently paid, assisted by elected councils." See ANS, 17G573, "Rapport Général d'Activité 1947–1950," présenté par Mamadou Madéïra Kéïta, Secrétaire Général du P.D.G. au Premier Congrès

Territorial du Parti Démocratique de Guinée (Section Guinéenne du Rassemblement Démocratique Africain), Conakry, 15–18 October 1950.

86.   Interview with Tourou Sylla, Kimbely, Mamou, 30 May 1991.

87.   ANS, 17G573, Guinée Française, Inspecteur des Affaires Administratives, Conakry, "Rapport sur la Manifestation R.D.A. au 18 Octobre 1949 à N'Zérékoré," 8 November 1949; Sidiki Kobélé Kéïta, *P.D.G.,* 1:219.

Mamadou Traoré was invariably known by his alias, "Ray Autra." Morgenthau notes that when the syllables are pronounced in reverse order, "Traoré" becomes "Ray-Au-tra." Morgenthau, *Political Parties,* p. 281 n. 1.

88.   AG, 5B47, Guinée Française, Gouverneur, Conakry, à Ministre, FOM, Paris, 27 November 1947, #778; ANS, 17G573, Inspecteur des Affaires Administratives, " . . . Manifestation R.D.A. au 18 Octobre 1949 à N'Zérékoré."

89.   ANS, 17G573, Inspecteur des Affaires Administratives, " . . . Manifestation R.D.A. au 18 Octobre 1949 à N'Zérékoré"; 17G573, Guinée Française, Services de Police, Conakry, "Rapport Hebdomadaire, Semaine du 17 au 23 Septembre 1951," #1676/898, C/PS.2; CRDA, Documents, Guinée, R.G. 47–57, Gouverneur, Guinée Française, Conakry, à Haut Commissaire, Dakar, 21 December 1951, #503/APA.

90.   ANS, 17G573, Inspecteur des Affaires Administratives, " . . . Manifestation R.D.A. au 18 Octobre 1949 à N'Zérékoré."

91.   ANS, 17G573, Guinée Française, Services de Police, "Renseignements A/S Mission de Propagande R.D.A.," 29 July 1950, #893/500, C/PS.2.

The Dabola canton chief, Almamy Barry Aguibou, was the father of Barry Diawadou, a Ponty graduate, government clerk, and staunch political opponent of the RDA. See Morgenthau, *Political Parties,* pp. 221–222, 233, 240.

92.   ANS, 17G573, Guinée Française, Services de Police, "Renseignements A/S Activité Mamadou Traoré dit Ray Autra," 26 July 1950, #808/482, C/PS.

93.   Maka, "R.D.A. et . . . Pratiques Coutumières"; Sékou Touré, "Contre Tout Travail Forcé," *La Liberté,* 1 March 1955, p. 3.

94.   AG, 1E37, Gaoual, "Rapport Politique Annuel, 1947"; AG, MO-33, Sékou Mara, "La Lutte de Libération Nationale et la Chefferie dite Coutumière en Guinée Forestière" (Mémoire de Fin d'Études Supérieures, IPJN, Kankan, 1975–1976), p. 47.

95.   ANS, 17G573, Police, "Rapport Hebdomadaire, 17–23 Septembre 1951"; 17G573, Guinée Française, Services de Police, "Revue Trimestrielle, 3ème Trimestre 1951," 24 November 1951; 17G573, Comité Directeur, Parti Démocratique de Guinée, Conakry, à Gouverneur, Guinée Française, Conakry, 29 February 1952.

96.   ANS, 17G573, "Mémorandum Remis par la Sous-Section du Parti Démocratique de la Guinée Française (Section Guinéenne du R.D.A.) de N'Zérékoré au Ministre, FOM et des États Associés lors de son Passage à N'Zérékoré, sur la Situation Politique et Économique du Pays," n.d. (before July 1951). Also see ANS, 2G53/189, Gendarmerie Nationale, " . . . Situation . . . de la Guinée . . . 4ème Trimestre 1953."

97.   ANS, 17G573, Gendarmerie Nationale, Détachement de l'A.O.F.-Togo, Service des Recherches, Diffusion et Fichier, Dakar, "Fiche de Renseignements," ca. 19 October 1951, #181/4R.

For the usurpation of chiefly functions by RDA village committees, see Maka, interview, 25 February 1991; Ameillon, *Guinée,* p. 22; Thomas Hodgkin, *African Political Parties: An Introductory Guide* (Gloucester, Mass.: Peter Smith, 1971), pp. 145–146.

98.   Sidiki Kobélé Kéïta, *P.D.G.,* 1:332, 336.

99. CAOM, Carton 2143, dos. 7, PDG, Comité Directeur, Conakry, "Rapport à la Délégation du Comité de Coordination et Groupe Parlementaire R.D.A., Assemblée Nationale, Paris," 14 January 1952, #1.

100. CRDA, Claude Gérard, "Incidents en Guinée Française, 1954–1955," *Afrique Informations,* 15 March–1 April 1955, pp. 5–7; "Élections Législatives Partielles de Guinée," 17 June 1954, in *P.D.G.-R.D.A., Parti Démocratique de Guinée, 1947–1959: Activités—Répression—Élections;* Sidiki Kobélé Kéïta, *P.D.G.,* 1:333; Morgenthau, *Political Parties,* p. 240; Mara, "Lutte de Libération," p. 51; AG, AM-1339, Idiatou Camara, "La Contribution de la Femme de Guinée à la Lutte de Libération Nationale (1945–1958)" (Mémoire de Fin d'Études Supérieures, IPGAN, Conakry, 1979), p. 77.

101. See Morgenthau, *Political Parties,* pp. 234–235.

102. AG, 1E39, Guinée Française, Cercle de Mamou, "Rapport Politique Annuel, Année 1949."

103. Morgenthau, *Political Parties,* p. 236.

104. Morgenthau, *Political Parties,* pp. 234–235; Sidiki Kobélé Kéïta, *Ahmed Sékou Touré: L'Homme et son Combat Anti-Colonial (1922–1958)* (Conakry: Éditions S.K.K., 1998), pp. 22–24, 28–29.

105. Suret-Canale, "Fin de la Chefferie," p. 469.

106. AG, 5B43, Guinée Française, Chef de la Sûreté, Conakry, à Secrétaire Général à la Présidence de la République et de l'Union Française, Conakry, 28 March 1947; 5B43, Gouverneur à Gouverneur Général, 29 October 1947; 5B47, Guinée Française, Gouverneur, Conakry, à Procureur de la République, Affaires Politiques et Administratives, 20 December 1947, #852/APA; Morgenthau, *Political Parties,* pp. 235–236, 250; Sidiki Kobélé Kéïta, *P.D.G.,* 1:165, 184–187.

Although the *grand chérif* initially opposed the RDA, he later reconciled with the party. Before his death in September 1955, he blessed Sékou Touré. See ANS, 2G55/152, "Rapport Politique Annuel, 1955."

107. ANS, 17G573, Guinée Française, Services de Police, "Renseignements de Kankan, A/S Passage de Ray Autra (R.D.A.)," 29 November 1949, #2428/73, C/PS.

108. ANS, 17G573, Guinée Française, Services de Police, Kankan, "Renseignements A/S Démissions du R.D.A.," 7 September 1950, #1064/602, C/PS.2.

109. AG, 1E41, Guinée Française, Services de Police, Maréchal-des-Logis-Chef Ceret, Commandant la Brigade, Kankan, "Rapport," 7 October 1951, #61/4.

110. ANS, 17G586, Guinée Française, Services de Police, Kankan, "Renseignements A/S Section RDA de Kankan—Assemblée Extraordinaire des Notables et des Délégués RDA chez le Chef de Canton, Alpha Amadou Kaba, 24–10–54," 3 November 1954, #2884/1112, C/PS.2.

111. ANS, 17G573, Ray Autra, Comité Directeur du *P.D.G.,* "Rapport sur la Situation Politique du Cercle de N'Zérékoré," N'Zérékoré, 1 March 1951.

112. ANS, 17G573, Parti Démocratique de Guinée à Gouverneur, 29 February 1952.

113. Claude Gérard, "Lettre Ouverte à Sékou Touré," *La Liberté,* 15 March 1955; CRDA, Gérard, "Incidents en Guinée . . . ," pp. 3–7; ANS, 20G136, Haut Commissaire, Dakar, à tous Gouverneurs, A.O.F., ca. November 1956; Morgenthau, *Political Parties,* pp. 103, 106, 240; Sidiki Kobélé Kéïta, *P.D.G.,* 1:315–318, 347.

114. Morgenthau, *Political Parties,* pp. 221–222, 233, 240.

115. Sidiki Kobélé Kéïta, *P.D.G.,* 1:245, 327–328, 334.

116. Mara, "Lutte de Libération," p. 47.

117. ANS, 17G586, Guinée Française, Services de Police, "Renseignements *Objet:* Incidents en Brousse," 13 November 1954, #2934/1140, C/PS.2.

118. ANS, 17G586, Guinée Française, Gendarmerie Nationale, Conakry, "Fiche de Renseignements," ca. 13 November 1954, #13/4.

119. ANS, 2G54/159, Guinée Française, Gouverneur, Conakry, à Haut Commissaire, Dakar, "Revue des Événements du 3ème Trimestre 1954," 22 January 1955, #40 CAB/APA.

120. Sidiki Kobélé Kéïta, *P.D.G.,* 1:337. Also see ANS, 2G55/151, "Revue des Événements du 4ème Trimestre 1955."

121. ANS, 2G55/152, "Rapport Politique Annuel, 1955."

122. Ibid.; ANS, 2G55/150, Guinée Française, Gouverneur, "Rapport Politique Mensuel, Juin 1955," 10 August 1955.

123. ANS, 2G55/152, "Rapport Politique Annuel, 1955."

124. ANS, 2G55/150, "Rapport Politique Mensuel, Juin 1955."

125. ANS, 2G55/152, "Rapport Politique Annuel, 1955"; CAOM, Carton 2143, dos. 9, Claude Gérard, "Dans L'Ouest Africain, Après les Incidents de . . . Conakry," *Interafrique Presse,* 10 March 1955; Moricandian Savané, "Les Grandioses Obsèques de Camara M'Ballia," *La Liberté,* 1 March 1955.

126. ANS, 2G55/152, "Rapport Politique Annuel, 1955."

127. Ibid. Also see Suret-Canale, "Fin de la Chefferie," p. 484.

128. ANS, 2G55/152, "Rapport Politique Annuel, 1955."

129. Informant quoted in Morgenthau, *Political Parties,* p. 235. Also see Klein, *Slavery and Colonial Rule,* p. 238.

CHAPTER 5: WOMEN TAKE THE LEAD: FEMALE EMANCIPATION AND THE NATIONALIST MOVEMENT, 1949–1954

1. Interview with Aissatou N'Diaye, Sandervalia, Conakry, 8 April 1991.

2. See Elizabeth Schmidt, " 'Emancipate Your Husbands!': Women and Nationalism in Guinea, 1953–1958," in *Women in African Colonial Histories,* ed. Jean Allman, Susan Geiger, and Nakanyike Musisi (Bloomington: Indiana University Press, 2002), pp. 282–304.

3. Madéïra Kéïta, secretary-general of the Guinean branch of the RDA, quoted in ANS, 17G573, Guinée Française, Services de Police, Conakry, "Renseignements A/S Réunion Générale du R.D.A.," 15 September 1948, #KE/989/5.

4. Interview with Léon Maka and Mira Baldé (Mme. Maka), Sangoyah, Conakry, 25 February 1991. For a discussion of RDA women in the French Soudan, see Jane Turrittin, "Aoua Kéita and the Nascent Women's Movement in the French Soudan," *African Studies Review* 36, no. 1 (April 1993): pp. 59–89.

5. Maka and Baldé, interview, 25 February 1991.

6. ANS, 17G573, Guinée Française, Services de Police, "En Marge de la Conférence d'Arboussier," written before 13 December 1949, #2444/77, C/PS/I; 17G573, Gouvernement Général de l'A.O.F., Cabinet, Bureau Technique de Liaison et de Coordination, "Note de Renseignements *Objet:* Activité Politique et Sociale en Guinée pendant le Mois de Décembre 1949," 15 January 1950, #141, CAB/LC/DK; Ruth Schachter Morgenthau, *Political Parties in French-Speaking West Africa* (Oxford: Clarendon Press, 1964), p. 98; Sidiki Kobélé Kéïta, *Le P.D.G.: Artisan de l'Indépendance Nationale en Guinée (1947–1958)* (Conakry: I.N.R.D.G., Bibliothèque Nationale, 1978), 1:338. Compare to

Susan Geiger, *TANU Women: Gender and Culture in the Making of Tanganyikan Nationalism, 1955–1965* (Portsmouth, N.H.: Heinemann; Oxford, James Currey, 1997), p. 57.

7.   ANS, 17G573, Gouvernement Général, "... Activité Politique et Sociale en Guinée ... Décembre 1949"; 17G573, Guinée Française, Services de Police, "Compte-Rendu de la Réunion Publique tenue au Cinéma 'Rialto' à Conakry, le 6 Décembre 1949," 6 December 1949, #2443/76, C/PS/I.

8.   Ibid.; 17G573, Guinée Française, Services de Police, "Renseignements A/S Visite de d'Arboussier à Conakry," 8 December 1949, #2485/80, C/PS.2; 17G573, Police, "... Conférence d'Arboussier," written before 13 December 1949; interview with Bocar Biro Barry, Camayenne, Conakry, 21 January 1991; AG, AM-1339, Idiatou Camara, "La Contribution de la Femme de Guinée à la Lutte de Libération Nationale (1945–1958)" (Mémoire de Fin d'Études Supérieures, IPGAN, Conakry, 1979), pp. 41, 44; Sidiki Kobélé Kéïta, *P.D.G.*, 1:338.

9.   ANS, 17G573, Guinée Française, Services de Police, Conakry, "Compte-Rendu de la Réunion Publique du Parti Démocratique de Guinée Française (P.D.G.)—Ex-R.D.A.—tenue au Domicile d'Amara Soumah le 24 Octobre 1950 de 18h30 à 20 Heures," 25 October 1950, #1248/221, C/PS/BM; interview with Sidiki Kobélé Kéïta, Donka, Conakry, 9 April 1991; Sidiki Kobélé Kéïta, *P.D.G.*, 1:339; Idiatou Camara, "Contribution de la Femme," pp. 41, 55, 57, 67.

10.   Sidiki Kobélé Kéïta, *P.D.G.*, 1:338; Idiatou Camara, "Contribution de la Femme," p. 41.

11.   ANS, 17G613, Guinée Française, Services de Police, Conakry, "Renseignements A/S Réunion des Comités R.D.A. de Conakry, le Mercredi 8 Mai Dernier à 20 Heures," 10 May 1957, #1065/423, C/PS.2; interviews with Mamady Kaba, Donka, Conakry, 15 January 1991; Fatou Diarra, Lansanaya, Conakry, 17 March 1991; Fatou Kéïta, Km 43, Conakry, 7 April 1991; Siba N. Grovogui, personal communication, 6 March 1998; Idiatou Camara, "Contribution de la Femme," pp. 38–39, 62.

12.   Maka, interview, 20 February 1991; Fatou Kéïta, interview, 7 April 1991; interview with Néné Diallo, Conakry, 11 April 1991; Idiatou Camara, "Contribution de la Femme," p. 14. Also see Thomas Hodgkin, *Nationalism in Colonial Africa* (New York: New York University Press, 1957), p. 90.

13.   N'Diaye, interview, 8 April 1991; Diallo, interview, 11 April 1991; Fatou Kéïta, interview, 28 April and 24 May 1991.

14.   See songs, below.

15.   CAOM, Carton 2144, dos. 1, Ministre, FOM, "Rapport Pruvost," 31 March 1955.

16.   ANS, 17G586, Guinée Française, Services de Police, Labé, "Renseignements *Objet:* Situation Politique à Labé dans la Première Quinzaine de Novembre 1954," 23 November 1954, #2999/1180, C/PS.2; Maka, interview, 20 February 1991; Fatou Diarra, interview, 17 March 1991; Fatou Kéïta, interview, 7 April and 24 May 1991; Sidiki Kobélé Kéïta, interview, 9 April 1991; Idiatou Camara, "Contribution de la Femme," pp. 41, 55, 57, 67; Sidiki Kobélé Kéïta, *P.D.G.*, 1:339. Also see Thomas Hodgkin, *African Political Parties: An Introductory Guide* (Gloucester, Mass.: Peter Smith, 1971), pp. 120–121, 135. For a similar discussion pertaining to Tanganyika, see Susan Geiger, "Tanganyikan Nationalism as 'Women's Work': Life Histories, Collective Biography and Changing Historiography," *Journal of African History* 37, no. 3 (1996): pp. 470, 472; Geiger, *TANU Women*, pp. 58, 72.

17.   Diallo, interview, 11 April 1991. Also see Maka, interview, 20 February 1991; Idiatou Camara, "Contribution de la Femme," p. 42.

18. For a discussion of "female" versus "feminist" consciousness, see Temma Kaplan, "Female Consciousness and Collective Action: The Case of Barcelona, 1910–1918," *Signs: Journal of Women in Culture and Society* 7, no. 3 (Spring 1982): pp. 545–566. For African women's collective action in response to threats to family well-being and economic survival, see Nina Emma Mba, *Nigerian Women Mobilized: Women's Political Activity in Southern Nigeria, 1900–1965,* Research Series, no. 48 (Berkeley: Institute of International Studies, University of California, 1982), pp. 297, 299; Cheryl Johnson, "Grassroots Organizing: Women in Anti-Colonial Activity in Southwestern Nigeria," *African Studies Review* 25, no. 2 (September 1982): pp. 140–141, 143, 148; Julia C. Wells, "Why Women Rebel: A Comparative Study of South African Women's Resistance in Bloemfontein (1913) and Johannesburg (1958)," *Journal of Southern African Studies* 10, no. 1 (October 1983): pp. 55–70.

19. For women's collective action in response to violations of their rights or threats to their interests, see Mba, *Nigerian Women Mobilized;* Cheryl Johnson, "Grassroots Organizing," pp. 137–157; Cheryl Johnson, "Madam Alimotu Pelewura and the Lagos Market Women," *Tarikh* 7, no. 1 (1981): pp. 1–10; Shirley Ardener, "Sexual Insult and Female Militancy," in *Perceiving Women,* ed. Shirley Ardener (London: Malaby Press, 1975), pp. 29–53; Caroline Ifeka-Moller, "Female Militancy and Colonial Revolt: The Women's War of 1929, Eastern Nigeria," in *Perceiving Women,* pp. 127–157; Judith Van Allen, " 'Aba Riots' or Igbo 'Women's War'?: Ideology, Stratification, and the Invisibility of Women," in *Women in Africa: Studies in Social and Economic Change,* ed. Nancy J. Hafkin and Edna G. Bay (Stanford, Calif.: Stanford University Press, 1976), pp. 59–85; Cherryl Walker, *Women and Resistance in South Africa* (London: Onyx Press, 1982), pp. 158, 163; LaRay Denzer, "Women in Freetown Politics, 1914–61: A Preliminary Study," *Africa* 57, no. 4 (1987): pp. 447–448.

20. ANS, 17G573, Guinée Française, Services de Police, Kankan, "Renseignements A/S Réunion du R.D.A. Section Kankan le 5 Octobre 1947," 6 October 1947, #1082/105 C; "La Population Féminine de Canton de Kaporo Écrit à M. le Médecin-Colonel-Directeur de la Santé Publique de la Guinée Française à Conakry," *La Liberté,* 18 January 1955, p. 3; R.D.A. Sous-Section de Mamou, "Résolution," *La Liberté,* 1 February 1955, p. 2; R.D.A. Sous-Section de Dinguiraye, "Motion Relative à l'Affectation d'une Sage-Femme à Dinguiraye," *La Liberté,* 25 September 1956, p. 4; Fatou Kéïta, interview, 28 April 1991; Idiatou Camara, "Contribution de la Femme," pp. 39–40, 66–67; Hodgkin, *African Political Parties,* pp. 37, 121. For comparison with Tanganyika, see Geiger, *TANU Women,* pp. 78, 94–96, 118.

21. See below.

22. Jean Suret-Canale, *French Colonialism in Tropical Africa, 1900–1945,* trans. Till Gottheiner (New York: Pica Press, 1971), pp. 406–407. For an excellent case study, see Myron Echenberg, *Black Death, White Medicine: Bubonic Plague and the Politics of Public Health in Colonial Senegal, 1914–1945* (Portsmouth, N.H.: Heinemann, 2002).

23. ANS, 21G101, Guinée Française, Service de la Sûreté, "Compte-Rendu de la Réunion Publique Organisée au Cinéma 'Rialto' le Dimanche 21 Décembre 1947 par la Section Guinéenne du Rassemblement Démocratique Africain," 22 December 1947, #1490/Y7 C/PS. See similar demands in ANS, 17G573, "Rapport Général d'Activité 1947–1950," présenté par Mamadou Madéïra Kéïta, Secrétaire Général du P.D.G. au Premier Congrès Territorial du Parti Démocratique de Guinée (Section Guinéenne du Rassemblement Démocratique Africain), Conakry, 15–18 October 1950.

24. AG, 5B47, Guinée Française, Gouverneur, Conakry, à Ministre, FOM, Paris, 25 October 1947, #711/APA; Suret-Canale, *French Colonialism,* p. 412.

25. Suret-Canale, *French Colonialism,* pp. 406–407.

26. ANS, 2G46/50, Guinée Française, Inspecteur du Travail, "Rapport Annuel du Travail, 1946," Conakry, 15 February 1947, #66/IT.GV; CAOM, Carton 2181, dos. 6, "Note sur la Guinée," 6 May 1958; Morgenthau, *Political Parties,* p. 400; Virginia Thompson and Richard Adloff, *French West Africa* (New York: Greenwood Press, 1969), p. 555.

27. Sidiki Kobélé Kéïta, *P.D.G.,* 1:245–246, 348–349. Also see ANS, 21G101, Sûreté, "... Réunion [RDA] ... au Cinéma 'Rialto' ... 21 Décembre 1947"; 17G573, Guinée Française, Services de Police, "Renseignements A/S Réunion Publique Organisée à Kindia le 1er Février par le R.D.A.," 2 February 1948, #159/55 C; 17G277, Guinée Française, Services de Police, "Renseignements *Objet:* Réunion R.D.A.," 9 February 1954, #254/148, C/PS.2; "Résolution Sociale," *La Liberté,* 16 August 1955, pp. 2; Modibo Kéïta, "Les Travaux du Comité de Coordination du R.D.A., Rapport Social," *La Liberté,* 30 August 1955, p. 1.

28. R.D.A. Mamou, "Résolution." Also see Sidiki Kobélé Kéïta, *P.D.G.,* 1:338.

29. R.D.A. Dinguiraye, "Motion ... Sage-Femme à Dinguiraye."

30. "Population Féminine de ... Kaporo." Also see Idiatou Camara, "Contribution de la Femme," p. 66.

31. ANS, 17G573, Police, Kankan, "... Réunion du R.D.A .... Kankan le 5 Octobre 1947." Also see Fatou Kéïta, interview, 24 May 1991.

32. ANS, 17G573, Police, "... Réunion [RDA] ... à Kindia le 1er Février [1948]."

33. "Résolution Sociale," p. 2; Sidiki Kobélé Kéïta, *P.D.G.,* 1:246, 348–349.

34. Modibo Kéïta, "Les Travaux du Comité de Coordination du R.D.A., Rapport Social," *La Liberté,* 16 September 1955, pp. 3, 4.

35. ANS, 21G101, Sûreté, "... Réunion [RDA] ... au Cinéma 'Rialto' ... 21 Décembre 1947."

36. Fatou Kéïta, interview, 7 April and 24 May 1991; Fatou Diarra, interview, 17 March 1991.

37. ANS, 21G101, Sûreté, "... Réunion [RDA] ... au Cinéma 'Rialto' ... 21 Décembre 1947."

38. Ibid.

39. ANS, 17G573, Police, "... Réunion ... Parti Démocratique de Guinée ... au Domicile d'Amara Soumah le 24 Octobre 1950 ... "; 17G277, Police, "... Réunion R.D.A.," 9 February 1954; 2G55/152, Guinée Française, Gouverneur, "Rapport Politique pour l'Année 1955," #281/APA; 17G613, Guinée Française, Services de Police, N'Zérékoré, "Renseignements A/S Conférence Publique Électorale tenue le Vendredi, 13 (15?) Mars 1957, au Centre Culturel de N'Zérékoré, par le P.D.G.-R.D.A.," 21 March 1957, #653/284, C/PS.2; Sidiki Kobélé Kéïta, *P.D.G.,* 1:245.

40. ANS, 17G586, Guinée Française, Services de Police, Kankan, "Renseignements *Objet:* Conférence Publique du RDA à Kankan," 28 December 1954, #3252/1300, C/PS.2.

41. ANS, 17G573, Guinée Française, Services de Police, "Renseignements A/S Activité R.D.A.," 31 May 1948, #627/213 C; 17G573, "Rapport Général d'Activité 1947–1950," P.D.G., 15–18 October 1950.

42. ANS, 17G573, Police, "... Réunion [RDA] ... à Kindia le 1er Février [1948]."

43. ANS, 17G573, "Rapport Général d'Activité 1947–1950," P.D.G., 15–18 October 1950.

44. ANS, 17G573, Police, "... Réunion ... Parti Démocratique de Guinée ... au Domicile d'Amara Soumah le 24 Octobre 1950 ... "; Maka, interview, 20 February 1991.

45. ANS, 17G586, Guinée Française, Services de Police, "Renseignements *Objet:* Réunion R.D.A. à Conakry," 9 August 1954, #2424/866, C/PS.2; Maka, interview, 20 February 1991.

46. ANS, 17G586, Guinée Française, Services de Police, Kindia, "Renseignements *Objet:* Réunion R.D.A. à Kindia," 3 June 1955, #1088/456, C/PS.2.

47. ANS, 17G573, Police, ". . . Activité R.D.A.," 31 May 1948; 17G573, Police, ". . . Réunion . . . Parti Démocratique de Guinée . . . au Domicile d'Amara Soumah le 24 Octobre 1950 . . . "; 17G586, Police, Kankan, ". . . Conférence Publique du RDA à Kankan," 28 December 1954; 2G55/150, Guinée Française, Gouverneur, "Rapport Politique Mensuel, Octobre 1955," 21 November 1955, #549/APA/CAB; Sidiki Kobélé Kéïta, *P.D.G.,* 1:245.

48. ANS, 17G573, Police, ". . . Réunion . . . Parti Démocratique de Guinée . . . au Domicile d'Amara Soumah le 24 Octobre 1950 . . . "; 17G586, Police, Kankan, ". . . Conférence Publique du RDA à Kankan," 28 December 1954.

49. Sidiki Kobélé Kéïta, *P.D.G.,* 1:245–246, 348–349. Also see ANS, 17G277, Police, ". . . Réunion R.D.A.," 9 February 1954; CRDA, "Résolution Sociale"; Modibo Kéïta, ". . . Comité de Coordination . . . Rapport Social," 30 August 1955.

50. ANS, 17G573, Police, ". . . Activité R.D.A.," 31 May 1948; 17G573, "Rapport Général d'Activité 1947–1950," P.D.G., 15–18 October 1950; Idiatou Camara, "Contribution de la Femme," p. 25.

51. ANS, 21G101, Sûreté, ". . . Réunion [RDA] . . . au Cinéma 'Rialto' . . . 21 Décembre 1947."

52. Fatou Kéïta, interview, 24 May 1991. Also see Sidiki Kobélé Kéïta, *P.D.G.,* 1:338.

53. Fatou Kéïta, interview, 24 May 1991. Also see Fatou Diarra, interview, 17 March 1991; Idiatou Camara, "Contribution de la Femme," p. 40.

54. ANS, 17G586, Guinée Française, Services de Police, Kankan, "Renseignements *Objet:* Réunion R.D.A. à Kankan," 18 February 1955, #384/159, C/PS.2.

55. Barry, interview, 29 January 1991.

56. Fatou Diarra, interview, 17 March 1991. Also see interview with Mamadou Bela Doumbouya, Camayenne, Conakry, 26 January 1991; Barry, interview, 29 January 1991; Baldé, interview, 25 February 1991; Fatou Kéïta, interview, 28 April 1991. For Tanganyika, see Geiger, *TANU Women,* pp. 75, 78.

57. ANS, 17G586, Guinée Française, Services de Police, Kankan, "Renseignements *Objet:* Conférence Publique R.D.A. à Kankan," 4 March 1955, #511/203, C/PS.2.

58. Barry, interview, 29 January 1991; Doumbouya, interview, 26 January 1991; interview with Tourou Sylla, Kimbely, Mamou, 30 May 1991. See the June 1954 photograph of Mafory Bangoura standing on a chair, addressing an RDA meeting in Conakry, in Sidiki Kobélé Kéita, *Ahmed Sékou Touré: L'Homme et son Combat Anti-Colonial (1922–1958)* (Conakry: Éditions S.K.K., 1998), photograph following p. 136.

59. Diallo, interview, 11 April 1991.

60. Fatou Kéïta, interview, 7 and 28 April 1991. Also see Fatou Diarra, interview, 17 March 1991; Baldé, interview, 25 February 1991.

61. Diallo, interview, 11 April 1991. Also see Baldé, interview, 25 February 1991; ANS, 2G55/152, "Rapport Politique Annuel, 1955," p. 81. For similar sentiments in Tanganyika, see Geiger, *TANU Women,* pp. 75, 78, 91, 95–96, 118, 143.

62. Quoted in Morgenthau, *Political Parties,* p. 238.

63. "Les Femmes s'Organisent," *La Liberté,* 18 August 1954, p. 4; Sidiki Kobélé Kéïta, *P.D.G.,* 1:340; Idiatou Camara, "Contribution de la Femme," pp. 43–44.

64. Fatou Kéïta, interview, 7 April 1991; Fatou Diarra, interview, 17 March 1991; interview with Kadiatou Meunier (pseud.), Minière, Conakry, 18 January 1991.

65. "Les Femmes s'Organisent"; Barry, interview, 29 January 1991; Maka, interview, 20 February 1991; N'Diaye, interview, 8 April 1991; Sidiki Kobélé Kéïta, *P.D.G.*, 1:340, 345; Idiatou Camara, "Contribution de la Femme," pp. 43–44.

66. Idiatou Camara, "Contribution de la Femme," p. 44.

67. Sidiki Kobélé Kéïta, *P.D.G.*, 1:340; Idiatou Camara, "Contribution de la Femme," p. 44.

68. Doumbouya, interview, 26 January 1991; Sidiki Kobélé Kéïta, *P.D.G.*, 1:326, 340; Idiatou Camara, "Contribution de la Femme," p. 44.

69. ANS, 17G586, Guinée Française, Services de Police, "Renseignements *Objet:* Création de Sections R.D.A. à Kindia," 7 August 1954, #2417/864, C/PS.2; Fatou Kéïta, interview, 7 April 1991; Diallo, interview, 11 April 1991; Doumbouya, interview, 26 January 1991; Sidiki Kobélé Kéïta, *P.D.G.*, 1:326, 340; Idiatou Camara, "Contribution de la Femme," p. 44.

70. ANS, 17G586, Guinée Française, Services de Police, "Renseignements *Objet:* Réception de Sékou Touré à Kankan le 9/8/1954," 19 August 1954, #2481/895, C/PS.2; 17G586, Guinée Française, Services de Police, "Renseignements *Objet:* Réunion Publique R.D.A. à Kankan le 10/8/54," 19 August 1954, #2483/896, C/PS.2.

71. ANS, 17G586, Guinée Française, Services de Police, "Renseignements *Objet:* Réunion Publique R.D.A. à Conakry et ses Suites," 8 September 1954, #2606/942, C/PS.2; Maka and Baldé, interview, 25 February 1991.
Turrittin notes that "In the French Soudan, militant activity by women in support of the independence movement rarely extended beyond the actions of a small number of elite women, such as Aoua Kéita, and wives of Union Soudanaise party leaders." Turrittin, "Aoua Kéita," p. 77. Also see Morgenthau, *Political Parties*, p. 287.

72. ANS, 17G586, Guinée Française, Services de Police, "Renseignements A/S Lettre-Circulaire de Sékou Touré," 7 October 1954, #2766/1034, C/PS.2; N'Diaye, interview, 8 April 1991.

73. Doumbouya, interview, 26 January 1991; Sidiki Kobélé Kéïta, *P.D.G.*, 1:326.

74. Baldé, interview, 25 February 1991. Also see Maka, interview, 20 February 1991.

75. Geiger, "Tanganyikan Nationalism," pp. 465, 467, 469, 471–472; Geiger, *TANU Women*, p. 162. Also see Hodgkin, *African Political Parties*, p. 135.

76. Idiatou Camara, "Contribution de la Femme," p. 65.

77. Mamadou Tounkara, "Autour d'une Musique," *La Liberté*, 9 November 1954, p. 3; Idiatou Camara, "Contribution de la Femme," p. 67. Also see Hodgkin, *African Political Parties*, p. 135. For comparisons with Nigeria, see Mba, *Nigerian Women Mobilized*, p. 194; Ifeka-Moller, "Female Militancy," p. 132; Van Allen, "Aba Riots," pp. 68–69, 71–73.

78. Idiatou Camara, "Contribution de la Femme," pp. 39–40, 65.

79. Fatou Kéïta, interview, 24 May 1991. Also see Idiatou Camara, "Contribution de la Femme," p. 67.

80. Idiatou Camara, "Contribution de la Femme," p. 69; Barry, interview, 29 January 1991; interview with Mabalo Sakho, Conakry, 19 June 1991.
For a similar description of market structure in Lagos, Nigeria, see Mba, *Nigerian Women Mobilized*, pp. 193–194. For Kumasi, Ghana, see Gracia Clark, *Onions Are My Husband: Survival and Accumulation by West African Market Women* (Chicago: University of Chicago Press, 1994), pp. 6–7, 252–274, 319; Steve Morrison and Claudia Milne, *Asante Market Women* (New York: Filmakers Library, 1982).

81. Mabalo Sakho, interview, 19 June 1991.

82. Interview with Hawa Fofana, Conakry, 7 April 1991.

83. Diallo, interview, 11 April 1991.

84. Fatou Kéïta, interview, 24 May 1991. Also see Maka, interview, 20 February 1991.

85. Fatou Diarra, interview, 17 March 1991. Also see Idiatou Camara, "Contribution de la Femme," p. 80.

86. N'Diaye, interview, 8 April 1991.

87. Maka, interview, 20 February 1991; Maka and Baldé, interview, 25 February 1991; Fatou Kéïta, interview, 7 April 1991; ANS, 17G586, Guinée Française, Services de Police, "Renseignements," 8 September 1954.

For similar use of song elsewhere in Africa, see Ardener, "Sexual Insult," pp. 29–30, 36–37; Ifeka-Moller, "Female Militancy," pp. 132–133; Van Allen, "Aba Riots," pp. 60–61; Mba, *Nigerian Women Mobilized,* p. 150; Geiger, "Tanganyikan Nationalism," p. 473.

The feminization of colonized males, and women's ridicule of them, is discussed in Partha Chatterjee, *The Nation and Its Fragments: Colonial and Postcolonial Histories* (Princeton, N.J.: Princeton University Press, 1993), pp. 69–71.

88. Grovogui, personal communication, June 1989 and October 1991.

Grovogui claims that in some dances, Susu women bared their bottoms to men they wished to shame. Similarly, Parker notes that in colonial Ghana, Ga women publicly disrobed in front of men they deemed cowardly. Their lack of shame implied that the cowards were not real men and thus no threat to women's modesty. John Parker, *Making the Town: Ga State and Society in Early Colonial Accra* (Portsmouth, N.H.: Heinemann; Oxford: James Currey, 2000), p. 52.

89. Meunier, interview, 18 January 1991.

For a discussion of evolving notions of masculinity in the French Soudan, see Gregory Mann, "Old Soldiers, Young Men: Masculinity, Islam, and Military Veterans in Late 1950s Soudan Français (Mali)," in *Men and Masculinities in Modern Africa,* ed. Lisa A. Lindsay and Stephan F. Miescher (Portsmouth, N.H.: Heinemann, 2003), p. 74.

Similar norms existed among the Asante and Ga of precolonial and colonial Ghana. Asante and Ga women also challenged men they deemed cowardly and, thus, effeminate in the face of British colonialism. See Pashington Obeng, "Gendered Nationalism: Forms of Masculinity in Modern Asante of Ghana," in *Men and Masculinities,* pp. 193, 202–204; Parker, *Making the Town,* pp. 52, 71.

Physical strength, aggression, bravery, courage, and perseverance were prized masculine traits among the Igbo of Nigeria as well. See Carolyn A. Brown, "A 'Man' in the Village is a 'Boy' in the Workplace: Colonial Racism, Worker Militance, and Igbo Notions of Masculinity in the Nigerian Coal Industry, 1930–1945," in *Men and Masculinities,* pp. 161–162.

90. Fatou Kéïta, interview, 7 April and 24 May 1991.

91. ANS, 17G586, Police, " . . . Réunion Publique R.D.A. à Conakry . . . ," 8 September 1954. For similar sentiments in the French Soudan, see Turrittin, "Aoua Kéïta," p. 72. For Tanganyika, see Geiger, *TANU Women,* p. 126.

92. ANS, 17G586, Police, " . . . Réunion Publique R.D.A. à Conakry . . . ," 8 September 1954; Fatou Diarra, interview, 17 March 1991.

93. ANS, 17G586, Guinée Française, Services de Police, "Renseignements A/S R.D.A. Conakry," 19 April 1955, #811/332, C/PS.2; 17G586, Guinée Française, Services de Police, "Renseignements *Objet:* RDA à Conakry," 27 April 1955, #867/353, C/PS.2; 17G586, Guinée Française, Services de Police, "Renseignements *Objet:* Incidents en Guinée," 3 June 1955, #1095/463, C/PS.2; 17G586, Guinée Française, Services de Police,

"Renseignements *Objet:* R.D.A. à Conakry," 6 June 1955, #1106/469, C/PS.2. Also see 17G573, Guinée Française, Services de Police, "Renseignements A/S Attroupement R.D.A. devant le Commissariat de Police de Mamou, le 15 Mai 1956," 19 May 1956, #929/324, C/PS.2; AG, 1E41, Guinée Française, Services de Police, "Renseignements A/S Conférence Publique tenue le Lundi 14 Janvier 1957 à Conakry, Salle du Cinéma 'Vox', par le P.D.G.-R.D.A.," 15 January 1957, #89/50/C/PS.2.

94. ANS, 17G586, Guinée Française, Services de Police, "Renseignements *Objet:* R.D.A. Conakry," 14 June 1955, #1158/490, C/PS. The Susu songs were transcribed and translated into French by the police. English translations are the author's.

95. Morgenthau, *Political Parties,* pp. 222, 240.

96. ANS, 17G586, Police, " . . . R.D.A. Conakry," 14 June 1955.

97. Diallo, interview, 11 April 1991.

98. N'Diaye, interview, 8 April 1991.

99. Fatou Kéïta, interview, 7 April 1991.

100. N'Diaye, interview, 8 April 1991. Also see Diallo, interview, 11 April 1991; Idiatou Camara, "Contribution de la Femme," p. 111. For Tanganyika, see Geiger, *TANU Women,* pp. 59, 81, 84; Geiger, "Tanganyikan Nationalism," pp. 472–473.

101. Mamayimbe Bangoura, as quoted in Idiatou Camara, "Contribution de la Femme," p. 58.

The following discussion owes much to the work of Idiatou Camara. Camara conducted extensive interviews with female activists in the mid-1970s, the results of which appear in her undergraduate thesis. See "Contribution de la Femme," pp. 52–65.

102. Idiatou Camara, "Contribution de la Femme," pp. 52, 61–65, 111.

The Guinean branch of the RDA published three successive periodicals during the period under consideration: *Le Phare de Guinée* (1947–1949), *Coup de Bambou* (1950), and *La Liberté* (1951–1960). Source: IFAN, Dakar, Senegal.

103. Idiatou Camara, "Contribution de la Femme," pp. 61–65, 111; Sidiki Kobélé Kéïta, *P.D.G.,* 1:326; ANS, 17G586, Guinée Française, Services de Police, "Renseignements *Objet:* Réunion Privée du Comité R.D.A. à Conakry," 25 September 1954, #2709/998, C/PS.2.

104. Idiatou Camara, "Contribution de la Femme," pp. 61–63, 65.

105. Fatou Kéïta, interview, 7 April 1991.

106. Ibid.; Idiatou Camara, "Contribution de la Femme," pp. 63–64.

107. ANS, 17G586, Guinée Française, Services de Police, "Renseignements *Objet:* Militants RDA Arrêtés à la suite d'Incidents," 18 March 1955, #605/250, C/PS.2. Also see Idiatou Camara, "Contribution de la Femme," p. 88.

108. Idiatou Camara, "Contribution de la Femme," pp. 63–64.

109. Ibid., p. 89.

110. Fatou Diarra, interview, 17 March 1991. Also see ANS, 17586, R.D.A., S/Section de Mamou, "Procès Verbal," Mamou, 21 August 1954, #1 RDA/SSM; Margarita Dobert, "Civic and Political Participation of Women in French-Speaking West Africa" (Ph.D. diss., George Washington University, 1970), p. 78.

111. Idiatou Camara, "Contribution de la Femme," p. 82; Sidiki Kobélé Kéïta, *P.D.G.,* 1:341.

112. Idiatou Camara, "Contribution de la Femme," p. 83; Mamady Kaba, interview, 15 January 1991; interview with Namankoumba Kouyaté, Conakry, 31 January 1991.

113. Idiatou Camara, "Contribution de la Femme," p. 63.

114. Grovogui, personal communication, October 1991.

115. Van Allen, "Aba Riots," pp. 61–62.

116. Ibid., p. 73.

For a similar practice among Ga women in colonial Ghana, see Parker, *Making the Town,* pp. 52, 60–61.

117. Van Allen, "Aba Riots," pp. 60, 62, 71–72.

118. Idiatou Camara, "Contribution de la Femme," pp. 82–84, 111, 128; Sidiki Kobélé Kéïta, *P.D.G.,* 1:341.

119. Morgenthau, *Political Parties,* pp. 232–233, 240–242, 247, 251–252.

120. N'Diaye, interview, 8 April 1991; Mamady Kaba, interview, 15 January 1991; Maka, interview, 25 February 1991.

121. Idiatou Camara, "Contribution de la Femme," pp. 84–85.

122. Maka, interview, 25 February 1991.

123. N'Diaye, interview, 8 April 1991. This incident is corroborated in ANS, 17G586, Guinée Française, Services de Police, "Renseignements à Propos de Décisions Judiciaires Rendues à Conakry," 26 May 1955, #1057/440, C/PS.2.

124. Idiatou Camara, "Contribution de la Femme," pp. 83–85; *La Liberté,* 12 April 1955; ANS, 17G586, Police, " . . . Décisions Judiciaires Rendues à Conakry," 26 May 1955.

125. Quoted in Idiatou Camara, "Contribution de la Femme," pp. 86–87.

126. ANS, 17G613, Guinée Française, Services de Police, Conakry, "Renseignements A/S Exclusion du R.D.A. Prononcée le 13 Mars 1957 contre Mafory *Bangoura,* Présidente Territoriale du R.D.A. et son Mari *Bangoura* Badara (Suite nos Rgts. #2656/962/C/PS/2, 8/5C/PS.2 et 13/9/C/PS.2, en dates des 29 Décembre, 3 et 4 Janvier 1957)," 14 March 1957, #598/262, C/PS.2; Sidiki Kobélé Kéïta, *P.D.G.,* 1:345.

127. ANS, 17G613, Police, " . . . Exclusion du R.D.A. . . . contre Mafory *Bangoura* . . . ," 14 March 1957; 2G55/150, Guinée Française, Gouverneur, "Rapport Politique Mensuel, Juillet 1955," #435/APAS/CAB; 2G55/150, Guinée Française, Gouverneur, "Rapport Politique Mensuel, Août 1955," 28 September 1955, #487/APAS/CAB; Idiatou Camara, "Contribution de la Femme," pp. 89–91, 128; Sidiki Kobélé Kéïta, *P.D.G.,* 1:346.

128. ANS, 2G55/150, "Rapport Politique Mensuel, Août 1955"; Idiatou Camara, "Contribution de la Femme," p. 91; Sidiki Kobélé Kéïta, *P.D.G.,* 1:345–346.

129. ANS, 2G56/138, Guinée Française, Gouverneur, "Rapport Politique Mensuel, Mars 1956," 19 April 1956, #185/APA; 17G586, Guinée Française, Services de Police, "Renseignements A/S Activités B.A.G.," 24 October 1956, #2187/762, C/PS.2; 17G613, Police, " . . . Exclusion du R.D.A. . . . contre Mafory *Bangoura* . . . ," 14 March 1957.

130. Doumbouya, interview, 26 January 1991.

131. Baldé, interview, 19 May 1991. Also see Maka, interview, 20 February 1991. For Tanganyika, see Geiger, *TANU Women,* pp. 57, 68, 75, 143.

132. Maka, interview, 20 February 1991.

133. Tourou Sylla, interview, 30 May 1991.

134. Barry, interview, 21 and 29 January 1991. Also see Tourou Sylla, interview, 30 May 1991.

135. Tourou Sylla, interview, 30 May 1991.

136. The following saga was recounted by Bocar Biro Barry on 29 January 1991.

137. Tourou Sylla, interview, 30 May 1991.

138. Fatou Kéïta, interview, 7 April 1991.

139. See interview with Nima Bah, Conakry, 31 January 1991; Fatou Kéïta, interview, 7 April 1991; N'Diaye, interview, 8 April 1991.

140. Fatou Diarra, interview, 17 March 1991. Also see N'Diaye, interview, 8 April 1991; Diallo, interview, 11 April 1991; Barry, interview, 29 January 1991; Kouyaté, interview, 31 January 1991; Maka, interview, 20 February 1991; Mabalo Sakho, interview, 19 June 1991; ANS, 2G55/152, "Rapport Politique Annuel, 1955," p. 81; Idiatou Camara, "Contribution de la Femme," p. 57. For a similar situation in Tanganyika, see Geiger, *TANU Women,* pp. 77–78, 82, 101–103.

141. N'Diaye, interview, 8 April 1991.

142. Fatou Kéïta, interview, 7 April 1991. Also see Geiger, *TANU Women,* p. 101.

143. Note the romantic nature of the songs women sang about Sékou Touré and/or *Syli.* Barry, interview, 29 January 1991; Fatou Kéïta, interview, 7 April 1991; Idiatou Camara, "Contribution de la Femme," p. 59. Also see Geiger, *TANU Women,* p. 103.

144. Fatou Kéïta, interview, 7 April 1991. Also see Geiger, *TANU Women,* p. 68.

145. Barry, interview, 29 January 1991.

146. Maka, interview, 20 February 1991.

147. Barry, interview, 29 January 1991. Also see Doumbouya, interview, 26 January 1991. For Tanganyika, see Geiger, *TANU Women,* p. 103.

148. Barry, interview, 21 January 1991; Idiatou Camara, "Contribution de la Femme," p. 42; Grovogui, personal communication, 1988.

Independent and mobile female nationalists in Tanganyika and Kenya risked similar condemnation. See Geiger, *TANU Women,* pp. 45, 59–60, 76, 93, 139; Cora Ann Presley, *Kikuyu Women, the Mau Mau Rebellion, and Social Change in Kenya* (Boulder, Colo.: Westview, 1992), pp. 158–159.

149. ANS, 17G586, Guinée Française, Services de Police, "Renseignements A/S KOUYATÉ Kémoko," 27 September 1954, #2715/1000, C/PS.2.

150. Idiatou Camara, "Contribution de la Femme," p. 57.

151. AG, 1E41, Guinée Française, Services de Police, "Renseignements A/S Création d'une Association Féminine," 20 November 1951, #2219/C/PS.2.

152. ANS, 17G565, Guinée Française, Gouverneur, Conakry, à Haut Commissaire, Dakar, 3 June 1950, #188, PS.

153. Diallo, interview, 11 April 1991.

154. N'Diaye, interview, 8 April 1991. Also see Geiger, *TANU Women,* pp. 77, 101.

155. N'Diaye, interview, 8 April 1991; Maka, interview, 20 February 1991; Kouyaté, interview, 31 January 1991.

156. Fatou Diarra, interview, 17 March 1991; Morgenthau, *Political Parties,* p. 233.

157. Fatou Kéïta, interview, 7 April and 24 May 1991.

158. Quoted in Claude Rivière, "La Promotion de la Femme Guinéenne," *Cahiers d'É-tudes Africaines* 8, no. 31 (1968): p. 408. Also see Idiatou Camara, "Contribution de la Femme," pp. 56–57; Barry, interview, 29 January 1991.

159. ANS, 17G586, Police, "Renseignements," 8 September 1954. Also see Idiatou Camara, "Contribution de la Femme," pp. 56–57.

160. Barry, interview, 29 January 1991; Meunier, interview, 18 January 1991; Idiatou Camara, "Contribution de la Femme," p. 56.

161. Barry, interview, 29 January 1991.

162. Unlike wage-earning men in the public and private sectors, nonliterate women in the informal sector rarely risked losing their jobs as a result of their political activities. This disparity may account for some of such women's seemingly more militant behavior. For a parallel in the French Soudan, see Turrittin, "Aoua Kéita," p. 72. For Tanganyika, see Geiger, *TANU Women,* pp. 59, 68, 82, 103, 126.

163. Barry, interview, 29 January 1991. Also see Idiatou Camara, "Contribution de la Femme," pp. 56–57.

164. Baldé, interview, 20 and 25 February 1991.

165. Idiatou Camara, "Contribution de la Femme," p. 59.

166. Tourou Sylla, interview, 30 May 1991. Also see Diallo, interview, 11 April 1991.

167. Maka, interview, 20 February 1991.

168. N'Diaye, interview, 8 April 1991.

169. Doumbouya's family spirited her away before an agreed-upon interview could take place. It was not clear if the decision was Doumbouya's or her family's. Notes on thwarted interview with N'Youla Doumbouya, Conakry, April 1991.

170. Kéïta's family, like Doumbouya's, seemed to play a role in silencing her. Fatou Kéïta, interview, 7 and 28 April and 24 May 1991.

CHAPTER 6: ETHNICITY, CLASS, AND VIOLENCE: INTERNAL DISSENT IN THE RDA, 1955–1956

1.   The period 1951–1956 witnessed a dramatic increase in the number of registered voters in Guinea. Between the legislative elections of June 1951 and January 1956, the size of the electorate more than doubled. There were 393,623 registered voters in May 1951 and 476,503 in June 1954. By January 1956, the electorate was 975,119 strong. It was the RDA that benefited the most from this explosion; the vast majority of new recruits had been mobilized by the RDA.

CRDA, "Élections de Guinée," *Afrique Nouvelle,* 22 December 1954; CRDA, Claude Gérard, "Incidents en Guinée Française, 1954–1955," *Afrique Informations,* 15 March–1 April 1955, pp. 3–5; ANS, 2G55/152, Guinée Française, Gouverneur, "Rapport Politique pour l'Année 1955," #281/APA. Also see ANS, 20G123, Télégramme Départ, Haut Commissaire, Dakar, à FOM, Paris, 20 December 1955, #769; Sidiki Kobélé Kéïta, *Le P.D.G.: Artisan de l'Indépendance Nationale en Guinée (1947–1958)* (Conakry: I.N.R.D.G., Bibliothèque Nationale, 1978), 2:11; Ruth Schachter Morgenthau, *Political Parties in French-Speaking West Africa* (Oxford: Clarendon Press, 1964), pp. 240, 397.

The governor's figures vary slightly from those cited above. His report indicates that there were 393,628 registered voters in May 1951 and 472,837 in June 1954. See ANS, 2G55/152, "Rapport Politique Annuel, 1955."

2.   Interview with Néné Diallo, Conakry, 11 April 1991.

3.   Ibid.

4.   Interview with Léon Maka, Sangoyah, Conakry, 20 February 1991. Also see interview with Mira Baldé (Mme. Maka), Sangoyah, Conakry, 19 May 1991.

5.   Baldé, interview, 19 May 1991.

6.   Interview with Siaka Sylla, Conakry, 5 April 1991.

7.   See Morgenthau, *Political Parties,* p. 238.

8.   Diallo, interview, 11 April 1991.

9.   Ibid.

In Guinea, most Diallos come from the Labé region, an area heavily populated by people of slave origin. After emancipation, many former slaves emigrated from the region. Given Néné Diallo's low-status profession—cloth dying was considered dirty and fit only for former slaves—it is likely that she was of slave ancestry.

See Martin Klein, *Slavery and Colonial Rule in French West Africa* (New York: Cambridge University Press, 1998), pp. 190, 253; William Derman, *Serfs, Peasants, and*

Socialists: A Former Serf Village in the Republic of Guinea (Berkeley: University of California Press, 1973), pp. 8–9, 14; Siba N. Grovogui, personal communication, 1991.

10.   Diallo, interview, 11 April 1991.

The DSG leader, Ibrahima Barry, was known as "Barry III."

11.   Interview with Aissatou N'Diaye, Kaloum, Sandervalia, Conakry, 8 April 1991.

12.   Klein, *Slavery and Colonial Rule,* pp. 155, 253.

13.   Ibid., p. 253; Jean Suret-Canale, *La République de Guinée* (Paris: Éditions Sociales, 1970), p. 89.

14.   Klein, *Slavery and Colonial Rule,* pp. 45, 188; Derman, *Serfs,* pp. 12–13, 30; Jean Suret-Canale, "La Fin de la Chefferie en Guinée," *Journal of African History* 7, no. 3 (1966): pp. 464–465; Walter Rodney, "Jihad and Social Revolution in Futa Djalon in the Eighteenth Century," *Journal of the Historical Society of Nigeria* 4, no. 2 (June 1968): pp. 269–284.

The term "Jallonke," or "men of the Jallon," refers to the people of a region, rather than an ethnic group. The Jallonke trace their roots to several populations. The Susu, part of the greater Mande group, settled in the Futa Jallon in the thirteenth century. They displaced or absorbed most of the original inhabitants, including the Limbas, Landumas, Bagas, and Bassaris. The resulting population is referred to collectively as the Jallonke. Rodney, "Jihad," p. 270.

15.   Suret-Canale, *République,* p. 89.

16.   Klein, *Slavery and Colonial Rule,* pp. 155–156, 187, 192–193.

17.   Ibid., pp. 250–251.

18.   Interview with Bocar Biro Barry, Camayenne, Conakry, 29 January 1991.

19.   Klein, *Slavery and Colonial Rule,* pp. 252–255, 316 n. 7, 341.

20.   Barry, interview, 29 January 1991.

21.   ANS, 17G586, Guinée Française, Services de Police, Labé, "Renseignements *Objet:* Section R.D.A. de Labé," 29 October 1954, #2870/1102, C/PS.2. Also see Barry, interview, 29 January 1991; Klein, *Slavery and Colonial Rule,* pp. 250–251.

22.   Suret-Canale, "Fin de la Chefferie," pp. 464–465; Rodney, "Jihad," p. 278; Derman, *Serfs,* pp. 2, 16–17; Barry, interview, 29 January 1991.

23.   Andrew F. Clark, *From Frontier to Backwater: Economy and Society in the Upper Senegal Valley (West Africa), 1850–1920* (Lanham, Md.: University Press of America, 1999), p. 47; Barry, interview, 29 January 1991.

24.   Klein, *Slavery and Colonial Rule,* p. 194; Andrew F. Clark, *Frontier to Backwater,* p. 47; Siba N. Grovogui, personal communication, 1991.

25.   Klein, *Slavery and Colonial Rule,* pp. 194, 227, 250; Rodney, "Jihad," p. 274, 278; Suret-Canale, *République,* p. 88; Derman, *Serfs,* pp. 17, 37–39; Grovogui, personal communication, 1991.

26.   Suret-Canale, *République,* p. 92; Derman, *Serfs,* pp. 8, 15; Barry, interview, 29 January 1991.

27.   ANS, 17G586, Police, Labé, " . . . Section R.D.A. de Labé," 29 October 1954.

28.   ANS, 17G586, Guinée Française, Services de Police, Labé, "Renseignements *Objet:* Les A.C. et le R.D.A. dans le Cercle de Labé," 17 February 1955, #374/150, C/PS.2.

For a similar trend in Pita circle, see ANS, 17G586, Guinée Française, Gendarmerie Nationale, Pita, "Fiche de Renseignements sur une Réunion Publique du Parti Démocratique de Guinée—Section de Pita," 15 November 1954, #55/4.

29.   Malinke blacksmiths were often identified by the family name Kanté. Barry, interview, 29 January 1991.

30. ANS, 2G55/150, Guinée Française, Gouverneur, "Rapport Politique Mensuel, Juin 1955," 10 August 1955.

31. Barry, interview, 29 January 1991; R. W. Johnson, "The Parti Démocratique de Guinée and the Mamou 'Deviation,' " in *African Perspectives: Papers in the History, Politics and Economics of Africa Presented to Thomas Hodgkin,* ed. Christopher Allen and R. W. Johnson (Cambridge: Cambridge University Press, 1970), p. 350.

32. Barry, interview, 29 January 1991.

33. Ibid.

34. ANS, 17G277, Guinée Française, Services de Police, "Renseignements *Objet:* Comité Propagande Barry Diawadou à Labé," 25 August 1954, #2534/916, C/PS.2; 17G586, Guinée Française, Services de Police, "Renseignements A/S Création S/Section Féminine du R.D.A. à Labé," 30 August 1954, #2558/925, C/PS.2; Barry, interview, 29 January 1991.

35. ANS, 17G586, Police, " . . . Création S/Section Féminine du R.D.A. à Labé," 30 August 1954.

36. Barry, interview, 29 January 1991; interview with Tourou Sylla, Kimbely, Mamou, 30 May 1991; R. W. Johnson, "Parti Démocratique de Guinée," p. 351; Grovogui, personal communication, 1991.

For a discussion of low-status professions, see Klein, *Slavery and Colonial Rule,* pp. 3, 194, 227, 250.

The Soninke and Malinke peoples are part of the greater Mande group. The Soninke are sometimes referred to as Saracolet or Maraka. Andrew F. Clark, *Frontier to Backwater,* p. 43.

37. Barry, interview, 29 January 1991.

38. Quoted in R. W. Johnson, "Parti Démocratique de Guinée," p. 351.

39. Tourou Sylla, interview, 30 May 1991. Also see Barry, interview, 29 January 1991.

40. Tourou Sylla, interview, 30 May 1991.

41. "Composition S/Section, Pita," *La Liberté,* 14 December 1954, p. 4.

42. See membership list in AG, AM-1339, Idiatou Camara, "La Contribution de la Femme de Guinée à la Lutte de Libération Nationale (1945–1958)" (Mémoire de Fin d'Études Supérieures, IPGAN, Conakry, 1979), p. 126.

43. Barry, interview, 29 January 1991.

44. ANS, 17G586, Police, Labé, " . . . Les A.C. et le R.D.A. dans le Cercle de Labé," 17 February 1955.

45. From the early days of French rule, school attendance was compulsory for the sons of chiefs. However, chiefs frequently substituted slaves' sons for those from chiefly or aristocratic families. Thus, the sons of Jallonke slaves, rather than the Peul aristocracy, formed the core of the "modernizing" elite, dominating the first groups of teachers and other civil servants. By the 1950s, the Pulaar-speaking Jallonke were generally designated "Peul."

Jean Suret-Canale, *French Colonialism in Tropical Africa, 1900–1945,* trans. Till Gottheiner (New York: Pica Press, 1971), pp. 341, 374–375, 377, 381, 384, 388, 393 n. 30, 31; Suret-Canale, *République,* pp. 136–137; Sidiki Kobélé Kéïta, *P.D.G.,* 1:73; Klein, *Slavery and Colonial Rule,* p. 251; Grovogui, personal communication, 24 October 1991.

46. Rodney, "Jihad," p. 278; Derman, *Serfs,* pp. 2, 13–14, 16.

47. Barry, interview, 29 January 1991.

48. Barry, interview, 21 January 1991; personal archives of Bocar Biro Barry, "Nouveau Bureau Directeur [Syndicat du Personnel Enseignant Africain de Guinée]," *L'École Guinéenne,* no. 1 (1957–1958); Suret-Canale, "Fin de la Chefferie," pp. 464–468; Klein,

Slavery and Colonial Rule, pp. 147–148; Derman, *Serfs,* pp. 2, 12–14; Morgenthau, *Political Parties,* p. 240.

Two lineages competed for the position of Almamy of the Futa Jallon: the Soriya line (which included Bokar Biro) and the Alfaya line. In an attempt to destroy their power, the French moved the Soriyas from their capital at Timbo to Dabola, and the Alfayas from their capital at Ditinn to Mamou. In the 1950s, the Soriyas were represented by the Dabola canton chief Almamy Barry Aguibou, while the Alfayas were represented by the Mamou canton chief Almamy Ibrahima Sory Dara. In 1950, the Mamou canton chief was designated "paramount chief of the Futa Jallon" by the colonial administration. R. W. Johnson, "Parti Démocratique de Guinée," p. 349; Suret-Canale, "Fin de la Chefferie," pp. 465–468; Klein, *Slavery and Colonial Rule,* pp. 147–148.

49. Morgenthau, *Political Parties,* pp. 19, 243, 246, 345; Suret-Canale, "Fin de la Chefferie," pp. 464–468; Klein, *Slavery and Colonial Rule,* pp. 147–148; R. W. Johnson, "Parti Démocratique de Guinée," p. 351; John H. Morrow, *First American Ambassador to Guinea* (New Brunswick, N.J.: Rutgers University Press, 1968), p. 66; Aly Gilbert Iffono, *Lexique Historique de la Guinée-Conakry* (Paris: L'Harmattan, 1992), p. 48; Barry, interview, 29 January 1991; N'Diaye, interview, 8 April 1991.

50. "Encore des Incidents Sanglants à Conakry et à Tondon; Les Agresseurs sont Libres et des Innocents Arrêtés," *La Liberté,* 15 February 1955, pp. 1–2.

51. For a general discussion of these issues, see Thomas Hodgkin, *African Political Parties: An Introductory Guide* (Gloucester, Mass.: Peter Smith, 1971), pp. 125–133.

52. Quoted in Morgenthau, *Political Parties,* pp. 238–239.

53. Quoted in Ibid., p. 239.

54. Ibid., p. 237. Also see Maka, interview, 20 February 1991.

55. Quoted in Morgenthau, *Political Parties,* p. 238.

56. Ibid.

57. AG, 1E39, Guinée Française, Cercle de N'Zérékoré, "Rapport Politique Annuel, Année 1949"; ANS, 17G573, Gouvernement Général de l'A.O.F., Cabinet, Bureau Technique de Liaison et de Coordination, "Note de Renseignements *Objet:* Activité Politique et Sociale en Guinée Pendant le Mois de Décembre 1949," 15 January 1950, #141, CAB/LC/DK. Also see membership list in Idiatou Camara, "Contribution de la Femme," p. 126; "Composition du Bureau Féminin de Kissidougou," *La Liberté,* 4 January 1955, p. 4.

58. ANS, 17G586, Guinée Française, Services de Police, "Renseignements *Objet:* Création de Sous-Sections Féminines R.D.A. à Kassa," 2 March 1955, #498/197, C/PS.2; 17G586, Guinée Française, Services de Police, "Renseignements *Objet:* Activité R.D.A. à Kassa, (Suite à Notre #498/197, 2 Mars 1955)," 9 March 1955, #537/212, C/PS.2.

59. ANS, 2G55/151, Guinée Française, Gouverneur, Conakry, à Haut Commissaire, Dakar, "Revue des Événements du 4ème Trimestre 1955," February 1956, #131/APA; 2G55/152, "Rapport Politique Annuel, 1955." Also see Hodgkin, *African Political Parties,* pp. 130–131.

60. See, for instance, ANS, 17G586, Guinée Française, Services de Police, Kankan, "Renseignements *Objet:* Provocations R.D.A. à Kankan," 26 January 1955, #208/81, C/PS.2; 17G586, Guinée Française, Services de Police, Kankan, "Renseignements *Objet:* Conférence Publique R.D.A. à Kankan," 4 March 1955, #511/203, C/PS.2; 17G586, Guinée Française, Services de Police, Kankan, "Renseignements *Objet:* Conférence Publique R.D.A. à Kankan," 18 March 1955, #601/247, C/PS.2; 2G55/150, Guinée Française, Gouverneur, "Rapport Politique Mensuel, Novembre 1955," 28 December 1955, #587/APA.

61. ANS, 17G573, Guinée Française, Services de Police, Conakry, "Compte-Rendu de la Réunion Publique du Parti Démocratique de Guinée Française (P.D.G.)—Ex-R.D.A.—tenue au Domicile d'Amara Soumah le 24 Octobre 1950 de 18h30 a 20 Heures," 25 October 1950, #1248/221, C/PS/BM; Sidiki Kobélé Kéïta, *P.D.G,* 1:238; Sidiki Kobélé Kéïta, *P.D.G.,* 2:113.

62. AG, 2Z16, "Rassemblement de la Jeunesse Démocratique Africaine," Récépissé de Déclaration d'Association, 1 March 1955, #263; Sidiki Kobélé Kéïta, *P.D.G.,* 2:111.

63. See Hodgkin, *African Political Parties,* pp. 122–123.

64. Virginia Thompson and Richard Adloff, *French West Africa* (New York: Greenwood Press, 1969), p. 139.

65. CRDA, Gérard, "Incidents en Guinée Française, 1954–1955," pp. 11–12; Morgenthau, *Political Parties,* pp. 103–104, 106, 243.

66. ANS, 17G586, Guinée Française, Services de Police, "Renseignements *Objet:* La Validation de l'Élection de Barry Diawadou et le RDA de Guinée," 24 January 1955, #187/75, C/PS.2.

67. ANS, 17G586, Guinée Française, Services de Police, "Renseignements *Objet:* Suite aux Incidents de Tondon," 18 February 1955, #389/160, C/PS.2; 2G55/150, Guinée Française, Gouverneur, "Rapport Politique Mensuel, Mars 1955"; Moricandian Savané, "Les Grandioses Obsèques de Camara M'Ballia," *La Liberté,* 1 March 1955; Comité Directeur, RDA-Guinée, "Rester Calmes," *La Liberté,* 1 March 1955.

68. ANS, 17G586, Guinée Française, Services de Police, Conakry, "Renseignements *Objet:* Activité RDA à Conakry," 7 March 1955, #523/207, C/PS.2; Morgenthau, *Political Parties,* p. 19; Thompson and Adloff, *French West Africa,* p. 94.

69. ANS, 17G586, Police, " . . . Activité RDA à Conakry," 7 March 1955.

70. ANS, 17G586, Guinée Française, Services de Police, "Renseignements *Objet:* Activité R.D.A. à Conakry," 10 March 1955, #543/216, C/PS.2; "À l'Ordre du Compagnon de l'Indépendance," *La Liberté,* 23 November 1959, p. 7; Idiatou Camara, "Contribution de la Femme," bibliography (alphabetical list of informants).

71. ANS, 2G55/150, "Rapport Politique Mensuel, Mars 1955."

72. CRDA, Gérard, "Incidents en Guinée Française, 1954–1955," pp. 13, 18; CRDA, "Troubles en Guinée," Extrait d'*Afrique Nouvelle,* 15 February 1955, p. 1; CAOM, Carton 2143, dos. 9, Télégramme Arrivée, Délégaof, Paris. Envoyée par Gouverneur, Guinée Française, Conakry, 6 February 1955, #57; Carton 2143, dos. 9, Télégramme Arrivée, FOM, Paris. Envoyée par Mission d'Inspection (Pruvost), Conakry, 20 February 1955, #2; Carton 2143, dos. 9, Télégramme Arrivée, FOM, Paris. Envoyée par Afcour, Dakar, 23 February 1955, #116–117; Carton 2144, dos. 1, Ministre, FOM, "Rapport Pruvost," 31 March 1955; Carton 2143, dos. 7, Télégramme Officielle, Haut Commissaire, Dakar, à Gouverneur, Guinée Française, Conakry, 11 October 1955; Carton 2143, dos. 8., Gouverneur, Guinée Française, Conakry, à Haut Commissaire, Dakar, 22 October 1955, #520/CAB/APA; ANS, 2G55/150, Guinée Française, Gouverneur, "Rapport Politique Mensuel, Octobre 1955," 21 November 1955, #549/APA/CAB.

73. CAOM, Carton 2143, dos. 9, Télégramme Arrivée, FOM, Paris. Envoyée par Haut Commissaire, Dakar, 10 February 1955, #94–98; Carton 2143, dos. 9, Télégramme Arrivée, FOM, Paris. Envoyée par Afcour, Dakar, 11 February 1955, #104; Carton 2143, dos. 9, "Incidents dans le Cercle de Dubréka," *Agence France-Presse (AFP), Spécial Outre Mer,* 15 February 1955; Carton 2143, dos. 9, H. Bernard, Procureur Général près la Cour d'Appel de Dakar, à Ministre, FOM, Paris, 23 February 1955, #1779; Carton 2143, dos. 9, Claude Gérard, "Dans L'Ouest Africain, Après les Incidents de . . . Conakry," *Interafrique Presse,* 10 March 1955.

74.   ANS, 17G586, Police, Kankan, " . . . Conférence Publique R.D.A. à Kankan," 4 March 1955. Also see 17G586, Police, Kankan, " . . . Provocations R.D.A. à Kankan," 26 January 1955.

75.   ANS, 17G586, Police, Kankan, " . . . Conférence Publique R.D.A. à Kankan," 18 March 1955.

76.   ANS, 2G55/150, "Rapport Politique Mensuel, Novembre 1955."

77.   ANS, 2G55/150, Gouverneur, Guinée Française, Conakry, "Rapport Politique Mensuel, Juillet 1955," #435/APAS; Morgenthau, *Political Parties,* p. 241; Thompson and Adloff, *French West Africa,* p. 94.

As "the supreme directing organ" of the RDA, the Coordinating Committee was superior in authority to the parliamentarians' ad hoc group. Thus, all binding decisions had to be approved by the Coordinating Committee. See the political resolution of the 1949 RDA Congress in Abidjan, quoted in Morgenthau, *Political Parties,* p. 98. Also see Sidiki Kobélé Kéïta, *P.D.G.,* 1:236; ANS, 17G573, Guinée Française, Services de Police, Conakry, "Rapport Hebdomadaire, Semaine du 23 au 30 Septembre 1951, Semaine du 1er au 7 Octobre 1951," #1794/984, C/PS.2.

78.   ANS, 2G55/150, "Rapport Politique Mensuel, Juillet 1955." Also see Hodgkin, *African Political Parties,* p. 71; Morgenthau, *Political Parties,* p. 309.

79.   Morgenthau, *Political Parties,* p. 241; Thompson and Adloff, *French West Africa,* p. 94.

80.   CAOM, Carton 2144, dos. 1, Ministre, FOM, "Rapport Pruvost," 31 March 1955. Also see Hodgkin, *African Political Parties,* p. 137.

81.   ANS, 2G55/150, "Rapport Politique Mensuel, Juillet 1955."

82.   ANS, 17G573, "Les Partis Politiques en Guinée, 1er Semestre 1951." Also see Frederick Cooper, *Decolonization and African Society: The Labor Question in French and British Africa* (New York: Cambridge University Press, 1996), pp. 409–410.

83.   See CAOM, Carton 2144, dos. 1, Ministre, FOM, "Rapport Pruvost," 31 March 1955.

84.   ANS, 17G573, Guinée Française, Services de Police, incomplete reference, 16 October 1951, #1863, C/PS.2; 17G573, Guinée Française, Services de Police, Conakry, "Rapport Hebdomadaire, Semaine du 15 au 21 Octobre 1951," #1907/1053, C/PS.2; 17G573, "Partis Politiques . . . 1er Semestre 1951"; Morgenthau, *Political Parties,* pp. 98, 241; Sidiki Kobélé Kéïta, *P.D.G.,* 2:119; R. W. Johnson, "Parti Démocratique de Guinée," p. 347.

85.   ANS, 21G13, Guinée Française, Service de la Sûreté, "État d'Esprit de la Population," 1–15 December 1950; CRDA, Ministre, FOM, Paris, à Haut Commissaire, Dakar, 21 March 1952; 17G573, Haut Commissaire, Dakar, à Ministre, FOM, Paris, 28 April 1952, #471, INT/AP.2; Morgenthau, *Political Parties,* p. 242; Cooper, *Decolonization,* p. 409.

86.   ANS, 2G55/150, "Rapport Politique Mensuel, Juillet 1955."

87.   Morgenthau, *Political Parties,* p. 241; Thompson and Adloff, *French West Africa,* p. 94.

88.   ANS, 2G55/150, "Rapport Politique Mensuel, Juillet 1955."

89.   ANS, 2G55/152, "Rapport Politique Annuel, 1955."

90.   ANS, 2G55/150, "Rapport Politique Mensuel, Juillet 1955."

91.   Although his full name was Pléah Koniba Coulibaly, the Mamou activist was generally known as Pléah Koniba.

92.   CRDA, P.D.G., Bureau Directeur, Sous-Section de Mamou, au Comité Directeur, P.D.G., Conakry, 1 August 1955, in *P.D.G.-R.D.A., Parti* Démocratique *de Guinée, 1947–1960: Les Sections—Les Syndicats;* interview with Ibrahima Fofana, Lansanaya, Conakry, 24 May 1991.

93. CRDA, P.D.G., Bureau Directeur, Sous-Section de Mamou, au Comité Directeur, P.D.G., Conakry, 19 August 1955, #22, in *P.D.G.-R.D.A.*

94. ANS, 2G55/150, Guinée Française, Gouverneur, "Rapport Politique Mensuel, Août 1955," 28 September 1955, #487/APAS/CAB.

95. ANS, 2G55/151, "Revue des Événements du 4ème Trimestre 1955."

96. Morgenthau, *Political Parties,* p. 243.

97. *La Liberté,* December 22 and/or 27, 1955, quoted in Morgenthau, *Political Parties,* pp. 243, 345; Hodgkin, *African Political Parties,* p. 72.

98. Morgenthau, *Political Parties,* p. 244.

99. Suret-Canale, *République,* p. 163.

100. ANS, 20G123, Directeur des Services de Sécurité, Dakar, à tous Chefs de Sûreté, A.O.F., Circulaire #07800/INT/S/DA, 12 December 1955.

101. ANS, 20G123, "Élections Législatives du 2 Janvier 1956, Liste du Rassemblement Démocratique Africain."

102. ANS, 20G122, Gouverneur, Guinée Française, Conakry, "Rapport Politique Mensuel, Decembre 1955," 2 February 1956, #50/APA; 2G55/152, "Rapport Politique Annuel, 1955." Also see Hodgkin, *African Political Parties,* p. 37.

103. ANS, 20G122, Gouverneur, Guinée Française, Conakry, à Haut Commissaire, Dakar, 6 January 1956, #6/CAB. Also see Hodgkin, *African Political Parties,* pp. 35–36.

104. ANS, 20G122, Gouverneur à Haut Commissaire, 6 January 1956; Morgenthau, *Political Parties,* p. 244.

105. ANS, 2G55/152, "Rapport Politique Annuel, 1955."

106. ANS, 20G122, "Rapport Politique Mensuel, Décembre 1955."

107. Morgenthau, *Political Parties,* p. 244.

108. Idiatou Camara, "Contribution de la Femme," p. 99.

109. ANS, 20G122, "Rapport Politique Mensuel, Décembre 1955."
Christopher Hayden has pointed out that nurses engaged in rural vaccination and sleeping-sickness eradication campaigns were highly mobile and thus ideal recruiters for the party. Christopher Hayden, e-mail communication, 26 October 2001.

110. Morgenthau, *Political Parties,* p. 244. Also see Hodgkin, *African Political Parties,* pp. 71–72, 143.

111. Morgenthau, *Political Parties,* p. 244; interview with Fatou Diarra, Lansanaya, Conakry, 17 March 1991.

112. Fatou Diarra, interview, 17 March 1991.

113. ANS, 20G122, Guinée Française, "Résultats, Élections Législatives, 2 Janvier 1956."

114. ANS, 2G55/152, "Rapport Politique Annuel, 1955."

115. ANS, 20G122, "Rapport Politique Mensuel, Décembre 1955"; 2G55/152, "Rapport Politique Annuel, 1955"; Morgenthau, *Political Parties,* pp. 246, 394; Sidiki Kobélé Kéïta, *P.D.G.,* 2:21.

116. ANS, 2G56/138, Guinée Française, Gouverneur, "Rapport Politique Mensuel, Janvier 1956." Also see Hodgkin, *African Political Parties,* pp. 130–131.

117. ANS, 2G56/138, "Rapport Politique Mensuel, Janvier 1956."

118. Ibid. Also see 17G586, Gouverneur, Guinée Française, Conakry, à Haut Commissaire, Cabinet-Militaire, Dakar, 16 October 1956, #2726/CAB/Mil.

119. ANS, 2G56/138, Guinée Française, Gouverneur, "Rapport Politique Mensuel, Février 1956."

120. ANS, 2G56/138, "Rapport Politique Mensuel, Janvier 1956."

121. Ibid.

122. ANS, 2G56/138, "Rapport Politique Mensuel, Février 1956."

123. Ibid.; ANS, 2G56/138, Guinée Française, Gouverneur, "Rapport Politique Mensuel, Mars 1956," 19 April 1956, #185/APA. Also see ANS, 17G586, Guinée Française, Services de Police, Kankan, "Renseignements A/S Réunion RDA à Kankan le 24–10–1954," 3 November 1954, #2885/1113, C/PS.2; 17G586, Guinée Française, Services de Police, Kankan, "Renseignements A/S Entretien à Kankan de Sékou Touré (Sily) avec Magassouba Moriba et Touré Sékou (Chavanel) sur Cas Lamine Kaba et Instructions sur Organisation Intérieure Sections R.D.A.," 17 November 1954, #2955/1158, C/PS.2; Morgenthau, *Political Parties*, pp. 236, 250–251.

124. ANS, 2G55/150, "Rapport Politique Mensuel, Juin 1955"; 2G55/152, "Rapport Politique Annuel, 1955"; 2G56/138, "Rapport Politique Mensuel, Février 1956"; 2G56/138, "Rapport Politique Mensuel, Mars 1956."

125. ANS, 17G586, Guinée Française, Services de Police, Kindia, "Renseignements A/S Passage à Kindia du Député *Diallo* Sayfoulaye et Compte-Rendu de Mandat de ce Parlementaire," 17 July 1956, #1396/503, C/PS.2.

126. ANS, 17G586, Guinée Française, Services de Police, Mamou, "Renseignements A/S Visite Parlementaire à Mamou," 23 July 1956, #1444/512, C/PS.2.

127. ANS, 17G586, Guinée Française, Services de Police, N'Zérékoré, "Renseignements A/S Réunion tenue à N'Zérékoré, le 6 Août 1956, par le Député R.D.A. *Diallo* Sayfoulaye," 18 August 1956, #1650/582, C/PS.2; 17G586, Guinée Française, Services de Police, Conakry, "Renseignements A/S Réunion Publique d'Informations tenue le Jeudi 30 Août 1956, par le Député *Diallo* Saifoulaye, à Conakry, Salle de Cinéma 'VOX'," 31 August 1956, #1761/619, C/PS.2.

128. ANS, 17G586, Guinée Française, Services de Police, Conakry, "Renseignements A/S Conférence Publique d'Information, tenue le 16 Septembre 1956 par le P.D.G.-R.D.A. au Cinéma 'VOX' à Conakry," 17 September 1956, #1907/658, C/PS.2.

129. ANS, 17G586, Guinée Française, Services de Police, Conakry, "Renseignements A/S Tension à Conakry, entre Soussous et Foulahs," 6 September 1956, #1808/629, C/PS.2; 17G586, Guinée Française, Services de Police, Conakry, "Renseignements A/S Tension entre Foulahs et Soussous en Banlieue (Suite mon R.G. #1808/629, C/PS.2, 6 Septembre 1956)," 7 September 1956, #1812/630, C/PS.2; 17G586, Guinée Française, Services de Police, Conakry, "Renseignements A/S Petit Incident entre Femmes Bagistes et R.D.A., au Marché de Madina (Banlieue)," 7 September 1956, #1813/631, C/PS.2; 17G586, Guinée Française, Services de Police, Conakry, "Renseignements A/S Agression dans la Nuit du 7 au 8 Septembre 1956 à Coronthie, Contre le B.A.G. *Camara* Mamadou," 8 September 1956, #1816/632, C/PS.2; 17G586, Guinée Française, Services de Police, P. Humbert, Commissaire Divisionnaire, Conakry, à Gouverneur, Guinée Française, Conakry, 19 September 1956, #1924, C/PS.2; 17G586, Administrateur en Chef de la FOM, Commandant de Cercle de Conakry et Administrateur-Maire, Conakry, "Rapport sur les Incidents de Conakry (29 Septembre–5 Octobre 1956)," 7 October 1956; 17G586, Guinée Française, Services de Police, Conakry, "Renseignements A/S Commentaires sur les Incidents des 29, 30 Septembre et 1er, 2ème, 3ème Octobre Derniers à Conakry," 10 October 1956, #2091/729, C/PS.2; 17G586, Gouverneur à Haut Commissaire, 16 October 1956; CAOM, Carton 2143, dos. 8, Télégramme Arrivée, FOM, Paris. Envoyée par Afcour, Dakar, 2 October 1956, #711–712; Carton 2143, dos. 8, Télégramme Arrivée, FOM, Paris. Envoyée par Gouverneur, Guinée Française, Conakry, 7 October 1956, #40.121–40.125; Idiatou Camara, "Contribution de la Femme," pp. 101–102.

130. ANS, 17G586, Administrateur en Chef de la FOM, " . . . Incidents de Conakry (29 Septembre–5 Octobre 1956)."

131. ANS, 17G586, Gouverneur à Haut Commissaire, 16 October 1956.

132. ANS, 17G586, Administrateur en Chef de la FOM, " . . . Incidents de Conakry (29 Septembre–5 Octobre 1956); 17G586, Gouverneur à Haut Commissaire, 16 October 1956.

133. ANS, 17G586, Guinée Française, Services de Police, Conakry, "Renseignements A/S Propagande R.D.A.," 9 October 1956, #2073/723, C/PS.2.

134. Ibid.; 17G586, Guinée Française, Services de Police, Conakry, "Renseignements Conférence du R.D.A. sur les Prochaines Élections Municipales," 29 October 1956, #2224/773, C/PS.2.

135. ANS, 17G586, Guinée Française, Services de Police, Conakry, "Renseignements A/S Réunion Publique au Cinéma 'Matam' Organisée par le R.D.A. le 1er Octobre 1956 à 18 Heures," 2 October 1956, #2047/710, C/PS.2. Also see Morgenthau, *Political Parties,* p. 243.

136. ANS, 17G586, Police, " . . . Conférence du R.D.A. sur les Prochaines Élections Municipales," 29 October 1956; 17G586, Guinée Française, Services de Police, Kankan, "Renseignements A/S Conférence Publique R.D.A. le 31 Octobre 1956 à Kankan," 6 November 1956, #2288/799, C/PS.2.

137. Morgenthau, *Political Parties,* p. 249.

138. Sidiki Kobélé Kéïta, *P.D.G.,* 1:241; Sidiki Kobélé Kéïta, *P.D.G.,* 2:113, 178–179; Morgenthau, *Political Parties,* p. 249; R. W. Johnson, "Parti Démocratique de Guinée," p. 355; B. Ameillon, *La Guinée: Bilan d'une Indépendance,* Cahiers Libres nos. 58–59 (Paris: François Maspero, 1964), p. 21.

Some ethnic committees lingered through 1957. Prior to the November 3, 1957, subsection bureau elections, the party leadership requested that all remaining ethnic committees be dissolved "in order to make disappear all local particularisms." ANS, 17G622, Guinée Française, Services de Police, "Renseignements A/S Conférence Publique d'Information, tenue à Conakry, Salle du Cinéma 'VOX', le Vendredi 18 Octobre 1957, sur les Travaux du Congrès de Bamako et les Prochaines Élections aux Bureaux-Directeurs des S/Sections P.D.G.," 19 October 1957, #2350/875, C/PS.2.

139. Morgenthau, *Political Parties,* p. 249.

140. Moriba Magassouba, "À la Suite des Incidents de Conakry, La Presse de Guinée Doit Être Poursuivie pour Excitation à la Guerre Civile et Atteinte à la Sécurité Intérieure de l'État," *La Liberté,* 26 October 1956, pp. 1–2. Also see Morgenthau, *Political Parties,* p. 249.

141. Tibou Tounkara, "Halte au Régionalisme Rétrograde," *La Liberté,* 12 February 1957.

142. ANS, 17G586, Gouverneur à Haut Commissaire, 16 October 1956. Also see Hodgkin, *African Political Parties,* pp. 130–131.

143. CAOM, Carton 2143, dos. 8, Gouverneur à Haut Commissaire, 22 October 1955.

144. Magassouba, " . . . Incidents de Conakry, La Presse . . . Doit Être Poursuivie. . . ."

145. ANS, 17G586, Police, " . . . Propagande R.D.A.," 9 October 1956. Also see Tounkara, "Halte au Régionalisme. . . . "

146. ANS, 17G586, Police, " . . . Conférence du R.D.A. sur les Prochaines Élections Municipales," 29 October 1956; 17G586, Kankan, " . . . Conférence Publique R.D.A. le 31 Octobre 1956 à Kankan."

The BAG had made similar charges against Sékou Touré the previous year, charges the governor concluded were unfounded. See CAOM, Carton 2143, dos. 7, Télégramme Officielle, Gouverneur, Guinée Française, Conakry, à Haut Commissaire, Dakar, 14 October 1955; Carton 2143, dos. 8, Gouverneur à Haut Commissaire, 22 October 1955.

147. CAOM, Carton 2143, dos. 8, Comité Directeur, P.D.G., "Circulaires à Toutes les Sous Sections," Conakry, 19 October 1955.

148. Ibid.

CHAPTER 7: INDEPENDENCE NOW: THE RESURGENCE OF THE LEFT AND THE MOVE TOWARD INDEPENDENCE, 1956–1958

1. Ruth Schachter Morgenthau, *Political Parties in French-Speaking West Africa* (Oxford: Clarendon Press, 1964), pp. 66, 71, 72; Ivan Hrbek, "North Africa and the Horn," in *General History of Africa,* vol. 8: *Africa since 1935,* ed. Ali A. Mazrui and C. Wondji (Berkeley: University of California Press, 1999), pp. 129, 132–135.

2. ANS, 20G136, Télégramme Départ, Afcours, à tous Gouverneurs, 4 July 1956, #80237; 20G136, Télégramme Départ, Haut Commissaire, Dakar, à tous Gouverneurs, 20 July 1956, #80266; 20G136, Gouverneur, Guinée Française, Conakry, à Haut Commissaire, Dakar, "*Objet*: Suffrage Universel dans les T.O.M.," 3 August 1956, #2072, CB/SL.

3. Morgenthau, *Political Parties,* p. 70; Frederick Cooper, *Decolonization and African Society: The Labor Question in French and British Africa* (New York: Cambridge University Press, 1996), pp. 407–408.

4. Morgenthau, *Political Parties,* p. 67.

5. Ibid., pp. 66–68, 246; Jean Suret-Canale, *La République de Guinée* (Paris: Éditions Sociales, 1970), p. 164; ANS, 17G613, Guinée Française, Services de Police, N'Zérékoré, "Renseignements A/S Passage à N'Zérékoré du Député-Maire Touré Sékou," 26 March 1957, #722/311, C/PS.

6. ANS, 20G122, Gouverneur, Guinée Française, Conakry, "Rapport Politique Mensuel, Décembre 1955," 2 February 1956, #50/APA; 20G136, Gouverneur, " . . . Suffrage Universel dans les T.O.M."; Morgenthau, *Political Parties,* pp. 43, 56, 66; Virginia Thompson and Richard Adloff, *French West Africa* (New York: Greenwood Press, 1969), pp. 45–46, 54–55.

7. Morgenthau, *Political Parties,* p. 68.

8. Ibid., pp. 66, 72–73.

9. Ibid., p. 15.

10. ANS, 17G586, Guinée Française, Services de Police, Conakry, "Renseignements A/S Conférence Publique d'Information, tenue le 16 Septembre 1956 par le P.D.G.-R.D.A. au Cinéma 'VOX' à Conakry," 17 September 1956, #1907/658, C/PS.2; 17G586, Guinée Française, Services de Police, P. Humbert, Commissaire Divisionnaire, Conakry, à Gouverneur, Guinée Française, Conakry, 19 September 1956, #1924, C/PS.2. Also see Thomas Hodgkin, *African Political Parties: An Introductory Guide* (Gloucester, Mass.: Peter Smith, 1971), pp. 122–123.

11. ANS, 17G586, Guinée Française, Services de Police, Conakry, "Renseignements A/S Meeting Public tenu le Samedi 1er Décembre 1956, à Conakry, Stade Cornut-Gentille, par le P.D.G.-R.D.A.," 3 December 1956, #2468/881, C/PS.2. Also see 17G586, Police, " . . . Conférence Publique d'Information, tenue le 16 Septembre 1956 par le P.D.G.-R.D.A. . . ."

12. ANS, 17G613, Guinée Française, Services de Police, Gendarmerie, Conakry, "Renseignements A/S Vie Politique à l'Intérieur du Pays," 22 March 1957, #669/290, C/PS.2.

13. ANS, 17G586, Guinée Française, Services de Police, Kankan, "Renseignements A/S Conférence Publique R.D.A. le 31 Octobre 1956 à Kankan," 6 November 1956, #2288/799, C/PS.2; 20G132, Gouverneur, Guinée Française, Conakry à Ministre, FOM,

Paris, 26 November 1956, #341/APAS; Sidiki Kobélé Kéïta, *Le P.D.G.: Artisan de l'Indépendance Nationale en Guinée (1947–1958)* (Conakry: I.N.R.D.G., Bibliothèque Nationale, 1978), 2:39.

14. ANS, 20G136, Gouverneur " . . . Suffrage Universel dans les T.O.M."; Sidiki Kobélé Kéïta, *P.D.G.,* 2:39.

15. ANS, 17G586, Guinée Française, Services de Police, Kindia, "Renseignements A/S Conférence Publique tenue par la Section R.D.A. de Kindia, au Cinéma 'VOX' le 11 Novembre 1956," 13 November 1956, #2325/817, C/PS.2; 20G132, Gouverneur à Ministre, FOM, 26 November 1956; AG, AM-1339, Idiatou Camara, "La Contribution de la Femme de Guinée à la Lutte de Libération Nationale (1945–1958)" (Mémoire de Fin d'Études Supérieures, IPGAN, Conakry, 1979), p. 100.

16. ANS, 20G132, Gouverneur à Ministre, FOM, 26 November 1956. Also see 20G132, "Élections Municipales 1956, Communes de Plein Exercice, Résultats"; 20G132, Télégramme Arrivée, Haut Commissaire, Dakar. Envoyée de Gouverneur, Guinée Française, Conakry, 19–22 November 1956, #50.689–#50.696, #50.713.

17. Sidiki Kobélé Kéïta, *Ahmed Sékou Touré: L'Homme du 28 Septembre 1958,* 2nd ed. (Conakry: I.N.R.D.G., Bibliothèque Nationale, 1977), pp. 64–65; Morgenthau, *Political Parties,* p. 246; Idiatou Camara, "Contribution de la Femme," p. 101.

18. ANS, 20G136, Gouverneur " . . . Suffrage Universel dans les T.O.M."; 20G136, "Suffrage Universel," unidentified press clipping, before 31 March 1957.

19. Morgenthau, *Political Parties,* p. 246; Sidiki Kobélé Kéïta, *P.D.G.,* 2:51.

20. CAOM, Carton 2181, dos. 6, Télégramme Arrivée, FOM, Paris. Envoyée par Gouverneur, Guinée Française, Conakry, 17 September 1958, #355–356; Morgenthau, *Political Parties,* p. 246; Sidiki Kobélé Kéïta, *P.D.G.,* 2:55; Suret-Canale, *République,* p. 164.

21. Morgenthau, *Political Parties,* pp. 246, 425; Suret-Canale, *République,* p. 164; R. W. Johnson, "The Parti Démocratique de Guinée and the Mamou 'Deviation,' " in *African Perspectives: Papers in the History, Politics and Economics of Africa Presented to Thomas Hodgkin,* ed. Christopher Allen and R. W. Johnson (Cambridge: Cambridge University Press, 1970), p. 349.

22. Idiatou Camara, "Contribution de la Femme," p. 107; Suret-Canale, *République,* p. 164.

23. Suret-Canale, *République,* p. 164.

24. CAOM, Carton 2181, dos. 6, FOM Gouverneur, Guinée Française, Conakry, à Ministre, FOM, Paris, "Discours Prononcé par le Président Sékou Touré, le 14 Septembre 1958," 15 September 1958, #0191/CAB. Also see "Unanimement le 28 Septembre la Guinée Votera Non," *La Liberté,* 23 September 1958, pp. 1–2; CRDA, Fodéba Kéïta, "Rapport du IVème Congrès sur les Reformes Administatives et les Nouvelles Structures," *La Liberté,* 25 July 1958, p. 3; Morgenthau, *Political Parties,* p. 250.

25. Suret-Canale, *République,* p. 164.

In Ghana, in contrast, the nationalist movement and government co-opted, reformulated, and incorporated a radically disempowered chieftaincy. See Richard Rathbone, *Nkrumah and the Chiefs: The Politics of Chieftaincy in Ghana, 1951–60* (Athens: Ohio University Press, 2000).

26. Interview with Léon Maka, Sangoyah, Conakry, 25 February 1991; Sidiki Kobélé Kéïta, *P.D.G.,* 2:66; Morgenthau, *Political Parties,* p. 250; Présence Africaine, *Guinée: Prélude à l'Indépendance* (Paris: Présence Africaine, 1958), p. 17. The text of the conference proceedings is reproduced in *Guinée: Prélude à l'Indépendance.*

27. Jean Suret-Canale, "La Fin de la Chefferie en Guinée," *Journal of African History* 7, no. 3 (1966): p. 489; Suret-Canale, *République,* p. 166; Présence Africaine, *Guinée,* pp.

21–24; Maka, interview, 25 February 1991; interview with Mamadou Bela Doumbouya, Camayenne, Conakry, 26 January 1991.

Also see Mory Camara, "La Chefferie Coutumière doit Disparaître," *La Liberté,* 18 July 1957, p. 1; ANS, 17G622, Guinée Française, Services de Police, "Renseignements A/S Voyage à Conakry de l'Almamy de Mamou, Ibrahima Sory Dara Barry, ex–Grand Conseiller et Conseiller Territorial," 23 July 1957, #1620/630, C/PS.2; 17G622, Guinée Française, Services de Police, "Renseignements A/S Bruit Courant en Ville sur la Suppression Totale de la Chefferie Coutumière en Guinée," 31 July 1957, #1699/660, C/PS.2.

28. Présence Africaine, *Guinée,* p. 22.

29. Sidiki Kobélé Kéïta, *P.D.G.,* 2:69; CRDA, Fodéba Kéïta, "Rapport."

30. Suret-Canale, "Fin de la Chefferie," pp. 459, 490; Sidiki Kobélé Kéïta, *P.D.G.,* 2:67; AG, MO-33, Sékou Mara, "La Lutte de Libération Nationale et la Chefferie dite Coutumière en Guinée Forestière" (Mémoire de Fin d'Études Supérieures, IPJN, Kankan, 1975–76), p. 66.

31. Suret-Canale, "Fin de la Chefferie," pp. 460, 490, 493.

32. Suret-Canale, "Fin de la Chefferie," pp. 459–460, 492; Sidiki Kobélé Kéïta, *P.D.G.,* 2:147; Doumbouya, interview, 26 January 1991.

33. ANS, 2G56/138, Guinée Française, Gouverneur, "Rapport Politique Mensuel, Janvier 1956."

34. ANS, 17G586, Guinée Française, Services de Police, Conakry, "Renseignements Conférence du R.D.A. sur les Prochaines Élections Municipales," 29 October 1956, #2224/773, C/PS.2; 17G586, Guinée Française, Services de Police, Conakry, "Renseignements A/S Réunion Publique tenue le 8 Novembre 1956, à Conakry Cinéma 'VOX' par le P.D.G.-R.D.A., pour l'Ouverture de la Campagne Électorale," 9 November 1956, #2301/804, C/PS.2. Also see Hodgkin, *African Political Parties,* p. 103. For a similar situation in Senegal, see Kenneth Robinson, "Senegal: The Elections to the Territorial Assembly, March 1957," in *Five Elections in Africa,* ed. W.J.M. MacKenzie and Kenneth Robinson (Oxford: Oxford University Press, 1960), p. 343.

35. ANS, 17G586, Police, Kankan, " . . . Conférence Publique R.D.A. le 31 Octobre 1956 à Kankan."

36. ANS, 17G586, Guinée Française, Services de Police, Conakry, "Renseignements A/S Réunion Publique Électorale tenue par le B.A.G. au Cinéma 'VOX' à Conakry, le Mercredi 14 Novembre 1956," 15 November 1956, #2345/822, C/PS.2.

37. ANS, 17G586, Police, Kindia, " . . . Conférence Publique tenue par la Section R.D.A. de Kindia . . . le 11 Novembre 1956." Also see Hodgkin, *African Political Parties,* p. 103; Kenneth Robinson, "Senegal," p. 343.

38. ANS, 17G613, Guinée Française, Services de Police, Kindia, "Renseignements A/S Conférence Publique Électorale tenue à Kindia, par la S/Section P.D.G.-R.D.A., au Cinéma 'VOX' le 18 Mars 1957," 21 March 1957, #654/285, C/PS.2.

39. ANS, 17G586, Police, " . . . Meeting Public tenu le . . . 1er Décembre 1956, à Conakry . . . par le P.D.G.-R.D.A.," 3 December 1956.

40. ANS, 17G586, Police, Kankan, " . . . Conférence Publique R.D.A. le 31 Octobre 1956 à Kankan."

41. ANS, 17G586, Police, Kindia, " . . . Conférence Publique tenue par la Section R.D.A. de Kindia . . . le 11 Novembre 1956."

42. ANS, 17G586, Police, " . . . Réunion Publique tenue le 8 Novembre 1956 . . . par le P.D.G.-R.D.A . . . ." Also see 17G586, Police, " . . . Conférence du R.D.A. sur les Prochaines Élections Municipales," 29 October 1956; 17G586, Police, Kindia, " . . . Con-

férence Publique tenue par la Section R.D.A. de Kindia . . . le 11 Novembre 1956." For a list of female councillors, see Idiatou Camara, "Contribution de la Femme," p. 47.

43. ANS, 17G586, Police, Kindia, " . . . Conférence Publique tenue par la Section R.D.A. de Kindia . . . le 11 Novembre 1956."

For discussions of women whose candidacies were successful, see ANS, 17G586, Police, " . . . Réunion Publique tenue le 8 Novembre 1956 . . . par le P.D.G.-R.D.A . . . ."; 17G586, Guinée Française, Services de Police, Conakry, "Renseignements A/S Réunion Publique Électorale tenue le Lundi 12 Novembre 1956 à Conakry, Cinéma 'VOX' par le P.D.G.-R.D.A.," 12 November 1956, #2321/813, C/PS.2; 17G613, Guinée Française, Services de Police, Mamou, "Renseignements A/S Première Réunion du Conseil Municipal de Mamou, le 7 Janvier 1957," 11 January 1957, #80/46, C/PS.2.

44. ANS, 17G586, Police, " . . . Réunion Publique tenue le 8 Novembre 1956 . . . par le P.D.G.-R.D.A . . . ."; CAOM, Carton 2169, dos. 5, "À Propos des Élections Municipales à Conakry," *La République,* September 1956. *La République* was the BAG newspaper. See Morgenthau, *Political Parties,* p. 233.

45. ANS, 17G586, Police, " . . . Réunion Publique Électorale tenue par le B.A.G. . . . à Conakry, le Mercredi 14 Novembre 1956."

46. CAOM, Carton 2169, dos. 5, " . . . Élections Municipales à Conakry."

Although an RDA activist, Bocar Biro Barry gave some credence to the BAG's claims. He noted that Sékou Touré felt particularly threatened by BAG president Koumandian Kéïta, who was also secretary-general of the African teachers' union, both at the territorial and interterritorial levels. See interview with Bocar Biro Barry, Camayenne, Conakry, 21 January 1991; Sidiki Kobélé Kéïta, *P.D.G.,* 2:99; R. W. Johnson, "Part Démocratique de Guinée," p. 358; ANS, 17G622, Guinée Française, Services de Police, "Renseignements A/S 6ème Congrès des Enseignants Africains qui s'est Ouvert à Mamou, le 6 Août Dernier," 10 August 1957, #1800/692, C/PS.2; 17G622, Guinée Française, Services de Police, "Renseignements A/S Conférence Publique tenue dans la Salle du Cinéma de Mamou, par les Enseignants, le Samedi 10 Août Dernier," 16 August 1957, #1837/709, C/PS.2; 2G57/128, Guinée Française, Police et Sûreté, "Synthèse Mensuelle de Renseignements, Novembre 1957," Conakry, 25 November 1957, #2593/C/PS.2.

47. ANS, 17G586, Guinée Française, Services de Police, Conakry, "Renseignements A/S Conférence Publique Électorale tenue le Samedi 17 Novembre 1956, à Conakry, Cinéma 'VOX', par le P.D.G.-R.D.A.," 18 November 1956, #2374/836, C/PS.2.

48. ANS, 17G586, Police, " . . . Réunion Publique Électorale tenue par le B.A.G. . . . à Conakry, le Mercredi 14 Novembre 1956."

49. ANS, 17G586, Police, " . . . Réunion Publique tenue le 8 Novembre 1956 . . . par le P.D.G.-R.D.A. . . . "

50. ANS, 17G586, Guinée Française, Services de Police, Kankan, "Renseignements A/S B.A.G. et Élections Municipales," 24 October 1956, #2200/763, C/PS.2.

51. ANS, 17G613, Guinée Française, Services de Police, Conakry, "Renseignements A/S Position R.D.A. vis à vis du Congrès Socialiste de Conakry," 10 January 1957, #64/40, C/PS.2.

52. ANS, 17G613, Guinée Française, Services de Police, Conakry, "Renseignements A/S Seconde Conférence Territoriale du P.D.G.-R.D.A. tenue à Labé, les 23 et 24 Février 1957," 28 February 1957, #478/210, C/PS.2.

53. Ibid.

54. Ibid. Also see Morgenthau, *Political Parties,* p. 412.

55. ANS, 17G613, Police, " . . . Seconde Conférence Territoriale du P.D.G.-R.D.A. . . . les 23 et 24 Février 1957."

56. ANS, 17G613, Guinée Française, Services de Police, Conakry, "Renseignements A/S Conférence Publique d'Informations tenue à Conakry, Salle du Cinéma 'VOX', le Lundi 11 Mars 1957, par le P.D.G.-R.D.A.," 12 March 1957, #565/249, C/PS.2.

Martinique, a French overseas department, was an integral part of the French Republic. As such, it was superior in status to the French overseas territories, which were merely members of the French Union.

57. ANS, 17G613, Police, ". . . Seconde Conférence Territoriale du P.D.G.-R.D.A. . . . les 23 et 24 Février 1957."

Sékou Touré reiterated these themes throughout the election campaign. See 17G613, Guinée Française, Services de Police, Conakry, "Renseignements A/S Situation en Guinée, à la Veille du Dépôt des Listes aux Élections Cantonales du 31 Mars Prochain," 9 March 1957, #555/247, C/PS.2; 17G613, Police, Kindia, ". . . Conférence Publique Électorale tenue à Kindia, par la S/Section P.D.G.-R.D.A. . . . le 18 Mars 1957." Also see 17G586, Police, Kankan, ". . . Conférence Publique R.D.A. le 31 Octobre 1956 à Kankan."

58. ANS, 17G613, Police, ". . . Seconde Conférence Territoriale du P.D.G.-R.D.A. . . . les 23 et 24 Février 1957"; 17G613, Guinée Française, Services de Police, Kankan, "Renseignements A/S Conférence Publique R.D.A. à Kankan le 3 Mars 1957," 11 March 1957, #554/246, C/PS.2.

59. ANS, 17G613, Guinée Française, Services de Police, Conakry, "Renseignements A/S Commentaires sur la Libération de David *Sylla*, ex–Chef de Canton de Tondon," 15 February 1957, #395/173, C/PS.2.

60. ANS, 17G613, Police, Kindia, ". . . Conférence Publique Électorale tenue à Kindia, par la S/Section P.D.G.-R.D.A. . . . le 18 Mars 1957."

For assistance rendered by European lawyers, see 17G613, Guinée Française, Services de Police, N'Zérékoré, "Renseignements A/S Vie Politique à N'Zérékoré," 3 May 1957, #998/401, C/PS.2.

61. ANS, 17G613, Guinée Française, Services de Police, Gendarmerie, Conakry, "Renseignements A/S Vie Politique à l'Intérieur du Territoire," 23 March 1957, #682/292, C/PS.2.

62. ANS, 17G613, Guinée Française, Services de Police, Gendarmerie, Conakry, "Renseignements A/S Vie Politique à l'Intérieur du Territoire," 2 April 1957, #767/329, C/PS.2.

63. ANS, 17G613, Police, ". . . Situation en Guinée . . . Dépôt des Listes aux Élections Cantonales . . . ," 9 March 1957.

64. ANS, 17G613, Guinée Française, Services de Police, Conakry, "Renseignements A/S Prochaines Élections Cantonales," 5 March 1957, #514/232, C/PS.2; 17G613, Guinée Française, Services de Police, Conakry, "Renseignements A/S Rumeurs R.D.A. Concernant les Prochaines Élections Cantonales," 13 February 1957, #373/164, C/PS.2; 17G613, Guinée Française, Services de Police, Conakry, "Renseignements A/S Conférence Publique tenue à Conakry-Banlieue, Salle du Cinéma 'Matam' le Mercredi 13 Mars 1957, par le P.D.G.-R.D.A.," 14 March 1957, #595/260, C/PS.2.

65. ANS, 17G613, Police, ". . . Situation en Guinée . . . Dépôt des Listes aux Élections Cantonales . . . ," 9 March 1957. See similar criticisms by RDA opponents in 17G613, Guinée Française, Services de Police, Conakry, "Renseignements A/S Conférence Publique Électorale, tenue le Dimanche 24 Mars 1957, à Conakry, Salle du Cinéma 'VOX', par le Démocratie Socialiste de Guinée," 25 March 1957, #696/300, C/PS.2.

The RDA's final list contained some BAG members, including canton chiefs. See 17G613, Police, ". . . Conférence Publique d'Informations . . . 11 Mars 1957, par le P.D.G.-R.D.A."

66.   17G613, Police, " . . . Conférence Publique d'Informations . . . 11 Mars 1957, par le P.D.G.-R.D.A."; Sidiki Kobélé Kéïta, *P.D.G.,* 2:58–60.

67.   ANS, 17G622, Guinée Française, Services de Police, "Renseignements A/S Exclusion du P.D.G./R.D.A. de Plusieurs Dirigeants de la S/Section de Mamou," 15 November 1957, #25[ ]/941, C/PS.2; 17G622, Guinée Française, Services de Police, "Renseignements A/S Conférence Publique tenue à Mamou, le 14 Novembre 1957, par l'Ex-Sous-Section du P.D.G./R.D.A.," 19 November 1957, #2565/954, C/PS.2; 2G57/128, Police et Sûreté, "Synthèse Mensuelle de Renseignements, Novembre 1957"; Fanta Diarra (Mme. Fofana) and Ibrahima Fofana, Lansanya, Conakry, 24 May 1991; R. W. Johnson, "Part Démocratique de Guinée," pp. 347, 352, 362; Thompson and Adloff, *French West Africa,* p. 95; Hodgkin, *African Political Parties,* pp. 122–123.

68.   ANS, 17G586, Police, Commissaire Divisionnaire, Conakry, à Gouverneur, 19 September 1956; 17G622, Guinée Française, Services de Police, "Renseignements A/S Entrevue ayant eu lieu 17 Juillet Dernier, à l'Assemblée Territoriale à Conakry, entre le Comité Directeur du P.D.G. et le Bureau de l'Union Générale des Étudiants et Élèves de Guinée (U.G.E.E.G.)," 23 July 1957, #1624/634, C/PS.2; 17G622, Guinée Française, Services de Police, "Renseignements A/S Réunion tenue le Lundi 22 Juillet 1957, à Conakry, par la S/Section R.D.A. du Quartier Almamya (Prise de Position Contre les Étudiants Africains)," 23 July 1957, #1627/636, C/PS.2; 17G622, Guinée Française, Services de Police, "Renseignements A/S Commentaires sur le Congrès Fédéral R.D.A. de Bamako," 9 October 1957, #2257/838, C/PS.2. Also see Tony Chafer, *The End of Empire in French West Africa: France's Successful Decolonization?* (New York: Berg, 2002), pp. 109, 125–137, 143, 145, 149–150, 157–158, 193, 202–207, 217.

69.   ANS, 17G586, Guinée Française, Services de Police, Kankan, "Renseignements A/S P.D.G. et Congrès de Dabola," 24 September 1956, #1965/682, C/PS.2.

70.   ANS, 2G53/187, Guinée Française, Secrétaire Général, "Revues Trimestrielles des Événements, 3ème Trimestre 1953," 12 September 1953, #862/APA; 17G613, Guinée Française, Services de Police, Conakry, "Renseignements A/S Mécontentement Regnant Chez les Évolués Guinéens, Après la Parution des Décrets d'Application de la Loi-Cadre Modifiés par le Conseil de la République," 30 April 1957, #966/393, C/PS.2; R. W. Johnson, "Parti Démocratique de Guinée," pp. 347–348, 354, 358; Sidiki Kobélé Kéïta, *P.D.G.,* 2:101; Thompson and Adloff, *French West Africa,* p. 95; Hodgkin, *African Political Parties,* pp. 122–123; Chafer, *End of Empire,* pp. 193–217.

For similar challenges by Asante "youngmen" in colonial Ghana, see Richard Rathbone, "Businessmen in Politics: Party Struggle in Ghana, 1949–1957," *Journal of Development Studies* 9, no. 3 (1973): pp. 398–399; Jean Marie Allman, "The Youngmen and the Porcupine: Class, Nationalism and Asante's Struggle for Self-Determination, 1954–1957," *Journal of African History* 31, no. 2 (1990): pp. 263–279; Jean Marie Allman, *The Quills of the Porcupine: Asante Nationalism in an Emergent Ghana* (Madison: University of Wisconsin Press, 1993), pp. 8, 28–36; Pashington Obeng, "Gendered Nationalism: Forms of Masculinity in Modern Asante of Ghana," in *Men and Masculinities in Modern Africa,* ed. Lisa A. Lindsay and Stephan F. Miescher (Portsmouth, N.H.: Heinemann, 2003), pp. 192, 202, 205.

71.   ANS, 17G613, Police, " . . . Mécontentement Regnant Chez les Évolués Guinéens . . . ," 30 April 1957; 17G622, Police, " . . . 6ème Congrès des Enseignants Africains . . . ," 10 August 1957; 17G622, Police, " . . . Conférence Publique . . . par les Enseignants . . . ," 16 August 1957; 17G622, Guinée Française, Services de Police, "Renseignements A/S Conférence Publique tenue le Samedi 17 Août Dernier, par la S/Section P.D.G.-R.D.A. de Kindia," 28 August 1957, #1920/734, C/PS.2; 17G622, Police,

" . . . Exclusion du P.D.G./R.D.A. . . . Dirigeants de la S/Section de Mamou," 15 November 1957; 2G57/128, Police et Sûreté, "Synthèse Mensuelle de Renseignements, Novembre 1957"; personal archives of Bocar Biro Barry, "Travaux du Congrès de Mamou (6–10 Août 1957): Motion sur la Loi-Cadre," *L'École Guinéenne*, 1957–1958, p. 1; R. W. Johnson, "Parti Démocratique de Guinée," pp. 358, 364.

72.   ANS, 17G586, Police, Kankan, " . . . P.D.G. et Congrès de Dabola," 24 September 1956.

73.   Suret-Canale, *République*, p. 169; Sidiki Kobélé Kéïta, *P.D.G.*, 2:108, 131.

74.   Suret-Canale, *République*, p. 170.

75.   Morgenthau, *Political Parties*, pp. 252–253; Charles Diané, *La F.E.A.N.F. et Les Grandes Heures du Mouvement Syndical Étudiant Noir*, vol. 5 of *Afrique Contemporaine* (Paris: Éditions Chaka, 1990), pp. 118–119; "La Résolution," *La Liberté*, 23 September 1958, p. 2.

76.   CAOM, Carton 2194, dos. 4, Ministre, FOM, Paris, "Bulletin de Renseignements," 19 April 1958, #1012/Be.; ANS, 17G622, Guinée Française, Services de Police, "Renseignements A/S Réunion Privée tenue à Conakry, le 26 Avril 1958, par les Militantes du P.R.A.," 29 April 1958, #832/285, C/PS.2; Morgenthau, *Political Parties*, pp. 310–311.

77.   ANS, 17G622, Guinée Française, Services de Police, "Renseignements A/S Diffusion d'une Circulaire du P.R.A.," 25 April 1958, #808/280, C/PS.2; 17G622, Police, " . . . Réunion Privée . . . le 26 Avril 1958, par . . . P.R.A.," 29 April 1958; CAOM, Carton 2194, dos. 4, Ministre, FOM, "Bulletin de Renseignements," 19 April 1958; Carton 2194, dos. 4, Haut Commissaire, Dakar, à Ministre, FOM, Paris, "Incidents de Mai" [Guinée Française], 10 September 1958, #10238; "Annexe: Incidents de Conakry (22 Avril au 5 Mai 1958)"; Carton 2181, dos. 6, "L'U.P.G.-P.R.A. se Prononce pour le 'Non' au Référendum," *Agence France-Presse*, 16 September 1958; Morgenthau, *Political Parties*, p. 253; Sidiki Kobélé Kéïta, *P.D.G.*, 2:51–52.

78.   Jean-Pierre Rioux, *The Fourth Republic, 1944–1958*, trans. Godfrey Rogers (New York: Cambridge University Press, 1987), pp. 266, 271, 282–283; Morgenthau, *Political Parties*, p. 82.

79.   Rioux, *Fourth Republic*, pp. 283, 296.

80.   Ibid., p. 297.

81.   Ibid., pp. 281, 285–300.

82.   Charles de Gaulle, *Memoirs of Hope: Renewal and Endeavor*, trans. Terence Kilmartin (New York: Simon and Schuster, 1971), pp. 17, 21; Rioux, *Fourth Republic*, pp. 286, 289, 295, 298, 301, 467; Morgenthau, *Political Parties*, p. 102.

83.   Rioux, *Fourth Republic*, pp. 299–303, 305; Pierre Messmer, *Après Tant de Batailles: Mémoires* (Paris: Albin Michel, 1992), pp. 231–232.

84.   Rioux, *Fourth Republic*, pp. 306–307; de Gaulle, *Memoirs of Hope*, p. 24.

85.   Rioux, *Fourth Republic*, pp. 308–309; de Gaulle, *Memoirs of Hope*, p. 26.

86.   Sidiki Kobélé Kéïta, *P.D.G.*, 2:132–133; Morgenthau, *Political Parties*, pp. 73, 388–390; de Gaulle, *Memoirs of Hope*, p. 66.

For the definitive text of the 1958 Constitution, see Morgenthau, *Political Parties*, pp. 385–392.

87.   Morgenthau, *Political Parties*, p. 73.

88.   Ibid., pp. 71, 75, 77.

89.   Ibid., pp. 72, 113–114.

90.   Sidiki Kobélé Kéïta, *P.D.G.*, 2:129–130, 137; Morgenthau, *Political Parties*, p. 426; Rioux, *Fourth Republic*, p. 309; Georges Chaffard, *Les Carnets Secrets de la Décolonisation* (Paris: Calmann-Lévy, 1967), 2:177–178, 181.

91. Morgenthau, *Political Parties,* pp. 71, 311; Sidiki Kobélé Kéïta, *P.D.G.,* 2:132–133.

92. Sidiki Kobélé Kéïta, *P.D.G.,* 2:108, 131.

93. Morgenthau, *Political Parties,* pp. 253, 309, 311, 317; Suret-Canale, *République,* p. 172; Chaffard, *Carnets,* 2:176, 182; Jacques Foccart, *Foccart Parle: Entretiens avec Philippe Gaillard* (Paris: Fayard/Jeune Afrique, 1995), 1:158–159.

94. Sékou Touré, "L'Afrique et le Référendum," *La Liberté,* 25 July 1958, p. 1.

95. Sidiki Kobélé Kéïta, *P.D.G.,* 2:131.

96. Quoted in Chaffard, *Carnets,* 2:189. Also see Foccart, *Foccart Parle,* 1:159, 166.

97. Chaffard, *Carnets,* 2:176–177; Messmer, *Tant de Batailles,* p. 233.

98. Chaffard, *Carnets,* 2:191–193; Sidiki Kobélé Kéïta, *P.D.G.,* 2:131; Morgenthau, *Political Parties,* pp. 73, 387–388, 390; Foccart, *Foccart Parle,* 1:161; Lansiné Kaba, *Le "Non" de la Guinée à De Gaulle,* vol. 1 of *Afrique Contemporaine* (Paris: Éditions Chaka, 1989), p. 76.

See Constitutional Articles 72, 76, and 86 in Morgenthau, *Political Parties,* pp. 387–388, 390.

99. Chaffard, *Carnets,* 2:194–196; Lansiné Kaba, *"Non" de la Guinée,* p. 86; Suret-Canale, *République,* p. 170; Foccart, *Foccart Parle,* 1:162; Messmer, *Tant de Batailles,* pp. 234–235.

100. Suret-Canale, *République,* p. 170.

101. Quoted in Chaffard, *Carnets,* 2:197–198. Also see Sékou Touré, "Les Conditions de Notre Vote," *La Liberté,* 25 August 1958, pp. 1–2.

102. Quoted in Suret-Canale, *République,* p. 170; Chaffard, *Carnets,* 2:198. Also see CAOM, Carton 2181, dos. 6, Gouverneur, Guinée Française, Conakry, à Ministre, FOM, Paris, "Motion du Parti Démocratique de la Guinée en Date du 14 Septembre 1958," 15 September 1958, #0191/CAB; retrospective view in de Gaulle, *Memoirs of Hope,* p. 55.

103. Chaffard, *Carnets,* 2:195, 206; Foccart, *Foccart Parle,* 1:165; Messmer, *Tant de Batailles,* p. 235.

104. Chaffard, *Carnets,* 2:206.

105. CAOM, Carton 2181, dos. 6, Télégramme Arrivée, FOM, Paris. Envoyée par Gouverneur, Guinée Française, Conakry, 29 August 1958, #242–244; Carton 2181, dos. 6, Bordereau à Ministre, FOM, Paris, de M. Remondière, Chef du Cabinet Militaire, Conakry, "Extraits du Bulletin de l'Agence France-Presse du 18 Septembre," 19 September 1958, #1244/CAB; Diané, *F.E.A.N.F.,* p. 126; Sidiki Kobélé Kéïta, *P.D.G.,* 2:142; Chaffard, *Carnets,* 2:202; Barry, interview, 21 January 1991.

106. CAOM, Carton 2181, dos. 6, Télégramme Arrivée, FOM, Paris. Envoyée par Gouverneur, Guinée Française, Conakry, 6 September 1958, #276–277; Carton 2181, dos. 6, "Extraits . . . de l'Agence France-Presse du 18 Septembre [1958]"; Sidiki Kobélé Kéïta, *P.D.G.,* 2:142.

107. CAOM, Carton 2181, dos. 6, Télégramme Arrivée, FOM, Paris. Envoyée par Gouverneur, Guinée Française, Conakry, 1 September 1958, #259–260.

108. CAOM, Carton 2181, dos. 6, "Motion du Parti Démocratique de la Guinée . . . 14 Septembre 1958"; Carton 2181, dos. 6, Bordereau à Ministre, FOM, Paris, de G. Gilbert (pour le Gouverneur de la Guinée Française), "Nouvelles Locales Reçues de l'A.F.P. en Date du 19 Septembre 1958," 19 September 1958, #2276/CAB; Chaffard, *Carnets,* 2:204, 206; Morgenthau, *Political Parties,* p. 219.

109. Chaffard, *Carnets,* 2:206.

110. Barry, interview, 21 January 1991. Former university student leader Charles Diané also claims that Sékou Touré opted for the "No" vote in the eleventh hour—pushed by the student movement. See Diané, *F.E.A.N.F.,* pp. 128–129.

111. Barry, interview, 21 January 1991.

In his September 14 address, Sékou Touré made reference to the proindependence positions already taken by these groups. CAOM, Carton 2181, dos. 6, "Discours Prononcé par le Président Sékou Touré, le 14 Septembre 1958." Also see "Unanimement le 28 Septembre la Guinée Votera Non."

112. CAOM, Carton 2181, dos. 6, "Discours Prononcé par le Président Sékou Touré, le 14 Septembre 1958"; Carton 2181, dos. 6, "Motion du Parti Démocratique de la Guinée . . . du 14 Septembre 1958"; "La Résolution" and "Unanimement le 28 Septembre la Guinée Votera Non"; Morgenthau, *Political Parties,* p. 219; Chaffard, *Carnets,* 2:206.

113. CAOM, Carton 2181, dos. 6, "Communiqué du Conseil de Gouvernement," *Agence France-Presse,* 16 September 1958.

For the conflicting attitudes of military veterans, see CAOM, Carton 2181, dos. 6, Télégramme Arrivée, FOM, 29 August 1958.

114. CAOM, Carton 2181, dos. 6, Télégramme Arrivée, FOM, Paris. Envoyée par Gouverneur, Guinée Française, Conakry, 18 September 1958, #375; Carton 2181, dos. 6, "Nouvelles Locales . . . de l'A.F.P. . . . du 19 Septembre 1958."

115. Suret-Canale, *République,* p. 172; Sidiki Kobélé Kéïta, *P.D.G.,* 2:166, 190–191.

116. Rioux, *Fourth Republic,* p. 312.

117. Sidiki Kobélé Kéïta, *P.D.G.,* 2:147; Suret-Canale, "Fin de la Chefferie," pp. 459–460, 492; Doumbouya, interview, 26 January 1991.

118. "Les Résultats du Scrutin," *La Liberté,* 4 October 1958, p. 5; Sidiki Kobélé Kéïta, *P.D.G.,* 2:147–148; Morgenthau, *Political Parties,* pp. 219, 399; Suret-Canale, *République,* p. 172.

119. Sidiki Kobélé Kéïta, *P.D.G.,* 2:148; Chaffard, *Carnets,* 2:212; Morgenthau, *Political Parties,* p. 312.

BIBLIOGRAPHY

INTERVIEWS CONDUCTED BY ELIZABETH SCHMIDT AND SIBA N. GROVOGUI

Bah, Nima (Mme. Sow). Conakry. 31 January 1991.

Baldé, Mira (Mme. Maka). Sangoyah, Conakry. 25 February, 19 May 1991.

Barry, Bocar Biro. Camayenne, Conakry. 21 and 29 January 1991.

Bomboh, Émile. Conakry. 23 March 1991.

Camara, Louis Marquis. Conakry. 27 March 1991.

Cissé, Oumou. Kimbely, Mamou. 28 May 1991.

Diakhaby, Tiguidanké. Donka, Conakry. 12 January 1991.

Diallo, Néné. Conakry. 11 April 1991.

Diarra, Fanta (Mme. Fofana). Lansanaya, Conakry. 24 May 1991.

Diarra, Fatou. Lansanaya, Conakry. 17 March 1991.

Diop, Adama. Conakry. 14 and 18 March 1991.

Doumbouya, Mamadou Bela. Camayenne, Conakry. 26 January 1991.

Fofana, Hawa. Conakry. 7 April 1991.

Fofana, Ibrahima. Lansanaya, Conakry. 17 March, 5 and 24 May 1991.

Kaba, Mamady. Donka, Conakry. 15 January 1991.

Kéïta, Fatou. Km 43, Conakry. 7 and 28 April, 24 May 1991.

Kéïta, Sidiki Kobélé. Donka, Conakry. 20 October 1990, 9 April 1991.

Kouyaté, Namankoumba. Conakry. 31 January 1991.

Maka, Léon. Sangoyah, Conakry. 20 and 25 February 1991.

Meunier, Kadiatou (pseud.). Minière, Conakry. 18 January, 19 February, 5 March 1991.

Montlouis, Joseph. Coléah, Conakry. 28 February, 3 and 6 March 1991.

N'Diaye, Aissatou. Kaloum, Sandervalia, Conakry. 8 April 1991.

Sakho, Fatou, Mahawa Sakho, and Mabalo Sakho. Conakry. 19 June 1991.

Sylla, Siaka. Conakry. 5 April 1991.

Sylla, Tourou. Kimbely, Mamou. 30 May 1991.

Touré, Fodé Mamadou. Ratoma, Conakry. 13 March 1991.

ARCHIVES

In Guinea

Archives de Guinée (AG), Conakry
Personal archives of Bocar Biro Barry, Conakry
Personal archives of Adama Diop, Conakry
Personal archives of Joseph Montlouis, Conakry

In Senegal

Archives Nationales du Sénégal (ANS), Dakar
Institut Fondamental d'Afrique Noire (IFAN), Dakar

In France

Centre d'Accueil et de Recherche des Archives Nationales (CARAN), Paris
Centre des Archives d'Outre-Mer, Archives Nationales (CAOM), Aix-en-Provence
Centre de Recherche et de Documentation Africaine (CRDA), Paris

PUBLISHED PRIMARY SOURCES

Periodicals housed at IFAN and CRDA

Coup de Bambou, 1950.
La Liberté, 1951–60.
Le Phare de Guinée, 1947–1949.
Réveil, 1946–1950.

"The Atlantic Charter, Joint Declaration by the President and the Prime Minister, Declaration of Principles, Known as the Atlantic Charter," 14 August 1941, U.S.-U.K., 55 Stat. app. 1603. http://www1.umn.edu/humanrts/education/FDRjointdec.html.
"Charter of the United Nations," San Francisco, 26 June 1945. http://www.un.org/aboutun/charter.
"Declaration by United Nations," 1 January 1942. http://www.ibiblio.org/pha/policy/1942/420101a.html.
"General Act of the Conference of Berlin (1885)." In *Colonial Rule in Africa: Readings from Primary Sources,* edited by Bruce Fetter, pp. 34–38. Madison: University of Wisconsin Press, 1979.
"Nouveau Bureau Directeur [Syndicat du Personnel Enseignant Africain de Guinée]," *L'École Guinéenne,* 1957–1958. Personal archives of Bocar Biro Barry.
Présence Africaine. *Guinée: Prélude à l'Indépendance.* Paris: Présence Africaine, 1958.
"Recommendations Adopted by the Brazzaville Conference." In *Colonial Rule in Africa: Readings from Primary Sources,* edited by Bruce Fetter, pp. 168–173. Madison: University of Wisconsin Press, 1979.
"Travaux du Congrès de Mamou (6–10 Août 1957): Motion sur la Loi-Cadre," *L'École Guinéenne,* 1957–1958, p. 1. Personal archives of Bocar Biro Barry.

SECONDARY SOURCES

Ajayi, Jacob F. "The Place of African History and Culture in the Process of Nation-Building in Africa South of the Sahara." *Journal of Negro Education* 30, no. 3 (1960): 206–213.

Allman, Jean Marie. *The Quills of the Porcupine: Asante Nationalism in an Emergent Ghana.* Madison: University of Wisconsin Press, 1993.

———. "The Youngmen and the Porcupine: Class, Nationalism and Asante's Struggle for Self-Determination, 1954–1957." *Journal of African History* 31, no. 2 (1990): 263–279.

Ameillon, B. *La Guinée: Bilan d'une Indépendance.* Cahiers Libres, nos. 58–59. Paris: François Maspero, 1964.

Anderson, Benedict. *Imagined Communities: Reflections on the Origin and Spread of Nationalism.* 2nd ed. New York: Verso, 1991.

Apter, David. *Ghana in Transition.* Princeton, N.J.: Princeton University Press, 1963.

Ardener, Shirley. "Sexual Insult and Female Militancy." In *Perceiving Women,* edited by Shirley Ardener, pp. 29–53. London: Malaby Press, 1975.

Beinart, William, and Colin Bundy. *Hidden Struggles in Rural South Africa: Politics and Popular Movements in the Transkei and Eastern Cape, 1890–1930.* Berkeley: University of California Press, 1987.

———. "State Intervention and Rural Resistance: The Transkei, 1900–1965." In *Peasants in Africa: Historical and Contemporary Perspectives,* edited by Martin Klein, pp. 270–315. Beverly Hills, Calif.: Sage Publications, 1980.

Breuilly, John. *Nationalism and the State.* 2nd ed. Chicago: University of Chicago Press, 1994.

Brown, Carolyn A. "A 'Man' in the Village is a 'Boy' in the Workplace: Colonial Racism, Worker Militance, and Igbo Notions of Masculinity in the Nigerian Coal Industry, 1930–1945." In *Men and Masculinities in Modern Africa,* edited by Lisa A. Lindsay and Stephan F. Miescher, pp. 156–174. Portsmouth, N.H.: Heinemann, 2003.

Bujra, Janet M. "Women 'Entrepreneurs' of Early Nairobi." *Canadian Journal of African Studies* 9, no. 2 (1975): 213–234.

Bukh, Jette. *The Village Woman in Ghana.* Uppsala, Sweden: Scandinavian Institute of African Studies, 1979.

Burawoy, Michael. *The Colour of Class on the Copper Mines: From African Advancement to Zambianization.* Zambian Papers, no. 7. Lusaka: University of Zambia, Institute for African Studies, 1972.

Chafer, Tony. *The End of Empire in French West Africa: France's Successful Decolonization?* New York: Berg, 2002.

Chaffard, Georges. *Les Carnets Secrets de la Décolonisation.* Vol. 1. Paris: Calmann-Lévy, 1965.

———. *Les Carnets Secrets de la Décolonisation.* Vol. 2. Paris: Calmann-Lévy, 1967.

Chatterjee, Partha. *The Nation and Its Fragments: Colonial and Postcolonial Histories.* Princeton, N.J.: Princeton University Press, 1993.

Chauncey, George Jr. "The Locus of Reproduction: Women's Labour in the Zambian Copperbelt, 1927–1953." *Journal of Southern African Studies* 7, no. 2 (April 1981): 135–164.

Clark, Andrew F. *From Frontier to Backwater: Economy and Society in the Upper Senegal Valley (West Africa), 1850–1920.* Lanham, Md.: University Press of America, 1999.

Clark, Gracia. *Onions Are My Husband: Survival and Accumulation by West African Market Women.* Chicago: University of Chicago Press, 1994.

Coleman, James S. "Nationalism in Tropical Africa," *American Political Science Review* 48, no. 2 (June 1954): 404–426.

————. *Nigeria: Background to Nationalism.* Berkeley: University of California Press, 1958.

Cooper, Frederick. *Decolonization and African Society: The Labor Question in French and British Africa.* New York: Cambridge University Press, 1996.

————. "From Free Labor to Family Allowances: Labor and African Society in Colonial Discourse." *American Ethnologist* 16, no. 4 (November 1989): 745–765.

————. "Industrial Man Goes to Africa." In *Men and Masculinities in Modern Africa,* edited by Lisa A. Lindsay and Stephan F. Miescher, pp. 128–137. Portsmouth, N.H.: Heinemann, 2003.

————. *On the African Waterfront: Urban Disorder and the Transformation of Work in Colonial Mombasa.* New Haven, Conn.: Yale University Press, 1987.

————. " 'Our Strike': Equality, Anticolonial Politics and the 1947–48 Railway Strike in French West Africa." *Journal of African History* 37, no. 1 (1996): 81–118.

Coquery-Vidrovitch, Catherine. "Nationalité et Citoyenneté en Afrique Occidentale Français[e]: Originaires et Citoyens dans Le Sénégal Colonial." *Journal of African History* 42, no. 2 (2001): 285–305.

Curtin, Philip, Steven Feierman, Leonard Thompson, and Jan Vansina. *African History: From Earliest Times to Independence.* 2nd ed. New York: Longman, 1995.

de Gaulle, Charles. *Memoirs of Hope: Renewal and Endeavor.* Translated by Terence Kilmartin. New York: Simon and Schuster, 1971.

————. *The War Memoirs of Charles de Gaulle: Salvation, 1944–1946.* New York: Simon and Schuster, 1960.

————. *The War Memoirs of Charles de Gaulle: Unity, 1942–1944.* New York: Simon and Schuster, 1959.

————. *War Memoirs: The Call to Honour, 1940–1942.* New York: Viking Press, 1955.

Denzer, LaRay. "Constance A. Cummings-John of Sierra Leone: Her Early Political Career." *Tarikh* 7, no. 1 (1981): 20–32.

————. "Towards a Study of the History of West African Women's Participation in Nationalist Politics: The Early Phase, 1935–1950." *Africana Research Bulletin* 6, no. 4 (1976): 65–85.

————. "Women in Freetown Politics, 1914–61: A Preliminary Study." *Africa* 57, no. 4 (1987): 439–456.

Derman, William. *Serfs, Peasants, and Socialists: A Former Serf Village in the Republic of Guinea.* Berkeley: University of California Press, 1973.

Deutsch, Karl W. *Nationalism and Social Communication: An Inquiry into the Foundations of Nationality.* 2nd ed. Cambridge, Mass.: M.I.T. Press, 1966.

Diané, Charles. *La F.E.A.N.F. et Les Grandes Heures du Mouvement Syndical Étudiant Noir.* Vol. 5 of *Afrique Contemporaine.* Paris: Éditions Chaka, 1990.

Duara, Prasenjit. "Historicizing National Identity, or Who Imagines What and When." In *Becoming National: A Reader,* edited by Geoff Eley and Ronald Grigor Suny, pp. 151–177. New York: Oxford University Press, 1996.

Echenberg, Myron. *Black Death, White Medicine: Bubonic Plague and the Politics of Public Health in Colonial Senegal, 1914–1945.* Portsmouth, N.H.: Heinemann; Oxford: James Currey, 2002.

————. *Colonial Conscripts: The Tirailleurs Sénégalais in French West Africa, 1857–1960.* Portsmouth, N.H.: Heinemann; London: James Currey, 1991.

————. " 'Morts Pour La France': The African Soldier in France during the Second World War." *Journal of African History* 26, no. 4 (1985): 363–380.

———. "Tragedy at Thiaroye: The Senegalese Soldiers' Uprising of 1944." In *African Labor History,* edited by Peter C. W. Gutkind, Robin Cohen, and Jean Copans, pp. 109–128. Beverly Hills, Calif.: Sage Publications, 1978.

Eley, Geoff, and Ronald Grigor Suny. "Introduction: From the Moment of Social History to the Work of Cultural Representation." In *Becoming National: A Reader,* edited by Geoff Eley and Ronald Grigor Suny, pp. 3–37. New York: Oxford University Press, 1996.

Fall, Babacar. *Le Travail Forcé en Afrique-Occidentale Française (1900–1945).* Paris: Éditions Karthala, 1993.

Foccart, Jacques. *Foccart Parle: Entretiens avec Philippe Gaillard.* 2 vols. Paris: Fayard/Jeune Afrique, 1995.

Geiger, Susan. "Anti-Colonial Protest in Africa: A Female Strategy Reconsidered." *Heresies* 9, no. 3 (1980): 22–25.

———. "Engendering and Gendering African Nationalism: Rethinking the Case of Tanganyika (Tanzania)." *Social Identities* 5, no. 3 (1999): 331–343.

———. "Tanganyikan Nationalism as 'Women's Work': Life Histories, Collective Biography and Changing Historiography," *Journal of African History* 37, no. 3 (1996): 465–478.

———. *TANU Women: Gender and Culture in the Making of Tanganyikan Nationalism, 1955–1965.* Portsmouth, N.H.: Heinemann; Oxford: James Currey, 1997.

———. "Women and African Nationalism." *Journal of Women's History* 2, no. 1 (1990): 227–244.

———. "Women in Nationalist Struggle: TANU Activists in Dar es Salaam." *International Journal of African Historical Studies* 20, no. 1 (1987): 1–26.

Gellner, Ernest. *Nations and Nationalism.* Ithaca, N.Y.: Cornell University Press, 1983.

Hargreaves, John D. *Decolonization in Africa.* 2nd ed. New York: Longman, 1996.

Hay, Margaret Jean. "Luo Women and Economic Change during the Colonial Period." In *Women in Africa: Studies in Social and Economic Change,* edited by Nancy J. Hafkin and Edna G. Bay, pp. 87–109. Stanford, Calif.: Stanford University Press, 1976.

Headrick, Daniel R. *The Tools of Empire: Technology and European Imperialism in the Nineteenth Century.* New York: Oxford University Press, 1981.

Henley, David E. F. "Ethnogeographic Integration and Exclusion in Anticolonial Nationalism: Indonesia and Indochina," *Comparative Studies in Society and History* 37, no. 2 (April 1995): 286–324.

Hobsbawm, E. J. *The Age of Revolution: Europe, 1789–1848.* London: Weidenfeld and Nicolson, 1962.

———. *Nations and Nationalism since 1780: Program, Myth, Reality.* 2nd ed. Cambridge: Cambridge University Press, 1992.

Hodgkin, Thomas. *African Political Parties: An Introductory Guide.* Gloucester, Mass.: Peter Smith, 1971.

———. *Nationalism in Colonial Africa.* New York: New York University Press, 1957.

Horne, Alistair. *To Lose a Battle: France 1940.* Boston: Little, Brown, 1969.

Hrbek, Ivan. "North Africa and the Horn." In *General History of Africa,* vol. 8: *Africa since 1935,* edited by Ali A. Mazrui and C. Wondji, pp. 127–160. Berkeley: University of California Press, 1999.

Hroch, Miroslav. "From National Movement to the Fully-Formed Nation: The Nation-Building Process in Europe." In *Becoming National: A Reader,* edited by Geoff

Eley and Ronald Grigor Suny, pp. 60–77. New York: Oxford University Press, 1996.

———. *Social Preconditions of National Revival in Europe: A Comparative Analysis of the Social Composition of Patriotic Groups among the Smaller European Nations.* Translated by Ben Fowkes. Cambridge: Cambridge University Press, 1985.

Ifeka-Moller, Caroline. "Female Militancy and Colonial Revolt: The Women's War of 1929, Eastern Nigeria." In *Perceiving Women,* edited by Shirley Ardener, pp. 127–157. London: Malaby Press, 1975.

Iffono, Aly Gilbert. *Lexique Historique de la Guinée-Conakry.* Paris: L'Harmattan, 1992.

Isaacman, Allen. "Chiefs, Rural Differentiation and Peasant Protest: The Mozambican Forced Cotton Regime, 1938–61." *African Economic History* 14 (1985): 15–56.

———. "Coercion, Paternalism and the Labor Process: The Mozambican Cotton Regime, 1938–1961." *Journal of Southern African Studies* 18, no. 3 (1992): 487–526.

———. *Cotton Is the Mother of Poverty: Peasants, Work, and Rural Struggle in Colonial Mozambique, 1938–1961.* Portsmouth, N.H.: Heinemann; London: James Currey, 1996.

———. "Peasants and Rural Social Protest in Africa." *African Studies Review* 33 (1990): 1–120.

Isaacman, Allen, Michael Stephen, Yussuf Adam, Maria João Homen, Eugenio Macamo, and Augustinho Pililão. " 'Cotton Is the Mother of Poverty': Peasant Resistance to Forced Cotton Production in Mozambique, 1938–1961." *International Journal of African Historical Studies* 13 (1980): 581–615.

Johnson, Cheryl. "Grassroots Organizing: Women in Anti-Colonial Activity in Southwestern Nigeria." *African Studies Review* 25, no. 2 (September 1982): 137–157.

———. "Madam Alimotu Pelewura and the Lagos Market Women." *Tarikh* 7, no. 1 (1981): 1–10.

Johnson, R. W. "The Parti Démocratique de Guinée and the Mamou 'Deviation.' " In *African Perspectives: Papers in the History, Politics and Economics of Africa Presented to Thomas Hodgkin,* edited by Christopher Allen and R. W. Johnson, pp. 347–369. Cambridge: Cambridge University Press, 1970.

Johnson-Odim, Cheryl, and Nina Emma Mba. *For Women and the Nation: Funmilayo Ransome-Kuti of Nigeria.* Urbana: University of Illinois Press, 1997.

Jones, James A. *Industrial Labor in the Colonial World: Workers of the Chemin de Fer Dakar-Niger, 1881–1963.* Portsmouth, N.H.: Heinemann, 2002.

Kaba, Lansiné. *Le "Non" de la Guinée à De Gaulle.* Vol. 1 of *Afrique Contemporaine.* Paris: Éditions Chaka, 1989.

Kanya-Forstner, A. S. *The Conquest of the Western Sudan: A Study in French Military Imperialism.* Cambridge: Cambridge University Press, 1969.

———. "Mali-Tukulor." In *West African Resistance: The Military Response to Colonial Occupation,* edited by Michael Crowder, pp. 53–79. New York: Africana Publishing Corp., 1971.

Kaplan, Temma. "Female Consciousness and Collective Action: The Case of Barcelona, 1910–1918." *Signs: Journal of Women in Culture and Society* 7, no. 3 (Spring 1982): 545–566.

Kéïta, Sidiki Kobélé. *Ahmed Sékou Touré: L'Homme du 28 Septembre 1958.* 2nd ed. Conakry: I.N.R.D.G., Bibliothèque Nationale, 1977.

———. *Ahmed Sékou Touré: L'Homme et son Combat Anti-Colonial (1922–1958).* Conakry: Éditions S.K.K., 1998.

————. *Le P.D.G.: Artisan de l'Indépendance Nationale en Guinée (1947–1958).* 2 vols. Conakry: I.N.R.D.G., Bibliothèque Nationale, 1978.

Kipré, Pierre. *Le Congrès de Bamako ou La Naissance du RDA en 1946.* Vol. 3 of *Afrique Contemporaine.* Paris: Éditions Chaka, 1989.

Klein, Martin. *Slavery and Colonial Rule in French West Africa.* New York: Cambridge University Press, 1998.

Lawler, Nancy Ellen. *Soldiers of Misfortune: Ivoirien Tirailleurs of World War II.* Athens: Ohio University Press, 1992.

Lindsay, Lisa A. "Domesticity and Difference: Male Breadwinners, Working Women, and Colonial Citizenship in the 1945 Nigerian General Strike." *American Historical Review* 104, no. 3 (June 1999): 783–812.

————. "Money, Marriage, and Masculinity on the Colonial Nigerian Railway." In *Men and Masculinities in Modern Africa,* edited by Lisa A. Lindsay and Stephan F. Miescher, pp. 138–155. Portsmouth, N.H.: Heinemann, 2003.

————. " 'No Need . . . to Think of Home?': Masculinity and Domestic Life on the Nigerian Railway, c. 1940–61." *Journal of African History* 39, no. 3 (1998): 439–466.

————. *Working with Gender: Wage Labor and Social Change in Southwestern Nigeria, 1930–1964.* Portsmouth, N.H.: Heinemann, 2003.

Lindsay, Lisa A., and Stephan F. Miescher, eds. *Men and Masculinities in Modern Africa.* Portsmouth, N.H.: Heinemann, 2003.

Lonsdale, John. "The Emergence of African Nations: A Historiographical Analysis." *African Affairs* 67, no. 266 (1968): 11–28.

————. "Some Origins of Nationalism in East Africa." *Journal of African History* 9, no. 1 (1968): 119–146.

Lunn, Joe. *Memoirs of the Maelstrom: A Senegalese Oral History of the First World War.* Portsmouth, N.H.: Heinemann; Oxford: James Currey, 1999.

Mamdani, Mahmood. *Citizen and Subject: Contemporary Africa and the Legacy of Late Colonialism.* Princeton, N.J.: Princeton University Press, 1996.

Mandala, Elias. "Peasant Cotton Agriculture, Gender and Inter-Generational Relationships: The Lower Tchiri (Shire) Valley of Malawi, 1906–1940." *African Studies Review* 25, nos. 2/3 (June/September 1982): 27–44.

Mann, Gregory. "Old Soldiers, Young Men: Masculinity, Islam, and Military Veterans in Late 1950s Soudan Français (Mali)." In *Men and Masculinities in Modern Africa,* edited by Lisa A. Lindsay and Stephan F. Miescher, pp. 69–85. Portsmouth, N.H.: Heinemann, 2003.

Manning, Patrick. *Francophone Sub-Saharan Africa, 1880–1985.* New York: Cambridge University Press, 1988.

Mba, Nina Emma. *Nigerian Women Mobilized: Women's Political Activity in Southern Nigeria, 1900–1965.* Research Series, no. 48. Berkeley: Institute of International Studies, University of California, 1982.

Messmer, Pierre. *Après Tant de Batailles: Mémoires.* Paris: Albin Michel, 1992.

Meynaud, Jean, and Anisse Salah Bey. *Trade Unionism in Africa: A Study of Its Growth and Orientation.* Translated by Angela Brench. London: Methuen, 1967.

Miescher, Stephan F., and Lisa A. Lindsay. "Introduction: Men and Masculinities in Modern African History." In *Men and Masculinities in Modern Africa,* edited by Lisa A. Lindsay and Stephan F. Miescher, pp. 1–29. Portsmouth, N.H.: Heinemann, 2003.

Moodie, T. Dunbar. "The Moral Economy of the Black Miners' Strike of 1946." *Journal of Southern African Studies* 13, no. 1 (October 1986): 1–35.

Morgenthau, Ruth Schachter. *Political Parties in French-Speaking West Africa.* Oxford: Clarendon Press, 1964.

Morrison, Steve, and Claudia Milne. *Asante Market Women.* New York: Filmakers Library, 1982.

Morrow, John H. *First American Ambassador to Guinea.* New Brunswick, N.J.: Rutgers University Press, 1968.

Mortimer, Edward. *France and the Africans, 1944–1960: A Political History.* New York: Walker, 1969.

Obeng, Pashington. "Gendered Nationalism: Forms of Masculinity in Modern Asante of Ghana." In *Men and Masculinities in Modern Africa,* edited by Lisa A. Lindsay and Stephan F. Miescher, pp. 192–208. Portsmouth, N.H.: Heinemann, 2003.

O'Meara, Dan. "The 1946 African Mine Workers' Strike and the Political Economy of South Africa." *Journal of Commonwealth and Comparative Politics* 13, no. 1 (March 1975): 146–173.

Parker, John. *Making the Town: Ga State and Society in Early Colonial Accra.* Portsmouth, N.H.: Heinemann; Oxford: James Currey, 2000.

Parpart, Jane L. "The Household and the Mine Shaft: Gender and Class Struggles on the Zambian Copperbelt, 1926–64." *Journal of Southern African Studies* 13, no. 1 (October 1986): 36–56.

Parsons, Timothy H. *The African Rank-and-File: Social Implications of Colonial Military Service in the King's African Rifles, 1902–1964.* Portsmouth, N.H.: Heinemann; Oxford: James Currey, 1999.

Person, Yves. "Guinea-Samori." Translated by Joan White. In *West African Resistance: The Military Response to Colonial Occupation,* edited by Michael Crowder, pp. 111–143. New York: Africana Publishing Corp., 1971.

———. *Samori: Une Révolution Dyula.* 3 vols. Dakar, Senegal: IFAN, 1968–1975.

Phimister, Ian. *An Economic and Social History of Zimbabwe, 1890–1948: Capital Accumulation and Class Struggle.* New York: Longman, 1988.

———. *Wangi Kolia: Coal, Capital and Labour in Colonial Zimbabwe, 1894–1954.* Harare, Zimbabwe: Baobab Books; Johannesburg, South Africa: Witwatersrand University Press, 1994.

Popular Memory Group. "Popular Memory: Theory, Politics, Method." In *Making Histories: Studies in History-Writing and Politics,* edited by Richard Johnson, Gregor McLennan, Bill Schwarz, and David Sutton, pp. 205–252. Minneapolis: University of Minnesota Press, 1982.

Presley, Cora Ann. *Kikuyu Women, the Mau Mau Rebellion, and Social Change in Kenya.* Boulder, Colo.: Westview, 1992.

Rathbone, Richard. "Businessmen in Politics: Party Struggle in Ghana, 1949–1957." *Journal of Development Studies* 9, no. 3 (1973): 390–401.

———. *Nkrumah and the Chiefs: The Politics of Chieftaincy in Ghana, 1951–60.* Athens: Ohio University Press, 2000.

Richard-Molard, Jacques. *Afrique Occidentale Française.* Paris: Éditions Berger-Levrault, 1952.

Rioux, Jean-Pierre. *The Fourth Republic, 1944–1958.* Translated by Godfrey Rogers. New York: Cambridge University Press, 1987.

Rivière, Claude. *Guinea: The Mobilization of a People.* Translated by Virginia Thompson and Richard Adloff. Ithaca, N.Y.: Cornell University Press, 1977.

———. "La Promotion de la Femme Guinéenne." *Cahiers d'Études Africaines* 8, no. 31 (1968): 406–427.

Robertson, Claire C. *Sharing the Same Bowl: A Socioeconomic History of Women and Class in Accra, Ghana.* Bloomington: Indiana University Press, 1984.

———. *Trouble Showed the Way: Women, Men, and Trade in the Nairobi Area, 1890–1990.* Bloomington: Indiana University Press, 1997.

Robinson, David. *The Holy War of Umar Tal: The Western Sudan in the Mid-Nineteenth Century.* Oxford: Oxford University Press, 1985.

Robinson, Kenneth. "Senegal: The Elections to the Territorial Assembly, March 1957." In *Five Elections in Africa,* edited by W.J.M. MacKenzie and Kenneth Robinson, pp. 281–390. Oxford: Oxford University Press, 1960.

Rodney, Walter. "Jihad and Social Revolution in Futa Djalon in the Eighteenth Century." *Journal of the Historical Society of Nigeria* 4, no. 2 (June 1968): 269–284.

Rosberg, Carl G., and John Nottingham. *The Myth of "Mau Mau": Nationalism in Kenya.* Stanford, Calif.: Hoover Institution Press, 1966.

Rotberg, Robert I. *The Rise of Nationalism in Central Africa: The Making of Malawi and Zambia, 1873–1964.* Cambridge, Mass.: Harvard University Press, 1965.

Scarnecchia, Timothy. "Poor Women and Nationalist Politics: Alliances and Fissures in the Formation of a Nationalist Political Movement in Salisbury, Rhodesia, 1950–6." *Journal of African History* 37, no. 2 (1996): 283–310.

Schmidt, Elizabeth. " 'Emancipate Your Husbands!': Women and Nationalism in Guinea, 1953–1958." In *Women in African Colonial Histories,* edited by Jean Allman, Susan Geiger, and Nakanyike Musisi, pp. 282–304. Bloomington: Indiana University Press, 2002.

———. *Peasants, Traders, and Wives: Shona Women in the History of Zimbabwe, 1870–1939.* Portsmouth, N.H.: Heinemann; London: James Currey, 1992.

Scott, James C. *Weapons of the Weak: Everyday Forms of Peasant Resistance.* New Haven, Conn.: Yale University Press, 1985.

Sembene, Ousmane. *God's Bits of Wood.* Translated by Francis Price. Portsmouth, N.H.: Heinemann, 1986.

Seton-Watson, Hugh. *Nations and States: An Enquiry into the Origins of Nations and the Politics of Nationalism.* Boulder, Colo.: Westview Press, 1977.

Sikainga, Ahmad Alawad. *"City of Steel and Fire": A Social History of Atbara, Sudan's Railway Town, 1906–1984.* Portsmouth, N.H.: Heinemann; Oxford: James Currey, 2002.

Smith, Anthony D. "The Origins of Nations." In *Becoming National: A Reader,* edited by Geoff Eley and Ronald Grigor Suny, pp. 106–130. New York: Oxford University Press, 1996.

———. *State and Nation in the Third World: The Western State and African Nationalism.* New York: St. Martin's Press, 1983.

Suret-Canale, Jean. "La Fin de la Chefferie en Guinée." *Journal of African History* 7, no. 3 (1966): 459–493.

———. *French Colonialism in Tropical Africa, 1900–1945.* Translated by Till Gottheiner. New York: Pica Press, 1971.

———. "The French West African Railway Workers' Strike, 1947–1948." In *African Labor History,* edited by Peter C. W. Gutkind, Robin Cohen, and Jean Copans, pp. 129–154. Beverly Hills, Calif.: Sage Publications, 1978.

———. *La République de Guinée.* Paris: Éditions Sociales, 1970.

Thompson, Virginia, and Richard Adloff. *French West Africa.* New York: Greenwood Press, 1969.

Touré, Ahmed Sékou. *L'Afrique et la Révolution.* Vol. 13. Geneva: Imprimerie en Suisse, 1966.

Turrittin, Jane. "Aoua Kéita and the Nascent Women's Movement in the French Soudan." *African Studies Review* 36, no. 1 (April 1993): 59–89.

Van Allen, Judith. " 'Aba Riots' or Igbo 'Women's War'?: Ideology, Stratification, and the Invisibility of Women." In *Women in Africa: Studies in Social and Economic Change,* edited by Nancy J. Hafkin and Edna G. Bay, pp. 59–85. Stanford, Calif.: Stanford University Press, 1976.

Walker, Cherryl. *Women and Resistance in South Africa.* London: Onyx Press, 1982.

Wells, Julia C. "Why Women Rebel: A Comparative Study of South African Women's Resistance in Bloemfontein (1913) and Johannesburg (1958)." *Journal of Southern African Studies* 10, no. 1 (October 1983): 55–70.

White, Luise. "A Colonial State and an African Petty Bourgeoisie: Prostitution, Property, and Class Struggle in Nairobi, 1936–1940." In *Struggle for the City: Migrant Labor, Capital, and the State in Urban Africa,* edited by Frederick Cooper, pp. 167–194. Beverly Hills, Calif.: Sage Publications, 1983.

————. *The Comforts of Home: Prostitution in Colonial Nairobi.* Chicago: University of Chicago Press, 1990.

Wright, Marcia. "Technology, Marriage and Women's Work in the History of Maize-Growers in Mazabuka, Zambia: A Reconnaissance." *Journal of Southern African Studies* 10, no. 1 (October 1983): 71–85.

UNPUBLISHED THESES, PAPERS, AND MANUSCRIPTS

Camara, Idiatou. "La Contribution de la Femme de Guinée à la Lutte de Libération Nationale (1945–1958)." Mémoire de Fin d'Études Supérieures. IPGAN, Conakry, 1979. AG, AM-1339.

Dobert, Margarita. "Civic and Political Participation of Women in French-Speaking West Africa." Ph.D. diss., George Washington University, 1970.

Geiger, Susan. "The Concept of Nationalism Revisited (Again): Culture and Politics in Tanzanian Women's Life Histories." Paper presented at the Annual Meeting of the African Studies Association, Denver, Colo., 21 November 1987.

Mara, Sékou. "La Lutte de Libération Nationale et la Chefferie dite Coutumière en Guinée Forestière." Mémoire de Fin d'Études Supérieures. IPJN, Kankan, 1975–76. AG, MO-33.

Schmidt, Elizabeth. "Cold War and Decolonization in Guinea, 1946–1958." Unpublished book manuscript.

————. "Top Down or Bottom Up?: Nationalist Mobilization Reconsidered, with Special Reference to Guinea (French West Africa)." Under consideration by the *American Historical Review.*

INDEX

Abidjan, 177, 189, 255 n.77
Afrique Occidentale Française (AOF).
    See French West Africa
Aguibou, Barry. *See* Barry, Almamy
    Aguibou
Alfaya Line, 253 n.48
Algeria, 172, 184
Almamy: of the Futa Jallon, 253 n.48; of
    Timbo, 154. *See also* Alfaya Line;
    Soriya Line
Amicale Gilbert Vieillard, 34, 212 n.53
Anderson, Benedict, 16, 198 n.12, 221 n.56
Aribot, Mamadou, 179
Asante, 246 n.89, 264 n.70
Assimilation, 28, 33, 55, 70, 74, 76, 82,
    90, 194
Association des Anciens Combattants de
    la Guinée Français, 45
Association des Anciens Combattants et
    Anciens Militaires Africains de la
    Guinée, 45, 50
Association des Anciens Combattants et
    Victimes de Guerre de l'Afrique Occi-
    dentale Française (AACVGAOF),
    43–44, 51
Association des Anciens Militaires
    Africains de Guinée, 45
Association Générale des Amputés et
    Grands Blessés de l'Afrique Occiden-
    tale Française (AGAGBAOF), 43
Association Unique des Anciens Combat-
    tants et Victimes de la Guerre de la
    Guinée, 49–50

Atlantic Charter, 8, 28–29
Autonomy, African. *See* Government,
    local; *Loi-cadre*
Autra, Ray 73, 104–5, 108, 118, 123, 238
    n.87
Auxiliary workers. *See* Civil servants,
    auxiliaries; Strikes: French West
    African Railway Strike (1947–1948)

Baga, 17, 156, 167, 179, 182, 251 n.14
Bah, Tierno Ibrahima, 96
Baldé, Mira, 115, 126, 137, 141, 147
Ballay Hospital, 118
Bamako, 189; Congress of (October
    1946), 32–34, 107, 154; trade union
    conference (1953), 77
Bambara, 155, 181
Bangoura, Aissata, 134
Bangoura, Fodé, 157
Bangoura, Karim, 148, 178
Bangoura, Khady, 134–35
Bangoura, Mafory, 12, 85, 88–89, 126,
    133–36, 141, 146, 157, 244 n.58
Bangoura, Mamayimbe, 132, 247
    n.101
Bangoura, Sayon, 135
Baro Plantation, 25
Barry, Almamy Aguibou, 105, 109, 131,
    154, 238 n.91, 253 n.48
Barry, Bobo, 153
Barry, Bocar Biro, 124, 137, 139, 141,
    149, 151–52, 154, 189–90, 248 n.136,
    262 n.46

Barry, Diawadou, 73, 109–11, 130–31, 147–48, 153–54, 156, 161, 163, 178–79, 184, 238 n.91
Barry III (Barry, Ibrahima), 147–48, 153, 161, 184, 251 n.10
Bassari, 17, 251 n.14
Béavogui, Louis Lansana, 161–62, 166
Benefits. *See* Trade unions: benefits; Veterans: benefits
Bérété, Framoi, 73
Berlin Conference (1884–1885), 17
Beyla, 47, 101, 105, 108, 110, 162, 164–65, 236 n.50
Beyla-Faranah (canton), 47
Binani (canton), 96–97
Biro, Bokar, 154, 253 n.48
Bissikrima, 34
Bloc Africain de Guinée (BAG): 110, 125, 132, 135, 140, 147–48, 153–55, 163, 165–66, 168, 177–79, 182, 184, 258 n.146, 262 n.44, 262 n.46, 263 n.65
Boffa, 103, 109–10, 179
Boké, 25, 27, 99, 102, 125, 146, 179, 181, 224 n.85, 234 n.30
Boola (village), 164
Boulbinet: neighborhood, Conakry, 131, 134–35, 157, 179, 189; neighborhood, Mamou, 153
Bouzié (canton), 100
Brazzaville Conference (1944), 29–32, 35, 55–56, 58

Caba, Lamine. *See* Kaba, Lamine
Camara, Aissata, 153
Camara, Baba, 73, 105
Camara, Bengaly, 157, 164, 166
Camara, Idiatou, 5, 127, 132, 135, 247 n.101
Camara, Louis Marquis, 86
Camara, M'Balia, 157
Camara, Mohamed, 116
Camara, Moustapha, 181
Camara, Sékou "François," 165
Camara, Terrin, 153
Camayenne (suburb, Conakry), 86
Cameroon, 1, 33
Caribbean, 180. *See also* Guadeloupe; Martinique
Cellou, Ex-Sergeant-Major, 97

Chérif, Karamoko Boubacar Sidiki, 107
Chiefs: abolition of the chieftaincy, 7, 104, 109, 146, 175–76, 192, 194, 260 n.25; abuses of, 2, 58, 92–94, 99, 102, 104–6, 108, 175; appointment of, 41, 94–99, 104, 236 n.50; authority crisis, 95–100, 110; canton, 20, 24–25, 52, 92–95, 102–4, 106, 108, 110, 131, 146, 154, 165, 175–76, 182, 192, 238 n.91, 263 n.65; and the colonial administration, 30, 46, 92, 95–96, 103–4, 106–9, 131, 135, 137, 175–76, 234 n.30; and conspicuous consumption, 96, 99, 109, 234 n.27; and crop requisition, 24, 46, 92–94, 99, 194, 200 n.29; education of, 96–97, 234 n.30, 252 n.45; and forced labor, 25, 75, 92–95, 101, 105–6, 108, 111, 149, 194; in the forest region, 98–101, 104–5, 108, 110; in the Futa Jallon, 94, 96–98, 104–6, 108, 110–11, 146, 149, 154, 252 n.45, 253 n.48; in the General Council/Territorial Assembly, 78, 96–97, 182, 263 n.65; and military conscription, 20, 92, 95, 149; political base, 103–4, 135, 179, 184, 225 n.104; precolonial restrictions on, 94, 98–99, 104; punishment of, 24, 92, 232 n.5; and the RDA, 1, 9, 34, 87, 91, 103–11, 146, 157, 159, 166, 171, 175–76, 182, 192, 194, 237 n.85; 238 n.91; 238 n.97; 263 n.65; and taxation, 9, 26, 46, 52, 92–93, 100, 102–3, 106, 110–11, 134; usurpation of functions of, 52, 102, 106, 238 n.97; village, 25, 52, 92, 95, 100, 102–4, 106; and the war effort, 15–16, 24–28, 35, 46, 91, 95–96, 99, 194, 205 n.66; women's work for, 75, 91, 94–95, 194. *See also* Elites: "traditional"; Kaba, Lamine: partisans' resistance to chiefs; Peasants, resistance: to chiefs; Veterans: appointment as chiefs; Veterans: resistance to chiefs; Women: resistance to chiefs
Christians/Christianity, 16–17, 59, 69, 72, 96, 100, 161, 224 n.85. *See also* Confédération Française des Travailleurs Chrétiens (CFTC)
Cinéma Rialto, 88
Cissé, Kitiba Fanta, 140

Cissé, Oumou, 133, 153
Citizenship, French, 8, 28, 30–32, 44, 48, 53, 55, 57, 74, 95, 173, 182, 192
Civil servants, African: 17, 30, 101, 107; auxiliaries, 60–62, 66, 68, 218 n.26; ranks, 60, 136; and the RDA, 33, 69, 116, 126, 136, 140–41, 153, 162, 171, 178, 182; slave origins, 96–97, 252 n.45; trade union activities, 7–8, 56, 60, 67–69, 80, 87, 136; wages and benefits, 68–69, 76, 80, 228 n.146. *See also* Clerks; Medical workers; Teachers
Class: alliances, 2, 7–8, 10, 13, 15–16, 34, 56, 60–62, 69, 71, 90, 111, 113, 143, 145, 147, 162–63, 167–68, 171–72, 176, 193, 195; bias, 145–46, 148–49, 168, 178, 193, 262 n.46; divisions, 5, 10, 14, 18, 63–64, 99, 104, 145, 147, 171–72, 176–77, 183, 194–95; and ethnicity, 146–54; and gender, 114, 152. *See also* Rassemblement Démocratique Africain (RDA), Guinean Branch: on class; Rassemblement Démocratique Africain (RDA), Guinean Branch: divisions within
Clerks, 8, 11, 33, 59–60, 69, 96, 100, 109, 157, 182, 236 n.50, 238 n.91. *See also* Civil servants; Elites: "modernizing"
Coké, 110
Coléah (suburb, Conakry), 157
Comité d'Entente Guinéenne, 73, 225 n.104
Comité des Anciens Combattants de la Section de Kankan, 49
Comité d'Études Franco-Africain de Résistance, 34
Communism. *See* Parti Communiste Français (PCF)
Conakry, 26, 34, 45–46, 59, 62–63, 65–66, 70–71, 73–75, 78–80, 84–86, 88, 105, 115–16, 118–23, 125–26, 130–31, 133–36, 141, 147, 156–60, 162, 165–68, 176–79, 182, 187, 189–90
Conakry-Niger Railway, 25–26, 57, 63, 65, 68, 105. *See also* Fédération des Syndicats des Cheminots Africains de l'A.O.F. (FSCA); Strikes: French West African Railway Strike (1947–1948)
Condé, Ex-Sergeant-Major Sako, 49

Confédération Française des Travailleurs Chrétiens (CFTC), 69–70, 72, 74, 77–78, 80
Confédération Générale du Travail (CGT), 33, 58–61, 67–72, 74–75, 77–80, 159–60; and the RDA: 8, 33–34, 56, 60, 67–68, 72–73, 77, 80. *See also* Parti Communiste Français (PCF): and the CGT; Strikes; Trade unions; Union des Syndicats Confédérés de Guinée (USCG)
Confédération Générale du Travail-Force Ouvrière. *See* Force Ouvrière (FO)
Coniagui, 151, 167
Constitutions, French: April 1946, 30–31, 206 n.88; October 1946, 31–32, 50, 74, 76, 207 n.94; September 1958, 1, 10, 172, 184–89, 192, 196, 265 n.86. *See also* Fourth Republic; Fifth Republic; Referendums
Cooper, Frederick, 8, 64, 76, 212 n.48, 226 n.127, 228 n.146, 231 n.213, 231 n.214
Coronthie (neighborhood, Conakry), 87, 135
Cotonou, 189
Coulibaly, Ouezzin, 157–58, 160
Coulibaly, Pléah Koniba. *See* Koniba, Pléah
Counibale (village), 109
Coup de Bambou, 105, 132, 247 n.102
Crop requisitions. *See* World War II: crop requisitions
Customary obligations, 93–94, 101–2, 106, 233 n.13. *See also* Labor: customary; Law, customary; World War II: crop requisitions

Dabola, 34, 48, 63, 65, 105, 109, 131, 151, 154, 238 n.91, 253 n.48
Dafila, 65
Dahomey, 65, 75, 116
Dakar, 11, 20–22, 39, 43, 65–66, 70, 73–74, 80, 105, 135–36, 140, 160, 173
Dalaba, 110, 153
Dama, Soriba, 45
Dara, Almamy Ibrahima Sory, 253 n.48
d'Arboussier, Gabriel, 115–16, 208 n.120
de Gaulle, Charles, 29, 38–39, 184, 186–89

Delsol Plantation, 25
Démocratie Socialiste de Guinée (DSG),
110, 140, 147, 153, 161, 163, 165–66,
178–79, 184, 251 n.10
Dia, Mouctar, 165
Diakabi, M'Bemba, 151
Diakité, Moussa, 181
Dialakoro (canton), 24
Diallo, Abdoulaye, 126
Diallo, Alfa Yaya, 154
Diallo, Alpha Bocar, 154
Diallo, Néné, 84–85, 87, 89, 117, 125,
128, 131, 140, 146–47, 250 n.9
Diallo, Saïfoulaye, 154, 161–63, 165–66,
175, 178
Diallo, Yacine, 64, 148
Diané, Charles, 267 n.110
Diané, Lansana, 183
Diané, Sarata, 116
Diané, Yayé, 65
Diarra, Fatou, 124, 128, 133, 138,
140–41
Diawadou, Barry. *See* Barry, Diawadou
Diawara, Mamby, 65
Dinguiraye, 54, 119, 137, 147, 201 n.7
Diop, Adama, 61, 65–66, 68, 77, 81, 218
n.25
Diori, Hamani, 51
Dioubaté, Diémory, 50
Diouf, Yama, 153
Ditinn, 253 n.48
Dixinn (suburb, Conakry), 119
Doumbouya, Mamadou Bela, 126, 136
Doumbouya, N'Youla, 89, 134–35, 142,
250 n.169, 250 n.170
Dowo-Sare (neighborhood, Labé), 151
Dubréka, 110, 179
Duoulou, Gbato. *See* Gbato, Duoulou

Echenberg, Myron, 8, 39, 97
École Normale William Ponty. *See* Ponty,
William (federal school)
Economy: cost of living, 44, 61, 68–70,
81, 149; impact of strikes on, 62–64,
67–68, 71, 78, 85; impact of war on, 2,
15, 20–21, 23, 25–28, 55–57, 68,
95–96, 195; inflation, 15, 55, 68, 70,
95–96, 195; price controls, 70, 73,
80–81

Education, political: 80, 145, 162–63,
177, 179–80, 182, 195
Education, Western: 2, 33, 41–42, 96,
119–20, 172–73, 176, 178, 180–82,
185, 252 n.45; of girls, 117, 120, 123,
125; literacy, 3–4, 8, 128; of women, 9,
87, 120, 127, 195; women's concerns
about, 85, 88, 114, 117, 120, 126, 195
Elections: 7, 46, 51, 66, 213 n.59; dual
electoral college, 30–32, 173; fraud, 91,
106, 109, 111, 129–31, 145, 176; General Council (1946), 41–42, 103, 213
n.59; Municipal Council (1956) 165,
174–79, 181–82; National Assembly
(1951, 1954, 1956), 108–11, 126,
129–31, 133, 153, 156–58, 161–64,
168; single electoral college, 32, 173;
Territorial Assembly (1957), 171, 175,
179–82, 263 n.57, 263 n.65. *See also*
Government, federal; Government,
French; Government, local; *Loi-cadre*;
Rassemblement Démocratique Africain
(RDA), Guinean Branch, women's
involvement in: suffrage; Suffrage
Elites: "modernizing," 2–8, 10, 12, 15–16,
30, 33, 35, 40–42, 48–49, 52–54, 56,
58, 61, 69, 87, 96–97, 101, 104–6, 111,
115–16, 125–26, 128, 135–36, 153–54,
161, 164–65, 171–72, 178, 180, 184,
193–94, 196, 218 n.25, 234 n.30, 245
n.71, 252 n.45; "traditional," 1–2, 30,
33, 46–47, 61, 63–64, 78–79, 94–98,
100–101, 103–4, 106–8, 111, 124, 135,
137, 147–50, 152–54, 161, 166, 171,
175, 179, 182, 225 n.104. 234 n.30;
252 n.45. *See also* Chiefs; Civil servants; Clerks; Education, Western;
Medical workers; Peul: aristocrats;
Teachers; Veterans: as elites
Equality Law (1950), 53–54
Ethnic (and Regional) associations: 6, 42,
88–89, 103, 116, 225; and the RDA,
33–35, 89, 117. *See also* Amicale
Gilbert Vieillard; Foyer des Jeunes de
la Basse-Guinée; Union de la Basse-
Guinée; Union des Métis; Union du
Mandé; Union Forestière;
Ethnic groups. *See* Baga, Bambara, Bas-
sari, Coniagui, Fula/Fulani/Fulbe,

Jakhanke, Kissi, Kpelle, Landuma, Limba, Loma, Malinke, Mandegine, Maraka/Soninke, Peul, Susu, Tukulor, Wolof

Ethnicity: ethnic alliances, 2, 4–5, 7, 10, 13–17, 34, 43, 56, 59–61, 88, 90, 111, 113, 143, 145–48, 154, 162, 165–68, 171, 176, 193, 195; ethnic exclusivism, 2, 12–14, 16, 33, 87, 100, 103–4, 135, 145, 147, 155–56, 168, 178–79, 193; ethnic tensions, 2, 5, 18, 42, 80, 99, 154, 161, 165–68, 195. *See also* Class: and ethnicity; Ethnic (and Regional) associations; names of specific ethnic groups; Rassemblement Démocratique Africain (RDA), Guinean Branch: divisions within; Rassemblement Démocratique Africain (RDA), Guinean Branch: on ethnicity; Violence: ethnic Europeans. *See* Rassemblement Démocratique Africain (RDA), Guinean Branch: on race; Trade unions: parity with Europeans; Veterans: parity with Europeans

Évolués. See Assimilation; Elites: "modernizing"

Family allowances. *See* Trade unions: family allowances

Faranah, 27, 105

Fédération des Syndicats des Cheminots Africains de l'A.O.F. (FSCA), 56, 60–62, 65, 69–70, 72, 74, 77–78, 183, 218 n.25. *See also* Conakry-Niger Railway; Independence: and trade unions; *Loi-cadre:* critiques of; Strikes: French West African Railway Strike (1947–1948)

Fédération Nationale des Prisonniers de Guerre (FNPG), 44

Fifth Republic, 1, 172, 184–86, 192. *See also* Constitutions, French: September 1958; Referendums: September 1958

Fofana, Fatoumata, 153

Fofana, Hawa, 12

Fofana, Ibrahima, 97–98

Fofana, Sékou, 177

Force Ouvrière (FO), 75

Forécariah, 27, 100, 109–10

Forest Region, 17, 25, 27, 33–34, 47–48, 98–100, 104–5, 108–10, 113, 134, 151, 156, 159, 161, 165–66, 183, 201 n.7, 233 n.22

Foromo, Ibrahima, 105

Fourth Republic, 30, 32. *See also* Constitutions, French: April 1946; Constitutions, French: October 1946; Referendums: May 1946; Referendums: October 1946

Foyer des Jeunes de la Basse-Guinée, 80, 88

Franco-African Community. *See* French Community

Free French, 18, 23–24, 26, 29, 38, 58

French Communist Party. *See* Parti Communiste Français (PCF)

French Community, 1, 34, 184–88, 192, 196. *See also* Constitutions, French: September 1958

French Equatorial Africa, 1, 30, 33, 38, 174, 185–87

French Republic. *See* Government, French

French Revolution, 6–7, 161, 174

French Soudan, 32–33, 40, 47, 75, 116, 155, 161, 208 n.120, 210 n.16, 235 n.36, 246 n.89; RDA women in, 115, 126, 231 n.208, 240 n.4, 245 n.71, 249 n.162. *See also* Bamako

French Union, 31, 33, 76, 183, 185, 190, 263 n.56; Assembly of the, 51, 178, 185, 208 n.120, 215 n.98

French West Africa, 1, 8, 11, 20–21, 23, 27, 29–30, 32–33, 38, 42–46, 51, 53, 57–62, 65–66, 68–69, 74–78, 81–83, 90, 116, 123, 159, 173–74, 183, 185–87, 192, 196, 217 n.16, 222 n.65, 231 n.213; high commissioner (governor-general) of, 11, 20, 23, 27, 39, 45, 48–49, 53, 71, 73, 78, 80–83, 140, 160, 173, 204 n.35; inspector general of labor for, 62, 66, 70–73, 82, 222 n.65. *See also* Government, federal

Front de Libération Nationale (FLN). *See* Algeria

Fula/Fulani/Fulbe, 17, 149, 155, 201 n.5. *See also* Peul; Tukulor

Futa Jallon, 17, 25, 27, 34, 42, 48, 50–51, 58, 94–97, 104–6, 108, 110–11,

124–25, 136–37, 146–54, 161–62, 165–66, 178, 201 n.5, 201 n.7, 230 n.192, 234 n.32, 251 n.14, 253 n.48. *See also* Chiefs: in the Futa Jallon; Jallonke; Peul; Slavery: in the Futa Jallon; Women: in the Futa Jallon
Futa Toro, 201 n.5

Ga, women: 246 n.88, 246 n.89, 248 n.116
Gaoual, 27, 95–97, 151
Gbato, Duoulou, 100
Geiger, Susan, 4, 127
Gender: alliance, 2, 5, 15, 56, 111, 113, 143, 145, 162, 167–68, 171, 193, 195; "big men," 40–41, 97, 210 n.18; male norms/masculinity, 15, 40–41, 47, 97, 104, 130–31, 210 n.18, 246 n.87, 246 n.88, 246 n.89. *See also* Class: and gender; Generations, tensions between; Rassemblement Démocratique Africain (RDA), Guinean Branch: on gender; Rassemblement Démocratique Africain (RDA), Guinean Branch, women's involvement in: assumption of male roles/clothing; Women: acceptance of gender norms; Women: emancipation of; Women: ridicule of men; Women: violation of gender norms
Generations, tensions between, 104, 172, 183, 264 n.70. *See* Gender; Youth
Germany, 29, 38, 42
Ghana (Gold Coast), 28, 201 n.7, 222 n.66, 231 n.213, 237 n.83, 245 n.80, 246 n.88, 246 n.89, 248 n.116, 260 n.25, 264 n.70
Government, federal: federal executive, 185, 187; Grand Council, 81, 173, 185
Government, French: Constituent Assemblies, 30–32, 213 n.59; Council of the Republic (Senate), 74–75, 173, 185; National Assembly, 31–32, 51, 64, 69, 74–75, 109, 131, 146, 154, 156, 161, 163, 172–73, 175, 180, 185, 213 n.59. *See also* Constitutions, French; Fourth Republic; Fifth Republic; Free French; French Community; French Union; Popular Front government; Referendums; Vichy

Government, local: African autonomy, 1–2, 33, 169, 172, 174, 183, 185; General Council, 32, 50–51, 72–73, 96–97, 103, 213 n.59, 216 n.103; municipal councils, 165, 174–78; Territorial Assembly, 30, 32, 51, 78, 162, 171, 173, 175, 178, 180, 182, 185, 187–89, 195, 216 n.103. *See also* Chiefs; Elections: General Council; Government, federal; Government, French; *Loi-cadre*
Governor-General. *See* French West Africa: high commissioner
Grand Chérif. See Mady, Fanta
Great Britain, 28
Groupes d'Études Communistes (GEC), 32, 34, 154, 161, 208 n.117
Grovogui, Siba N., 200 n.32, 246 n.88
Guadeloupe, 59
Guéckédou, 27, 108, 110
Guèye, Doudou, 34
Guèye, Lamine. *See* Lamine Guèye Law
Guirila (canton), 47

Haidara, Nabya, 134–35, 142
Hayden, Christopher, 256 n.109
Health and hygiene, 114, 117–20, 126, 195
Horefello, Fatoumata, 153
Houphouët-Boigny, Félix, 64, 157, 160, 189–90
Houphouët-Boigny Law (1946), 31, 55, 57, 101
Hroch, Miroslav, 16

Igbo: masculine norms, 210 n.18, 226 n.120, 226 n.127, 246 n.89; women, 134, 222 n.66, 242 n.19, 245 n.77, 246 n.87
Imperialism, "enlightened," 7–8, 28–29, 35, 44–45, 54–56, 69, 90, 172–73, 184, 194
Independence: and divisions within the RDA, 169, 174,182–83, 185–86, 188–92; and the PRA, 183–86, 189, 190–92; and students, 172, 183, 190, 267 n.110; and trade unions, 189–90, 192; and veterans, 192, 267 n.113; and women, 172, 189; and youth, 172, 174, 188–90, 192
Indigénat, 18, 30–31, 60, 101–2, 233 n.13
Indochina, 42, 171. *See also* Vietnam

Institut Français d'Afrique Noire, 33
Islam: 13, 46–47, 100–101, 115, 124,
    136–38, 142; in precolonial Guinea, 17,
    107, 147, 149, 154, 194, 201 n.7, 234
    n.32; and the RDA, 13, 16–17, 87, 89,
    107, 109, 122–25, 136–38, 140,
    147–48, 150, 155–56, 161–62; and
    trade, 17, 98; and trade unions/strikes,
    59, 79–80. *See also* Kaba, Lamine: reli-
    gious background; Peul: religious con-
    servatism; Touré, Sékou: and Islam;
    Women: in the Futa Jallon
Italy, 38, 42
Ivory Coast, 8, 63–65, 75, 82, 100, 116,
    208 n.120

Jakhanke, 150–51, 153
Jallonke, 17, 96, 149–51, 234 n.32, 251
    n.14, 252 n.45
Johnson, R.W., 152

Kaba, Alpha Amadou, 107–8
Kaba, Ansa, 107
Kaba, Daye, 107
Kaba, Diaka, 140
Kaba, Gnamakoron, 124
Kaba, Kéritou, 140
Kaba, Kiaka, 140
Kaba, Lamine: Kankan Revolt, 46–50;
    partisans' resistance to chiefs, 46–49,
    100–101; partisans' resistance to taxes,
    46, 100, 103; political activities, 46–47,
    49–50, 52, 101, 103, 107, 165, 213
    n.59; religious background, 46–47,
    107; and veterans, 46–50. *See also* Parti
    Républicain Socialiste de Guinée
    (PRSG); Veterans: protests
Kaba, N'Faly, 140
Kaba, Sayon Mady, 158
Kaba, Sinkoun, 157
Kaba family, 107, 140, 177
Kaback (island), 110
Kabila. See Women: organizations
Kakossa (island), 110
Kankan, 24–25, 34, 46–52, 59, 63, 65–66,
    80, 100–101, 107–8, 120, 124, 128–29,
    140, 158, 164–65, 177, 179, 181
Kankan Revolt. *See* Kaba, Lamine:
    Kankan Revolt; Veterans: protests

Kaplan, Temma, 117, 242 n.18
Kaporo (suburb, Conakry), 119–20
Karagoua (canton), 47
Karfamoriah (village), 107
Karim, Ex-Lieutenant Abdou, 54
Kassa (island), 156
Kéita, Aoua, 254 n.71. *See also* French
    Soudan: RDA women in
Kéïta, Fatou, 82, 84–86, 88–89, 123, 125,
    127–28, 131, 138–39, 141–42, 250
    n.170
Kéïta, Koumandian, 262 n.46
Kéïta, Madéïra, 33–34, 73, 108, 115–16
Kéïta, Mamadou, 65
Kéïta, Nassirou, 153
Kéïta, N'Famara, 177
Kéïta, Sidiki Kobélé, 5, 199 n.18
Kenya, 231 n.213, 249 n.148
Kimbely (neighborhood, Mamou), 152
Kindia, 27, 34, 50, 59, 63, 65, 105, 120,
    122, 177, 181
Kissi, 16, 151, 167
Kissidougou, 24, 47, 100
Konaté, Aissata, 153
Konaté, El Hadj, 79
Koniba, Pléah, 160, 255 n.91
Kononkoro-Malinké (canton), 100, 236
    n.50
Kourouma, Mamady, 50
Kourouma, Mariama, 116
Kourouma, Nankoria, 116
Kouroussa, 24–25, 34, 47–48, 63, 100
Kouyaté, Kémoko, 140
Kpelle, 16, 100, 151, 167

Laba. See Women: organizations
Labaya (canton), 110
Labé, 34, 48, 51, 93, 95, 105, 110, 122,
    147, 149–51, 153–55, 164, 250 n.9
Labor: customary, 48, 52, 75, 94, 101–2,
    105–6, 233 n.13; forced, 7–9, 15, 18,
    20, 23, 25–31, 35, 39, 48, 55–58, 60,
    74; plantation 25–26, 58, 62–64; resis-
    tance, 8, 15, 26–28, 48, 52, 55–58. *See
    also* Chiefs: and forced labor; Peasants,
    resistance: to forced labor; Strikes;
    Trade unions
Labor Code. *See* Overseas Labor Code
La Fayette, Marquis de, 161

Lamine Guèye Law: First (1946), 31, 57,
74, 182; Second (1950), 69, 76, 80, 228
n.146
Landuma, 17, 156, 167, 251 n.14
Law, customary, 31, 40, 176, 207 n.96
Lawler, Nancy, 8
Lebano-Syrians, 67, 179–80, 196
Lelouma (canton), 110
Liberia, 27, 99–100, 233 n.22
La Liberté, 119, 132, 135, 154, 157, 161,
167, 179, 181, 186, 247 n.102
Liger, Henri: campaign (1948–1952),
53–54. *See also* Veterans: pensions
Limba, 17, 251 n.14
Lindsay, Lisa A., 84, 210 n.18, 219 n.29,
222 n.65, 222 n.66, 226 n.120, 226
n.127, 228 n.153, 229 n.159, 229 n.171,
231 n.213
Linkeny Banana Plantations, 25
Loi-cadre, 172–75, 177, 180, 183, 185; cri-
tiques of, 169, 172, 183, 196; provisions
of, 173. *See also* Chiefs: abolition of the
chieftaincy; Elections: single electoral
college; Students; Suffrage: universal;
Teachers; Trade unions; Youth
Loma, 16, 98, 151, 161, 166–67
Lonsdale, John 4
Lower-Guinea, 25–27, 34, 64, 80, 88,
100, 105, 109–10, 117, 125–26,
146–47, 151, 159, 162–63, 165–66

Macenta, 27, 45, 47, 48, 98–100, 236 n.50
Madina-Kouta (village), 93
Mady, Fanta (*grand chérif*), 80, 107, 227
n.144, 239 n.106
Magassouba, Moriba, 158, 167, 183
Maka, Léon, 50, 52 88, 95, 103, 115, 126,
135, 137, 139, 147
Mali (subdivision), 27, 93, 110–111
Malinke, 13–14, 16–18, 33–34, 59, 98,
100–101, 105, 107, 113, 116–17, 124,
137, 146–47, 150–53, 155–56, 161,
163, 165–67, 179, 200 n.32, 201 n.5,
236 n.50, 251 n.29, 252 n.36
Mamaya. See Women: organizations
Mamou, 34, 59, 63, 65, 75, 78, 85, 104–6,
119, 133, 136, 151–53, 160–61,
164–65, 178, 253 n.48, 255 n.91

Mande, 34, 150, 201 n.5. *See also*
Malinke
Mandegine, 156
Mandinka/Mandinga/Mandingo. *See*
Malinke
Mandougou (canton), 100
Manéah, 122
Maninka, 16, 147, 201 n.5, 251 n.14, 252
n.36. *See also* Malinke
Mann, Gregory, 47, 210 n.16, 235 n.36,
246 n.89
Maraka/Soninke, 152, 252 n.36
Market women. *See* Occupations: market
women; Strikes: French West African
General Strike (1953): women's role in;
Strikes: French West African Railway
Strike (1947–1948): women's role in;
Women: economic roles
Martin, Jeanne, 116
Martinique, 178, 180, 182, 263 n.56
Mauritania, 75
Medical workers: 8, 11, 118–19, 178;
assistant-doctors, 118–19, 160, 182;
assistant-veterinarians, 182; midwives,
87, 114–16, 119–20; nurses, 118–20,
132, 163, 182, 256 n.109. *See also*
Civil servants; Elites: "modernizing"
Métis, 34, 176, 179–80, 182. *See also*
Rassemblement Démocratique Africain
(RDA), Guinean Branch: on race;
Union des Métis
Meunier, Kadiatou, 84, 87, 130
Military: regime, 11–14. *See also*
Tirailleurs Sénégalais; Veterans; World
War II
Molota (village), 177
Montgomery, General Bernard Law,
134–35
Montlouis, Joseph, 59
Morébayah, 110
Morébayah Kaback (canton), 110
Morgenthau, Ruth Schachter, 4–5, 160,
167
Morocco, 172
Mouvement Républicain Démocrate, 34
Mozambique, 200 n.29, 233 n.13, 235
n.46
Muso Sere. See Women: organizations

Nationalism, 3–4, 6–7, 15–18, 54–55, 127, 145, 161, 166, 172, 193–94, 198 n.12, 199 n.22
N'Diaye, Aissatou, 86–89, 104, 113, 131, 135, 138, 140, 142, 147, 230 n.192
N'Diaye, Yombo, 146
Niamey, 189
Niger, 51, 63, 75, 161; river, 7. *See also* Conakry-Niger Railway
Nigeria, 28, 210 n.18, 219 n.29, 222 n.65, 226 n.120, 226 n.127, 228 n.153, 229 n.159, 231 n.213, 246 n.89; women, 84, 127, 134, 222 n.66, 229 n.171, 242 n.19, 245 n.77, 245 n.80, 246 n.87. *See also* Igbo
North Africa, 21, 38. *See also* Algeria; Morocco; Tunisia
N'Zérékoré, 27, 48, 51, 100, 104–5, 108, 233 n.22

Occupations: artisans, 113, 150, 153, 156, 162, 182, 252 n.36; blacksmiths, 125, 150–51, 251 n.29; butchers, 150, 152; carpenters, 151; cattle herders, 150, 153; cloth dyers, 9, 13, 75, 84–85, 88, 124–26, 147, 150, 152, 250 n.9; griots, 34, 50, 150, 162; market women, 9, 13, 67, 75, 84, 86–87, 118, 121–22, 127–29, 132, 179, 222 n.66, 245 n.80; merchants, 63, 66–67, 120, 122, 162, 182; planters, 63–64, 96; seamstresses, 9, 75, 85, 88, 125–26, 132; tailors, 150; traders, 66–67, 98, 101, 122, 150, 156, 163; transporters, 162–63, 182; weavers, 150. *See also* Civil servants; Clerks; Medical workers; Peasants; Teachers; Women: economic roles
Ounah (canton), 105
Ourouyakoré (village), 105
Overseas Labor Code, 57, 73–77, 81, 83, 126, 162. *See also* Trade unions: family allowances
Overseas Territories, 28, 31, 50–51, 57, 59, 172–74, 183, 185–86, 192, 263 n.56; minister of, 82–83, 105–6, 109, 173

Paris, 11, 19–20, 23, 30–31, 51, 72, 81, 158, 160, 172–73, 180, 185
Paris-Dakar, 65
Parker, John, 246 n.88, 246 n.89, 248 n.116
Parti Communiste Français (PCF), 29, 32, 44; break with the RDA, 159–60; and the CGT, 33, 56, 58, 67, 69, 71–72, 75–76, 159–60; collaboration with the RDA, 32, 34, 51, 67, 69, 71, 76
Parti Démocratique de Guinée (PDG), 34, 136. *See also* Rassemblement Démocratique Africain (RDA), Guinean Branch
Parti du Regroupement Africain (PRA), 183–86, 189, 190–92. *See also* Independence: and the PRA; Union Progressiste Guinéenne
Parti Progressiste de Guinée (PPG), 32–34
Parti Républicain Socialiste de Guinée (PRSG), 47, 49. *See also* Kaba, Lamine: political activities
Peasants, and the RDA, 91, 103–6, 109–11
Peasants, resistance: to chiefs, 2, 9, 16, 18, 27, 46–47, 52, 91, 95, 99–101, 109–11, 194, 200 n.29, 235 n.46; to crop requisitions, 27, 95, 99–100, 200 n.29; to forced labor, 26–27, 52, 56–58, 91, 95, 101–2, 111; to taxation, 26–27, 46, 91, 95, 99–100, 102–3, 110–11
Pélisson, Pierre, 66
Peul, 13, 17–18, 33–34, 59, 64, 113, 116, 125, 146–47, 155–56, 161, 165–68, 178, 181, 184, 201 n.5; aristocrats, 96, 105–7, 124, 135, 137–38, 146–50, 152–54, 161, 252 n.45; "bush" or "cow," 150; free, 106, 149–50; gender hierarchy, 124, 136–38, 147, 151–52; political institutions, 17, 154, 201 n.7, 253 n.48; religious conservatism, 124, 136–37, 147; slaves, 42, 96–98, 106, 111, 146–53, 234 n.32, 250 n.9, 252 n.45; social hierarchy, 96, 105–7, 111, 124, 136–37, 146–50, 152–54. *See also* Chiefs: in the Futa Jallon; Futa Jal-

lon; Slaves: in the Futa Jallon; Women:
in the Futa Jallon

Le Phare de Guinée, 132, 247 n.102

Pita, 34, 96, 110, 153, 168, 251 n.28

Pléah, Koniba. *See* Koniba, Pléah

Pleven, René, 23, 39, 204 n.35

Political parties. *See* names of specific
parties

Ponty, William (federal school), 105, 109,
153–54, 238 n.91. *See also* Civil servants; Education, Western; Elites:
"modernizing"; Teachers

Popular Front government, 58

Portuguese Territory, 27. *See also*
Mozambique

Postes, Télégraphes, Téléphones (PTT).
See Strikes, Guinean PTT Strike
(1945); Syndicat Professionel des
Agents et Sous-Agents Indigènes du
Service des Transmissions de la Guinée
Français; Touré, Sékou: and the PTT
workers' union

Poudrière (neighborhood, Mamou), 153

Pré, Roland, 70

Pruvost, H.: as inspector of colonies, 57;
as secretary of state for Overseas
France, 117, 157, 159

Pulaar, 16, 146–47, 149, 165, 179, 201
n.5, 252 n.45. *See also* Peul

Race. *See* Rassemblement Démocratique
Africain (RDA), Guinean Branch: divisions within; Rassemblement Démocratique Africain (RDA), Guinean
Branch: on race; Trade unions: parity
with Europeans; Veterans: parity with
Europeans

Railways. *See* Conakry-Niger Railway;
Fédération des Syndicats des
Cheminots Africains de l'A.O.F.
(FSCA); Independence: and trade
unions; Strikes: French West African
Railway Strike (1947–1948)

Rassemblement de la Jeunesse Démocratique Africaine (RJDA), 156. *See also*
Youth

Rassemblement Démocratique Africain
(RDA), Guinean Branch: on class, 2, 5,
171–72, 176–77, 180–82; collaboration

with the colonial administration,
160–61, 164, 183, 196; conferences and
congresses, 34, 116, 125–26, 156, 177,
180–81, 183, 185, 188–90; conflicts
with the interterritorial RDA, 2, 172,
185, 188–92; divisions within, 2, 5, 7,
10, 114–15, 136–42, 145, 154–61,
163–69, 171, 174, 176–83, 193–96; on
ethnicity, 2, 5, 7, 10, 32–34, 56, 80,
145–48, 151, 153–54, 161–62, 165–68,
176–83, 193–94; on gender, 9, 15, 56,
104, 117, 119, 124, 136–42, 145,
176–78, 181, 193, 195; on race, 166,
176–80, 182–83, 196; on regionalism,
166–68, 176–79, 181–82; state repression of, 69, 71, 90, 106, 108–9, 111,
116, 126, 131, 145–46, 168; on violence, 154–61, 163–68, 194; voter registration, 162, 174, 250 n.1. *See also*
Chiefs: and the RDA; Civil servants:
and the RDA; Class: alliances; Class:
divisions; Confédération Générale du
Travail (CGT): and the RDA; *Coup de
Bambou*; Education, political; Elections; Ethnic (and Regional) associa-
tions: and the RDA; French Soudan:
RDA women in; Independence: and the
RDA; Islam: and the RDA; *La Liberté*;
Loi-cadre; Parti Communiste Français
(PCF): break with the RDA; Parti Com-
muniste Français (PCF): collaboration
with the RDA; Peasants, and the RDA;
Le Phare de Guinée; Slaves: and the
RDA; Strikes: French West African
General Strike (1953): RDA's role in;
Strikes: French West African Railway
Strike (1947–1948): RDA's role in;
Strikes: Guinean General Strike (1950):
RDA's role in; Taxes: and the RDA;
Teachers: and the RDA; Touré, Sékou:
and the RDA; Veterans: and the RDA;
Violence: ethnic; Violence: political;
Youth

Rassemblement Démocratique Africain
(RDA), Guinean Branch, women's
involvement in: 5–7, 9, 12–13, 56, 89,
113–16, 125–26, 162, 172, 189; arrests
and imprisonment, 135–36; assumption
of male roles/clothing, 130, 133–35,

142; clandestine activities, 131–32, 140–41; committees, 126, 148, 151, 153, 156, 163, 172, 189; concerns and demands, 2, 9, 114, 117–26, 143, 193, 195; intelligence gathering and security, 132–33; mobilizing methods, 127–28, 143, 146, 148, 162–63; noms de guerre, 132, 134–35; political office, 176–78, 262 n.42, 262 n.43; Red Cross committees, 133; reputation of, 1, 136, 139–40, 142, 249 n.148; respect and status of, 9, 13, 104, 114, 117, 124–26, 244 n.61; sale of party cards, 131–32; sexual extortion, 141; shock troops, 133–36, 141; songs, 3, 14, 114, 127–31, 134–36, 139–42, 155–56, 179, 194, 246 n.87, 247 n.94, 249 n.143; suffrage, 161–63, 178; uniforms, 3, 114, 194. *See also* Touré, Sékou: and women; Women

Rassemblement Démocratique Africain (RDA), Interterritorial: 1, 32–33, 115–16, 208 n.120; collaboration with chiefs/colonial administration, 63–64, 155, 157, 159–61, 188–89; congresses, 32–34, 107, 154, 159–60; coordinating committee, 159–60, 168; parliamentarians, 159. *See also* Bamako, Congress of (October 1946); Coulibaly, Ouezzin; d'Arboussier, Gabriel; Houphouët-Boigny, Félix; Parti Communiste Français (PCF): break with the RDA; Parti Communiste Français (PCF): collaboration with the RDA; Rassemblement Démocratique Africain (RDA), Guinean Branch: conflicts with the interterritorial RDA; *Réveil*

Rassemblement du Peuple Français, 66

Referendums: May 1946, 31; October 1946, 32; September 1958, 1, 172, 176, 186–88, 190, 192, 196. *See also* Constitutions, French; Fourth Republic; Fifth Republic; Independence; Parti du Regroupement Africain (PRA); Rassemblement Démocratique Africain (RDA), Guinean Branch

Regional associations. *See* Ethnic (and Regional) associations

Regionalism. *See* Rassemblement Démocratique Africain (RDA), Guinean Branch: divisions within; Rassemblement Démocratique Africain (RDA), Guinean Branch: on regionalism

Religion, indigenous, 16–17, 98, 100. *See also* Christians/Christianity; Islam

La République. *See* Bloc Africain de Guinée

Resistance. *See* Kaba, Lamine: partisans' resistance to chiefs; Kaba, Lamine: partisans' resistance to taxes; Labor: resistance; Peasants, resistance; Rassemblement Démocratique Africain (RDA), Guinean Branch; Rassemblement Démocratique Africain (RDA), Guinean Branch, women's involvement in; Strikes; Veterans: resistance to chiefs; Women: resistance to chiefs

Réveil, 51, 67–68, 72, 237 n.81

Richard-Molard, Jacques, 24, 26, 205 n.66

Rivière, Claude, 5

Safé, Samba, 149

Sakho, Mabalo, 127–28

Samou (canton), 100

Sandé, Marie, 148

Sandervalia (neighborhood, Conakry), 88, 134–36

Sané, Fanta, 153

Sanitation. *See* Health and hygiene

Sankaran (canton), 48

Saracolet. *See* Maraka/Soninke

Sarr, Ibrahima, 61, 65

Savané, Moricandian, 50

Self-determination. *See* Constitutions, French: September 1958; Independence; *Loi-cadre*; Referendums: September 1958

Self-government. *See* Government, local; *Loi-cadre*

Sembene, Ousmane, 222 n.65

Senegal, 11, 20–22, 25, 27, 44–45, 59, 65, 75, 84, 116, 155, 181–82, 201 n.5, 201 n.7, 203 n.27, 208 n.120, 210 n.16, 218 n.25, 261 n.34. *See also* Dakar

Sidibe, Ousmane, 47

Sierra Leone, 28

Siguiri, 25, 47, 100, 109, 140, 174
Simandougou: canton, 236 n.50; RDA subsection, 110, 165
Slaves: discrimination against, 146, 149–50; emancipation of, 148–49, 250 n.9; in the Futa Jallon, 146, 148–49, 250 n.9, 252 n.45; and low status professions, 150–52, 250 n.9; and the RDA, 146–47, 149–53; slave villages, 150, 153. *See also* Civil servants: slave origins; Teachers: slave origins; Veterans: slave origins
Socialist Party. *See* Démocratie Socialiste de Guinée (DSG)
Société Indigène de Prévoyance (SIP), 102, 162, 175
Songs. *See* Strikes: French West African General Strike (1953): songs; Rassemblement Démocratique Africain (RDA), Guinean Branch, women's involvement in: songs
Soninke. *See* Maraka/Soninke
Soriya Line, 253 n.48
Soumah, El Hadji Alkaly Ibrahima, 87
Soumah, Almamy, 65
Soumah, Amara, 72–73, 78–80, 87, 116, 179
Soumah, David, 72, 77, 79–80
Soumah, Kadiatou, 153
Soumah, Mabinty, 157
Soumah, Néné, 134
Soumah, Nnady, 135
Strikes: French West African General Strike (1952), 75
Strikes: French West African General Strike (1953), 8, 77–89; RDA's role in, 77–80, 89–90; songs, 86–87; women's role in, 8–9, 56, 83–90, 113, 116–17, 125–26, 195. *See also* Overseas Labor Code; Touré, Sékou: and the 1953 general strike; Trade unions: family allowances
Strikes: French West African Railway Strike (1947–1948), 8, 60–68; CGT involvement in, 60–61, 67; class cleavages, 63–64; community support for, 65–68; economic impact of, 62–63; in Guinea, 62–63, 65, 67–68; Mikado derailment, 65; RDA's role in, 61,

67–68; women's role in, 8–9, 56, 61, 67, 195, 222 n.66. *See* Conakry-Niger Railway; Fédération des Syndicats des Cheminots Africains de l'A.O.F. (FSCA)
Strikes: Guinean General Strike (1950), 8, 69–73; RDA's role in, 71–73. *See also* Touré, Sékou: and the 1950 general strike
Strikes: Guinean PTT Strike (1945), 59–60. *See also* Syndicat Professionel des Agents et Sous-Agents Indigènes du Service des Transmissions de la Guinée Français; Touré, Sékou: and the PTT workers' union
Students, critiques of *loi-cadre*, 172, 183, 196. *See also* Independence: and students; Independence: and youth; Youth: critiques of *loi-cadre*; Youth: and independence
Subjects, French, 8, 18–20, 27, 29–31, 38, 74, 92–93, 233 n.13
Sub-Saharan Africa, 39, 84, 171, 185, 192
Suffrage: limited, 30–31, 41, 178, 250 n.1; universal, 30–31, 104, 173–75, 178. *See also Loi-cadre*; Rassemblement Démocratique Africain (RDA), Guinean Branch: and voter registration; Rassemblement Démocratique Africain (RDA), Guinean Branch, women's involvement in: suffrage
Suret-Canale, Jean, 4–5, 176
Susu, 13–14, 16–18, 33–34, 59, 65, 113, 116–17, 125, 129–30, 135, 146–47, 151, 153, 155–56, 162, 165–68, 177, 179, 182, 200 n.32, 230 n.190, 246 n.88, 247 n.94, 251 n.14
Syli, 86, 117, 129–30, 140–41, 179, 230 n.190, 249 n.143
Sylla, Aissata, 153
Sylla, David, 110, 157
Sylla, Karimou, 40
Sylla, Lamine, 100
Sylla, Maciré, 153
Sylla, Siaka, 147
Sylla, Tourou, 85, 104, 124, 137–38, 142, 152–53
Syndicat Professionel des Agents et Sous-Agents Indigènes du Service des Trans-

missions de la Guinée Français (PTT workers' union), 8, 33, 59–60, 65, 67, 69. *See also* Strikes: Guinean PTT Strike (1945); Touré, Sékou: and the PTT workers' union

Tall, El-Hadj Umar b. Said, 17, 147, 201 n.7
Tanganyika/Tanzania, women, 4, 127, 241 n.16, 242 n.20, 244 n.56, 244 n.61, 246 n.91, 247 n.100, 248 n.131, 249 n.140, 249 n.147, 249 n.148, 249 n.162
Taxes, 18, 92–94, 102, 122; and the RDA, 52, 91, 106, 110–11, 122–23, 126, 162; and the war effort, 9, 26; and women, 91–93, 122–23, 126. *See also* Chiefs: and taxation; Kaba, Lamine: partisans' resistance to taxes; Peasants, resistance: to taxation; Veterans: and taxation; World War II: crop requisitions
Teachers: and chiefs, 96; critiques of *loi-cadre*, 172, 183; and independence, 10, 189–90; and the RDA, 87, 104–5, 114–16, 133, 153–54, 162–63, 181–82, 189–90; slave origins, 96, 252 n.45; trade union, 8, 56, 69, 154, 172, 183, 189–90, 262 n.46. *See also* Civil servants; Elites: "modernizing"; Ponty, William (federal school)
Télimélé, 153
Thiaroye. *See* Veterans: protests
Timbi-Touni (canton), 96
Timbo, 154, 253 n.48
Tinki (canton), 24
Tirailleurs Sénégalais, 19–22; career soldiers, 40, 42–43, 96–97; and combat in World War II, 7, 18, 21, 37–38, 50; conscription of, 7, 9, 15, 18–21, 35, 149; conscripts, 40, 42–43; prisoners of war, 18, 38–39; relationship with French civilians, 7, 18, 22, 42–43, 52; relationship with French soldiers, 22, 42–43, 194; role in the liberation of France, 8, 18, 21, 23, 38–39, 42–43, 48, 50, 194. *See also* World War II: military conscription; Veterans
Togba, Fahan, 100
Togo, 1, 27, 33, 155
Tombo, 86

Tondon, 110, 157–58
Tougué, 48, 111
Toumania, 153
Tounkara, Tibou, 167
Touré, Faciné, 65
Touré, Ismaël, 180
Touré, Mahawa, 134–35
Touré, Moussa, 116
Touré, Samori, 17, 107–8, 111, 201 n.7
Touré, Sékou: and the 1950 general strike, 69, 72–73; and the 1953 general strike, 77–80; and class, 178, 180, 262 n.46, 263 n.57; co-optation of, 159–61; and de Gaulle, 188; and ethnicity, racism, and regionalism, 146, 155–56, 161–62, 164–66, 168, 177, 179–81, 258 n.146; and independence, 174, 186, 188–91, 267 n.110, 267 n.111; and Islam, 79–80, 124, 155, 239 n.106; and law and order, 157–58, 160, 258 n.146; and the *loi-cadre* government, 174–75; personality cult, 117, 159–60; and the PTT workers' union, 33, 59; and the RDA, 12–14, 32–34, 67–68, 77–78, 89, 107, 109, 111, 159–63, 230 n.190; and the USCG/CGT, 13, 33–34, 60, 67–69, 72–73, 77–78, 89, 159–60; and women, 13, 87–89, 117, 120–26, 130–32, 134–35, 139–42, 147, 155–56, 178, 249 n.143. *See also* Strikes: French West African General Strike (1953); Strikes: Guinean General Strike (1950); Strikes: Guinean PTT Strike (1945)
Touré, Soriba, 67, 177, 179
Touré, Yakha, 153
Touré family, 107, 140, 177
Trade. *See* Islam: and trade; Occupations: market women; Occupations: traders
Trade unions: benefits, 2, 9, 55–56, 61–62, 65, 68–70, 74, 76–78, 81–82; critiques of *loi-cadre*, 172, 183, 196; family allowances, 56, 61–62, 69, 74–78, 82–85, 88, 114, 126, 194, 226 n.127; food rations, 26, 83, 117, 120, 122–23, 126, 195; parity with Europeans, 59–62, 65, 68, 70, 73–78, 82, 84, 90, 194–95; wages, 2, 9, 26, 55–56, 59–61, 65, 68–74, 76–78, 80–83, 85, 194–95. *See also* Confédération

Générale du Travail (CGT): and the
RDA; Independence: and trade unions;
Labor; names of specific trade unions;
Overseas Labor Code; Strikes
Traoré, Fatoumata, 140
Traoré, Jacques, 65–66
Traoré, Mama, 153
Traoré, Mamadou. *See* Autra, Ray
Tugnifili (canton), 110
Tukulor, 17, 201 n.5
Tunisia, 172, 184
Turrittin, Jane, 245 n.71

Union de la Basse-Guinée, 34, 80
Union des Métis, 34
Union des Syndicats Confédérés de
Guinée (USCG), 33, 60, 69, 72, 77. *See
also* Confédération Générale du Travail
(CGT)
Union du Mandé, 34
Union Forestière, 34
Union Progressiste Guinéenne, 184. *See
also* Parti du Regroupement Africain
(PRA)
United Nations: Charter, 207–8 n.108;
trusts, 1, 33
United States, 28–29
Universalism, French claims to, 8, 28, 33,
37, 42, 44, 55, 61, 82, 212 n.48
Upper-Guinea, 17, 25, 27, 34, 47–48, 58,
66, 100, 103–5, 107–9, 130, 151, 159,
161, 166, 183, 201 n.7
Upper Volta, 75

Van Allen, Judith, 134
Vepo (canton), 100
Veterans: appointment as chiefs, 41,
96–97; associations, 43–46, 49–51, 61,
190–92; attitudes toward France, 18,
23, 37, 41–43, 47, 52, 54, 267 n.113;
benefits, 8, 37, 40–46, 50–51, 53–54,
97, 194; co-optation of, 8, 37–38,
40–41, 49–54, 56, 97, 194–95; as elites,
8, 15–16, 40–42, 44, 47–49, 52–54,
96–97, 111, 194, 210 n.16, 235 n.36;
ex–POWs, 40, 42–44, 53; noncommissioned officers, 42, 45, 47–49, 54, 97,
101, 110; parity with Europeans, 2,
7–8, 21, 23, 37, 39, 41–45, 50–51,

53–55, 61, 80, 90, 194, 214 n.82; pensions, 40, 43–46, 50–51, 53, 97, 194;
privileges, 30, 37, 40–42, 54; protests,
39–40, 42–43, 45–51; and the RDA,
5–6, 8, 23, 35, 37–38, 50–56, 71, 91,
111, 151, 162, 182, 190–93; resistance
to chiefs, 6–9, 15–16, 37–38, 41,
46–49, 52–54, 91, 101–2, 110–11, 165,
194, 214 n.70; slave origins, 40, 42,
96–97, 149, 151; surveillance of,
43–44, 50; and taxation, 52, 102, 110;
and trade unions, 61, 80; wages, 39, 44,
50–51; wounded, 24, 40, 42–43. *See
also* Chiefs: and military conscription;
Elites: "modernizing"; Independence:
and veterans; Kaba, Lamine: Kankan
Revolt; Kaba, Lamine: and veterans;
Liger, Henri: campaign (1948–1952);
names of specific veterans' associations; Tirailleurs Sénégalais; World War
II: military conscription
Vichy, 18, 23, 25, 29, 38, 58
Vietnam, 172. *See also* Indochina
Violence: ethnic, 2, 7, 10, 145–46,
154–61, 165–68, 195; political, 2, 10,
145–46, 154–61, 163–68, 194–95. *See
also* Education, political; Rassemble-
ment Démocratique Africain (RDA),
Guinean Branch: divisions within;
Rassemblement Démocratique Africain
(RDA), Guinean Branch: on ethnicity;
Rassemblement Démocratique Africain
(RDA), Guinean Branch: on violence
*La Voix des Combattants et Victimes des
Guerres de l'A.O.F. See* Association des
Anciens Combattants et Victimes de
Guerre de l'Afrique Occidentale
Française (AACVGAOF)

Wages. *See* Trade unions: wages
West Africa (magazine), 75
Wolof, 147, 151, 153, 155
Women: acceptance of gender norms, 84,
114–15, 117, 130, 133, 135, 138–39,
141–43, 145, 195, 229 n.171; collective
action, 84, 117, 134, 141, 242 n.18, 242
n.19; dances, 4, 116, 127, 130, 163, 246
n.88; divorce, 1, 9, 138–41; economic
roles, 2, 75–76, 84–88, 114, 124, 150,

152, 195, 229 n.174, 249 n.162; elite, 87, 114–16, 125–26; emancipation of, 13, 114–15, 117, 124, 145, 178, 195; in the Futa Jallon, 124, 136–37, 147, 150–53; historiography of, 3–5, 11–12, 14; marital tensions, 114–15, 136, 138–39, 141; as mothers, 2, 15, 84–85, 88, 114, 117, 126, 195; nonliterate, 1, 7, 9, 12–13, 87–88, 111, 114, 125–28, 162, 171, 193–94; organizations, 5, 9–10, 12, 88–89, 114, 116–17, 132; prostitution, 1, 136, 139–40; resistance to chiefs, 9, 91, 109–11, 113, 131, 134, 137–38, 153; ridicule of men, 67, 129–31, 141–42, 231 n.208, 246 n.87, 246 n.88, 246 n.89; violation of gender norms, 9, 13, 84, 88, 114–15, 117, 124–25, 130, 133–38, 141–42, 145, 152, 195, 231 n.208, 244 n.58; violence against, 123, 138, 140, 157; and World War II, 15, 24–25, 40, 95. *See also* Chiefs: women's work for; Education, Western; French Soudan: RDA women in; Ga, women; Gender; Igbo: women; Independence: and women; Kenya; Nigeria: women; Occupations; Rassemblement Démocratique Africain (RDA), Guinean Branch, women's involvement in; Strikes: women's role in; Tanganyika/Tanzania, women; Taxes: and women; Touré, Sékou: and women

World Federation of Trade Unions, 160

World War II: crop requisitions, 23–26; forced labor, 25–26; military conscription, 7, 9, 15, 18–21, 35. *See also* Chiefs: and the war effort; de Gaulle, Charles; Free French; Tirailleurs Sénégalais; Veterans; Vichy; Women: and World War II

Yandi (village), 93

Yaya, Alfa. *See* Diallo, Alfa Yaya

Youkounkoun, 151

Youldé, Ex-Lieutenant, 45–46

Youth: 264 n.70; critiques of *loi-cadre*, 172, 183, 196; and independence, 172, 174, 188–90. *See also* Generations, tensions between; Independence: and youth; Rassemblement de la Jeunesse Démocratique Africaine (RJDA); Students; Teachers

About the Author

ELIZABETH SCHMIDT is Professor of History at Loyola College in Maryland. She is author of *Decoding Corporate Camouflage: U.S. Business Support for Apartheid* (Institute for Policy Studies 1980) and *Peasants, Traders, and Wives: Shona Women in the History of Zimbabwe, 1870–1939* (Heinemann 1992).